Theories of Man and Culture

Theories of Man and Culture

ELVIN HATCH

Columbia University Press

New York & London

1973

301.2
H28π
90260
oct 1974

Library of Congress Cataloging in Publication Data
Hatch, Elvin
 Theories of man and culture.

 Bibliography: p. 359
 1. Ethnology. 2. Anthropologists. I. Title.
GN315.H36   301.2   73-1250
ISBN 0-231-03638-8

To Raymond K. Hatch

PREFACE

In this book I present the ideas of ten major anthropologists. Each of them offers a fundamentally different interpretation of human behavior, which is to say that if they were to observe the same person at the same time they would not fully agree on what he is doing. My goal in this work is to reveal the differences of interpretation they would offer, or the type of meaning which they see in human affairs. I begin with one of the leading anthropologists of the last century, E. B. Tylor. I then discuss the works of nine other writers, a few of whom began their work prior to 1900, but all of whom expressed distinctly twentieth-century views about man: Franz Boas, Ruth Benedict, A. L. Kroeber, Julian Steward, Leslie White, Emile Durkheim, A. R. Radcliffe-Brown, E. E. Evans-Pritchard, and Bronislaw Malinowski.

This volume owes a great deal to many people, but much of their influence has been so diffuse that it is difficult to acknowledge. However, there are several to whom I owe a particularly heavy and immediate intellectual debt. Among these is William C. Beatty, who is responsible for my decision to enter anthropology. Another is M. G. Smith, whose seminars on social anthropology were among the most enlightening experiences I have had. I also owe a special debt to several other teachers, including Hilda Kuper, Pedro Carrasco, William A. Lessa, and John Horton.

Several people have read portions of the manuscript and have offered valuable suggestions for its improvement. I am particularly indebted to Charles Erasmus, whose enthusiasm for the project has been invaluable to me. I also owe thanks to Professor George Stocking, who read the manuscript in its entirety; this work has benefited considerably from his suggestions. Thanks are also due to Elman Service, David Brokensha, Donald Brown, Barbara Voorhies, and Denis Dutton, each of whom read parts of the manuscript and offered helpful criticisms. In some cases I took the advice that was offered me, and in others I did not; I alone am responsible for what I have written.

This book grew out of a lecture course I taught on history and theory of anthropology, and many of the ideas contained here were first tried on my students. To them I owe a special debt. Some of this material was developed in my seminars, both graduate and undergraduate; the students who participated have been enormously helpful in providing me with a stimulating and challenging forum.

A number of people have provided me with clerical and bibliographical assistance; to them I also owe a word of thanks: Anne Klingelhofer, Phyllis Frezin, Donna Haas, Linda Silbert, and Jeanette Woodward. I thank the University of California at Santa Barbara for funds for clerical assistance, and for the award of a Summer Faculty Fellowship in partial support of this project. I also gratefully acknowledge the permission of The Macmillan Company in allowing me to reproduce two illustrations from Boas' *Race, Language and Culture.*

CONTENTS

Theories of Man and Culture

INTRODUCTION

The success or failure of anthropological fieldwork often hinges on the investigator's grasp of the local meaning of a few key words (Evans-Pritchard 1951a:80), and the same is true of the historical study of ideas. One of the most basic words to understand in twentieth-century anthropology is *culture*. Even though the term has been discussed in countless books and articles, there is still a large degree of uncertainty in its use—anthropologists employ the notion in fundamentally different ways, frequently without noticing it. To some, culture is a finely tuned instrument which serves man's material needs, whereas others tacitly assume that it is virtually autonomous from the exigencies of life and varies almost randomly with respect to them. Some take for granted that institutions are actively used and manipulated by the members of society, whereas others suppose that the governing principles behind culture are located at a level beyond the grasp of the individual. Some contend that culture is rooted in the conditons of the present, and still others hold that it is a product of historical contingency.

A topic which is closely related to the culture concept is that of the nature of the human animal. Culture entails behavior, and consequently a writer's ideas about custom have implications for the image of man which he employs. Basic disagreements exist within anthropology over the nature of the individual, and particularly over the way in which culture affects or transforms him. Some view the individual as a formless mass which is almost entirely shaped by his cultural milieu; others see him as a bundle of needs and drives which culture serves but does not substantially modify; yet others view him as egoistic and impulsive, and in constant need of moral constraint.

In this book I undertake a study of the works of ten anthropologists who have been prominent in the development of the discipline, and I do so in order to reveal the ideas of culture and the images of man which they have employed. My purpose is to contribute to an understanding of what anthropologists do. On the one hand, I hope to inform the non-anthropologist about what I believe have been—and continue to be—some of the critical issues within the discipline. Too often it is thought that anthropology concentrates on trivial and esoteric matters, such as routes of diffusion or the kin terms which are employed by distant and little-known societies. I shall attempt to show that frequently issues of fundamental importance are contained within discussions which seem trifling. On the other hand, I hope to increase the anthropologist's self-awareness and to bring new light on the research in which he is engaged. The culture concept and the image of man which an anthropologist employs are fundamental to his professional work.

There is more to say about the type of analysis I will undertake, but first I need to introduce the people whose writings I discuss.

Anthropology is a young discipline. During most of European history there was comparatively little interest in foreign peoples, and little thought was given to the systematic study of other ways of life. This indifference gradually gave way following Columbus' travels to the New World, however, because a concomitant of European exploration and expansion was a growing curiosity about "strange" and "exotic" customs, and about peoples who looked and even smelled different from those at home. Nevertheless, the field of anthropology itself was not born until the 1860s, when the first professional specialists appeared. It was somewhat later, during the final two or three decades of the last century, that a few anthropologists first received appointments at universities and museums in Europe and the United States. Graduate programs for the training of students did not come into existence until almost the turn of the century; and the practice whereby the anthropologist collects his own data during more or less extensive field expeditions was not instituted until about the same time. In short, the last four decades of the 1800s may be spoken of as the period of emergence of the new discipline.

One of the towering figures in anthropology during the period of its emergence was Edward B. Tylor. Tylor, an Englishman, began his anthropological researches in the early 1860s, and when he received an appointment at Oxford in 1883 he became one of the first academic anthropologists in the world. His approach constitutes an intellectualistic theory of culture, and it is fairly representative of the kind of thinking which predominated among English-speaking anthropologists of the last century.

Tylor's ideas seem decidedly old-fashioned from today's point of view, and his works are now read primarily for their historical interest. Nevertheless, an understanding of his thought is important for a full appreciation of the modern views about culture and the individual, for the frames of reference of the twentieth century developed largely in *response* to ideas similar to his own. The work of Franz Boas, who is the second person I shall consider, illustrates this dialectical process.

Boas was a German by birth, but in the 1880s he emigrated to the United States. During the 1890s he instituted the department of anthropology at Columbia University, which soon became the center of the discipline in this country. Boas is commonly regarded as the founder of American anthropology. Boas' work may seem tedious and esoteric when considered by itself, but it acquires significance when viewed in the context of the changes taking place in anthropological thought during about the turn of this century. His ideas belong to the movement in the social sciences which is sometimes referred to as anti-intellectualism, and his concept of culture may be seen as an attempt to establish a new definition of the nature and meaning of human affairs.

Boas laid the foundations for much of the anthropological thought which developed in the United States. The next four scholars that I consider built upon and modified a few of his key ideas, and in doing so they contributed to the growing diversity of the discipline in this country. The first of these is Ruth Benedict, a student of Boas' who later joined him on the faculty at Columbia. Benedict's account of the Zuni, Kwakiutl, and Dobuans is one of the most famous studies ever made by an anthropologist. Second is A. L. Kroeber, who took his first course in anthropology from Boas in 1896. Five years later, in 1901, Kroeber received his Ph.D. under Boas, and he went on to become one of the most eminent figures in the discipline. The next writer I discuss is Julian Steward, a student of Kroeber, whose theory of cultural ecology has stimulated an extensive body of anthropological research. Fourth is Leslie White, who studied under some of Boas' prominent followers in New York and Chicago. Although White sees little continuity between Boas' thought and his own, the culture concept and image of man which he employs may be conceived as the elaboration and modification of some of Boas' most fundamental ideas.

The next person on my list of characters is Emile Durkheim, who was a contemporary of Boas'. Durkheim taught education and sociology at the University of Bordeaux and, later, the Sorbonne. He was a leading intellectual in France, and his influence was felt in fields as diverse as law, history, economics, and

archaeology. Durkheim's work, like Boas', may be seen as a reaction to certain nineteenth-century views about the nature of
human affairs, and in elaborating his scheme he developed an
image of man, society, and culture which resembled Boas' in
some respects and which was in radical opposition to Tylor's.

In about 1909–10 a young British anthropologist, A. R. Radcliffe-Brown, happened upon Durkheim's work, and he quickly
became a stanch supporter. He taught at a variety of universities around the world, most notably at Cape Town, Sydney,
Chicago, and Oxford. Radcliffe-Brown helped set the direction
of anthropology in Great Britain after about the first quarter of
this century, and his impact has been felt in the United States
as well, although less decisively.

Another distinguished British anthropologist who traces his
intellectual roots to Durkheim, and the ninth to be dealt with
in this work, is E. E. Evans-Pritchard. Evans-Pritchard began
the study of anthropology at the London School of Economics
in the mid-twenties. He has since occupied several teaching and
research posts in both Africa and England, and in 1946 was selected to succeed Radcliffe-Brown in the chair at Oxford.
Evans-Pritchard eventually arrived at what may be termed an
idealistic view of culture, society, and human behavior, and his
work has provided an important alternative to the positivism
which traditionally has dominated British anthropology.

The last person to be discussed is Bronislaw Malinowski. Although Polish by birth, Malinowski traveled to England in
1910 to undertake the study of anthropology. Shortly thereafter
he conducted fieldwork among the Trobriand Islanders, whom
he has immortalized through his writings. Following World
War I Malinowski returned to England to teach at the London
School of Economics, where he remained almost until his death
in the early 1940s. Malinowski was a commanding figure
within the discipline—virtually every anthropologist trained in
Britain during the 20s and 30s came under his influence—and
his works appealed to a large popular audience as well. Mali-

nowski's approach entails an image of man and culture different from any of the others considered in this book.

In my selection of writers I have been guided in part by temporal considerations. Tylor, of course, was chosen to provide historical perspective, for his scheme represents a point of view which was common in the late 1800s. The other theories I deal with are all of the twentieth century, which signifies more than mere placement in time: each of these schemes, except Tylor's, shares a few common assumptions about human affairs. For example, each holds that culture is governed by something other than man's rational faculties, that the human animal is dominated more by emotion than reason, and that culture is grounded primarily in emotional processes. Even Boas and Durkheim, whose early writings straddle the century mark, present comparatively modern images of man and culture.

Although focusing primarily on writers of this century, I have avoided very recent developments in the field. I have chosen people whose ideas matured, or were nearly mature, prior to the end of the Second World War. Time provides a perspective of its own, and many of the post-World War II developments are still too close to permit detached evaluation.

Another consideration guiding my choice of writers is a desire to focus upon people whose ideas represent a certain range of differences. Each of the twentieth-century schemes which I consider is built upon the same set of notions—such as the view that man is an emotional animal—but these basic ideas have been elaborated quite differently. The result is a set of fundamentally different interpretations of human affairs. The theories which I consider represent variations on a common theme, and collectively they make up a series of alternative approaches to the same set of issues. For example, I shall distinguish between monistic and dualistic images of man, and between irrational and utilitarian versions of culture.

I have tried to select people whose works have been

important in themselves. I have given preference to those whose names are familiar even beyond anthropology, who have also had a decisive influence within the discipline, and whose writings illustrate issues which I believe are of lasting and fundamental significance.

The anthropologists considered here have elaborated a wide variety of approaches in explaining cultural phenomena. For example, Boas developed a historical framework; he accounted for the existence of a culture trait among a people by showing that it had been diffused from somewhere else, and he explained the distinct form which the trait assumed by showing that it had been modified to fit its cultural context. Steward proposed a causal framework, and he explained such phenomena as political organization and property rights by reference to cultural ecological determinants. Radcliffe-Brown analyzed kinship systems, religious patterns, and the like, by reference to their role in promoting a stable and cohesive society.

In spite of the diversity of approaches, each of the schemes is alike in one respect. At least implicitly, each supplies the meaning of behavior. The theories which I discuss not only explain why phenomena exist, how they developed, why they assume one form rather than another, and how they behave, but they also make human actions and institutions intelligible.

A hypothetical example will illustrate what is meant. Suppose I am rummaging through an attic and come across an old mechanical device which I have never seen before. It is a puzzle to me, an enigma. What is puzzling is not how the device got into the attic, or the causal factors which explain its origin. What is puzzling, rather, is that the contraption seems to make no sense. I decide to take it to an antique dealer to ask him what it is, and he tells me that it was once part of an old sewing machine. He has supplied an explanation of the device merely by identifying it.

Understanding a culture trait or an institution is a similar procedure. If I am in a primitive society and observe a pattern of behavior which is unintelligible, I immediately begin to search for the meaning which is behind it. Perhaps I observe a man hovering over a few oddments, apparently mumbling to himself. I inquire what he is doing and am told that he is performing a rite. I begin to understand. Next I find that the rite is intended to promote the vigorous growth of the man's gardens, and that it is but a small part of a larger system of magic. My understanding is increased. Later I recognize that the magical rite which I observed performs an important social function, for it reinforces the social bonds between the magician and others who have an interest in the productivity of his gardens. I now feel that I have achieved considerable understanding of this cultural feature.

Intelligibility or understanding of this type is achieved by seeing an event as part of a larger context and by tracing its relations with the other phenomena which make up that context. The mechanical device becomes intelligible when seen as part of a sewing machine, and the magician's actions become intelligible when seen in the context of cultural beliefs and social relations. This form of explanation is quite similar to that which is often used by the historian:

the historian and his reader initially confront what looks like a largely unconnected mass of material, and the historian then goes on to show that sense can be made of it by revealing certain pervasive themes or developments (Walsh 1967b:75).

Dray writes that in an inquiry of this kind "the burden of explanation is in the synthesis of the parts into a new whole" (1964:20; see also 1959).

The culture concept and image of man which an anthropologist employs guide him in his synthesis of the data and in the meaning which he sees in human affairs. For example, some have a cynical image of man and interpret the individual's conduct by viewing it in relation to self-interested motives. The

8

individual is conceived as using and manipulating his cultural norms for his own advantage. Others have an optimistic view of behavior and interpret human action in terms of a disinterested commitment to moral values.

The culture concept which an anthropologist employs is particularly important in influencing the way in which he orders his data and the interpretation which he makes of them. For example, Steward conceived culture largely as an adaptive response to environmental and subsistence factors, and in his study of the Shoshone Indians he portrayed the family organization of those people by viewing it in relation to practical concerns. Ruth Benedict would have seen this institution in an entirely different light. She had little to say about the Shoshone, but in her accounts of other societies she interpreted the family in relation to what she called the cultural pattern or configuration. This is an emotional theme which, in her view, tends to pervade a culture and is free to vary almost randomly with respect to man's physical needs. Benedict would have viewed the Shoshone family as an "irrational" culture trait which is relatively arbitrary with respect to man's material interests.

The form of understanding that I am referring to as the interpretation of meaning may be distinguished from scientific explanation, according to which the occurrence of an event is accounted for in terms of a general covering law. The contrast between the two forms of explanation is perhaps clearest when considering the issue of predictions. Scientific analysis attempts to establish the causal factors behind a phenomenon in such a way that when the necessary conditions exist, the event can always be anticipated. Scientific explanations "render predictable what is explained by subsuming it under universal empirical laws" (Dray 1964:5). When the anthropologist explains a phenomenon by elucidating its meaning, on the other hand, the issue of prediction does not arise. The example of the primitive magician is illustrative, for in that case the explanation did not necessarily imply that this particular rite would ever again be performed in this particular way. The explanation simply made sense of a man's actions which otherwise seemed opaque.

It is not at all uncommon for anthropologists to seek causal, scientific explanations in their work. Steward is an example, for he commonly focused upon cultural ecological factors in an attempt to locate the necessary laws which govern culture history. Even when a person undertakes a scientific analysis of this kind, however, he is likely to supply a meaningful interpretation of the phenomena he is studying, if only implicitly. An instance is Steward's analysis of the Shoshone family. Although Steward attempted to arrive at the causal factors behind the development of this institution, he also supplied a meaningful interpretation, for he viewed the family organization of these people as a practical rather than an arbitrary phenomenon. He portrayed it in a certain light by relating it to one context rather than another. If the causal aspect of this account were entirely eliminated from his analysis, his portrayal of the Shoshone family as a practical institution would remain. It is possible to cite other cases in Steward's work in which he did not attempt causal analyses and endeavored only to describe cultural phenomena. In these cases, too, his framework led him to see the data in a distinct light and to make sense of them in a particular way.

Since a diversity of culture concepts and images of man is in common use, it follows that two different observers of the behavior of the same person need not agree on what that person is doing. Similarly, two different observers need not agree on their identification or assessment of the same institution. One of my chief goals in this book is to uncover the meaning which a variety of writers see when observing human affairs.

Description and explanation are not entirely objective, for they are conditioned by the subjective point of view by which the investigator apprehends his material. This idea is not new, but its importance needs to be stressed. It has been forcefully illustrated by Thomas S. Kuhn, an historian of science.

According to Kuhn, facts can be understood only when they are viewed within a conceptual or theoretical context, and this context is so crucial that the distinction between fact and theory is "exceedingly artificial" (1962:52). For example, three different men may be said to have "discovered" oxygen, but this discovery could not be fully comprehended until conceptual changes took place which provided a frame of reference for viewing the gas (1962:53–56). Kuhn argues that a fact which is understood within the context of one theory is not the same fact at all when viewed from some other perspective. He writes:

Examining the record of past research from the vantage of contemporary historiography, the historian of science may be tempted to exclaim that when paradigms change, the world itself changes with them. Led by a new paradigm, scientists adopt new instuments and look in new places. Even more important, during [scientific] revolutions scientists see new and different things when looking with familiar instruments in places they have looked before. It is rather as if the professional community had been suddenly transported to another planet where familiar objects are seen in a different light and are joined by unfamiliar ones as well (1962:110).

According to this version of science, "the facts" can never be objectively ascertained, because they can only be apprehended according to subjective categories and perspectives which order the world and make it intelligible. By assuming a different theoretical position from someone else, you are, in essence, investigating a different world from his. Kuhn illustrates this principle with the example of switches in visual gestalt, whereby a person looking at a black-and-white cutout can change his frame of reference so that what is foreground one instant becomes background the next (1962:110). The scientist's subjective perspective leads him to focus on particular aspects of the real world and to leave others as background.

If subjective perspective has an important influence on how

the anthropologist interprets his data, then this perspective itself becomes a prime topic for research. Arguments over the meaning of abstract terms like culture have an immediate bearing on the understanding of concrete facts.

THE RISE OF THE ANTI-INTELLECTUAL

E. B. TYLOR AND FRANZ BOAS

In this chapter we examine the meaning of human affairs as conceived by Tylor and Boas. I bring these two writers together specifically to emphasize the contrast between them: they are representative, respectively, of late nineteenth- and early twentieth-century thought. Tylor's work exhibits what may be regarded as an intellectualistic and pre-modern version of culture, whereas Boas is representative of anti-intellectualism and of the modern view of behavior. By comparing the ideas of these two writers it is possible both to show the importance of the changes taking place in anthropological thought at about the turn of the century and to present these developments in their historical context.

E. B. TYLOR

EVOLUTION, INTELLECTUALISM AND POSITIVISM. The idea that progress applied to the field of human activity was central to eighteenth-century Enlightenment thought, but during the first half of the nineteenth-century it seems to have dropped almost out of sight, to return—in full force—during the 1860s and 1870s. These two decades constitute the beginning of anthropology as a self-conscious, professional discipline, and Tylor was one of its principal founders. The central focus of the budding and controversial new science, and the central issue in Tylor's work as well, was cultural evolution.

Much of the evolutionary thought which appeared during the last half of the nineteenth century was the elaboration of a few key principles which had been inherited from the Enlightenment. Two of these are particularly important for an understanding of Tylor. The first is what may be called the intellectualistic view of human behavior, and the second is positivism.

The central element of the intellectualistic approach to human affairs is the assumption that the actor in society governs his behavior by rational principles. In other words, it assumes that if we are to understand a person's actions we must view them as products of his own rational thought. Similarly, according to this point of view, society and social institutions are conscious, rational creations and are entered into because it is sensible to do so. For example, according to Locke, people realized that as long as they lived outside of civil society they would be faced with a degree of uncertainty and injustice. Consequently, by means of the social contract, they established a system of government for their mutual benefit (cf. Parsons 1937:95ff.).

It was just as obvious to the intellectualistic writers of the past as it is to anthropologists today that not all actions and institutions are governed by reason; there are irrational elements in human life, and these were explained away by intellectualists as the result of ignorance and error:

Either the actor simply did not know certain facts relevent to his action and would have acted differently had he known them, or he based his action on considerations which a more extensive knowledge would have proved to be erroneous. He thought he knew, but in fact he did not (Parsons 1937:66).

According to this version of social theory, institutions are grounded in reason, and practices which are traditional, ritual, or symbolic—and hence "irrational"—are intrinsically unstable. They will be discarded once their fallaciousness becomes evident to the members of the society. Traditional beliefs and practices may have a tenacious hold on people's minds, but they will eventually give way to reason.

To the degree that institutions are not grounded in reason—and it is the task of the social sciences to determine whether or not they are—they are to be uprooted as ignorant traditions. The following description of Herbert Spencer's image of his own work reveals the intellectualistic viewpoint which prevailed in his time:

Man, freed at last from unreflecting subservience to immemorial customs and institutions, is about to take his future into his own hands and shape it, guided and instructed by science, in the image of rationality and justice. The taboos are broken, nothing is unquestionable. Obviously men born into a generation on the threshold of such achievements bear a heavy responsibility, and the young Spencer was fully aware of it (Burrow 1966:214).

The utopian society in Spencer's mind was to be based upon the principle of laissez-faire, according to which social relations would be essentially rational economic relations stripped of all traditional and irrational encumbrances. The actor in society was to be free to apply pure reason to his everyday affairs (Burrow 1966:205–6, 214–27).

The intellectualistic framework came under heavy attack during the last few years of the nineteenth century, and was replaced by a variety of new approaches which saw both human behavior and rationality in radically new ways (Parsons 1937; Hughes 1958).

Positivism is the second principle which helped inform much of the evolutionary theory which developed during the latter half of the nineteenth century. Whereas the intellectualistic framework has all but disappeared from modern anthropological thought, the same is not ture of positivism, for the latter is probably the dominant viewpoint within the discipline today.

Positivism has no doubts about the reality of the external world or that this world can be objectively apprehended and understood (cf. Dray 1964:21–23), and it therefore stands in opposition to all idealist and relativistic versions of social science and history. An important element of this realism is the view that the world operates according to natural laws, and that this is as true of society and social institutions as it is of molecules or living organisms. Accordingly, explanation in the social sciences is essentially the same as explanation in the natural sciences, and consists in subsuming the events to be explained under natural, empirical laws of the universe (Dray 1964:2, 5). For example, Herbert Spencer was an advocate of the "universality of causation": to him, all things are caused by natural laws, and scientific progress amounts to subsuming a greater number of phenomena under laws of increasing generality. Burrow argues that the notion of causal laws is a more fundamental aspect of Spencer's thought than the theory of evolution; Spencer's belief in causation *led* him to his evolutionary theory, since the idea of evolutionary sequences satisfied the needs of a cause-and-effect scheme (Burrow 1966:205–6).

Positivism implies some form of determinism: within limits, at least, it assumes that human institutions and human behavior are caused by natural laws. In fact, behavioral determinism is frequently taken as the definitive element of positivism (e.g., van Kaam 1969:15–18, and Bidney 1953:177–78).

BACKGROUND. Sir Edward B. Tylor was born in London in 1832. His father was a successful businessman, the owner-operator of a brass foundry, and Tylor left school at the age of sixteen to work for the family firm. He suffered from ill health, however, and while still in his early twenties, in 1855, his physician advised him to leave the business and devote his life to leisure and travel. This he did, supported comfortably by an allowance from home.

After spending nearly a year seeing the United States, Tylor met another traveler in Havana, Henry Christy. Christy was a well-known antiquarian and a prosperous banker; he was about to tour Mexico, and he persuaded Tylor to accompany him. From the perspective of a middle-class Britisher, Mexico was then an exotic place, a land of archaeological relics and curious traditions. The excursions which the two travelers made into the hinterlands brought the young Tylor face to face with these phenomena.

In 1861 Tylor published his *Anahuac,* an anecdotal travelogue about his Mexican tour. In this chatty and discursive book he gives clear evidence of a growing interest in antiquarian and anthropological matters. *Anahuac* was followed shortly by several articles on anthropological topics (cf. Freire-Marreco 1907:375), and in 1865 by his first substantial anthropological work, *Researches into the Early History of Mankind.* Although cultural evolution constitutes a central focus of this book, its design, as Stocking notes, is "as 'diffusionist' as it is 'evolutionist'" (1968a:79).

Tylor's ideas continued to develop in a series of lectures and articles on such topics as the development of religion and language, and in 1871 he published his monumental *Primitive Culture.* This work is an analysis of primitive religious beliefs and practices, among other things. Although both volumes of *Primitive Culture* are brimming with descriptive material, these data are directed toward the establishment of certain theoretical principles, the underlying one of which is that the culture of mankind is governed by definite laws of evolutionary development. This book had considerable impact on anthropology as a whole and may have served to shift the emphasis away from the study of such topics as law and archaeology toward religion (Burrow 1966:235–39). *Primitive Culture* was the capstone of Tylor's career; although he continued to lecture and write for a number of years after its publication, what followed contained little that he had not already said (Stocking 1968b:174). The only book-length work he was to publish subsequently was his *Anthropology* (1881), a general introduction to the field.

Tylor did not earn a university degree, yet he became one of the leading academic and professional anthropologists in England. In 1883 he was appointed Keeper of the University Museum at Oxford; shortly thereafter he was appointed to a readership in anthropology, and in 1896 he became Oxford's first professor of anthropology. He held that position until he retired in 1909.

Tylor is noted for his careful research, critical use of sources, and his tempered, well-reasoned theoretical stance. Even Lowie, one of the severest critics of the evolutionary school of thought, speaks approvingly of him: "the lapse of time has merely confirmed the earlier judgment of his greatness" (Lowie 1937:68). Tylor was also well regarded as an individual:

His simplicity, patience, and quiet humor made him popular as a teacher and organizer, and contributed to an easy, persuasive style which won a wide audience for his writings. His writings were always free of jargon or pretension of any kind, a consequence, perhaps, of the fact that he was taken from school at sixteen and never again became a "student" in the academic sense (Kardiner and Preble 1963:52).

REDUCTIONISM AND THE AUTONOMY OF CULTURE. Tylor's scheme is paradoxical. On one hand, it is reductionistic, for it explains culture in terms of the individual: to Tylor, the origin of institutions is to be sought in the natural thought processes of human beings. On the other, his scheme entails the view that human institutions are (at least within limits) *sui generis,* autonomous systems with a life of their own, for he held that there are occasions in which customs persist solely due to the force of tradition. In this sense they "fetter" human thought and determine the individual's behavior.

The intellectualistic view of behavior is fundamentally a reductionistic scheme. According to Locke, for example, government was consciously and rationally designed by individuals for their own ends. Even natural law, which was supposed to govern people's relations with one another, was conceived by him as the expression of individual reason. This theory of government is reductionist in a double sense: first, it views social institutions as purposefully designed for *individual ends;* second, it takes *individual reason* as the principle which regulates the form of these institutions.

Both types of reductionism are pronounced in Tylor's work. Concerning the purposefulness of human institutions, Tylor wrote:

It is, I think, a principle to be held fast in studying the early history of our race, that we ought always to look for practical and intelligible motives for the habits and opinions we find existing in the world. . . . The very assertion that [the savages'] actions are motiveless, and their opinions nonsense, is itself a theory, and, I hold, a profoundly false one . . . (1866:86; see also 1878:56).

The emphasis which Tylor placed on the purposiveness of behavior and institutions meant that he had a utilitarian view of culture. Institutions are consciously created to serve practical ends, and therefore their utility or usefulness is one of their primary features. For example, Tylor held that language can be explained as the product of a series of conscious choices guided by the principle of suitability or usefulness:

Language is one branch of the great art of sign-making or sign-choosing, and its business is to hit upon some sound as a suitable sign or symbol for each thought. Whenever a sound has been thus chosen there was no doubt a reason for the choice (1881:128).

Even grammar, Tylor said, is "but the result of man's efforts to get easier, fuller, and exacter expression for his thoughts" (1881:133). Similarly, law and morality were purposefully created by individuals for their own benefit. Tylor stated that the small clan or tribe is "the original lawgiving body enacting its laws for its common interest, the society which is ever sitting in committee and settling public opinion on utilitarian principles . . ." (1873:717).

To Tylor, the principle which guides mankind in devising his utilitarian institutions is that of reason, and social practices are explained by reference to rational processes of thought. Reason, therefore, is the key which we can apply to our own as well as to the most exotic beliefs and practices in order to gain understanding.

Closely associated with the principle of reason in Tylor's scheme is his view that human institutions can be studied in causal terms, as expressions of natural laws. In the opening pages of *Primitive Culture,* he noted that many people are repelled by the idea that human history is but one aspect of the history of nature, or that "our thoughts, wills, and actions accord with laws as definite as those which govern the motion of waves, the combination of acids and bases, and the growth of plants and animals" (1871, I:2). He argued that indeed natural laws do play a role in human behavior, and that he would take one aspect of man's history—Culture—and determine some of the causes which lay behind it (1871, I:5). That Tylor placed this argument concerning natural laws at the very beginning of his *magnum opus* reveals how central the issue was in his own mind.

To what features of the natural world did he look to discover these explanatory laws behind culture? Did he seek them in geography, in the conditions of the environment? Or perhaps in the structure of society itself? Not at all: he located them in a particular aspect of the human mind, in its rational as distinct from its emotional or affective components. The natural laws which explain culture are the natural processes of human reason. According to his theory of animism, for example, the basis of religion is the savage's attempt to explain to himself, by reason, such phenomena as life, death, dreams, and sleep. Animism did not arise but once, accidentally; it arose again and again in all parts of the world, and it is the expression of a natural law of human thought.

If Tylor saw human institutions as purposive and useful creations designed according to rational principles of thought, then he should have regarded customs as instruments eminently worthy of promoting a people's well-being. Tylor never arrived at this conclusion for at least two reasons. First, he held that experience and reason sometimes betray man, giving rise to such ill-conceived institutions as magic. I shall discuss the role of ignorance and error in Tylor's scheme shortly. Second, practices and beliefs sometimes acquire an authority and respect of their own and are adhered to on that basis in spite of their obvious inadequacies. In this sense Tylor regarded human institutions as sometimes autonomous, emergent, or *sui generis*. Speaking of the people of savage society, Tylor states that

the tyranny of tradition at every step imposes upon them thoughts and customs which have been inherited from a different stage of culture, and thus have lost a reasonableness which we may often see them to have possessed in their first origin (1866:86).

Elsewhere he states,

Whether a custom is plainly useful or not, and even when its purpose is no longer known, once established as a custom it must be conformed to. Savages may have finger-joints cut off, or undergo such long and severe fasts that many die; but often the only reason they can give for inflicting such suffering on themselves is that it was the custom of their ancestors (1881:4-9).

Although recognizing the relative autonomy of institutions, Tylor never pursued this issue systematically. He touched upon it frequently, but it was always a subsidiary and residual element in discussions about topics that he regarded as more important. He was not indifferent to traditional conservatism, however, for he regarded it as a morbid condition. He stated that "civilization is at a standstill where it is regulated by an-

21

cestral custom administered by great-grandfathers" (1881:430). Progress requires unfettered reason, the antithesis of which is traditionalism (cf. Stocking 1968a:82–83). Moreover, to Tylor, a main goal of anthropology is to show which beliefs and practices of civilized society are good and useful, and which are superstitions concealed "in the garb of modern knowledge." To him, "the science of culture is essentially a reformer's science," its role being to strip out moribund and stultifying ideas (1871, II:531, 539).

Traditional conservatism is much more pronounced in primitive than in civilized society, Tylor believed. The civilized peoples consciously improve their institutions by checking them systematically against their experiences, and also by reflecting upon them, whereas

among the lower races there is obstinate resistance to the most desirable reforms, and progress can only force its way with a slowness and difficulty which we of this century can hardly imagine (1881:439).

Tylor apparently did not discuss in detail how it is possible for a custom to have such a tenacious hold on the minds of a people; he never tried to account for the psychological or social mechanisms which insure the persistence of custom. It is perhaps understandable that he did not do so, since traditional conservatism was a residual issue in his mind. Nevertheless, I think that the essential feature of conservatism in Tylor's view can be summed up by the term "thoughtlessness." Traditional conservatism results when, for whatever reason, a people do not apply their minds to their traditional practices and beliefs, but adhere to them without conscious reflection. For example, Tylor occasionally wrote that the consensus of public opinion is a basis of conservatism: people often believe that "what everybody says must be true, what everybody does must be right" (1871, I:13). Tylor occasionally suggested that ecclesiastical authorities are a source of conservatism when they assign beliefs and practices to the realm of the sacred:

Egyptian mathematicians, being a priestly order, had come to regard their rules as sacred, and therefore not to be improved on, while their Greek disciples, bound by no such scientific orthodoxy, were free to go on further to more perfect methods (1881:319).

Tylor also held that conservatism is sometimes the result of the savage's regard for his ancestors:

[The savage's] tendency is to consider his ancestors as having handed down to him the perfection of wisdom, which it would be impiety to make the least alteration in (1881:439).

Whatever it may have been that Tylor took as the ultimate grounding or basis for conservative institutions, it is clear that he gave little emphasis to the role of emotion. In this respect he contrasts conspicuously with later writers, like Durkheim, who laid much weight on collective sentiments, and Boas, who regarded man as governed more by emotion and habit than reason. This is one of the principal contrasts between Tylor and later anthropologists.

To Tylor, culture is like a slow-growing but persistent plant trying to push its way through heavy soil. The minds of people in the early stages of development are severely limited by the conservative fetters of tradition, but rational thought is dogged and sooner or later will prevail. This is not to say that reason always results in progress, however, for errors in judgment are common, particularly in the early stages. Continuing the metaphor, it is as if the plant's growth process were occasionally to err and send the young bud in a sideward direction, or even deeper into the soil. Nevertheless, it is clear why Tylor was content to focus on the growth process itself rather than the binding fetters of tradition. Like the biologist interested in the growing plant rather than the earth through which it struggles, Tylor's central concern was always rational thought.

In summary, Tylor employed a reductionistic framework to explain the development and persistence of rational institutions. The worthwhile features of culture are understood by reference to individual ends and individual, rational thought. On the other hand, it is the morbid fetters of tradition which are emergent, for they are acquired from without and restrict people's thoughts and actions.

TYLOR'S EVOLUTIONISM. As the preceding suggests, Tylor's notion of culture is inextricably bound up with his idea of evolution, for he always conceived of human institutions within a developmental context.

Tylor's evolutionary theory is to be seen largely in relation to one of the leading issues facing anthropology during the 1860s: this was the debate between the degenerationists and progressionists (Stocking 1968a:74–81). The degenerationists argued that savage peoples once enjoyed a better condition, but, having fallen in the eyes of God, they degenerated to their present status. The degenerationist view was coupled with the notion that culture is not a natural phenomenon and that it falls beyond the reach of scientific analysis. Tylor was a leading exponent of the progressionist argument, which was that all societies and institutions go through a gradual—and natural—process of development, and that the various peoples of the world represent different levels of achievement along this line of evolutionary progression.

As crucial as these issues were in shaping the polemical thrust of Tylor's work, my interest here is in a somewhat different set of problems, which is the conceptual framework which underlies his evolutionary theory.

One can almost say that, whereas Durkheim and Spencer took the biological organism as their model for cultural analysis, Tylor, like Comte, took the development of science as the model for cultural evolution. In the process of arriving at truth, the sciences must pass through stages dominated by such erroneous theories as the belief in vitalism, alchemy, and astrology; these ill-reasoned beliefs are slowly transformed or eradicated as evidence mounts and thought develops. Similarly, culture, in its gradual course toward perfection, is characterized by false and inadequate knowledge which is slowly but relentlessly swept aside. Societies low on the scale of development are those which exhibit a high degree of ignorance and error.

The reason for the similarity between Tylor's conceptions of cultural and scientific development is clear enough: he thought that both are founded on rational thought. The savage puzzling over the inadequacies of his tools or laws, or over the natural phenomena of his environment, is like the scientist rationally and unemotionally pondering his problems in the laboratory (cf. Parsons 1937:58). The processes behind culture and science are much the same. For example, Tylor held that a principal difference between science and many of the myths devised by mankind is that science is true knowledge, whereas mythology is a false attempt at knowledge (e.g., cf. 1871, I:385). Even standards of morality have a rational and empirical basis. The "dull-minded barbarian has not power of thought enough to come up to the civilized man's best moral standard." The primitive quickly forgets the experiences of the past and fails to consider the future, for otherwise he would improve his behavior.

Much of the wrong-doing of the world comes from want of imagination. If the drunkard could see before him the misery of next year with something of the vividness of the present craving, it would over-balance it (1881:407).

Cultural evolution occurs because, in the long run, reason prevails over error:

Loose and illogical as man's early reasonings may be, and slow as he may be to improve them under the check of experience, it is a law of human progress that thought tends to work itself clear (1881:341).

Elsewhere Tylor states that "through age after age there has gone on a slow process of natural selection, ever tending to thrust aside what is worthless, and to favour what is strong and

25

sound" (1867:93). The context of this statement leaves little doubt that the key to this natural selection is "the test of reason and experience" (1867:93). The result is that human institutions become progressively more true and useful.

Note that the test of institutions is not one of reason alone, but reason together with experience. Tylor was an empiricist (cf. 1881:49ff; 1871, I:240ff., 273ff., 368ff.), emphasizing experience as the source of what men think and believe. He even argued that mathematics is an inductive science, the fundamental truths of which are "based on actual experience." Tylor quotes approvingly from J. S. Mill, who contended that the principle of addition derives not from logic but from the senses, from having observed, say, that two objects added to three objects totals five (1871, I:240–41). I have already indicated the role of experience in the development of moral standards. Certain actions, such as drunkenness, have consequences which the individual recognizes, and when he does so he is on the path to a higher morality.

In addition to his empiricism, Tylor was a determined realist, believing that it is *objective* experience which, together with reason, is behind human behavior and institutions. Ideally, according to Tylor, all people should interpret the same experiences the same way. The savage, "forgetful of yesterday and careless of to-morrow, lolling in his hammock when his wants are satisfied" (1881:407), should react to his own behavior the same way as Tylor. That he does not is explained by the fact that the savage is unable to perceive or imagine the objective consequences of his actions.

In short, Tylor's theory has little more room for cultural relativity than it does for scientific relativity, and for the same reasons. Cultural institutions, like scientific theory, are based upon objective experience and reason. And cultural evolution, like scientific evolution, is uni-directional (although of course it is subject to occasional regressions).

The extent of Tylor's absolutism is sometimes difficult for

twentieth-century people to comprehend. For example, he even viewed art in terms of a single evolutionary scale. He spoke of the Egyptian wall-paintings as "a style half-way between the lowest and highest." In spite of their cleverness, the ancient Egyptians "have not quite left behind the savage stage of art." Theirs are "picture-writings rather than pictures," "coloured in childish daubs of colours." Tylor wrote that the landscapes painted by the ancient Greeks were "still in the picture-writing stage," for the forests, mountains, and houses were not faithful representations but "stood as signs of the world outside" (1881:300–5).

Tylor used two principal methods in charting the course of evolution—the comparative method and the analysis of survivals. The latter is a technique for tracing developmental sequences by means of the residues of past institutions remaining among extant peoples. In all societies, ancient patterns of thought and behavior have survived beyond the conditions which gave rise to them, and these patterns serve "as proofs and examples" of an earlier stage of development (1871, I:16). For example, bows, arrows, and slings are mere toys in modern society, but they provide a record of activities in which Europeans once engaged in dead earnest (1871, I:72ff.).

The second method which Tylor employed, the comparative method, is based upon what seemed to him a self-evident fact, that throughout the world the institutions of mankind exhibit remarkable similarities. Such cultural phenomena as stone implements, basket-making, and cooking practices differ in little more than detail from society to society and continent to continent. "Little respect need be had in such comparisons for date in history or for place on the map" (1871, I:6). Similar beliefs, practices, and implements may be gathered from all over the world, and then they may be organized into comprehensive classificatory schemes. Weapons may be organized into the categories of spear, club, sling, bow and arrow, and the like. Myths may be categorized into such classes as myths of sunrise, myths of sunset, earthquake myths, and so on (1871, I:6–8). Once classified in this manner, the data within each category are arranged to show patterns of progression or evolutionary development. For example, in studying firearms, the investigator begins with the early and crude forms of weapons, such as the flint-lock rifle, and moves on to the most modern and sophisticated ones (1871, I:14–16). The direction which evolution has taken is brought to light in this way.

Behind these two methodological principles is the assumption that, to explain cultural evolution, the anthropologist has to "re-think" the steps by which it has come about: since institutions are consciously and purposefully created by individuals for their own ends, it follows that, to understand them, and to discover their causes, one is to recreate the experiences and reasoning upon which they rest. Marett, in a discussion of Tylor's theory of language, notes that Tylor's method was to join minds with the savage, and that this amounted "to a sort of introjection" (Marett 1936:56). In brief, Tylor employed the subjective point of view (Parsons 1937:46) in tracing cultural development.

The subjective point of view entails a difficulty. To "re-think" an institution raises the possibility of imposing on the actor's thought features which are foreign to it. Tylor was quite aware of the problem of subjective understanding:

The reasoning of the savage is not to be judged by the rules which belong to a higher education; and what the ethnologist requires in such a case, is not to know what the facts prove to his own mind, but what inference the very differently trained mind of the savage may draw from them (1878:5).

To Tylor, the problem of subjective understanding is met by taking account of the fact that the rational principles behind savage institutions are those of "a mental condition of intense and inveterate ignorance" (1871, I:23). In other words, the principle which explains the divergence of savage thought from our own—and hence the reason why there is a problem of subjective understanding at all—is ignorance and error. Once the savage's errors in reasoning are recognized, even the most irrational, frivolous, and despicable beliefs and practices became intelligible.

Using ignorance and error as the key to subjective understanding, some cultural phenomena can be "re-thought" with comparatively little difficulty. This is particularly true of technical skills and inventions. The use and purpose of tools and techniques is self-evident, so a careful description itself contains a fairly adequate account of the reasoning upon which they are based: the anthropologist does not have to go to great lengths to understand what a hatchet or blow-gun is all about, for example. The ignorance and error which explains these techniques and artifacts is simply that savage societies have a more rudimentary knowledge of mechanics and physics than civilized people. Moreover, reasonable developmental sequences of technological phenomena can be constructed on fairly objective grounds: "no one comparing a long-bow and cross-bow would doubt that the cross-bow was a development arising from the simpler instrument" (Tylor 1871, I:15; cf. 1881:16–17). Technological evolution amounts to the simple, linear accumulation of inventions, a process occurring more rapidly among some peoples than others. One can understand why Tylor's discussions of technology appear to be purely descriptive and lacking in "psychological" explanatory principles. I think the "psychological" principles are there, however; they consist in the inventors' processes of reasoning but are implicit in Tylor's account.

Tylor's method of "re-thinking" institutions is much less simple when applied to phenomena like mythology and religious beliefs; Tylor was led to develop fairly elaborate theoretical schemes in order to explain these, for the reasoning and supposed errors on which they rest are not self-evident. This may be illustrated by considering perhaps the most famous of his theories, his interpretation of animism.

Tylor noted that the "lower theologies" are frequently misunderstood by Europeans. He stated that these beliefs are hardly "a rubbish-heap of miscellaneous folly," but are consistent and logical to a high degree. Their formation and development rest upon rational principles, although the rationality that is involved is one of ignorant minds (1871, I:22–23).

Tylor asserted that there is no good evidence that any primitive society is totally without religion (1871, II:1ff.), and that as far as he could judge it is the belief in spiritual beings which is the religious belief common to all low races (1871, II:9). This belief, then, constitutes the very "groundwork of the Philosophy of Religion" (1871, II:10). Tylor's problem was to "rethink" this primitive philosophy: to "look for meaning, however crude or childish," to "search for the reasonable thought which once gave life to observances now become in seeming or reality the most abject and superstitious folly" (1871, II:5). Accordingly, he thought that the origin of belief in spiritual beings is to be found in the savages' attempts to explain two enigmas of life:

In the first place, what makes the difference between a living body and a dead one; what causes waking, sleep, trance, disease, death? In the second place, what are those human shapes which appear in dreams and visions (1871, II:12)?

The savage mind discovered a principle which explained all these phenomena at once: the doctrine of the human soul. The soul is able to leave the body temporarily during sleep, to wander about and undergo the experiences which are recorded in the mind as dreams; and it can depart for good, leaving the body without life.

It was not only the original doctrine of animism or belief in souls which Tylor explained by "re-thinking," however. He presented an enormous collection of beliefs and practices in his analysis, and each was interpreted as a logical extension of the original doctrine of souls. For example, "The doctrine of a Fu-

ture Life as held by the lower races is the all but necessary outcome of savage Animism" (1871, II:87). Human sacrifice, too,
is derived from the belief in souls; it is a rational inference
that, when a man dies, he may need or want others to accompany him in the next life (1871, II:42).

By using reason, or ignorance and error, as keys for subjective understanding, Tylor engaged in a subtle form of circular
thinking. He was living in a time of widespread confidence in
science, and as an individual he was firmly convinced of the
virtues of his own society; he spoke of his as "an enlightened
country," and of his age as one "scarcely approached by any
former age in the possession of actual knowledge and the stren-
uous pursuit of truth as the guiding principle of life" (1871,
II:536). He never seems to have seriously questioned the assumption that the institutions of Victorian England were, for
the most part, rational creations. However, when he applied
the principle of reason to savage beliefs and practices it was obvious that they usually did not measure up. The savage hunter
quietly but earnestly talking to his arrows before the kill, the
barbarian gardener offering sacrifices to the tubers he had just
planted—these are hardly examples of the flowering of rational
thought. The conclusion which Tylor drew from such evidence
was that savage thought is somehow defective. It did not occur
to him that the primitives may have appeared stupid because of
his own assumption that their institutions must be founded on
reason.

It is widely held that Tylor clearly distinguished between
culture and race, and that to him the only significant differences between people are of a cultural rather than a biological
order. The reason for this interpretation is easily discovered.
Again and again Tylor emphasized what has been called the
psychic unity of mankind. For example, in his *Researches* he
stated that when we consider the arts, knowledge, customs, and
superstitions of mankind we are struck by the recurrence of
similar forms in the most remote parts of the world. This, he

noted, "strikingly illustrates the extent of mental uniformity among mankind" (1873:373). At the beginning of *Primitive Culture* he stated:

For the present purpose it appears both possible and desirable to eliminate considerations of hereditary varieties or races of man, and to treat mankind as homogeneous in nature, though placed in different grades of civilization (1871, I:7).

And yet elsewhere Tylor made comments which are seemingly quite contradictory. For example, in his *Anthropology* he stated that "There seems to be in mankind inbred temperament and inbred capacity of mind." Some races, he commented, "have marched on in civilisation while others have stood still or fallen back," and this is due in part to "differences of intellectual and moral powers." He stated that the children of lower races appear to learn as well as white children until about the age of twelve, when they are left behind by the white children. "This fits with what anatomy teaches of the less development of brain in the Australian and African than in the European" (1881:60, 74–5; cf. also Harris 1968:140, Stocking 1968a:115–16, and White 1960a:iv). There seems little doubt that, at least by the time he wrote *Anthropology*, Tylor viewed the races of man as different in innate abilities.

How could he reconcile both notions? In Tylor's view the unity of mankind is one of potential, and some races have achieved more of this than others. Tylor probably held a Lamarckian conception of race, so the progress of civilization itself would be a cause of the similarities between the minds of people at like positions along the developmental scale.

CONTEXT AND MEANING. In what way did Tylor's ideas about culture influence his understanding or interpretation of concrete data? Tylor perceived human institutions in terms of the interaction of two opposing forces—the conservative fetters of tradition on one hand, and progressive, rational thought on the other. Accordingly, his interpretation of a datum took one of two forms, depending on whether he regarded the fact primarily as the expression of one force or the other.

Tylor viewed conservatism as a morbid condition, and he showed little sympathy when he came upon an example of it. Some anthropologists, like Durkheim, saw the fetters of tradition as a positive benefit; to Durkheim, the restraining force of tradition contributes to the cohesion and stability of society. Other anthropologists, including Benedict, tended to take a neutral position toward conservatism. To Benedict, traditionalism is simply a fact of life, unfortunate in some cases, perhaps, but not in most. Tylor could never regard conservatism as a neutral fact, let alone a positive benefit, without changing the core of his thought about mankind. To Tylor, the history of man is a record of achievement, and the restrictive fetters of tradition are the antithesis of both reason and progress.

Tylor actually devoted little space in his writings to cases of traditional conservatism, for he was more interested in progress than in the hindrances to it. One example he gave is illustrative, however. The incident occurred among the Dayaks of Borneo. When presented by the Europeans with a superior technique for chopping wood, the Dayaks resisted to the point of levying a fine on anyone caught using the new method. The superiority of the European innovation was obvious, nevertheless, and many of the Dayaks surreptitiously used it anyway. Tylor described this as "a striking instance of survival by ancestral authority in the very teeth of common sense" (1871, I:71).

An issue as important as Tylor's antipathy for conservatism is that of the grounds upon which he assigned a custom to that category. He classified as conservative all customs which persisted in use even though he could see no rational and utilitarian grounds for their doing so. Had he been able to shed his intellectualistic assumptions and view the same idata from some other perspective, however, he would have seen that the very customs he regarded as morbid made sense after all. For example, a Durkheimian interpretation of the Dayaks might have shown that these people were behaving quite reasonably. Durkheim would perhaps have seen the Dayaks' reaction as an example of a moral group clinging to a symbol of unity when faced with a disorganizing and threatening way of life. In short, not only did Tylor's perspective lead him to disapprove of conservatism; in addition, it dictated which customs were to be regarded as morbid and which were not.

Tylor's notion of culture also influenced his interpretation of rational (as opposed to conservative) institutions, for he assumed that the meaning of nontraditional social practices is to be seen in terms of the principles of reason and utility. This can be illustrated by his analysis of myth.

The New Zealanders believe[1] that Maui, a mythical hero, can ride or imprison all the winds but one, the West wind. Maui can neither catch the West wind nor find the cave in which it lives. From time to time, however, the hero nearly overtakes the West wind, which hides in its cave until the crisis has passed. It is during these brief periods that the prevailing westerly does not blow (Tylor 1871, I:360–61). Tylor interpreted this myth as a rational attempt by the New Zealanders to make sense of the world around them. It is a nature-myth, the purpose of which is to describe or explain "in personal shape the life of nature" (1871, I:367).

One comparatively modern framework for explaining myth is that which holds that tales are symbolic statements about social affairs. According to this interpretation, myths have important functions to perform at the level of the cultural or social system, in that they contribute to the solidarity of society, among other things.

Tylor did not ignore the relationship between myth and society. For example, he discussed a class of legends which he called "explanatory traditions":

[1] Throughout this book I frequently use the ethnographic present, in that I employ the present tense to describe cultural practices and conditions which were observed and described in the past and which may no longer exist.

When the attention of a man in the myth-making stage of intellect is drawn to any phenomenon or custom which has to him no obvious reason, he invents and tells a story to account for it . . . (1871, I:392).

Tylor cites the way in which the African Wakuafi account for their practice of cattle thievery. The Wakuafi assert that Heaven gave all the cattle to them, and whenever they come across an animal in someone else's possession it is "their call to go and seize it." Tylor describes this tale as an "ex post facto" legend which satisfies the "craving to know causes and reasons" (1871, I:392). To Tylor, the tale is a product of rational minds and fulfills the individual's need for explanation. The symbolic and functional significance of the belief is totally missed. In short, Tylor's analysis of "explanatory traditions" is precisely the same as that of nature-myths, and it bears little resemblance to the functional interpretations which proliferated after the turn of the century.

It was not only Tylor's interpretation of myth which was affected by his culture concept. For example, Tylor describes a custom of the North American Indians whereby a mother who has recently lost a baby makes a crude representation of the infant out of black feathers and quills. This is kept in a cradle which the woman carries around with her, and when she stops to work she talks to the infant's effigy as if it were the real child. Customs—or rituals—of this sort would soon be handled by the Durkheimians, and later by Radcliffe-Brown, as symbolic acts, the meaning of which could be reached only by seeing them in their social context. Tylor's interpretation, however, was much more simple and direct. To him, the feathers and quills are merely a rational device which enables the mother to remember her lost child. The savage mind is less developed than that of a civilized person, and it has greater need for material images to assist its thought (1878:106 ff.).

As a practitioner of the comparative method, Tylor has been criticized for wrenching ethnographic facts from their cultural contexts and thereby doing violence to them. Ruth Benedict describes Tylor's as "the anecdotal period of ethnology." She contrasts the anthropologists of his period with Franz Boas, who always insisted "that anthropological theory must take into account not detached items but human cultures as organic and functioning wholes" (1932:1). This criticism is essentially correct, but it misses the point. Tylor was quite concerned with context, although he regarded the *ethnographic* context as a relatively unimportant one within which to couch his material. To him, it is primarily within a comparative or historical context that the distinctive characteristics of a trait emerge. Tylor offered an admittedly trivial illustration, the European custom of wearing earrings. The earring, Tylor believed, is "a relic of a ruder mental condition," a condition in which such things as rings, bones, and feathers are inserted through the cartilage of the nose, or in which ivory studs are inserted in the corners of the mouth. The use of earrings is a custom located near the end of this developmental sequence, and, Tylor implied, it will ultimately die out altogether (1878:1–2). The customs and laws of savage and barbarous tribes "often explain to us, in ways we should otherwise have hardly guessed, the sense and reason of our own" (1881:401; see also 1873, Part II).

It is not only the beliefs and practices of civilized society to which the historical and comparative context is applicable:

The treatment of similar myths from different regions, by arranging them in large groups, makes it possible to trace in mythology the operation of imaginative processes recurring with the evident regularity of mental law; and thus stories of which a single instance would have been a mere isolated curiosity, take their place among well-marked and consistent structures of the human mind (1871, I:282).

The value of the comparative framework is that it allows the anthropologist to discover, through induction, the common processes of thought behind human institutions, and therefore their meaning.

One reason why Tylor could ignore the cultural or ethnographic context of a trait is that his was a reductionist theory, stressing the causal relations between individual mental processes and cultural phenomena. All traits which share the same cause belong together, regardless of where they are found. To argue that it is necessary to provide the ethnographic context of a trait in order to understand it rests on the assumption that it is the relations between cultural elements which are significant for understanding—that traits have properties which enable them to react upon one another. In short, it assumes that culture is an emergent system. To accuse Tylor of detaching his data from their cultural context amounts to accusing him of failing to achieve a culture concept which was quite foreign to his thought and to the intellectual tradition in which he worked.

FRANZ BOAS

The revolution in the social sciences which took place between about 1890 and 1930 laid the foundations of much of what constitutes present-day social thought (see Hughes 1958 and Parsons 1937). Hughes notes that the people most intimately involved in this revolution were of "the original 'heartland' of Western society: France, Germany (including Austria), and Italy" (1958: 12). Englishmen, Americans, Russians, and Eastern Europeans played little part. The geographical source of this revolution is significant, for the man who later became known as the founder of American anthropology, Franz Boas, was not an American at all, but was born, raised, and educated in Germany. Moreover, the years during which Boas' thought underwent the greatest change—the decade or so before the turn of the century and the years immediately following—were precisely those during which this revolution took place. In short, Boas should be seen in the context of this larger intellectual movement; he was one of the "turn-of-the-century thinkers who were creating the modern image of the human animal" (Stocking 1968a:160).

INTRODUCTION. Boas' academic training was undertaken within the natural sciences or *Naturwissenschaften,* and his anthropological theory was definitely shaped by a desire to approach culture with the rigor of the physical scientist. However, his work was also decidedly influenced by the German idealist tradition of thought. This was a tradition which placed greater emphasis on the subjective idea than on objective, phenomenal reality. Whereas the natural sciences dealt with the phenomenal world on a materialistic basis, the idealists held that the sphere of human activity could only be approached in terms of its "spiritual" or subjective qualities. History was not to be understood as the working out of natural and universal laws, but as the expression of ideas. The *Geist* or "spirit" became the organizing principle for the historian's data, and this *Geist* was a subjectively perceived whole. Each cultural tradition and each period was thought to have its own unique "spirit" which was qualitatively different from any other, and a person from one tradition was able to grasp the events and "spirit" of another through subjective understanding. German idealist writings tended to take one of two approaches. They either focused on the philosophy of history, or they took as their goal meticulously detailed historical accounts aimed at providing the fullest possible knowledge or understanding of a given period or event (Parsons 1937:473–87).

The turn-of-the-century revolution in social thought can be regarded—within limits and in very rough terms—as the infusion of certain elements of idealist thought into the mainstream of positivism. The nineteenth-century positivists held that a single standard of rationality could be used for evaluating human institutions. At that time it was thought that contemporary Western European society had achieved the highest expression of rational thought so far. German idealism, on the other hand, contained a degree of relativism. Each "spirit" was thought to be unique; it had to be understood in terms of itself and not in terms of a universal standard, and therefore the investigator had to leave his own ideas behind when embarking upon the study of another time and place.

Similarly, the turn-of-the-century revolution in social thought rejected the notion that departures from Western European rationality are to be seen solely or even primarily in terms of ignorance and error. This revolution stressed in particular that human institutions are not at bottom rational, but are founded on emotion. To understand another society the investigator has to forsake his own perspective and take up that of the people he is studying.

Rejected, then, were the image of man as rational and calculating, and the conception of human institutions as rationally conceived artifacts. In their place the view emerged that behavior is largely "irrational" and emotional, and that it is precisely these elements which must be taken into account in order to understand human affairs.

The view of man and society which appeared at about the beginning of the twentieth century is sometimes referred to as anti-intellectualism. This term is used by Crane Brinton, for example, who offers the following definition:

Basically, the anti-intellectual, in the sense we here use the term, does not regard the instrument of thought as *bad,* but among most men most of the time as *weak.* . . . [T]he anti-intellectual notes merely that thought seems often at the mercy of appetites, passions, prejudices, habits, conditioned reflexes, and a good deal else in human life that is not thinking (1963:213; emphasis in the original).

A prime representative of anti-intellectualism is Pavlov, according to whom behavior is governed by automatic reflexes far more than by conscious, rational thought; another is Freud, who conceived human thought and action as products of such "irrational" factors as drives and neuroses; a third is Pareto, whose focus was upon the nonrational features of behavior and society.

Brinton has attempted to place anti-intellectualism within a historical context of social and political events. He notes that ideas about the natural goodness and rationality of man and about the perfectibility of society reached their fullest and purest expression during the Enlightenment. It was believed that social institutions could be improved by conscious and intelligent effort; if people tried, they could bring about progress through political action. These ideas constituted the underpinnings of democratic society, with its belief that a free electorate has the intelligence and high-mindedness to govern itself wisely. The events of history severely challenged these notions, however. Due to such developments as the excesses of the French Revolution and the rise of Napoleon, a growing disillusionment and pessimism set in. Both the goodness of man and his propensity to follow the dictates of reason were subject to increasing doubts. The same blighted hopes and expectations, continuing into the twentieth century, resulted in anti-intellectualism, which Brinton describes as "one of the characteristic manifestations of the spirit of our age" (1963:212).

It was not only the image of the human actor and his society which were called into question by the innovators at about the beginning of this century. There was also a reexamination of the problem of the observer's understanding of his data, Max Weber's notion of ideal types being perhaps the best illustration (see Hughes 1958).

BIOGRAPHICAL. Boas was born in Minden, Germany, in 1858, the son of a comparatively well-to-do businessman. He studied a variety of subjects at several universities, and in 1881 received his doctorate from the University of Kiel. His degree was in physics, but he had a strong interest in geography, his minor. Not long after leaving Kiel, in 1883, he embarked upon a year-

long trip among the Eskimo to try to discover their knowledge
of local geography and the patterns of their migrations (Stocking 1968a:138–40). Although the problems he chose were geographical, strictly speaking, his investigations enabled him to
move into anthropology with little difficulty.

When Boas returned to Germany he received an appointment at the Royal Ethnographic Museum in Berlin, serving
under Bastian, and not long thereafter was appointed Docent
in geography at the University of Berlin. But very shortly he
left once again for field research, this time among the Bella
Coola of the Northwest Coast of North America. For the rest of
his life his ethnographic research would focus primarily (although not exclusively) on the Indians of this part of the
world.

Boas was a Jew, and for that reason, together with his "left-
liberal posture," he wanted to leave Germany for a more congenial social atmosphere (Lesser 1968:99–100; Stocking
1968a:149–50). Between 1887 and 1896 he received several appointments in New York, Worcester, and Chicago, each of
which enabled him to pursue his anthropological research. In
1896 he began teaching at Columbia University, where he remained for the most part until his retirement in 1937. He died
in New York in 1942.

Boas was a strong-willed man, and he frequently found himself chafing under the authority of those above him. But the
force of his personality and his determination were of inestima-
ble importance in the history of American anthropology. Boas
was absolutely dedicated to establishing anthropology as a fully
professional, rigorous, and research-oriented discipline, and almost single-handedly he trained and directed a corps of
students—such as Kroeber, Lowie, Radin, Spier, Benedict—
who would distinguish the field as a viable and productive addition to the social sciences. The department at Columbia,
strongly identified with Boas himself, soon became the heart of
anthropology in the United States.

It is next to impossible to give a capsule account of Boas' research and publications, for his interests covered the entire range of anthropology, and he was a prolific writer. He conducted significant research on human growth, anthropometry, mythology and folklore, linguistics, and primitive art, to name only the most important topics. His work in any one of these areas would have been enough to establish him as an important figure in anthropology. It is easier to appreciate this productivity when it is remembered that he was also quite active in shaping and organizing a new discipline and training its members.[2]

THE DEVELOPMENT OF BOAS' CULTURE CONCEPT. Although Boas began his university training with a rather "materialistic *Weltanschauung*," he soon began to question those assumptions (see Stocking 1968a:Chapter 7, and Kluckhohn and Prufer 1959). At least with regard to his thinking about human behavior, he showed signs of neo-Kantian and idealist influences early in his career. He was sufficiently interested in Kant to have a copy with him while among the Eskimo, and even before that he expressed an interest in the epistemological problem of the effect of the individual's mental state on perception. Before the end of the 1880s he had come to see "each culture as a subjectively perceived whole," and in the very early years of his development—still in the 1880s—he was turning in the direction of historicism, perhaps due to the influence of Dilthey (Stocking 1968a:137–44, 152–56).

Partly as a result of these idealist influences, Boas was in a good position to participate in the turn-of-the-century revolution described above. How, then, did he view the purpose of anthropology and the program of research which it was to follow, and how did he plan to change the discipline's focus? By

[2] For a sample of the range of Boas' interests, see his collection of articles in *Race, Language and Culture* (Boas 1940). For an appreciation of Boas' impact, see the articles contained in the two memoirs devoted to him (Kroeber *et al.*, 1943, and Goldschmidt 1959).

inquiring into these issues I can reveal some of the most important developments in his thought.

In a paper published in 1887 on "The Study of Geography" Boas distinguished between two fundamentally different scientific pursuits. The first seeks to discover general laws of the universe, and it considers a particular phenomenon of interest only for what it reveals about some natural law. The second form of science consists of "the study of phenomena for their own sake" (1887, in 1940:642). This approach seeks to understand phenomena as they appear to the human observer; interest is directed toward a thorough understanding of the phenomena themselves rather than toward the laws which they express. For example, if a geographer were to take the first approach, he would isolate the various geological, meteorological, or other elements of a region and relate them to other phenomena in other parts of the world which have the same cause. By the second approach he would take all the features of the local area as a unit and seek to understand them as a unique constellation of traits. Boas argued that the two forms of science are compatible and equally valid.

This division of scientific interest is reflected in Boas' early work in anthropology. He was quite explicit that the first form of science occupies an important place in the discipline. He wrote that "certain laws exist which govern the growth of human culture, and it is our endeavor to discover these laws" 1896, in 1940:276). Boas was critical of the earlier comparative method employed by the evolutionists (1896, in 1940:270ff.), however, and argued that a fresh approach was needed. The earlier method was to construct classificatory schemes with which to organize the ethnographic data; these schemes were based on the principle that the simpler and more "irrational" customs are earlier. In other words, the evolutionists assumed that their systems of classification represented history. Boas rejected this assumption, and he argued that the laws of evolution can be derived only from the analysis of the actual histories of delimited regions:

Thus we have come to understand that before we can build up the theory of the growth of all human culture, we must know the growth of cultures that we find here and there. . . . We must, so far as we can, reconstruct the actual history of mankind, before we can hope to discover the laws underlying that history (1898a:4).

In 1897 the Jesup North Pacific Expedition was organized under Boas' direction, and it followed his plan precisely: its purpose was to provide the detailed history of a limited area, the northern Asiatic and North American regions bordering the Pacific. More specifically, the expedition was to discover the degree of influence between the Asian and North American tribes (1898a:4–6).

It was characteristic of the period in which Boas wrote to regard human institutions as expressions of "mental life." Both the positivists and the idealists, in spite of their differences, agreed on this point. Consequently, it is not surprising that Boas believed that evolutionary laws were to be found in "the psychical laws of the human mind" (1896, in 1940:436). Like Tylor, Boas thought that culture could be reduced to individual mental processes.

The second form of science, that which is concerned not with the search for natural laws but with an understanding of phenomena for their own sake, played an even more important role in Boas' early anthropology. He held that the primary means for achieving this kind of understanding is the historical approach: it is possible to attain an "intelligent understanding" of culture by discovering how it came to be what it is (1936, in 1940:305; see also 1908:7–8). In his early work Boas returned again and again to the detailed historical accounts of particular regions, especially in his many articles on folklore.

The historical approach was not the only one which he used in order to achieve this form of understanding, however, for he also employed the principle of subjective interpretation. In 1885, for example, Boas was at the Royal Ethnographic Museum in Berlin, having just returned from his Eskimo trip. A collection of Alaskan and British Columbian Indian artifacts arrived at the museum, and, Boas states, "my fancy was first struck by the flight of imagination exhibited in the works of art of the British Columbians as compared to the severe sobriety of the eastern Eskimo." Later that year he had a chance to interview some Northwest Coast Indians who had been brought to Berlin, "and opportunity was thus given to cast a brief glance behind the veil that covered the life of those people." He commented that "the attraction became irresistible"; "with the financial aid of personal friends" he set off for research in British Columbia (1909:307). What attracted him so strongly was not history, but the desire to get "behind the veil" that stood between him and the thought of the Indians. An attempt to penetrate this veil is contained in an article on Northwest Coast face paintings published as part of the reports of the Jesup Expedition in 1898. In that essay Boas attempted to show the meaning of facial paintings and of Northwest Coast art in general as seen from the perspective of the Indians themselves (1898b).

All the research which Boas conducted for the Jesup Expedition was motivated to a degree by a desire to penetrate the Kwakiutl veil. In introducing his Kwakiutl ethnography, which resulted from the Jesup project, Boas states,

It seemed to me well to make the leading point of view of my discussion, on the one hand an investigation of the historical relations of the tribes to their neighbors, on the other hand a presentation of the culture as it appears to the Indian. For this reason I have spared no trouble to collect descriptions of customs and beliefs in the language of the Indian, because in these the points that seem important to him are emphasized, and the almost unavoidable distortion contained in the descriptions given by the casual visitor and student is eliminated (1909:309).

Boas' interest in the subjective side of culture constituted a major theme in his work, and the motivation behind this interest seems to have been the desire for understanding simply for the sake of understanding.

I have said that Boas saw two ways to pursue the second form of science in anthropology, or to arrive at an "intelligent understanding" of culture. One was to study culture history, the other was to achieve subjective understanding.

It appears that Boas did not regard these as clearly distinguishable approaches, for he believed that when people offer an interpretation of their customs they provide an explanation for their historical development as well. By inquiring into a people's ideas, then, the investigator can understand the past, and vice versa. His discussion of ceremonial masks is illustrative. In some societies, he writes, masks "are used for deceiving spirits," whereas in others "the wearer personifies a deceased person whose memory is to be recalled." These statements express the peoples' cultural explanations for the use of masks. However, Boas thought that these brief characterizations also provided a historical account of the respective customs, for he wrote that "These few data suffice to show that the same ethnical phenomena *may develop from different sources*" (1896, in 1940:273–75; emphasis mine). In his pursuit of history, Boas was led to explore the subjective side of culture, the domain of cultural ideas; and in studying cultural ideas he thought he was also studying history.[3]

Boas' original program of research had room to accommodate both forms of science as he conceived them. I now want to show some of the results of this program of research, for it led to revolutionary changes in Boas' thought; it led to the devel-

[3] Boas soon gave up the notion that the study of ideas is a safe approach to the study of history (e.g., 1903, in 1940:562, 563). In the first edition of *The Mind of Primitive Man* Boas again discussed the use of ceremonial masks, but he added a significant qualifying remark: "While it is not at all necessary to assume that these explanations given by the wearer of masks represent the actual historical development of the custom, the explanations themselves suggest the improbability of a single origin of the custom" (1911:187).

opment of a twentieth-century version of the culture concept. Although a variety of factors contributed to this emergence (see Stocking 1968a:Chapter 9), here I shall deal with three that are particularly important.

The first factor was Boas' desire to work out the detailed histories of delimited regions. The principal methodological technique he used for this was the study of the dissemination or diffusion of traits. For example, by an investigation of myths he concluded that, at least with respect to mythology, the Navaho were more strongly influenced from the northwest of North America than from the northeast or the Mississippi Basin area (Boas 1897). By means of distributional studies Boas was also able to conclude that the Alaskan Eskimo exhibited greater outside influences than the other Eskimo groups, and he speculated that the original homeland of these peoples was east of the Mackenzie River (1901a).

The 1890s was a decade in which Boas gave considerable attention to folklore studies; much of his effort was directed toward collecting and reporting the tales, but the ultimate purpose was to trace histories. This work eventually led him to a critical conclusion, which was that the ultimate cause of myths cannot be found in the processes of thought of individual human beings. The folklore of a people is built up by the "accretions of foreign material," and each diffused element is then adapted or modified to fit its new cultural context (1896, in 1940:429). Consequently, "the original significance of the myth"—the mental process which constitutes its origin—is necessarily obscure (1898, in 1940:423), and any "systematic explanation of mythological stories . . . [is] illusory" (1933, in 1940:450). In brief, myths are products of such complex histories that the search for origins is futile. The speculations of men like Tylor—who held, for example, that "nature-myths" originate in the savage's desire to understand the universe—can never be proved.

This conclusion was not restricted to folklore, but was soon extended to cover technology, art, social organization, and the rest of culture (e.g., 1924, in 1940:290–94); toward the end of his career Boas wrote,

the material of anthropology is such that it needs must be a historical science, one of the sciences the interest of which centers in the attempt to understand the individual phenomena rather than in the establishment of general laws which, on account of the complexity of the material, will be necessarily vague and, we might almost say, so self-evident that they are of little help to the real understanding (1932, in 1940:258).

The form of science which was motivated by a desire to understand phenomena for their own sake was to prevail in anthropology, not because of Boas' preference, necessarily, but because of the nature of the data.

Boas' views about the way in which history obscures the causes of cultural phenomena had fundamental implications for evolutionary theory. Boas argued that each culture trait has a complex past, and therefore the total cultural assemblage of a people "has its own unique history" (1920, in 1940:286). He rejected the notion of more or less uniform evolutionary stages (cf. 1911:Chapter 7) since the presence or absence of pottery, metallurgy, or the like in a given area "seems to be due more to geographical location than to general cultural causes" (1911:183; see also 1896, in 1940:270–80).

An even more fundamental result of Boas' conclusions regarding the complexity of history is that he came to regard culture as an emergent system. It is not to be understood as the product of natural mental operations of individual human beings, but as the result of its own *sui generis,* historical principles. In particular, culture traits are to be explained in terms of the principles of diffusion and modification, the latter of which is the process whereby a trait is reshaped to fit the new cultural context in which it is found. Boas' insistence that culture is "historically determined" amounts to saying that it is emergent (1920, in 1940:289).

Closely associated with the development of Boas' view that culture is an emergent system is the growth of his cultural determinism. If culture does not arise from within the human being, then it must come to him ready-made from without. Man learns rather than creates it; his behavior and beliefs reflect, not his native intelligence, but the cultural tradition in which he was raised. Boas' rejection of racial explanations of mental differences is famous, and this rejection "took place mainly because Boas . . . greatly elaborated the alternative explanation of mental differences in terms of cultural determinism" (Stocking 1968a:219). Boas' recognition of cultural determinism, of "the iron hold of culture upon the average individual" (1932, in 1940:259), also led him to see how thoroughly people are modified by tradition. He thought that personality differences between societies are so great that "for most mental phenomena we know only European psychology and no other" (1932, in 1940:250)—because psychologists had limited their research to European subjects.

Some feel that Boas did not go far enough in his views about the autonomy of culture. Leslie White, for example, argues that the guiding principles behind cultural dynamics are contained within the technological system, and that the ideational elements of culture are essentially epiphenomena of technological arrangements. Boas' thinking developed out of a tradition which regarded behavior and custom as expressions of thought; if anything, according to this viewpoint, economics are epiphenomena of ideas. Consequently, although Boas viewed cultural ideas as autonomous with respect to natural processes of thought, he "reduced" much of culture, including social structure, economics, and technology—what Goodenough has called the phenomenal order of culture as distinct from the ideational order (Goodenough 1964:11–13)—to the cultural ideas of a people. For example, Boas seems to have implied that political change among a people is limited primarily by the ideas the people have rather than by the structure of the society, the dis-

49

tribution of power, or the nature of the economic arrangements:

A political leader may add new ideas to old political forms, although the older forms will exert an influence upon his mind and limit the extent to which the new may become acceptable (1932:163).

Elsewhere Boas speaks of social structure being "based" on concepts (1935:171–72), and of "fundamental concepts underlying" social organization (1932:14–15).

A second important factor contributing to the emergence of Boas' culture concept was his fascination for getting behind the veil separating him from foreign modes of thought. Perhaps in part because of his early German historicist influences, Boas conceived of the problem of subjective understanding in terms radically different from those envisaged by Tylor—according to whom differences in belief between peoples turned essentially on the pivot of reason and mis-reason (or ignorance and error). Boas, like the German idealists, assumed that each people's system of thought is qualitatively different from any other; he had more respect than Tylor for the uniqueness of foreign ideas, and his approach was to understand them on their own terms without imposing a framework of rationality. Boas' analysis of art is an example. Instead of regarding the painting and carving of the Northwest Coast Indians as awkward attempts at realistic representation, as Tylor would have done, Boas tried to see them in terms of the principles which guided the eye and hand of the artist himself (see Codere 1966: xx–xxiii).

Boas' realization that the mental life of a people must be approached on its own terms was not limited to the issue of what people think, but was extended to cover their perception or experiencing of the world as well. An example is his article "On Alternating Sounds," published in 1889. At the time he wrote this essay many philologists believed that primitive languages were less precise than civilized tongues, and that this imprecision was evident in the phonetic systems of the simpler languages. It was found that savage speakers pronounced the same word in a variety of ways, and it was assumed that the existence of these "alternating sounds" in a language was a sign of indefiniteness and therefore primitiveness. Boas showed that the reason the investigator heard sounds as alternating was that the analyst's language did not classify phonetic sounds the same way as his subject's. Since the investigator's language made distinctions which were not meaningful in the foreign tongue, differences were heard which were not intended by the native speaker. In effect, Boas argued that to adequately understand a foreign language the investigator had to learn to think in terms of the phonetic distinctions of that tongue rather than his own. At a more general level, his argument was that experience—in this case, the experience of hearing sounds—was not objective, but was structured and in that sense determined by the cultural tradition in which the individual was raised (cf. Stocking 1968a:159).

By 1894 Boas' appreciation that the mental life of a people must be approached on its own terms resulted in an important criticism of evolutionary thought. Evolutionists like Tylor and Spencer believed that primitive societies are retarded or childlike in intellectual development, and this idea seemed to be confirmed when the principle of reason was applied to their thoroughly absurd customs. The savages' childlike nature also seemed to be corroborated by the reports of travelers and others who had observed primitives first-hand. Boas argued that these reports were unreliable. The observers usually did not know the languages of those about whom they were reporting, they seldom had the time to thoroughly enter into the "inner life" of foreign peoples, and their accounts were frequently biased. Boas singled out several "mental qualities" which were supposed to characterize the lower societies, including impulsiveness and fickleness, improvidence, inability to concentrate, and lack of originality. He discounted each as typical of primitives, and argued instead that travelers and others have erred in judging the behavior of foreign peoples according to European standards. Boas gave as an example the European traveler who hires native help for his journey. Since the traveler regards time as extremely valuable, he wants to reach his destination as soon as possible. But his savage employee is subject to an entirely different set of compulsions and does not feel the need to get started early. He delays, thoroughly irritating his employer, and as a result the traveler regards the savage as fickle and impulsive in work habits. Boas notes that it would be just as reasonable for the primitive to charge that it is the traveler who is impulsive and lacking in self control, because it is the traveler who becomes so "irritated by a trifling cause like loss of time" (1894:317–23).

The point of this argument was that what was widely interpreted as the hereditary inferiority of savages is really a difference arising from social causes. The technique Boas used in this polemic, however, was to show that the supposed inferiority vanishes when the investigator enters thoroughly into the primitive's "inner life" and achieves adequate understanding. In brief, the supposed inferiority of primitives is manifest only when the observer imposes Western European ideas on the savage's thought. The argument was repeated in other contexts and with respect to other facets of cultural life, such as language. Whereas some authorities held that primitive languages lack the "power of classification and abstraction," Boas countered that

Here, again, we are easily misled by our habit of using the classifications of our own language, and considering these, therefore, as the most natural ones, and by overlooking the principles of classification used in the languages of primitive people (1911:142).

I have already said that Boas arrived at the view that each culture has a complex history; the implication is that each culture is unique. His argument about the need for thorough subjective understanding brought him to the same conclusion. The exotic beliefs of primitive man cannot be apprehended by the imposition of foreign—European—standards of value and belief, including the criterion of reason, but must be understood in terms of their own distinctive principles:

> The activities of the mind . . . exhibit an infinite variety of form among the peoples of the world. In order to understand these clearly, the student must endeavor to divest himself entirely of opinions and emotions based upon the peculiar social environment into which he is born. He must adapt his own mind, so far as feasible, to that of the people whom he is studying. The more successful he is in freeing himself from the bias based on the group of ideas that constitute the civilization in which he lives, the more successful he will be in interpreting the beliefs and actions of man (1901b:1).

This amounts to an even more fundamental denial of Tylorian evolutionary theory than the failure to find evidence of developmental stages in the historical record. The fact that evolutionary stages are not apparent in the data does not mean that they will not appear some day, but the fact that each cultural system of thought is completely unique means that the evolutionary framework which is to explain these stages is untenable. European standards of rationality could no longer constitute the basis for a single framework for understanding and comparison, so even if evolutionary stages were to emerge from Boas' data they would have to be explained in terms quite different from Tylor's.

Boas' rejection of the European standard of rationality in anthropological analysis was accompanied by an innovation that was a central element in the turn-of-the-century revolution in social thought. In place of reason as the basis of human institutions, Boas substituted emotion. This was the third important factor in the emergence of his culture concept.

The emotional conception of behavior was firmly embedded in Boas' thought by the first decade of this century. Moreover, his early discussions about emotion and tradition were placed in juxtaposition to comments about reason; for example, in 1901 he wrote:

When we consider . . . the whole range of our daily life, we notice how strictly we are dependent upon tradition that cannot be accounted for by any logical reasoning (1901b:8; see also 1904, *passim*).

This suggests that he may have seen theories which emphasized emotion and those which emphasized reason as in contention with one another, and he may therefore have sensed the historical and theoretical significance of the innovation he was proposing.

The key to Boas' formulation of the role of emotion in culture is the word "habit." Boas thought that when an action is performed frequently over a period of time it becomes "automatic," in that its "performance is ordinarily not combined with any degree of consciousness" (1910:380). For example, a person learns to eat with a knife and fork, and this becomes so habitual that it seems natural. It becomes governed by unconscious rather than conscious thought.

In addition to being unconscious, habitual patterns acquire emotional associations: "Any action that differs from those performed by us habitually strikes us immediately as ridiculous or objectionable." For example, a dog taught to shake hands with his hind rather than front paw elicits amusement, and breaches of habitual standards of modesty are strongly resented. Even linguistic patterns acquire an emotional underpinning, in that "We resent deviations in pronunciation and in structure" of the language we speak. The intensity of the emotional reaction of a people when they are confronted by forms of thought and behavior which are not in accord with their own is illustrated by the persecution of heretics by the Church (1932:139ff.).

As Boas' thinking about emotion developed, he began to see human reason in a new light. According to Boas, habit and emotion are by far the more important principles behind human behavior: "Even in our civilization popular thought is primarily directed by emotion, not by reason" (1938c:210). This is not to say that the typical individual cannot *give* reasons for what he does. There are occasions in which a habitual pattern is brought into consciousness—such as when an individual observes a breach of custom, or is asked by a child why people perform an activity in a particular way—and he then attempts to provide an explanation. These explanations are no more than rationalizations, however, "secondary interpretations of customary actions" (1910:382). To Boas, reason is not the basis of human behavior and social institutions, for it is comparatively frail and powerless in the face of the dominating influence of emotion and habit.

This view of behavior entails a dramatic shift in the interpretation of the meaning of Western European social institutions, such as Western standards of morality, democracy, and the like. To Tylor and the other evolutionists, these institutions were historical summits, the highest expression so far of the application of reason to social affairs. To Boas, they were simply habitual patterns which Western peoples had grown accustomed to, and the arguments of churchmen and others about their objective reasonableness were illusory:

The fact which is taught by anthropology,—that man the world over *believes* that he follows the dictates of reason, no matter how unreasonably he may act,—and the knowledge of the existence of the tendency of the human mind to arrive at a conclusion first and to give reasons afterwards, will help us to open our eyes; so that we recognize that our philosophic views and our political convictions are to a great extent determined by our emotional inclinations, and that the reasons which we give are not the reasons by which we arrive at our conclusions, but the explanations which we give for our conclusions (1908:27).

The view that a people's conscious and rational understanding of their own behavior is deceptive was not a minor issue in Boas' mind. He stated,

In fact, my whole outlook upon social life is determined by the question: how can we recognize the shackles that tradition has laid upon us? For when we recognize them, we are also able to break them (1938a:202).

Boas felt that the evolutionary anthropologists' failure to recognize the shackles of tradition which bound their thoughts was a major defect in their work. In 1904 he noted that there was "a strong tendency" in anthropology toward the "subjective valuation of the various phases of [evolutionary] development, the present serving as a standard of comparison." Indeed, "the grand picture of nature" as a whole, not just the picture of the development of civilization, "is still obscured by a subjective element, emotional in its sources, which leads us to ascribe the highest value to that which is near and dear to us" (1904:515). In brief, one of the principal errors committed by the evolutionary anthropologists is that they mistook their cultural rationalizations for unfettered rational thought. Although they believed that both their theories and Western European social institutions were guided by reason, instead it was emotion.

Similarly, Boas implied that the reason why primitive institutions can depart so radically from the standard of rationality is not because the primitive himself is childlike or simple-minded. Like the evolutionary anthropologist, even the most gifted savage finds it difficult to break through the emotional fetters of tradition. This was another blow to the evolutionists' paradigm. A universal standard of rationality cannot be the basis of a comparative anthropological science precisely because the failure of institutions to live up to that standard is due, not to ignorance and error, but to man's irrational attachment to the customs he has inherited from the past.

In summary, in his early program of research Boas emphasized two different but related forms of science, and in engaging in each he was led toward the development of a modern version of the culture concept. The first type of study was the fairly detailed historical analysis of specific cultural phenomena. This brought him to the view that culture is an emergent system, since he was led to conclude that each culture trait has a complex history and that its origins cannot be traced to the natural operations of the human mind. Culture must be understood in terms of its own distinctive historical processes. Second, in his early research he tended to emphasize that other systems of thought must be understood in terms of their own principles rather than in terms of a single standard of rationality. In doing so he rejected the entire Tylorian evolutionary framework, which imposed Western European principles of thought, in the guise of rationality, on other peoples' beliefs—thereby making cross-cultural understanding impossible. There was a third important element in the development of Boas' culture concept, although its source cannot be traced to his early program of research. It was that the basis of culture is not reason at all, but emotion. In Boas' view, reason is subordinate to emotion, for it is the means by which people rationalize their habitual patterns of thought and behavior.

THE MEANING OF HUMAN AFFAIRS. Soon after Boas undertook the study of the development of culture he concluded that traits can seldom be explained by reference to their causal source, and that they are to be viewed instead in terms of the historical processes which began affecting them as soon as they came into existence and which eventually obscured their origins. Boas explicitly recognized two historical processes, diffusion and modification, and these became key principles for the explanation of culture and the interpretation of meaning.

According to Boas, the cultural inventory of a people is almost entirely the cumulative result of diffusion, a process which has been operating continuously since man first became a tradition-bearing animal. The fabric of a culture is made up of countless disparate threads, nearly all of which are of foreign origin. Once a new trait is acquired, however, it is molded to fit its new cultural context. Due to this process of modification or integration, the body of traits of a society tends to become welded into an integral whole: inconsistencies tend to be worked out over time, and the discrete elements making up the system tend to become interrelated.

It is only a tendency for cultures to become integrated, in Boas' view. For example, Northwest Coast culture is dominated by an emphasis upon social competition and the pursuit of prestige, and yet, Boas notes, there are some very "amiable qualities" in the family life of those people (1938b:685). Elsewhere he states that "in the same mind the most heterogeneous complexes of habits, thoughts and actions may lie side by side, without ever coming into conflict" (1911, in 1940:301). Integration is never complete largely because the process of diffusion never stops.

In virtually all of his analyses of modification or integration, Boas gave primacy to the ideational rather than the phenomenal (the manifest, observable, or nonideational) aspects of culture. Moreover, his work as a whole exhibits a similar emphasis on subjective factors, for he conceived human behavior and social institutions as the spelling out or manifestation of ideas. In short, he employed a subjective approach.[4]

Boas placed so much emphasis on viewing culture from the

[4] The importance of the subjective approach in Boas' work is highlighted by David Aberle's analysis of the influence of linguistics on American anthropology (Aberle 1960). Early in this century the Boasians achieved some remarkable results in the field of linguistics, and their accomplishments rebounded on the culture concept itself, according to Aberle. A number of American anthropologists, stimulated by successes in the study of language, were tempted to extend certain assumptions derived from linguistics to the study of the total cultural system; linguistics became a model for the further development and elaboration of cultural theory (Aberle 1960:4–5). For example, it was discovered that some of the most important patterns behind language are located at the unconscious level, and this conclusion contributed to the view that some of the key principles behind culture are located within the subjective sphere and are beyond the individual's awareness (pp. 7–8). The validity of Aberle's thesis is difficult to assess—one of its main defects is that it does not give adequate recognition to the German historicist roots of the Boasian school. Nevertheless, his analysis leaves little doubt about the importance of the subjective approach both in Boas' scheme and in the early development of American anthropology.

"inside"—in terms of subjective principles—that he tended to under-rate or ignore the significance of phenomenal features. An example is his analysis of the potlatch of the Northwest Coast Indians. The potlatch is a ceremonial feast at which the host, a man of chiefly rank, presents a grand display of wealth, which may either be destroyed or distributed to the guests. Boas devoted a great deal of attention to this institution, and yet it is not uncommon to read that he never fully grasped its significance. For example, George Dalton notes that Boas ignored several crucial changes which had taken place since the advent of Western culture in the Northwest Coast region, and that in doing so he failed to understand the potlatch. In particular, Boas did not recognize the rapid decrease in population following about 1840, as well as the increasing use of Western goods in Northwest Coast culture. Both of these changes had fundamental implications for the potlatch (Dalton 1965:63–64, n. 11). I suggest that Boas missed these features precisely because his focus was upon subjective culture. In his view, understanding is achieved by inquiring into the cultural ideas of a people, not by the analysis of systems of exchange or of population statistics.

In view of Boas' emphasis on ideational factors, it is not surprising that he conceived the principle of modification or integration primarily in subjective terms. Integration within the subjective sphere of culture consists in the process whereby traits are progressively modified according to a dominant idea or attitude. I have already mentioned one of the dominant attitudes of the Northwest Coast Indians:

The leading motive of their lives is the limitless pursuit of gaining social prestige and of holding on to what has been gained, and the intense feeling of inferiority and shame if even the slightest part of prestige has been lost (Boas 1938b:685).

One of the clearest illustrations of this cultural theme is the potlatch, which is a central element in the system of social competition of these people. Even the art of the Northwest Coast Indians is affected by their cultural motif, for the work of the Kwakiutl craftsman "consists in the glorification of the family crest or of family histories" (1938b:685).

Boas was explicit that an understanding of custom requires that it be viewed in subjective and integrational terms. For example, he stressed that the history of a culture trait can never be fully understood solely by reference to its distribution; the "historic source" of a trait

> may perhaps be determined by geographic-historical considerations, but its gradual development and ethnic significance in a psychological sense, as it occurs in each area, must be studied by means of psychological investigations in which the different interpretations and attitudes of the people themselves toward the phenomenon present the principal material (1911, in 1940:296).

For example, Boas found that the myths of the Tsimshian and Kwakiutl Indians are quite similar in some respects, as would be expected considering the proximity of the two peoples. But he went to great pains to show that each mythological system has "its own individuality" as a result of the different subjective emphases of the two cultures (1935:171).

One of Boas' earliest integrational analyses is contained in a paper published in 1897 in which he tried to explain how the Kwakiutl secret societies acquired "their peculiar characteristics." He suggests that both the secret societies and the clans in Kwakiutl culture exhibit parallel developments, for once they were borrowed from tribes living to the north they were shaped to fit the Kwakiutl emphasis on social honor and prestige. For example, each clan enjoys exclusive ownership of certain legends, and these tales are guarded with an intense jealousy. Boas states that "the same psychic factor that molded the clans into their present shape"—in other words, the competitive desire for social honor—"molded the secret societies" (1897, in 1940:380). One of the values of belonging to a secret society is that membership entails the acquisition of spirits; this cultural trait resembles the exclusiveness of clan legends, and it also expresses the competitive emphasis of Kwakiutl life.

Boas did not believe that the study of integration should be limited solely to the level of ideas and attitudes, for he recognized that the principle of modification applies to the level of phenomenal culture as well. To him, the problem of integration within the phenomenal sphere consists in the simple compatibility of traits. He writes, "It is advantageous to investigate those types of social conduct that are mutually contradictory and therefore cannot exist side by side" (1938b:679). Among the examples he cites are the incompatibility of a complex political organization with a sparse population; and small, isolated groups of people combined with an elaborate division of labor. Boas himself devoted little attention to the study of integration at the level of phenomenal culture; this remained an unexplored, residual issue in his scheme.

The principle of diffusion reveals the meaning of human affairs in the sense that a custom acquires significance when it is recognized as a local variant of a more widespread trait. For example, the design motifs or myths of the Kwakiutl Indians become intelligible when they are conceived as varieties of traits which are shared throughout the Northwest Coast region. The depth of understanding which is achieved by this method is not very great, however—little satisfaction is afforded by an explanation which asserts only that a pattern of behavior has been borrowed from neighboring tribes.

Another shortcoming of the principle of diffusion is that it tends to lead to the view that culture is utterly *without* meaning. Boas found that different traits exhibit very different distributional patterns, and that even elements which are closely associated in a particular culture often do not occur together in others. For example, Boas criticized the culture area approach, according to which a large region, usually a continent, was divided into cultural provinces (or culture areas) on the basis of similarities and dissimilarities in material culture. He stated that

61

the culture areas were assumed to be natural groups that divided mankind into so many cultural groups. Actually the student interested in religion, social organization, or some other aspect of culture would soon discover that the culture areas based on material culture do not coincide with those that would naturally result from his studies. . . . Attempts to map the distribution of cultural traits that occur over continuous areas prove that various forms overlap irregularly (1938b:671).

The conclusion which this suggests is that the traits of a culture are more or less independent of one another, or that a culture is "a congeries of disconnected traits, associated only by reason of a series of historical accidents" (Spier 1931:455). The principle of diffusion tends to foster the view that traits are wholly fortuitous and virtually without meaning.

Far more important in supplying the meaning of custom is the principle of modification or integration. This reveals the meaning of human affairs in that a custom becomes intelligible once it is recognized as part of a larger, coherent whole. For example, the Kwakiutl trait according to which certain legends are the exclusive property of clans may seem rather meaningless, but its significance becomes apparent when it is seen in the context of the cultural emphasis upon prestige and social competition. The potlatch is made intelligible when it is viewed against the same cultural backdrop. The principle of integration or modification constitutes the most important guide to the meaning of social institutions that Boas' scheme has to offer.

Since Boas held that each culture is unique, he was pessimistic about the possibility of arriving at a body of theory or universal laws pertaining to cultural integration. He felt that "attempts to develop general laws of integration of culture do not lead to significant results" (1930, in 1940:267). On one hand, he believed, cultures are never fully integrated because of the endless effects of diffusion, the constant flux of cultural process. In short, invariant relations between traits will never be found.

On the other hand, he felt that traits can combine in an almost unlimited number of ways. Boas argued that the anthropologist must be content to study "specific forms," like the astronomer interested in "the actual distribution, movements, and constitution of stars, not in generalized physical and chemical laws" (1930, in 1940:268). Boas compared anthropology to the study of the erosion of a mountainside. Although there are natural laws which explain erosion, they can never be used to make predictions because the phenomena are far too complex. A boulder may deflect a stream and cause changes in the water channel; the soil in one direction may be softer than in another. A similar situation obtains in culture. Hostile attacks from neighboring groups may force a society to migrate into a new area, an accident like that of the boulder which helped determine the erosion of the mountainside. "Even a hasty consideration of the history of man shows that accidents of this kind are the rule in every society" (1932:208–11). Each culture is a unique system, just as the erosional pattern of a particular mountainside is matched nowhere else in the world.

Boas' views about the contingency of history and human institutions present a striking contrast with the thought of Tylor, according to whom institutions are not at all vicissitudinous, but are grounded in certain objective conditions or exigencies of the present. To Tylor, the features of culture are anchored firmly in place by the principles of reason and utility. For example, moral principles arise from people's observations about the immediate consequences of their behavior. The moral norms proscribing drunkenness are prompted by the objective effects of drinking and are far from arbitrary. The effects which laziness and negligence of duty have on people's lives result in the development of standards of self-discipline.

Are there no limitations at all on the vicissitudes of historical or cultural development, in Boas' scheme? Do cultures reflect so much historical contingency that they are completely arbitrary with respect to the conditions or exigencies of the moment? Or are institutions rooted in the present somehow by a set of physical, objective factors?

In various places Boas distinguished between two types of force behind culture, "limiting factors" and "creative factors" (e.g., 1932:240, 242, 244; 1938c:174; 1940:255, 265–66). He makes a similar distinction between "static" and "dynamic" factors (1932, in 1940:258), and between "outer" and "inner" forces (e.g., 1932:211; 1930, in 1940:264; 1932, in 1940:257). According to Boas, it is within the subjective sphere of culture that we find the creative forces (or the inner or dynamic factors) behind institutions, and perhaps the most important of these creative elements is the tendency for a diffused trait to be modified or reinterpreted to fit its new cultural context (cf. Stocking 1968a:213–14).

The "static" or "outer" factors consist in the features of the physical environment, for the most part. The environment has a limiting but not a creative influence, for it has the capacity only to restrict the kinds of cultural development which may take place. Boas writes,

There is no doubt that the cultural life of man is in many and important ways limited by geographical conditions. The lack of vegetable products in the Arctic, and the absence of stone in extended parts of South America, the dearth of water in the desert, to mention only a few outstanding facts, limit the activities of man in definite ways (1930, in 1940:265–66).

Institutions are rooted in the present primarily by virtue of the limitations imposed by the physical world.

Even though Boas was quite clear that "every culture is strongly influenced by its [natural] environment" (1932, in 1940:256), he also insisted that this influence is always mediated by a set of cultural ideas:

We must remember that, no matter how great an influence we may ascribe to environment, that influence can become active only by being exerted on the mind; so that the characteristics of the mind must enter into the resultant forms of social activity (1911:163).

These "characteristics of the mind" are cultural for the most part. The mistake of geographical determinism, Boas argued, is that it failed to recognize that the members of society inherit traditional patterns of thought. All peoples do not respond the same way to a given environment because they do not share the same subjective culture (1932:241, 242). The implication of this view is that even the unbending, limiting conditions of the environment must be analyzed in terms of the subjective frame of reference of the people themselves.

Boas did little more than acknowledge the principle of environmental limitations, for he never pursued this mode of explanation in his own research. His focus seems to have been on the subjective sphere of culture. By all but ignoring the environment, Boas implied that it does not normally need to be taken into account for an understanding of institutions. He implied that the limitations of the environment are actually quite broad and permit a wide range of variations in culture.

In view of Boas' subjective approach and his idea that the creative forces behind culture are ideational, it is understandable that he regarded the study of the individual as an essential problem in anthropology. It is the individual mind which reinterprets and modifies newly acquired culture traits; it is also the individual who feels the stress of changing conditions, and, because of the pressures felt, sets out to alter his social practices along culturally acceptable lines. "The causal conditions of cultural happenings lie always in the interaction between individual and society," or, more properly, between the individual and his culture (1932, in 1940:257). In brief, the study of cultural dynamics must be a study of the individual in his cultural setting. In 1930 Boas called for a reorientation of American anthropology away from the historical reconstructions which had dominated research in the past toward the study of the individual (1930, in 1940:269). Boas states that in 1910 he himself turned from the study of diffusion to that of cultural dynamics (1936, in 1940:311), although Benedict writes that in personal conversations he gave 1922 as the date of this shift (Benedict 1943a:31). Boas' book on *Primitive Art* illustrates his interest in the dynamic features of culture; in that study he attempted to delineate the individual and cultural factors behind the work of the primitive artist.

Boas' work exhibits a very distinctive image of man, and this has considerable bearing on his conception of the meaning of human affairs. A most important characteristic of the individual, in Boas' view, is the tendency for behavior to become dominated by habit. An activity or thought carves a rut on the unconscious through repetition, and this pattern becomes automatic. Boas contrasted animal and human behavior by saying that the former is primarily instinctive in nature, while human behavior consists in an "enormously increased number of learned adjustments" (1930, in 1940:262). In spite of this difference, however, Boas noted an important similarity: neither an instinct nor a habit needs conscious effort to be expressed in overt behavior; both are "marked by an immediate, involuntary reaction" (1932:138). Man's conduct, like that of other animals, tends to be thoroughly unreflective.

Boas' view of the unreflective, automatic nature of behavior is illustrated by his theory of taboos. He suggests that taboos frequently develop when the general conditions of life change, throwing old, habitual forms of behavior into negative relief. He cites the case of the Eskimo taboo against eating caribou and seal meat on the same day. The Eskimo live alternately in coastal and inland regions. When they are inland, they can acquire no seal and eat only caribou; when on the coast, they hunt no caribou and eat only seal. This pattern has become so deeply inscribed on the Eskimo's mind that, even though it is sometimes both possible and practical to consume both at the same time, it is taboo to do so (1910:381–82).

A more elaborate illustration of Boas' conception of the unconscious and habitual basis of custom is his analysis of Alaskan needlecases, which are tubes used by the Eskimo to keep their

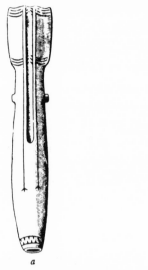

a   b

ALASKAN NEEDLECASES

(a) A "typical" Alaskan needlecase. (b) A needlecase on which the flanges have been carved to resemble walrus heads. (Reprinted with permission of The Macmillan Company from *Race, Language and Culture* by Franz Boas. Copyright 1940 by The Macmillan Company, renewed 1968 by Franziska Boas Michelson.)

needles from breaking (Boas 1908, in 1940). The needle is inserted in a skin which in turn is pulled into the tube. The tube is slightly bulging in the middle and has two winglike flanges at the upper end, separated by a long, narrow groove on front and back. It has two small knobs on either side immediately below the flanges. Etched on the surface of the flanges are a number of parallel lines cut approximately at right angles to the length of the tube. There is also a pair of lines which border each groove, extend beyond it, and end in two or three spurs. At the bottom of the needlecase is a band encircling the tube; it consists of a pair of lines with short spurs radiating from each (Boas 1908, in 1940:565–68). According to Boas, the

Eskimo needlecase represents a conventional style, and the production of these objects is not a purely creative act but is simply a response to the basic pattern which is contained in the artisan's mind.

Not all needlecases conform strictly to the "typical" pattern, however, for the imagination of the Eskimo craftsman often leads to elaborations and modifications of several kinds. For example, the etched decoration is frequently more elaborate than that of the "typical" needlecase; and the flanges may almost disappear, resulting in modifications of the incised design. Most interesting are instances in which certain portions of the needlecase are modified to look like animals, such as when the flanges are carved to look like walrus heads. These are "secondary interpretation [s] of the design," whereby "the imagination of the artist was stimulated" by the characteristics of the fundamental pattern (1908, in 1940:578–79, 580). Boas states that the elaborations and modifications "may be largely explained as results of the play of the imagination under the restricting influence of a fixed conventional style" (1908, in 1940:588–89).

The conclusion which I draw from a comparison of the types of needlecases here represented is that the flanged needlecase represents an old conventional style, which is ever present in the mind of the Eskimo artist who sets about to carve a needlecase. The various parts of the flanged needlecase excite his imagination; and a geometrical element here or there is developed by him, in accordance with the general tendencies of Eskimo art, into the representation of whole animals or of parts of animals. . . . Besides this, associations between animal forms and the form of the whole needlecase seem to have taken place, which have to a certain extent modified the manner of representing animal forms which were adapted to use as needlecases; so that the old form and style of the needlecase determined the treatment of the animal form (1908, in 1940:588).

Man's behavior is not totally determined by unconscious, habitual patterns, for culture traits are often reinterpreted and modified by means of the "play of imagination."

Nevertheless, to Boas, these elaborations and modifications are always structured and closely circumscribed by the basic unconscious pattern; the play of imagination actually operates within comparatively narrow limits. Boas' analysis of folklore is illustrative. New tales are continually added to a society's stock of traditions through diffusion, and the whole body of tales is reworked endlessly by "the play of imagination." The result is that the folklore of a given society "consist[s] of combinations and recombinations of old themes" (1914, in 1940:480). The creative process behind the reworking of tales is highly restricted, however; what takes place essentially is the reshuffling of elements from one context to another, and little is produced that is entirely new. Boas writes,

So far as our knowledge of mythology and folk-lore of modern peoples goes, we are justified in the opinion that the power of imagination of man is rather limited, that people much rather operate with the old stock of imaginative happenings than invent new ones (1916, in 1940:405–6).

Another feature of conscious thought to which Boas frequently alludes is the process of rationalization, discussed earlier, according to which habitual patterns acquire secondary explanations. For example, Boas showed that a particular variety of moccasin design is shared by a number of Indian tribes, but that each tribe has a different interpretation of what the design means. He concludes that the pattern of the design is older, the conscious interpretations later; "the design is primary, the idea secondary" (1903, in 1940:555). Elsewhere he states that "this tendency is not by any means confined to art," but characterizes mythology and ceremonialism as well: "in these also the outer form remains, while the accompanying interpretations are widely different" (1927:128).

These two features of conscious thought—imaginativeness and rationalization—are alike in that both are subordinate or secondary to the unconscious and emotional patterns contained in the mind. To Boas, the guiding force behind human behavior and institutions is located at the unconscious level, and to adequately explain and understand cultural phenomena the anthropologist has to penetrate the conscious veneer. This is as true for grasping social process as it is for understanding moccasin or needlecase designs.

Boas nowhere developed a theory of politics, but a telling illustration of his conception of the unconscious, habitual, and emotional basis of behavior is contained in what little he did say about political process. He held that political segmentation and competition cannot be viewed in terms of competing interest groups rationally calculating advantages in relation to others, as some anthropologists do today (e.g., see Barth 1959a, b). Much of the political strife in the world, Boas thought, is due to an emotional opposition to foreign ways of behaving and thinking, together with the belief that one's own culture is superior to all others. He compared the hostility between modern nations to that between "tribal units that considered every alien an enemy who must be slain" (1932:98).

It is not any rational cause that forms opposing groups, but solely the emotional appeal of an idea that holds together the members of each group and exalts their feeling of solidarity and greatness to such an extent that compromises with other groups become impossible (1932:102).

In political life just as in religion and everyday habits, "our actions are the results of emotional preferences" (1932:115). A person is Catholic or Jew or Presbyterian primarily because of early family influences, and similarly his political loyalties are essentially habitual responses:

When, on account of our early bringing up, we act with a certain political party, most of us are not prompted by a clear conviction of the justice of the principles of our party, but we do so because we have been taught to respect it as the right party to which to belong. Then only do we justify our standpoint by trying to convince ourselves that these principles are the correct ones. Without reasoning of this kind, the stability and geographical distribution of political parties as well as of church denominations would be entirely unintelligible (1910:383).

To Boas, only a limited degree of understanding can be achieved if behavior is viewed as the manifestation of conscious, willful thought. Far more important for assessing the meaning of human action is the concept of custom. Man's behavior is dominated by unconscious, customary patterns to which emotional associations have become attached. In order to understand the behavior of the participant in the Kwakiutl potlatch, or the actions of the Eskimo craftsman who is engaged in producing needlecases, or the voting preferences of the United States citizen, the investigator must inquire into the traditions of the society in question.

In summary, to Boas, culture is to be understood in terms of its own *sui generis* principles and not in terms of the natural properties of the human mind. The two principles which stand out in Boas' work are the processes of diffusion and modification. Both of these are subject to a great deal of historical contingency, and the result is that any cultural system is somewhat arbitrary in relation to the conditions and exigencies of the moment. There is a third principle behind culture which Boas sometimes noted but which he virtually ignored, the rather broad limitations of the environment. It is primarily by virtue of the environment that the institutions of mankind are rooted in the present. At the level of the individual himself, Boas gave little scope to the human will; it is culture which makes behavior intelligible, because, for the most part, human actions conform to traditional patterns.

CONCLUSION

To Tylor, traditionalism is the antithesis of progress, for in his view civilization is at a standstill when people accept their customs uncritically. It is unfettered rationality which is the basis for improvement. Tylor's vision was always directed toward civilization and its rational foundations, and he all but ignored tradition, for to him the purpose of anthropology was to chart the course that evolution—the progressive expression of rational thought—has taken.

Boas denied that culture is erected upon the principles of reason and utility. To him, virtually all human institutions are largely irrational, and this is as true of the beliefs and practices of Great Britain and the United States as it is of the Andamanese or Australian aborigines.

In rejecting Tylor's principle of reason, Boas expanded on its antonym. Whereas Tylor placed rationality at the center of his theoretical scheme, Boas gave that position to tradition. To Boas, a living culture is a museum of past forms of behavior, and each trait is comparatively thoughtless in both design and execution. The individual himself is a comparatively unthinking slave to the habitual patterns of behavior which he has acquired. Moreover, because of the emotional grounding of tradition, customs tend to persist in spite of their uselessness or even disutility—a view reminiscent of Tylor's notion of survivals; Boas wrote,

It may even be shown that old customs, that may have been in harmony with a certain type of environment, tend to survive under new conditions, where they are of disadvantage rather than of advantage to the people. An example of this kind, taken from our own civilization, is our failure to utilize unfamiliar kinds of food that may be found in newly settled countries. Another example is presented by the reindeer-breeding Chuckchee, who carry about in their nomadic life a tent of most complicated structure, which corresponds in its type to the older permanent house of the coast dwellers, and which contrasts in the most marked way with the simplicity and light weight of the Eskimo tent (1911:162).

Boas' culture concept is one which emphasizes the irrationality of custom and the binding of tradition. This image of culture and of man was a distinctive feature of American anthropology for many years, although it has not been unchallenged by those who believe that culture and the individual are in some sense rational after all (e.g., see Erasmus 1961:33ff., and Harris 1968:354ff.).

--◄{ III }►--

FROM IRRATIONALITY
TO UTILITY IN
CULTURAL INTEGRATION

BENEDICT, KROEBER, STEWARD, AND WHITE

Boas concentrated primarily on distributional studies in his early anthropological writings, and his purpose was to trace the history of culture. During the second or third decade of this century, however, he turned increasingly to the study of cultural dynamics, or the interaction between the individual and his cultural milieu. Others were beginning to change their focus as well; although American anthropology had never been very homogeneous, there seems to have been a process of diversification at work during the late 1920s and the 1930s. For example, this was the period in which both acculturation and culture and personality studies took root, and in which evolutionism began its revival.

One of the most logical lines of theoretical development that American anthropology could take was to elaborate the principle of integration, because it was this feature of Boas' culture concept which offered the greatest possibilities for locating meaning in human affairs. The limitations of the environment were too broad to be important in explaining custom, according to Boas, and the process of diffusion tended to lead to the idea that culture is wholly fortuitous and meaningless. According to the principle of integration, however, the investigator can provide the meaning of customs and beliefs by placing them in their cultural contexts.

In this chapter I deal with four writers—Ruth Benedict, Alfred L. Kroeber, Julian Steward, and Leslie White—who were trained either by avowed Boasians or by Boas himself. The work of each of these writers constitutes an important element in the aforesaid diversification in American anthropology and their schemes may be conceived as elaborations and modifications of Boas' concept of integration. Moreover, these four approaches represent a logical sequence, beginning with the Boasian view of the irrationality of custom and ending with the idea that culture is a highly useful or utilitarian instrument.

RUTH BENEDICT

Victor Barnouw, one of Benedict's graduate students at Columbia, describes the impression she made on him then. "Like most of Ruth Benedict's students, I looked up to her with a mixture of veneration and bewilderment." He speaks of her "silvery aura of prestige, dignity, and charm" (Barnouw 1949:241). This aura was partially due to her remoteness. She was hard of hearing, shy, and frequently melancholy, and consequently she tended to remain aloof from people. But she was also a remarkably generous person, for she gave freely of both her time and money to friends and students who were in need.

Benedict was born in New York City in 1887. Her father, a surgeon, died when she was two years old, leaving her mother to support the family as a teacher and librarian. Because of a scholarship, however, Ruth and her sister were able to attend Vassar, and they graduated together in 1909 (Mead 1959:537–

38). Ruth taught school for two years after graduation, and in 1914 married a biochemist at the Cornell Medical College.

Benedict was restless before her marriage, and she apparently hoped that her husband and new home would bring an end to her discontentment. But the life of a housewife turned out to be quite unsuitable for her. She engaged in a variety of diversionary activities, including rhythmic dancing and social work (Mead 1959:6). She even tried writing, especially poetry, an interest which she retained throughout her life. In 1919—still searching for a meaningful preoccupation—she began attending lectures in anthropology at the New School for Social Research in New York City. Anthropology met a response in her, and in 1921 she went to Columbia University to study under Franz Boas. She earned her Ph.D., the following year.

Benedict began teaching at Columbia after receiving her Ph.D., and she was untiring in the assistance she gave Boas in running the department. She continued in this role until Boas' retirement in 1937. During the war she went to Washington to work in the Office of War Information, conducting research on such strategically important peoples as the Japanese and Thai. After the war she returned to Columbia where she continued her research on large, complex societies. She died in 1948, after an eventful summer of traveling and teaching in Europe.

Benedict's culture concept may be summarized under two main headings: her ideas about integration, and about the *sui generis* nature of culture.

CULTURAL INTEGRATION. Not only are Benedict's views about integration the best-known features of her thought, they are also the most important elements of her theory, since, to her, cultural integration is the master concept for the analysis of cultural phenomena. In Benedict's mind just as in Boas', integration is the principal "creative force" behind culture; although a culture is the chance accumulation of so many "disparate elements fortuitously assembled from all directions by diffusion" (1932:2), the constituent elements are modified to form "a more or less consistent pattern of thought and action" (1934:46). Her emphasis is on the term consistent. She cites the example of Gothic architecture, which began as "hardly more than a preference for altitude and light," but which "by the operation of some canon of taste" developed into "the unique and homogeneous art of the thirteenth century."

What was at first no more than a slight bias in local forms and techniques expressed itself more and more forcibly, integrated itself in more and more definite standards, and eventuated in Gothic art (1934:47–48).

Like Boas, Benedict thought that the creative force of integration is located in the individual mind, and that it consists in the selection, rejection, and modification of culture traits by individuals according to the subjective standards of their culture. She never went into detail about the way in which integration takes place, but she did mention two mechanisms. First, each culture has its "favorite" or "most cherished" customs, such as the potlatch of the Northwest Coast Indians or the religious ceremonies of the Zuni. The individual tends to focus his attention on these customs and to elaborate them, and consequently they become the dominant features of the culture (see 1929:811 and 1956:189). Second, she held that some people by temperament find their culture more congenial than others. Those who fit their culture best are the most successful and tend to become influential. As a result, they leave a stronger impression on their culture than other people, and they tend to incline it even farther in the direction in which it is moving (see 1934:257 ff.).

Implicit in her discussion is a distinction between two levels at which the process of integration operates: the level of culture traits on one hand, and the level of emotional patterning on the other.

Considering first the level of traits, Benedict emphasized

again and again that culture elements occur in limitless combinations. In one society a particular culture element, such as an art form, may be incorporated into the religious system, whereas in another society the same trait may be redefined as a valuable commodity and become part of the system of economic exchange. "The possibilities are endless and the adjustments are often bizarre" (1934:37; cf. pp. 37–44).

In addition, there is an infinite number of possible emphases in a culture, since any trait or complex of traits can become a focal point and then be "elaborated past belief." For example, the Todas of India have singled out their buffalo herds and have made them the focus of their lives. Their religious ritual is essentially a dairy ritual, the dairymen are priests, and the sacred cowbell is the holy of holies (1929:811–12). The Australian aborigines have elaborated the restrictions of exogamy in unparalleled fashion. The Kurnai of Australia have such rigid marriage rules that it is typically impossible for a young man to find an acceptable bride, and as a result he has to elope, risking death at the hands of the pursuing villagers. The Kurnai, according to Benedict, "have extended and complicated a particular aspect of behavior until it is a social liability" (1934:34–35).

An important feature of Benedict's views about integration is that no two cultures are ever alike. The mode of integration of a culture is fortuitous, the product of the almost arbitrary and limitless recombination, reinterpretation, and elaboration of traits.

The view that cultural integration is fortuitous was the direct outgrowth of diffusion studies. When a trait is followed from one society to another it is patently evident that the trait *does* enter into different combinations, assume different forms, and receive different emphases; and these changes seem to follow no pattern. Benedict's Ph.D. thesis, published in 1923, is exemplary. She set out to test various theories about the origin of religion, hoping to determine if there were "some fixed causality which is at work" behind religious beliefs (1923:7). She focused on a trait which was found almost universally among North American Indians, the concept of the guardian spirit. Her problem was to determine which of its features were stable, and therefore necessary or causal. She concluded that nothing was stable in this complex; there was "no coalescence" or combination of traits "which we may regard as being other than fortuitous" (1923:84). Rather, she found a "fluid recombination" or "desultory association" of culture traits (1923:82, 80). Among the Thompson River Indians the guardian spirit complex was intimately associated with male puberty rites, whereas among the Kwakiutl the guardian spirit was a hereditary caste mark which was highly valued as a private possession. On the Great Plains the guardian spirit concept "developed along still different lines," for the Plains Indians imposed no limitation on the sex or age of the recipient of a guardian spirit, and the vision was obtained through isolation, fasting, and self-torture (1923:9ff; see also p. 84).

The diffusionist perspective which Benedict employed in this study was the immediate result of her training under Boas. Mead notes that Benedict began her graduate work at Columbia at a time when Boas was still having his students trace the diffusion of traits from culture to culture, "showing the changes which the trait or the complex of traits underwent" (1959:11).

The second level at which Benedict viewed cultural integration was that of emotion. The search for cross-cultural uniformities seemed fruitless to her, because in her view the conclusions of these studies would all be negative. Consequently, after completing her Ph.D. thesis she turned away from comparative studies and toward the problem of integration. She began to seek an abstract framework that would make sense of the general patterns which seemed to pervade each culture; she sought "some integrating principle" by which to explain the unity of culture which "she felt was there" (Mead 1959:204). In the summer of 1927 the idea which she sought finally came to her, and she set forth her theory during the late twenties and early thirties (Benedict 1928, 1932, 1934). Consistent with her Boasian background, she did not locate the organizing principle behind culture in the phenomenal world of environmental, economic, or social structural factors, but at the level of subjective thought. She hit upon the idea that the differences between cultures can be explained like the differences between people: like an individual, each culture tends to have a distinct temperament (Mead 1959:206). "Cultures from this point of view are individual psychology thrown large upon the screen, given gigantic proportions and a long time span" (Benedict 1932:24). Benedict called this integrating principle the cultural ethos or configuration.

Perhaps the best examples of Benedict's configurationalism are her analyses of the Pueblo and Plains Indians. Benedict characterized the Pueblo configuration as Apollonian; it stressed moderation and cooperation, and gave little or no place to excess, frenzy, and individualism. For example, the religious rituals of the Pueblos were meticulously regulated and organized and allowed little expression of emotion. The leader in Pueblo society almost had to be coerced into serving, because he was reluctant to set himself above and apart from his fellow community members. Benedict characterized the ethos of the Plains Indians as Dionysian. The individualism and emotional frenzy which the Pueblos virtually eliminated were capitalized upon by the Plains cultures. For example, a dominant feature of Plains Indian religion was the vision quest, which entailed self-torture, fasting, and emotional frenzy. Warfare was highly developed on the Plains; it was pursued aggressively and violently, and exploits in war were a means of attaining personal glory (see Benedict 1928, 1932, and 1934: Chapter 4).[1]

The integrating principle which Benedict hit upon—the

[1] Benedict is often severely criticized for distorting her data to make them fit her configurational analysis; for example, see Ray 1956:167–68.

cultural configuration—is essentially an *emotional* pattern: it consists of an emotional bent or attitude which in time tends to pervade a culture. The distinctive feature of the Dionysian ethos of the Plains was not simply a unique organization of traits, or the dominance of certain culture elements or activities. It was an emotional tone: intemperate, excessive individualism. Similarly, the Apollonian ethos of the Pueblos was the attitude of moderation, nondemonstrativeness, and group-orientation. It might be said that in searching for an integrating principle below the level of culture traits, Benedict simply pulled together two threads of Boas' thought: first, his view that one of the primary creative forces of culture is the tendency toward consistency within the subjective sphere, and second, his view that custom is at bottom emotional. Benedict's configuration is an emotional consistency in culture.[2]

Although Boas and others recognized the role of emotion in human behavior long before Benedict began working in anthropology, she is to be credited with carrying this insight a step farther by emphasizing the need for a systematic and thorough understanding of the emotional level of cultural life. She noted that Americans are likely to misunderstand the Pueblo snake dance if they fail to grasp the "emotional background" of the performance. To the American, the snake dance elicits a feeling of repulsion and horror, but for the Pueblo Indian "the whole procedure is upon the level of a dance with eagles or with kittens." Benedict argued that in the usual ethnographic monograph the "emotional background" of custom is not provided (1932:6–7). She stated that ethnographic descriptions "must include much that older fieldwork ignored, and without the relevant fieldwork all our propositions are pure romancing" (1932:27).

A distinguishing feature of Benedict's view of cultural inte-

[2] I believe that these comments apply not only to Benedict's configurational studies, but to her national character studies as well, and particularly to her analysis of the Japanese (Benedict 1946). In the latter, she located a pair of emotional patterns which lay behind and which explained Japanese behavior and institutions.

gration at the level of traits is that each culture has a different pattern of organization. The same is true at the level of emotion, for she held that each configuration is unique (cf. Benedict 1939a). It follows that anthropology cannot be a comparative science and that there is little possibility of developing a general body of theory that will apply to all peoples. For example, a political theory that would be applicable to the temperate and cooperative Pueblos would hardly apply to the excessively individualistic Plains Indians.

Some hold that Benedict's views about the incommensurability of cultures represent a dead-end in anthropology:

The difficulty with the assumption of "incommensurability" is that, if it is taken literally, scientific work becomes impossible. If two objects or events are truly incommensurable, then no further statements can be made about them in the same universe of discourse (Aberle 1960:9).

However, it would be a mistake to think that Benedict's scheme lacks explanatory power. The key to both anthropological explanation and the meaning of human affairs, in her view, is the concept of integration:

for there is no axiom of cultural study which is more clearly established than the fact that a whole array of familial, political, economic and religious institutions mutually condition one another and conversely are unintelligible when considered in isolation (1939b:570).

In Benedict's view, explanation amounts to showing the context of each trait, or how it fits within the total integrational pattern.

Benedict implicitly distinguished between two levels of integration, and accordingly there are two different contexts within which a cultural item can be viewed. First is the level of traits. The ceremonial system of the Toda is intelligible by reference to the cultural focus on buffalo herds; outside that context such features as the holy cowbell and the dairymen's role as

priests are without meaning. Similarly, the practice of elope-
ment among the Kurnai makes sense only when viewed in relation to the cultural focus on marriage regulations.

An even more important context to Benedict was that of the
cultural configuration, since, to her, integration at the level of
traits is governed largely by the principles contained at the
level of emotion: for example, because of the cultural ethos of
the Pueblo Indians, it would have been virtually inconceivable
for them to have elaborated the warfare complex the way the
Plains Indians did; and the emphasis placed on warfare by the
Plains cultures was quite consistent with their emotional
theme.

The explanatory potential of Benedict's configuration concept is particularly evident when applied to problems of culture history. Living near the Pueblo Indians were a number of
Dionysian peoples who employed alcohol and drugs extensively
in their religious ritual. The intoxicants and drugs were used
to achieve a religious experience or vision. However, "none of
these alcohol and drug-induced excitations have gained currency among the Pueblos" (Benedict 1928:251), because hallu-
cinatory religious experiences were uncongenial to the Pueblo
configuration. Moreover, the Pueblo religious functionaries
practiced fasting in connection with their ritual performances.
The fast was not used to induce visions as it was on the Plains
and elsewhere, however, but was simply "a requirement for ceremonial cleanness" (1928:254). This culture trait—fasting—
had been modified and brought into conformity with the ethos
of Pueblo society.

Benedict's configuration concept is an explanatory device in
a nonhistorical sense as well, for it supplies the meaning of
human affairs. To view a trait within its configurational context is to see it in terms of its emotional and attitudinal matrix,
and integrational analysis therefore amounts to a form of
subjective understanding. Customs and behavior which seem
absurd from the outside become quite reasonable once the

emotional pattern behind them is grasped. As ridiculous and inhumane as Plains warfare and self-torture seems to a Western European, these institutions make sense from the perspective of the emotional theme of Plains culture.

The singularity of this configurational form of subjective understanding is thrown into relief when contrasted with Tylor's mode of analysis. To Tylor, societies at different levels of evolution exhibit different degrees of reason, but the same standard of rationality is applicable to the institutions of all peoples. Like Boas, Benedict was tacitly proposing that reason is subordinate and in a sense epiphenomenal to emotion, for reason is thoroughly distorted by emotional bias. What appears to an American as an irrational, paranoid approach to life is perfectly reasonable given the emotional slant of Dobuan culture (Benedict 1934:Chapter 5). The same standard of rationality does not apply to all peoples, and in order to grasp the reasoning behind foreign institutions the emotional context must first be understood.

An important implication of Benedict's integrational approach is that it precludes the study of cultural institutions outside their larger context. In considering this issue it is again useful to distinguish between the two levels of integration implicit in her work, and to consider the level of traits first.

One of the primary assumptions of Radcliffe-Brown's approach is that social structure constitutes a system which can be studied and understood in terms of its internal principles. For example, he analyzed the structure of lineage systems by reference to such principles as unilineal descent and the equivalence of siblings. He also assumed that a cultural emphasis or de-emphasis on such features as art, puberty rites, and even economic activities is not important for his analysis, and if he brought the issue of cultural foci into his account he did so in order to explain them in terms of the social structure and not vice versa. To Radcliffe-Brown, understanding is achieved largely by reference to the principles of social structure.

Benedict's position was that each sector of culture has to be viewed in the context of the whole, for each is part of the larger system of integration and is subject to the principles which govern the whole. The Toda emphasized and elaborated a particular feature of their economic life, and the social structure had to be viewed in that context. Benedict would say that it was the focus on buffalo herds rather than the principles of social structure which explained the organization of Toda society.

To Benedict, integration at the level of emotion is even more basic than that at the level of traits, and she believed that the configurational context is essential for anthropological analysis:

The significant sociological unit . . . is not the institution but the cultural configuration. The studies of the family, of primitive economics, or of moral ideas need to be broken up into studies that emphasize the different configurations that in instance after instance have dominated these traits (1934:244).

The implications of this point of view for anthropological studies can be illustrated again by reference to Radcliffe-Brown's social structural framework. A number of anthropologists have attempted to show that the ease and frequency of divorce in society is a function of structural arrangements—in other words, that the principles of social structure explain differences in divorce patterns. In a society with strongly matrilineal lineages the jural rights in a woman are divided between the woman's matrilineal kin and her husband; consequently, the marital relationship is relatively unstable and divorce is comparatively easy and frequent. In strongly patrilineal societies the jural rights in a married woman are vested primarily in her affinal kin, particularly her husband, and as a result divorce tends to be infrequent and difficult (see Gluckman 1956:65ff.). To Benedict, it is not the social structure which explains divorce patterns, but the cultural configuration. Divorce was frequent and easy in Pueblo society, but not primarily because the villages were organized on the basis of strongly matrilineal kin groups. Rather, the Pueblo configuration stressed nondemonstrativeness and village-wide cooperation. There was little emphasis on institutions such as marriage and divorce which were "matters for the individual to attend to" (1934:73). Nor was there much room in Pueblo culture for jealousy, or for an emotional attachment between husband and wife "that refuses to accept dismissal" (1934:75): this was a culture in which institutions "effectively minimize the appearance of a violent emotion like jealousy" (1934:108). In short, marriage was easily dissolved because of the Apollonian ethos.[3,4]

Benedict's rejection of the possibility that institutions can be understood outside their integrational contexts recalls a point made earlier, that Benedict's approach denies the feasibility of comparative studies. To her, the pattern of integration of each culture is incommensurate. Anthropology can attempt to understand the features of specific cultures, but each cultural system has to be accounted for by a separate body of theory.

THE SUI GENERIS NATURE OF CULTURE. To Benedict, culture is to be understood in terms of its internal principles, and these are relatively autonomous from outside influences. The autonomy of culture emerges as an issue in her work in two separate contexts: in her views about the relationship between culture and the environment on one hand, and between culture and personality on the other.

Some anthropologists view culture in terms of its utilitarian functions, emphasizing its role in accommodating man to his natural habitat. According to this perspective the most impor-

---

[3] See also Benedict's discussion of divorce among the Dobu (Benedict 1934:138–39).

[4] Benedict personally found Radcliffe-Brown insufferable (cf. Mead 1959:326–28), although a paper she published in 1936 shows that he had at least a passing influence on her. In that paper she made a comparative analysis of the relationship between property rights and bilaterality, ignoring the configuration concept altogether. The point of that paper runs directly counter to the views expressed in *Patterns of Culture*, published only two years earlier.

tant cultural processes are those involved in the relationship between culture and the environment. For example, culture change is seen largely as a result of the progressive adaptation of the total system to local circumstances. To Benedict, however, it is the *sui generis* principles of cultural integration which hold the key to cultural dynamics, and culture change is essentially the progressive unfolding and application of these principles. Technology and cultural adaptation are like puberty rites, warfare, or social structure: they are features which can be emphasized and elaborated in one culture but virtually ignored in the next:

In one society technology is unbelievably slighted even in those aspects of life which seem necessary to insure survival; in another, equally simple, technological achievements are complex and fitted with admirable nicety to the situation (1934:24).

If the relationship between culture and environment is important in a particular society, it is so essentially by chance.

Benedict went yet farther, for she implied that the relationship between culture and habitat is frequently whimsical or even fantastic. She stated that, in elaborating the features of his culture, man "has a passion for extremes" (1929:813). Economic pursuits need not be directed toward providing the necessities of life at all, but "toward piling up in lavish display many times the necessary food supply of the people and allowing it to rot ostentatiously for pride's sake" (1934:243). The first menstruation of a young girl may involve "the redistribution of practically all the property of a tribe" (1934:244). The Plains Indians who received supernatural power through visions believed they were bullet-proof, and they went into battle convinced of their invulnerability (1923:23). Benedict writes that in his social institutions

Man can get by with a mammoth load of useless lumber. . . . After all, man has a fairly wide margin of safety, and he will not be forced to the wall even with a pitiful handicap (1929:813).

To Benedict, culture is hardly utilitarian in nature, designed for man's benefit. One of the things that anthropologists have made up their minds about, she wrote, is that "it is usually beside the point to argue the social usefulness of a custom" (1929:813). Indeed, in Benedict's view custom is frequently disadvantageous or impractical; in this sense it is irrational. Benedict's thought was very much like Boas' on this issue.

Benedict's view of the impracticality of custom is illustrated by her analysis of the potlatch of the Kwakiutl Indians. She interpreted the potlatch by reference to the cultural configuration of the Northwest Coast, which she characterized as megalomaniacal because of its emphasis on self-glorification and on the bettering and shaming of rivals. The chief who gave the potlatch strove both to demonstrate his superiority by distributing or destroying as much property as possible, and to shame those he had invited by the generosity of his gifts. Although the institution was understandable from the perspective of the cultural configuration, it was wasteful and costly from the practical point of view (Benedict 1934:173ff.).

The distinctiveness of Benedict's interpretation of the potlatch is highlighted when it is compared with some of the later studies (cf. Drucker and Heizer 1967). One of these suggests that the institution should be understood as an adaptive mechanism, a response to variations and fluctuations in food supply. According to this analysis, not only were there differences in food productivity between localities, but in addition all localities suffered periods of relative scarcity. The potlatch functioned to redistribute food and thereby to equalize its availability. The Kwakiutl drive to achieve prestige was necessary to keep the system operating, for it provided the motivation to ensure that the people participated; but it was not the reason for the existence of the potlatch (Suttles 1960).

The second context in which the *sui generis* nature of culture emerged as an issue in Benedict's thought was in her conception of the relationship between culture and personality. She held that culture is virtually autonomous from natural processes of thought, because the latter are highly circumscribed, almost obliterated, by culture. Benedict noted that as detailed descriptions of different peoples accumulated, anthropologists began to question the earlier ideas about "human nature"; what had been thought of as natural inclinations or reactions came to be interpreted as culturally determined responses:

In some societies adolescence was a period of rebellion, of stress and strain; in some societies it was a period of calm, a time when one especially enjoyed oneself. In some societies men were violent and quarrelsome; in some, no voice was raised above its wonted key and no man was known in all their memory to have struck another. The list of contrasts was endless, and the conclusion could not be avoided: a great deal of what had ordinarily been regarded as due to "human nature" was, instead, culturally determined (1942:245–46).

Thought is so thoroughly determined that the individual willingly follows the dictates of custom even when they go directly against reason or his own practical interests. Culture can make the Kwakiutl chief ambitious enough to waste his energy, time, and wealth on the potlatch, and it can make the Plains Indian truly believe that a hallucination makes him invulnerable to bullets.

The reason culture has such a powerful hold on man is because of its emotional foundations. The individual acquires such a strong emotional commitment to his customs and beliefs that it is virtually impossible for him to question them, let alone reject them:

Even given the freest scope by their institutions, men are never inventive enough to make more than minute changes. From the point of view of an outsider the most radical innovations in any culture amount to no more than a minor revision, and it is commonplace that prophets have been put to death for the difference between Tweedledum and Tweedledee (1934:84).

If the emotional features of the mind are so thoroughly affected by culture, then it follows that different cultures produce fundamentally different types of personality. Not only did the Plains Indians and Pueblos differ in their customs, but the people themselves were different. The Plains warrior or vision seeker was not merely playing a Dionysian role: he *was* Dionysian, and his customs fit him like a glove. His personality had been so thoroughly molded and reworked by his culture that it could almost be said that he was a different species of animal from the gentle and unassuming Pueblo villager.

A corollary of Benedict's emphasis on culture as a determinant of the personality is her view that the mind is a *tabula rasa* at birth. Either the natural, pre-cultural features of the personality are all but nonexistent, or they are so malleable that they are obliterated once the process of socialization is complete. Mead states that the *tabula rasa* assumption was only a working hypothesis for field research, and that if there are intrinsic principles or features of the mind which are not culturally determined, they should be discovered by comparative research (Mead 1942). I think Benedict would have agreed. In fact, however, the *tabula rasa* assumption was more than a working hypothesis in Benedict's work, for it had a major effect on her interpretation of data. Her analysis of the Pueblo Indians is illustrative.

Studies of Pueblo culture are numerous, and they have been classified by Bennett into two broad categories. The first he calls the organic theories, for they emphasize "the organic wholeness" of Pueblo life (1946:364). This interpretation regards Pueblo culture as a highly integrated system, exhibiting a set of harmonious and consistent values which pervade nearly all aspects of life (pp. 362–63). The organic theory holds that the Pueblo personality is one "which features the virtues of gentleness, non-aggression, cooperation, modesty, tranquillity, and so on" (p. 363). Benedict's analysis is organic in this sense. The other interpretation Bennett calls the repression theory, according to which Pueblo society is "marked by considerable *covert* tension, suspicion, anxiety, hostility, fear, and ambition" (p. 363). The culture is repressive and coercive, and the individual reacts to it with suppressed hostility.

Bennett relates this difference in interpretation to differences in value orientations held by the investigators. Those who adhere to the organic theory, he feels, "show a preference for homogeneous preliterate culture," whereas those who hold the repression view have "a fairly clear bias in the direction of equalitarian democracy and non-neurotic, 'free' behavior" (p. 366). This controversy may be seen from another perspective as well. Benedict's organic interpretation assumes that the personality more or less passively accepts the shape that is given it by culture. It assumes that since Pueblo culture is Apollonian, the individual is as well. In brief, it assumes that culture is the primary determinant of the personality. On the other hand, the repression theory does not regard the personality as so completely determined or transformed by culture as Benedict believed; the individual, caught in a stifling and repressive milieu, reacts or fights back.[5]

A. L. KROEBER

A. L. Kroeber was one of Boas' first graduate students at Columbia. He preceded Benedict there by twenty-five years, and was already well established in the discipline by the time she undertook her graduate studies. The ideas of the two students clearly bear the stamp of their venerable teacher. In particular, both inherited the idea that culture is a *sui generis*

[5] Benedict progressively modified her views about the degree to which culture determines the personality. She gave increasing weight to the idea that the personality system is sufficiently autonomous from culture that it can respond or react to the cultural milieu in which it finds itself. In the introduction to *Zuni Mythology* (1935) Benedict tried to explain why some Zuni myths do not accurately reflect Zuni culture, and she concluded that the discrepancies are due to compensatory daydreaming. For example, polygamy does not occur in Zuni society, although stories of plural marriage appear frequently in the folklore. Benedict contended that polygamy stories represent grandiose daydreams, autistic demonstrations of power or prowess. In brief, she explained the stories by the principles of individual psychology rather than culture. In her study of the Thai (1943b) she argued that certain features of Thai child rearing produce self-reliant adults. The Thai are not easy-going, friendly and unsuspicious because of the values of their society, but because the child normally responds in certain ways to his cultural milieu (see also Benedict 1948).

phenomenon which must be explained in terms of its own principles. They also developed similar ideas about cultural configurations, and these notions may be viewed as elaborations of Boas' principle of integration.

Alfred Louis Kroeber was born in 1876 in New Jersey, although he spent most of his youth in New York City.[6] The Kroeber family belonged to a distinctive and traditional segment of New York: it was German speaking and upper middle class, and was characterized by a strong intellectual orientation. His parents spoke German in the home, and Alfred was fluent in both English and German during his youth. His family also placed a high value on good books, music, and art, and they were careful that their children received the best education possible. The other families with whom they mixed, and the children with whom the young Kroeber played and went to school, shared the same bilingualism and cultural interests. It was a milieu which produced a remarkable number of eminent men of science and letters, and Alfred himself acquired an excellent grounding in the sciences, history, and art while still a boy.

In 1892 Kroeber entered Columbia College, where he earned his B.A. degree in literature. He took an M.A. in the same department the year after he graduated, and then became an assistant in English there. While working as an assistant he met Boas, who had just begun teaching at the university. Kroeber took a seminar from Boas on American Indian languages, and by the next year, 1897, decided to turn to anthropology. He received his Ph.D. in anthropology in 1901.

In 1900 Kroeber was invited to serve as anthropological curator for the Academy of Sciences in San Francisco. This marked the beginning of his lifelong association with both San Fran-

[6] The principal biographical and secondary sources on Kroeber are Beals 1968, Driver 1962, Harris 1968:Chapter 12, Hymes 1961, Lowie 1936, Rowe 1962, Theodora Kroeber 1970, and Steward 1961. Another important account of Kroeber's life and work (Steward 1973) was completed too late for me to draw upon it here.

cisco and Berkeley, and also his interest in the Indians of California, for he soon became dedicated to collecting and preserving the cultural materials of the indigenous peoples of the state.

His job lasted only a year, however, because the academy was unwilling to support the field research which Kroeber wanted to conduct. He returned to New York City, but soon he was back on the West Coast with an appointment in the newly created University of California Department and Museum of Anthropology at Berkeley. Mrs. Phoebe Hearst, mother of William Randolph, was a collector of fine arts and archaeological specimens. She decided to finance an anthropological museum which was to be located in San Francisco and run by the university. Kroeber was the first ethnologist appointed, and within a few years he was also the director. In addition to his museum duties he taught a course on anthropology at Berkeley. The department originally focused on undergraduate education, but by the early 1920s it offered a substantial graduate program as well. Due largely to Kroeber's guidance, the Berkeley department became one of the most distinguished in the world.

Kroeber himself enjoyed an eminent reputation, and within American anthropology he was second only to Boas. He was also a prolific writer. When he first entered anthropology at Columbia he was attracted by the possibilities of linguistic analysis, and throughout his career much of his work was devoted to studying the languages of non-Western societies. But his interests quickly broadened to cover the entire spectrum of cultural phenomena. He was a specialist on the North American Indians, and particularly on the peoples of California, but he also engaged in significant archaeological fieldwork in Peru. Later in his life he turned increasingly to the analysis of the higher civilizations, from ancient Egypt and Mesopotamia to modern Western society.

Kroeber retired in 1946 at the age of seventy. He did not stop working, however: he was visiting professor at Harvard,

Columbia, Brandeis, and Yale after his retirement; he traveled, attended conferences and meetings, and continued to write. He was active until the time of his death, in October, 1960, at the age of eighty-five.

SCIENCE AND HISTORY, REALITY AND VALUE CULTURE. According to Kroeber, two kinds of approach may be used in the study of phenomena (see especially 1935; 1936, in 1952:66ff.; 1938, in 1952:79ff.). The first, the scientific, is both analytic and generalizing. It is analytic in that it attempts to decompose or analyse things or events into their constituent processes, and it is generalizing in that it attempts to arrive at formulations which have application to phenomena beyond those which are under investigation: it seeks findings which are "independent of specific or particular time and place" (1936, in 1952:70). In short, the scientific approach "destroys the phenomena as phenomena by transmuting them into abstract concepts—laws, constants, mathematical relations, and the like" (1936, in 1952:69).

The second approach is the historical. This is synthetic, for it attempts to achieve "descriptive integration" (1935:545). It does not decompose the materials under investigation but views them as parts of larger wholes; it traces relations between elements. Two kinds of relations may be pursued. The first are diachronic or temporal, and the form of explanation which results consists in elucidating sequences of events, or providing the historical context of events. Second, synchronic relations may be pursued, in that the study may attempt to trace the interrelations between events within a single frame of time. In anthropology, the synchronic approach consists in placing an item in its cultural context.

In addition to being synthetic, the historical method attempts "to preserve as much as possible of the complexity of individual events" (1938, in 1952:79). Rather than attempting to achieve generalizations with broad applicability, it views phenomena in terms of their actual and unique appearances. Historical findings are always located in time and space.

The historical approach as defined by Kroeber is not employed solely by the discipline of history, for it may be applied to the study of any phenomenon. For example, geology gives descriptive and nongeneralizing explanations of geological formations, and astronomy produces accounts which depict the phenomena of the universe in terms of particular and concrete characteristics. Kroeber did believe, however, that the scientific approach is somewhat more suitable to the study of inorganic and organic phenomena than it is to culture and human behavior. He did not rule out the potential value of scientific studies in anthropology, but he was pessimistic about them; he also preferred the historical method on personal grounds, and he employed it exclusively in his own work.

Whereas science isolates process, the historical approach locates patterns. For example, the biologist identifies a new species of animal life by noting its distinctive pattern of organization. The historian explains an historical event by seeing it as part of a larger complex of trends and occurrences, the totality of which constitutes a pattern. The pattern concept is particularly important in anthropology because of the discipline's heavy reliance on the historical method. Kroeber defines cultural patterns as "those arrangements or systems of internal relationship which give to any culture its coherence or plan, and keep it from being a mere accumulation of random bits" (1948:311). The pattern concept leads to a form of integrational analysis in anthropology.

To Kroeber, the pattern approach can be applied to all facets of culture. He divided the cultural system into at least two components, however, and he thought that each exhibits a somewhat different set of characteristics. It follows that each also manifests somewhat different kinds of pattern.

Kroeber originally referred to these two components of culture as the basic and secondary features, although in his later writings he spoke of them as reality and value culture, respectively. The basic aspects of culture are directed toward the practical matters of life, and particularly toward the problem of making a living. They consist especially of those features having to do with subsistence (e.g., see 1958, in 1963:70).[7] The distinguishing characteristic of the secondary features of culture, on the other hand, is that they are expressions of creative impulses and playful experimentation. When a society places a high value on some aspect of its cultural inventory, such as basketry or ceremonial life, it tends to elaborate this in a fanciful but compulsive manner. Whereas basic culture, or reality culture, must "face reality," secondary culture, or value culture, "faces values" (1957:36). The secondary component of the cultural system "can be denoted as 'value culture,' on the ground of having value, or being an end in itself, and not merely means to practical ends" (1962:9).[8]

The secondary features may occupy a prominent place in a given cultural system, but in a sense they are a residuum left over after the more basic matters have been taken care of. Kroeber remarks, "every society exists in a conditioning environment, and its members have basic physiological necessities to satisfy. It is only after this that free stylization of culture can begin" (1957:102).

An early example of his use of the concepts of basic and secondary features is contained in his monograph on "Zuni Kin

---

[7] Kroeber also used the term "basic pattern" in another sense altogether (see especially 1943, in 1952:85ff.). This second usage referred to any set of interrelated features which exhibits historical stability, and was applied to both reality and value culture. For example, Kroeber spoke of the "basic pattern" behind women's formal dress fashions in Western society, and notes that it has continued relatively unchanged for a thousand years (1919, 1940).

[8] In his earlier writings Kroeber seems to have assumed that all sociocultural phenomena fall within the categories of basic and secondary culture. In his later years, however, he thought that social structure and language, at least, should be set apart. In short, he arrived at the view that reality and value culture are not exhaustive (see 1950/1951, in 1952:152–66). Kroeber eventually became especially uncertain about the relationship between social structure and culture (see 1958, in 1963:176–77).

and Clan" (1917). He notes that the clan plays a comparatively minor role in the normal, everyday life of the Zuni Indian: "The clan is not thought of in ordinary personal relations of man to man, or man to woman." Although the religious system of the village will be affected if the clans are removed, "the life and work of day to day, the contact of person with person, will go unaltered." Zuni clans do not constitute an essential aspect of the society:

The clans give color, variety, and interest to the life of the tribe. They serve an artistic need of the community. But they are only an ornamental excrescence upon Zuni society, whose warp is the family of actual blood relations and whose woof is the house (pp. 48–49).

Another example of Kroeber's use of the concepts of basic and secondary features is contained in his discussion of the social structures of the Australian tribes. The aborigines were hunters and gatherers living in small bands, and traditionally they have been regarded as among the simplest peoples in the world. Nevertheless, their societies were organized according to elaborate systems of kinship, marriage, and descent. According to Kroeber, what is basic in these societies is the fundamental local group patterns—"the primary patterns of group residence and subsistence associations." He suggests that the complex systems of kinship, marriage, and descent should be conceived as "secondary and often unstable embroideries on the primary patterns"; they are "secondary elaborations and shifting experiments"; they constitute a "field of experimentation or play on the part of the cultures" (1938, in 1952:217).

The analysis in Koreber's *Cultural and Natural Areas of Native North America* (1939) further illustrates the distinction between basic and secondary features of culture. This book consists primarily of an examination of the relationship between environmental factors, such as food supply, and the cultures of the American Indian. Kroeber was quite emphatic that an understanding of environmental phenomena is necessary for

97

a full understanding of North American cultures, and he cites the Indians of California in illustration. These were primarily hunters and gatherers rather than agriculturalists, and most of them depended largely on the acorn. Food was plentiful in California and allowed a comparatively high population density. Moreover, because of these favorable environmental characteristics, the cultures of California "were able to flourish with some vigor" (p. 205). The people were able to elaborate certain cultural features, such as basketry and ceremonialism, to a degree that was not possible among their less fortunate neighbors. For example, the level of cultural efflorescence was much higher in California than among the peoples of the Columbia-Fraser Plateau, which is a comparatively inhospitable and desolate region and which was marked by the virtual absence of cultural elaboration beyond the level of bare subsistence needs. Among the peoples of the Columbia-Fraser Plateau, the problem of survival left little room for the elaboration of secondary patterns, or value culture, whereas the subsistence base in California permitted a cultural luxuriance (p. 55).

Kroeber's distinction between the basic and secondary features appears in yet another context in his *Cultural and Natural Areas* book. A major thesis of this work was that culture areas tend to be characterized by one or more "cultural climaxes," localities at which customary practices achieve their most intense or richest development and their highest systematization. A climax appeared in California in a region north of San Francisco Bay. The Pomo, for example, developed a highly elaborate form of basketry. They became skillful at a variety of techniques, going well beyond their practical needs, and they turned their basketry work into an art form of high quality (pp. 54–55; see also 1925:244–47). A climax such as this represents the elaboration of a set of secondary elements, or of an aspect of value culture, to a relatively high point of development.

The distinction between basic and secondary features rests

on several bases. First, fundamentally different kinds of motivation lie behind the two spheres of culture. The basic features rest upon purely practical interests, whereas the secondary features spring from feelings of playfulness and creativity. Kroeber speaks of value culture as "embodying expressions or sublimations of play impulses" (1955, in 1963:209); he refers to "a very strong latent impulse toward cultural play, innovation, and experiment, a true originality and inventiveness" in man (1938, in 1952:218).

Second, reality culture and value culture are attached to the empirical world in different ways. Reality culture is grounded in the objective conditions of the present; it is fixed in nature, for it reflects the immediate and practical interests of people and the natural phenomena which they face. The subsistence patterns of the California Indians or of the Australian aborigines are bound up with the objective exigencies of life in those regions. On the other hand, the secondary features of culture tend to be governed by their own internal principles, which, in the limiting case, are autonomous from external factors (see 1963:62). For example, art styles tend to develop according to purely aesthetic values.

Third, basic and secondary features exhibit different patterns of historical development. The basic segment of culture tends to be cumulative; Kroeber writes,

That whole part of civilization which is concerned with survival and subsistence and welfare must in its nature face reality. Means once achieved are accordingly likely to be retained and added to. So the general course of this practical component of civilization is cumulative (1957:36).

On the other hand, the stylistic or secondary features of culture —such as Pomo basketry, Zuni clanship, Australian systems of kinship, marriage, and descent, and modern Western art—are noncumulative, for they reflect the fickleness of the creative impulse and the arbitrariness of the ends which it seeks. If the course of Pomo culture history had not been interrupted and eventually brought to an end by Western civilization, the imagination and creativity which those people lavished on their basket work might eventually have shifted to social organization or wood carving; their basketry would have atrophied and eventually become a purely utilitarian craft.

STYLES AND GROWTH CURVES. The pattern of historical development which characterizes the various styles making up secondary culture is the growth curve. Each stylistic pattern tends to progress through periods of growth, culmination, and decline; it "tends first to develop and progress, later to degenerate and die" (1958, in 1963:41).

One of Kroeber's most famous works, *Configurations of Culture Growth* (1944), was an attempt to document and chart the phenomenon of growth curves. This is a massive book, containing almost 850 pages of text, and it covers an extreme sweep of history: it deals with all the "higher" civilizations of the world, from ancient Egypt, Mesopotamia, India, and China, to modern, Western society. The focus is on aesthetic and intellectual achievements, including philosophy, science, philology, sculpture, painting, drama, literature, and political expansion.

Kroeber's analysis of philosophical thought (Chapter 2) illustrates what he meant by growth curves. A particular style of philosophy builds on the assumptions and the knowledge which are contained within a culture, and it does so within a definite institutional setting. The assumptions, knowledge, and setting constitute the basis upon which the system of thought grows, and they supply both the limitations and potentialities for its full development. Kroeber writes,

Such a [philosophical] system bears in itself certain specific potentialities, and also specific limitations, which enable it, even compel it, barring catastrophe from outside, to realize or fulfill itself to the terminus of these potentialities, but not to go beyond them (p. 90).

The period of growth is the phase in which the logical possibilities of the system are worked out. In the earliest stages progress may seem slow and uncertain, but as the process of growth builds and the main issues become clear, both the tempo and level of sophistication increase. Culmination occurs when activity and productivity are at their peak, and it is over once most of the logical possibilities have been explored. "When the given set of potentialities is exhausted, the growth ends" (p. 90). Decline then sets in. The period of decline may take a number of forms, such as the internal disintegration of the pattern, or a tendency toward mechanical repetitiousness.

Kroeber's views about the condition of the arts in modern Western society illustrate what he meant by the process of decline. He wrote, "All European fine arts since about 1880, and more strongly since 1900, have displayed increasing symptoms of what may be called pattern dissolution. . . ." A revolution is taking place whereby the artist is wrecking and upsetting the patterns of the past—he writes music which is characterized by dissonance, paints pictures which run directly counter to nature (he paints "hands on trees and cogwheels in men"), writes "plotless novels" and "lines of verse beginning with small letters or full of stammers." "[T]he pattern possibilities of the Goethe and Beethoven configurations are obviously exhausted." The extravagances which are taking place represent in part "the zeal of the revolutionist who needs first to wreck everything . . . before he can reconstruct"; and in part they constitute "responses to a condition in which, accepted patterns having gone stale, any upsetting novelty is rewarded for being startling" (pp. 764–65).

The method which Kroeber employed in this book was to plot the incidence of genius in the development of a pattern, for he assumed that the relative frequency of geniuses is an index of levels of achievement. Logically, geniuses should be equally distributed through time, but in actuality their incidence is uneven. For example, there were "no geniuses at all between 1450 and 1550" in England, whereas between 1550 and 1650 there appeared "a whole series of geniuses in literature, music, science, philosophy and politics" (pp. 10–11). This clustering phenomenon reflects the growth curve of patterns, since those whom posterity recognizes as geniuses are the ones whose talents were realized during a period of growth or culmination. Even the most gifted men and women are not likely to leave their mark in history if they have the misfortune of working during a period of decline or stagnation (pp. 7–16).

In writing this book Kroeber set out to investigate the possibility of establishing standard growth curves, or predictable cycles of rise and decline, by comparing the data of historically different patterns. However, he emerged at the end of this long study concluding that growth curves do not follow a standard form; they exhibit considerable historical variability:

> In reviewing the ground covered, I wish to say at the outset that I see no evidence of any true law in the phenomena dealt with; nothing cyclical, regularly repetitive, or necessary. There is nothing to show either that every culture must develop patterns within which a florescence of quality is possible, or that, having once so flowered, it must wither without chance of revival (p. 761).

Kroeber explicitly noted the relationship between his own analysis and Oswald Spengler's cyclical theory of historical change (pp. 825–33). Kroeber was probably far less critical of Spengler than most Boasians, but he disagreed with the German philosopher-historian on several fundamental issues. In particular, he rejected Spengler's view that "cultures necessarily develop through essentially parallel stages" and "that they die of themselves" (p. 828). To Kroeber, the life courses of civilizations are far less uniform and necessary than Spengler supposed.

To fully understand Kroeber's analysis in *Configurations* it is important to distinguish between stylistic patterns and growth curves. A pattern is the basic plan which is behind a philosophical system, art style, and the like; it is a set of assumptions, principles, and values which are elaborated by the creative impulses, and it is to be approached subjectively. On the other hand, a growth curve is simply the rise and decline in a pattern's level of achievement. The growth curve is an external manifestation of dynamic factors contained within the subjective pattern, and is explainable by reference to them. For example, the growth and culmination of Greek philosophy between about 585–280 B.C. is to be explained in terms of the working out of certain assumptions and principles contained within Greek philosophical thought.

Kroeber's book dealt with growth curves, and only incidentally with patterns: he concentrated almost entirely on plotting the rise and fall of achievement as measured by the incidence of genius. This is somewhat surprising, since it is the pattern which provides understanding; to study the growth curve is to focus on an external index or manifestation of a cultural phenomenon rather than on the phenomenon itself. Probably several factors helped divert Kroeber's attention from patterns in this book. For one, patterns are infinitely variable and hence incommensurate, whereas this is not true of growth curves (pp. 6–7). By charting and comparing configurations of growth, Kroeber could reveal fundamental similarities and differences in the rise, culmination, and decline of cultural phenomena. Moreover, the knowledge required to make intelligent analyses of the patterns of such diverse societies as ancient Mesopotamia and nineteenth-century Japan was probably beyond the capacity even of the learned Kroeber.

Probably the most important reason why Kroeber concentrated on growth curves rather than patterns is that his ideas were strongly rooted in the empirical tradition of Boasian anthropology: he seems to have wanted to avoid the intuitive approach which an account of patterns would have entailed, whereas he felt that by using genius as an index of growth curves he could arrive at comparatively objective conclusions. He did not have to rely on his own opinions about historical

peaks and depressions, but could use the evaluations of quali-
fied experts as to the stature of historical figures. Kroeber notes
a "fairly close" consensus among those who have discussed the
accomplishments of former artists, philosophers, and the like.
He also notes that he found textbooks particularly useful, "on
account of their timidity about departing from the accepted
norm" (p. 23).

Kroeber did not always retreat from the subjective interpretations of patterns, however. For example, in 1951 he published
a paper in which he attempted to characterize the values expressed in the major art forms of native South America (1951,
in 1952:289–96). An even more striking instance of his interest
in subjective patterns is contained in his study of fashions in
women's formal or evening dress, written with Jane Richardson
(1940; see also 1919).

This study was an attempt to chart historical variations in
the basic pattern which has characterized women's formal dress
in Western society during the last several centuries. Most of the
analysis focused on certain objective measurements, including
skirt length and width (or fullness of skirt at the hem), width
and height of the waist, and the width and depth of decolle-
tage. Kroeber drew upon fashion plates, magazines, engravings,
and the like for his data, which were good as far back as the
late 1780s and spotty but usable to 1630.

Kroeber discovered two significant features about the history
of women's fashion. First, the several measurements go through
pendulum-like swings lasting approximately 100 years. For example, skirt length goes through a cycle from long, to short, to
long again about every century. Second, superimposed on this
100-year cycle are periodic occurrences of fashion agitation or
unsettlement; these are periods marked by unusual amounts of
variability in style. For example, dress length sometimes exhibits comparatively wide fluctuations in the representative
specimens for a single year.

Kroeber noted that unsettlement appears at characteristic

points along the 100-year cycle. When the pendulum swings to short dresses, dress lengths exhibit considerable unsettlement, and when fashions swing back to long dresses again the unsettlement subsides. Similarly, when the waist moves very high, near the bustline, unsettlement appears; and when the waist moves near the hips, unsettlement appears once again; but when the waistline is in between, at its normal anatomical position, unsettlement all but vanishes.

Kroeber used this correlation of unsettlement and pendulum swing to define the "basic or ideal pattern" of women's evening dress (1940:145). When style departs too far from the ideal pattern, fashion comes under strain, which is manifested by agitation. The pressure to modify the style mounts; it is as if the people are not satisfied with the existing fashion. On the other hand, when the current fashion is in conformity with the basic pattern, the style "is felt to be satisfying" (p. 144) and the agitation disappears.

Once fashion is in conformity with the basic pattern, why do alterations not cease and dress styles remain stable? The reason is that style demands constant change. When the current fashion and the basic pattern are in harmony, superficial elements are modified for a time. For example, color, accessories, and frills may be altered. But when these possibilities are exhausted, the fundamental pattern itself is slowly worked upon under the constant pressure for stylistic change. Kroeber writes that the basic pattern is then "attacked and distorted by fashion" (1940:145).[9]

The basic or ideal pattern which Kroeber isolated consists of

[9] Kroeber also noted that sociopolitical instability and tension seem to affect dress fashions. Departures from the basic pattern—and hence increases in fashion unsettlement—are correlated with periods of social and political conflict. An example is the period stretching from the French Revolution to the years of post-Napoleonic tensions, and another is the twentieth century. These periods of conflict in society are precisely the periods in which the basic pattern was attacked most vigorously. On the other hand, during the period of relative peace which persisted through much of the nineteenth century, women's fashions conformed with the basic pattern, and little unsettlement or agitation was evident (see especially 1957:7–27).

a long skirt, reaching to the feet, which is also quite full. The waist is as slender as possible and is located at its normal anatomical position. A substantial portion of the upper breasts, shoulders, and arms is uncovered. Below the waist, the silhouette of the dress departs radically from the shape of the body, but from the waist up the contours of both body and dress are in close conformity (1940:145; 1957:19–20).

This basic pattern is "an ideal though unconscious pattern" (1940:147). It is a subjective framework which exists in people's minds and which guides them both in elaborating and choosing their styles of clothing. Kroeber writes, "This basic ideal pattern of Western women's dress, mediaeval and modern, has gone through a thousand years of constant remodeling without any fundamental change" (1957:20).

Kroeber notes that dress fashions do not exhibit the growth curves which characterize most of the other stylistic patterns of secondary culture, such as art. Western dress fashions do not constantly evolve toward some ideal or goal and then decay once the goal is reached. Rather, they seem to take the goal for granted; the basic pattern of women's formal dress wear is relatively stationary, although it is ceaselessly tampered with, "Tantalus-like, under the tyrannical spur of mode" (1957:21).

Kroeber dealt primarily with the patterns and growth curves of delimited segments of culture, such as pottery styles, architecture, philosophy, and dress fashions; but he also thought that total cultures or civilizations frequently exhibit distinctive stylistic tendencies. He thought that the styles of a given culture tend to exhibit "a certain consistency among themselves" (1951, in 1952:402). He wrote,

We can then construe a civilization as something that achieves a degree of unity, that works from a start of more or less randomness toward increasing coherence, and that moves from amorphousness toward definiteness, from fumbling trials to decision (1948, in 1963:22).

Kroeber referred to this total cultural pattern by a variety of terms, including master plan and super-style.

PATTERN, STYLE AND MEANING. One of the most interesting aspects of Kroeber's work is that he devoted his attention almost entirely to the patterns of secondary culture and virtually ignored the basic features. This seems surprising, since the terms "basic" and "secondary" imply that it is the former which is the more important and should be given priority in research. Kroeber was even explicit that the environmental and subsistence factors have crucial implications for the rest of culture—for example, he notes that because of the favorable conditions which existed in aboriginal California, the cultures there "were able to flourish with some vigor" (1939:205).

Nevertheless, on the whole, he seems to have regarded the subsistence base as little more than a limiting factor. An adequate economic system is necessary for a rich or elaborate value culture to develop, but once it does develop it pursues its own ends and responds to its own *sui generis* principles. Possibly Kroeber's thinking about the relative independence of value culture reflected the influence of Boas, to whom cultural phenomena are largely autonomous from the exigencies of life.

Even more important in understanding why Kroeber tended to neglect reality culture is that he viewed the secondary features in a distinct light, in that he placed a high value on them. To him, value culture is not truly "secondary" at all, for it represents that which is excellent or worthy of note in human society; it represents achievement. On the other hand, reality culture represents the mundane, humble, or menial side of life; it consists in elements which man needs if he is to survive, but which do not express his true human potential.

Kroeber's evaluations of basic and secondary culture—and the basis for his concentration on the latter—are apparent in his *Cultural and Natural Areas of Native North America*

(1939). A central focus of this book was the issue of cultural intensity, by which he meant the degree of elaboration of secondary elements. Kroeber attempted to characterize and compare the North American Indian groups in terms of the degrees of cultural intensity they exhibited, and the very terms he used in discussing these matters reveal his more or less implicit feelings about value culture. For example, throughout the study he referred to the "richness" and "luxuriance" of some cultures—those which achieved a high degree of elaboration; he used such phrases as the "finest flowerings" of cultural climaxes (p. 223), and the "flourishing" of cultures (p. 226). On the other hand, he spoke of "culture recession" (p. 223) and of the "declining" of cultures (p. 224). The cultures of the Mississippi Valley, he noted, reached a "modest peak," then "spread and shallowed" (p. 227). He referred to the Eskimo culture as one of the "lower-grade cultures in America" because of its preoccupation with subsistence matters, although he noted that it received "enrichment" from contacts with other groups (pp. 20, 25). He noted that the area of the Columbia-Fraser Plateau

failed to develop any great amount of culture of its own, [and] it has long, and on the whole correctly, been regarded as a region marked by negative traits, by absences, except for its more immediate subsistence adaptations (p. 55).

These cultures "failed" to develop the rich elaboration of ceremonial life which characterized some of the societies of nearby California, for example; they exhibited "negative traits" rather than cultural luxuriance.

Kroeber's more or less implicit value judgments concerning secondary culture are parallel to his evaluations of growth curves. He was explicit that subjective evaluations are required when charting the growth curves of a cultural pattern, such as an art form. For example, an art style is at its peak of development when originality and refinement are at their fullest expression, and decline has set in once the style is characterized by a lack of imagination or by a mechanical repetition of design. Similarly, the higher the level of cultural intensity, the greater the cultural achievement; if a society does no more than satisfy its subsistence needs, its cultural achievement is low.

Kroeber's interest in the higher civilizations is to be understood in the context of the value he placed on the secondary features of culture. The higher civilizations represent the richest flowering of creativity, the highest achievements of man, and are therefore particularly tempting to study.

It is expectable that the patterns of reality and value culture should exhibit somewhat different properties, since the former are rooted in the exigencies of life and the latter are not. Kroeber did not devote much attention to the basic features of culture, so little can be said about the way he conceived them. This is not true of value culture, however. To Kroeber, whatever is not immediately functional or utilitarian is somewhat fanciful and imaginative in nature, and is stamped with the quality of playfulness. He wrote, "A great deal of the total picture [of culture] suggests the play of earnest children, or the inventive vagaries of fashion" (1942, in 1952:244).

Among the most telling illustrations of the quality of playfulness which Kroeber saw in human institutions are his discussions of social structure (see especially 1938, in 1952:210ff.; 1942, in 1952:219ff.; 1948:395–99). He suggested that much of the formal social organization of primitive society consists in imaginative embroideries, experimentation, ingenuity, and play; this is true, he believed, of the societies of both Zuni and Australia, as I have noted. If one were to have asked him to describe the distinguishing quality of the Zuni clan system, he would not have stressed its functional value in maintaining social stability and cohesion, its role in the subsistence system, or even its purely traditional character; rather, he would have remarked upon its fanciful quality. Kroeber's interpretation of Plains culture is also illustrative. Unlike Benedict, he did not view Plains institutions in terms of a pervasive emotional theme. To Kroeber, the introduction of the horse onto the plains enabled the Indians there to become effective buffalo hunters; the subsistence base was drastically modified by the new food supply, and this in turn had "culturally intensifying consequences" (1939:77). Kroeber writes, "not only ritual complexes, but indeed all sorts of cultural patterns, quickly blossomed out in the plains after the introduction of the horse" (1939:78). The complex system of warfare and the spread of the Sun Dance, among other things, were "luxury manifestations" (1939:56); they were fanciful expressions of the creative impulse and were to be seen in that light.

Kroeber's ideas about the creative and playful quality of secondary culture had important implications for his interpretation of the behavior of the individual. Like Benedict, Kroeber inherited the Boasian notion that culture is enormously significant in shaping both thought and action, and he was the first American anthropologist to explicitly develop the thesis of cultural determinism. In an article published in 1917 (reprinted in 1952:22–51) he argued that culture is "superorganic," and that it is a "substance" which is irreducible to the level of the individual organism. He opposed the view that the great inventions or discoveries in the history of civilizations are to be explained as products of individual genius, for he maintained that these innovations are cultural events and should be seen as part of the flow of cultural change.

Kroeber later softened his views about the superorganic nature of culture (see 1948, in 1952:112; 1952:22–23), probably for several reasons. One factor, perhaps, was the tension between his cultural determinism and his ideas about creativity, for the two are fundamentally contradictory. To Kroeber, the individual does not merely reproduce the culture he has received; he works with it by attempting to elaborate and improve it. The human intellect has at least some capacity to stand apart from culture and work upon it from without. Kroeber eventually became aware of the contradiction between his notions of creativity and style on one hand and cultural determinism on the other. He wrote that his conception of the growth and decline of patterns "contains a concealed factor of striving and will, in the individuals through whom the realization is achieved. A creative urge and spark must be accorded them" (1952:9).

Kroeber's views represent a subtle departure from the Boasian image of man. He was implying that the individual's actions are not understandable solely in terms of habit and custom, for the playful impulse is an additional and important part of man's character (see 1948:390–91). For example, Kroeber implies that, to a degree, at least, it is the playful impulse which motivates the individual to pursue the ends laid down by his culture. It is in part the creative urge which propels the Australian aborigine and the Zuni Indian to engage in their rather elaborate social systems.

Boas, of course, did not totally ignore the playful impulse, for he emphasized the creative imaginativeness which is behind such phenomena as art and folklore. I have described his analysis of Alaskan needlecases, according to which an element of the needlecase design may excite the imagination of the Eskimo craftsman, who then elaborates that feature within the conventional limits of the art form. Similarly, Benedict did not ignore the element of creative elaboration; to her, a cultural configuration begins as a slight bias in a certain direction, and it is progressively developed and elaborated by the members of society. Nevertheless, Boas and Benedict thought that human imagination and creativity are highly restricted. To them, these do not play a fundamental role in human institutions, are not important in their interpretation, and do not stamp them with the quality of playfulness.

Although Kroeber's concept of value culture represents a departure from Boasian thought, it also bears a strong family resemblance to Boas' principle of cultural integration. According to Kroeber, the creative impulse concentrates on whatever is valued by society, and consequently cultures tend to become organized around and to exhibit distinct foci. The values of secondary culture define "toward what the cultures are slanted" and "around what they are organized" (1949, in 1952:131). What Boas or Benedict would have regarded as a pattern of integration was to Kroeber the product of playful impulses; it represented the efflorescence of value culture.

Earlier I suggested that Benedict's configuration concept was a result of the combination of Boas' principle of integration with his idea that culture is founded on emotion. Similarly, Kroeber's concept of value culture—which is the principal element in his work—may be conceived as the joining of Boas' idea of integration with his notion of creative imaginativeness.

JULIAN STEWARD

Steward was one of Kroeber's students at Berkeley, and the continuity between the work of the two writers is clear. Nevertheless, Steward modified Kroeber's ideas in several fundamental ways and arrived at a view of behavior and institutions which was quite at variance with that of his teacher. Kroeber focused primarily on value culture, which, as he conceived it, is composed of stylistic patterns that need to be apprehended subjectively. On the other hand, Steward focused on what Kroeber would have referred to as reality culture, and he insisted that it is to be seen from the objective point of view: it is to be understood from the perspective of the outside observer and not in terms of the categories and values of the individual in society.

Behind these differences separating the two writers was yet another: Kroeber was pessimistic about the scientific approach to culture and he preferred to employ the historical method in his own research, whereas Steward conceived anthropology as a science almost from the beginning of his career. In searching for the laws behind human institutions he looked beyond the level of subjective culture to the world outside the individual; he located them in the economic and environmental conditions which both Kroeber and Boas noted but which they left largely unexplored.

Steward was born in 1902 in Washington, D.C., the son of an official in the U.S. Patent Office. He attended both the University of California and Cornell as an undergraduate, receiving his B.A. at Cornell in 1925. After graduating he returned to Berkeley to study anthropology, and while he was there he came under the influence of both Kroeber and Carl Sauer—the latter a geographer with an interest in the relationship between culture and the environment. Steward received his Ph.D. at Berkeley in 1931.

The Depression years were difficult for young Ph.D.s, and Steward's case was no exception. Nevertheless, between 1931 and 1935 he was associated with three universities (Michigan, Utah, and California) and engaged in fieldwork in the western part of the United States. In 1935 he joined the staff of the Bureau of American Ethnology. Prior to that time he concentrated on the archaeology and ethnography of the Great Basin and Plateau regions of North America, but soon after 1935 he engaged in fieldwork in highland Peru and Ecuador and among the Carrier Indians of British Columbia.

In 1940 he undertook the monumental task of organizing and editing the six-volume *Handbook of the South American Indians*. This firmly established his reputation as a South Americanist. Between 1943 and 1946, while still working on the *Handbook*, he served as Director of the Smithsonian's Institute of Social Anthropology, the purpose of which was to promote teaching and field research in Latin America.

In 1946 Steward accepted a position at Columbia University. By now he had achieved worldwide prominence as an anthropologist, and he attracted a number of students who have since become leaders in the discipline. While at Columbia he took charge of an extensive research project on the peoples of Puerto Rico, the actual fieldwork being conducted primarily by his graduate students (Steward 1956a).

Although his years at Columbia were productive, the demands of teaching were a heavy burden on him, and in 1952 Steward moved to the University of Illinois where he had been offered a position as research professor. After moving to Illinois he authored a significant amount of work and participated in a variety of research programs, the most important of which was a project he directed on the effects of industrialization and urbanization in traditional societies (Steward 1967). In addition, he was involved in both graduate and undergraduate teaching at Illinois (Harris 1968:662; Shimkin 1964:1–8). Steward retired in 1969, and died three years later, at the age of seventy.

CULTURAL ECOLOGY. The key to Steward's ideas about culture is his concept of ecology, a term which he first began using in the 1930s but which received its fullest elaboration in his *Theory of Culture Change* (1955:Chapter 2). Steward writes that "The principal meaning of ecology is 'adaptation to environment'" (1955:30). For most animals adaptation is accomplished by means of their physical characteristics. An obvious example is the wings and sensory organs of the bat, a mammal which is able to exploit a very distinctive ecological niche. Man's adaptation, however, is achieved largely by means of culture:

Man enters the ecological scene . . . not merely as another organism which is related to other organisms in terms of his physical characteristics. He introduces the super-organic factor of culture (1955:31).

Cultural ecology is the study of the adjustment or relationship of culture to the natural environment, and two distinct orders of phenomena are involved: the features of the environment itself, and the cultural arrangements by which the environment is exploited, including technology and economic organization. Both sets of phenomena must be taken into account in a cultural ecological analysis. A given economy will function very differently in an unproductive environment than in a rich one; and the same environment will be exploited quite differently by a primitive economy than it will by a highly industrialized system.

Steward's approach was to analyze the ecology of a society in order to discover the manner in which the ecological framework determines other features of the culture. An example is a monograph he wrote on the Shoshonean peoples of the Basin-Plateau area (Steward 1938; summarized in 1955: Chapter 6), a rather extensive region which includes the Great Basin of the western United States as well as part of the Colorado Plateau to the south and the Columbia Plateau to the north. This territory includes the Columbia-Fraser Plateau referred to by Kroeber. The Basin-Plateau region is quite arid, supporting a meager plant and animal life. The Indian inhabitants of this environment employed a simple hunting and gathering economy and were forced to live at a bare subsistence level: "life was devoted almost exclusively to the unrelenting demands of the food quest" (1939:529).

One significant effect of the ecology was that large concentrations of people were impossible for other than brief periods. During most of the year the elementary family traveled alone in the hot, dry valleys in search of food. For a few months during the winter the supply of pine nuts in the mountains was sufficient for a few families to camp together, but these encampments tended to be located at different places each year and seldom consisted of exactly the same families the next year. The environment, together with a simple economy, served to make the elementary family an independent and self-sufficient unit.

The ecology had other effects, one of which was to favor (but not require) the development of polyandry. The exigencies of life made the food quest and economic cooperation within the family central concerns, and since both husband and wife were equally important in this sphere sex equality was the rule. In contrast, in most societies the male enjoys social dominance, and consequently he monopolizes sexual and marital privileges. Among most peoples who practice plural marriages, it is only the male who may take more than one spouse. However, the sex equality of the Shoshoneans made it possible for them to practice both polygyny and polyandry, since "the relationship of both sexes to plural marriage [was] almost identical" (1936b:561; see also 1938:242–43).

Property rights were also closely associated with the Basin-Plateau ecology. Among most of these peoples there was no exclusive ownership of land or resources, and families were free to wander at will. If a family were foraging in a particular area it had rights to that location on a "first come, first served" basis, and usually another group did not dispute this right by searching for food in the same place. This system of property rights was essential to survival, since the location of food was unpredictable; a given spot would be rich one year and meager the next, or have an abundance of game or seeds in the spring but be depleted by summer. Permanent and exclusive rights to land and resources would have been disastrous by restricting the mobility of family groups (Steward 1938:253–56; 1955: 107–8).

Although Steward regarded the ecology as an important causal factor behind social institutions, he was clear that not all features of culture can be explained in terms of ecological adaptation. He distinguished between the cultural core, "the constellation of features which are most closely related to subsistence activities and economic arrangements," such as political organization and in some cases religious patterns; and the secondary features of culture, those which are not strongly tied to the core and which "are determined to a greater extent by purely cultural-historical factors—by random innovations or by diffusion" (1955:37). This distinction parallels that which Kroeber made between reality and value culture.

Steward held that his causal and ecological framework provides the basis for a theory of cultural evolution. Boas, and most of the anthropologists he trained, held that each culture has a unique and complex history and that laws of evolutionary change either do not exist or are too complex to be discovered. According to Steward's scheme, however, environments necessitate distinctive forms of adaptation, so different cultures in similar environments should exhibit similar patterns of development. For example, if a people with a comparatively simple hunting and gathering economy were to have moved into the Basin-Plateau region in aboriginal times, either they would have adapted along the lines of the Shoshonean cultures or they would have perished. Much of Steward's research was devoted to working out parallels in ecological adaptation and evolutionary development of this kind (see Steward 1955: Chapters 6–11, and 1959).

Steward identified himself as an evolutionist since 1952 (Steward 1965:733), but he dissociated his theory from the work of the nineteenth-century anthropologists, such as Tylor, who attempted to construct a single, comprehensive scheme of evolutionary development (Steward 1955:15–16). Steward referred to his approach as a multilinear rather than a unilinear theory of evolution, for he believed that cultures have evolved along a variety of different lines. He stated that his approach "simply seeks cross-cultural regularities and explanations but it presupposes no universal schemes. According to this view, there may be many kinds of evolution and many unlike factors involved" (1965:733).

An idea which has become closely associated with Steward's evolutionary theory is his concept of levels of sociocultural integration. He maintained that differences between simple and complex societies are not merely quantitative; "systems of the higher level do not consist merely of more numerous and diversified parts" (1950:107). Rather, complex systems are qualitatively different from simple ones, for different degrees of complexity entail fundamentally different forms of integration and adaptation. The surplus of wealth in the United States permits a system of social stratification that was impossible among the Shoshoneans, and the industrial economy requires national institutions such as currency and banking which had no place in the simpler society. The elementary family of the aboriginal Eskimo is fundamentally different from that of the United States because the two societies are at different levels of development. The family in modern America has lost many of its primitive functions, and other functions which it has retained have been so modified that the household has acquired "unique meaning and relationships that are specific to the context of modern civilization" (1950:110). As a culture evolves, changes in levels of integration must be taken into account, for the successive types "are not only increasingly complex but . . . represent new emergent forms" (1955:41).

The concept of levels of integration was used by Steward as a typological device with evolutionary implications. For example, in his *Native Peoples of South America,* co-authored with Louis Faron, he presented a survey of South American cultures by arranging them along a single continuum, irrigation civilizations at the top and hunters and gatherers at the bottom. He does not suggest that this continuum represents the actual historical development of specific societies, but by the use of this typological scheme he is able to bring a wide variety of cultures together into a common framework.

BOASIAN TRACES IN STEWARD'S THOUGHT. Although Steward's ideas about culture represent a fundamental departure from the Boasian frame of reference, in certain respects it may be conceived as a continuation or elaboration of the same tradition of thought—a tradition which Steward inherited largely through Kroeber.

First, Steward's scheme may be regarded as the elaboration of

Boas' principle of the limitations of the environment. Boas never made a detailed analysis of the effects of these limiting conditions because his interest was always directed toward the subjective and creative features of culture. Benedict ignored the environmental influences as well, although she went even farther than Boas in doing so: in elaborating her view of the autonomy of culture she concluded that the limits imposed by the environment are so broad that they are unimportant. "After all," she wrote, "man has a fairly wide margin of safety" (1929:813). Similarly, to Kroeber, the stylistic patterns of which value culture is composed develop according to their own subjective principles and are largely autonomous from the exigencies of life.

In Steward's mind these limiting conditions are often much narrower and more important than Boas, Benedict, or Kroeber thought. To Steward, each people finds themselves boxed in by a set of inflexible limiting conditions: "any system may vary only within limits, otherwise the people will obviously not survive" (Steward 1938:261). Much of Steward's analysis of the Shoshoneans is an account of the limitations imposed by a harsh environment on a simple society; among the Shoshoneans

the activities involved in the exploitation of an arid environment by means of certain simple devices restricted the size and permanence of sociopolitical groups, prevented the formulation of concepts of property in real estate and the development of social classes, and placed comparatively narrow limits on the nature and function of such elements as houses, sweat houses, and garments (Steward 1940:494).[10]

Steward's formulation of the role of the environment goes beyond Boas' in at least one respect, for Steward was emphatic that the environment is a creative as well as a limiting factor

[10] Steward did not insist that all societies are as narrowly restricted as the Shoshoneans. He remarked that "These limits may be narrow or great and in turn permit small or large latitude in those cultural activities that depend upon them" (1938:261). For example, the ecology of the Carrier Indians permitted a fairly wide range of variation compared with that of the Shoshoneans (Steward 1941).

behind culture (e.g., 1955:34ff.). To Boas, a culture trait can be modified, recombined, and reinterpreted almost without end—it can vary almost randomly—as long as it remains within the broad limits imposed by the environment. To Steward, a variety of cultural forms may be possible within the context of a given environment, but some are more reasonable and adaptive than others and will tend to prevail. The environment is creative in the sense that it tends to select the most appropriate traits from among the possibilities. For example, many forms of land ownership were clearly ruled out by the Basin-Plateau ecology, but it is conceivable that some form other than that practiced by the Shoshoneans would have been possible; nevertheless, the system that did prevail was presumably the most suitable. To Steward, culture is subject to far less historical contingency than Boas believed; culture is rooted in the present conditions of the environment and is not merely limited by them.

Steward's concept of levels of sociocultural integration may be seen as an extension of this ecological framework. He noted that the ecological approach is less applicable to complex societies than to primitive ones, because a society with a sophisticated technology enjoys greater freedom from environmental limitations and hence a wider range of latitude (Steward 1955:40). However, this does not mean that the cultures of complex societies are more arbitrary; as early as 1938 Steward wrote, "In complex societies components of the social superstructure rather than ecology seem increasingly to be determinants of further developments" (1938:262). The conditions which enclose cultural forms progressively shift from the environment to the sociocultural system itself. The conditions to which a politically autonomous primitive village must adapt are primarily ecological in nature; but the peasant or folk community is a segment of a larger society, and the national institutions make up a crucial part of that village's "environment." The peasant villager must adjust not only to climate, soils, and the like, but to the legal, political, and economic systems of the

larger society as well (1950:110–12). In the Puerto Rican project which Steward directed, considerable attention was paid to
such features as credit—an important "environmental" factor
deriving from the larger sociocultural whole.

The second respect in which Steward's thought represents
the application rather than rejection of Boasian ideas is that his
ecological approach is actually a form of cultural integrationalism.

When Steward was developing his scheme in the 1930s, it
was a common view in American anthropology that culture is
"a congeries of disconnected traits, associated only by reason of
a series of historic accidents, the elements being functionally
unrelated" (Spier 1931:455). This "shreds and patches" image
of culture was largely a product of the diffusionist methodology, as I have noted. Benedict's configuration concept and
Kroeber's ideas about pattern and style were developed largely
in an attempt to rise above this position; both writers believed
that a thread of unity tends to pervade the customs of a people
and that traits are not completely disconnected from one another. Similarly, Steward's cultural ecological scheme was an attempt to locate the system within culture, and it was developed
in large part as a reaction to the view that culture is a ragbag of
traits. The following, although referring to culture change,
sums up his approach:

> culture is not an entirely fortuitous assemblage of unrelated elements
> but consists of parts which in some degree predetermine, condition,
> or delimit one another. The problem, then, is to ascertain the nature
> and degree of this interrelationship (Steward 1940:480).

The environmental conditions which circumscribe a culture
provide the frame of reference for making an integrational analysis, and explanation consists in showing the effects of adaptation on the sociocultural whole. In short, Steward's integrational approach may be conceived as an attempt to combine
Boas' principle of integration with that of the limitations of the
environment.

To clarify Steward's integrational approach it is useful to return briefly to the distinction between Benedict's view of culture and the utilitarian version mentioned above. In Benedict's view, culture is virtually autonomous from the exigencies of life and varies almost randomly with respect to them. In this sense hers was an irrational version of culture. According to the utilitarian version, however, the essential feature of a culture element is its contribution to the people's material well-being or to social cohesion. Culture is not autonomous from the exigencies of life, but is closely tied to them. Explanation consists in showing the utility of a trait.

Steward's scheme falls between these two points of view; his might be referred to as a practical rather than either an irrational or a utilitarian version of culture. To him, culture is not autonomous from the hard realities of life, for institutions are directly conditioned and limited by these realities. Nevertheless, the point of his research has never been to analyze the utilitarian functions of institutions, for it was the Boasian problem of integration which set the pattern for his work. His research was devoted to showing the unity and not the utility of culture.

The Puerto Rico project which Steward directed is illustrative (Steward 1956a). The field research consisted of four rural community studies together with an investigation of the wealthy and prominent families of the island. The analysis focused on the effects of ecological adaptation on such features as community stratification, attitudes toward mobility and education, and family structure. In one of the rural communities the family was typically an economic and land-holding unit; the father was the head of this unit and occupied an important position of authority. In another community the women worked in the fields for wages, and the basic unit of family life was the mother and her children. The economic importance of the husband was minimal and a matriarchal family was the result (Steward 1956a:474–75). This analysis did not attempt to explain the features of the local community as adaptive in a utilitarian sense; rather, differences in family structure were explained by showing the differences in the cultural and ecological contexts in which they were found.

In saying that the point of Steward's research was never to discover the utilitarian functions of institutions I do not mean that he totally ignored such functions or that he minimized their importance, for he did occasionally note the utility of specific traits (e.g., Steward 1955:118). Because of his focus on integration, however, the utility of traits was a residual issue in his mind. Steward was on the verge of revising the Boasian culture concept in a fundamental way, for he rejected the irrational image of institutions; but he stopped short of completing this revision.

STEWARD'S DEPARTURES FROM BOASIAN THOUGHT. Two features of Steward's thought betray his Boasian roots: his conception of the ecology as a set of external conditions which circumscribe culture, and his integrational form of analysis. But in other respects his scheme constitutes a major departure from Boas' culture concept. Three changes in particular are apparent.

First, whereas Boas held that human behavior and institutions should be understood subjectively, from the "inside," Steward took the objective point of view. He set out to analyze behavior and culture by using his own scientific categories rather than those of the people being studied.

Steward's objective point of view was not an accidental feature of his thought, but was a result of using the conditions of the environment as analytical reference points. Although the folk categories and beliefs about the world may be interesting, they are not essential to the analysis (but see Frake 1962). If an individual finds himself short of water in a hot, dry environment, he will either respond appropriately or suffer the consequences; this is true whether he is a university trained anthropologist or an illiterate hunter. Similarly, "any [cultural] system may vary only within limits, otherwise the people will obviously not survive" (1938:261). The Basin-Plateau environment presented conditions which had to be adjusted to, and an understanding of Shoshonean culture demanded the objective analysis of these factors.

In discarding Boas' subjective point of view, Steward tended to relegate the individual to a comparatively unimportant place in his work. A person should respond in characteristic ways to the objective conditions surrounding him, so the man and woman in society may be by-passed in giving an account of these conditions:

> Cultures, societies, and areas have distinctive traditions or histories and unique patterns, no two being alike in their totality. At the same time, it is possible to identify certain institutions and modes of behavior which are similar in different areas. . . . The problem, then, is one of specifying the particular conditions under which similar behavior patterns may be produced (1950:6).

Moreover, the total complex of conditions which impinge upon a culture, and the impact of the individual's behavior on the total sociocultural system, may be beyond a person's comprehension. Consequently, an account of ecological conditions and cultural adaptation *must* proceed above the level of the individual. For example, it is unlikely that those who were involved in the early development of irrigation agriculture were fully aware of the consequences of their acts:

> The food revolution that was the basis of these agrarian states resulted from the application of certain scientific knowledge, while state administration, conquest, and religious and aesthetic developments were all creative expressions of sorts. But it is doubtful whether anyone in the course of the rise of agrarian states was aware of their outcome, let alone consciously directed their growth beyond the pattern in which he was involved (1960:182; see also 1956b:73).

Steward's analyses tended to take the perspective of the observer who stands outside and above the sociocultural system, and who is able to achieve a comprehensive view; they usually avoided the perspective of the individual who lives within the system and who has a limited understanding of the whole.

The second modification of the Boasian culture concept has already been touched upon. Steward's version of culture may be characterized as practical rather than irrational, for in his view human institutions are to be understood in terms of their adjustments to the exigencies of life. They are not virtually autonomous from the environment or from human needs.

A corollary is that human behavior in general is less traditional and irrational than Benedict and Boas thought. The individual is less determined by culture and enjoys greater freedom to pursue his own interests, and what seems on the surface traditional behavior may in fact be quite practical. Steward noted that the tropical-forest peoples of South America are known primarily as horticulturalists, but that they ascribe a great deal of importance to hunting and fishing. He questioned the interpretation which viewed this cultural emphasis as a product of the vicissitudes of history or tradition; he suggested that it may be due to the unbalanced, starchy diet which would result if the people ate only what they raised in their gardens:

Any society will exploit wild resources to some extent, and when cultivated foods provide a badly unbalanced diet for which hunting and fishing can compensate, it is quite possible that the craving for meat, rather than mere tradition, led men to hunt (Steward 1959:292).

Steward's tendency to emphasize the practical rather than the traditional side of behavior would have had important consequences had he ever extended his ideas into the field of culture and personality, for he probably would have protested two trends which have dominated most of the research in this area: the emphasis on the importance of tradition in shaping the human personality, and the emphasis on the role of emotion in the personality system. But since he viewed culture and behavior largely as responses to local exigencies, it was these rather than the personality system which he was led to investigate. On the other hand, in Benedict's view, culture is relatively autonomous from these external conditions; to her, behavior is essentially a product of cultural conditioning, and it was the relationship between culture and personality which emerged as the critical research problem.

Steward's third departure from the Boasian frame of reference has to do with the structure of culture. Boas gave primacy to ideas in his culture concept; he viewed the phenomenal order of culture as the spelling out or manifestation of the ideational order. Benedict and Kroeber employed similar approaches, since they held that the principles or patterns which govern the whole are contained at the level of subjective culture. On the other hand, it was to the phenomenal world that Steward looked to find the guiding principles behind culture; he held that the subsistence patterns tend to govern the larger sociocultural system. For example, according to Steward, culture change is to be seen primarily in terms of ecological principles:

over the millennia cultures in different environments have changed tremendously, and these changes are basically traceable to new adaptations required by changing technology and productive arrangements (1955:37).

Two elements of Steward's thought led him to give primacy to the ecology rather than ideas. The first was his view that culture is circumscribed by a set of objective and inflexible conditions. Culture may be subject to fortuitous variations that are governed by subjective principles, but if a trait comes into conflict with the subsistence system, it simply must adjust. Even if a people elaborate the ceremonial or artistic features of their culture rather than subsistence, their cultural interests can only be pursued within the limits allowed by the ecological base. Consequently, changes in the subsistence system will often necessitate changes in the other features of culture, whereas the reverse is less frequently true. Second, Steward had a practical image of man. As a rule, the individual will give precedence to subsistence matters over less vital concerns, so the nonecological features of culture will be the first to give should an incompatibility exist between traits. Because of both these factors, the problem of ecological adjustment tends to have a prevailing influence on culture, and hence the ecology is the key to cultural integration and change.

Benedict's views were fundamentally incompatible with Steward's, for, to her, no sector of culture is inherently more basic than any other. A particular culture may emphasize ecological adaptation or it may not; if it does not, then ecological principles are comparatively unimportant for an understanding of the pattern of integration of that system.

It would appear to be a fairly simple problem to determine whether or not the subsistence system is the basic feature of culture, and it seems paradoxical that Benedict and Steward never came to an agreement on this issue—especially since they had command of roughly the same body of data. They received their Ph.D.s within ten years of each other, were trained within the Boasian intellectual tradition, and were both North Americanists.

The paradox is understandable in that Steward and Benedict could look at the same body of data and not agree on what they were looking at. Benedict approached her material convinced of the value of Boas' empiricism and nominalism. She felt that an analytical framework should emerge from the data and should not be supplied a priori by the investigator. Moreover, because of her acceptance of Boas' subjective approach, she thought that the analysis must employ the perspective of the people being studied. What is basic in each culture is whatever the people themselves feel is important—such as the Kurnai emphasis on marriage regulations, and the Kwakiutl emphasis on prestige.

On the other hand, Steward asserts that certain cultural features are more important than others, regardless of what the members of society may think. An elaborate development of religious ceremony, or art, or competition for prestige is possible only if the more basic subsistence factors permit. By using cultural ecology as his frame of reference, Steward felt that he could cut through the superficial and arbitrary features of culture and lay bare the more fundamental aspects.

In brief, Benedict and Steward did not agree on how to decide what *was* basic in a given culture. Steward's framework makes such data as property rights and population density stand out in bold relief, and it leaves such features as ceremonial patterns and myths as background. Benedict's approach throws an entirely different set of data into relief. Even if she had accepted Steward's analyses she must have thought them trivial, for they accounted for data which to her mind were often of secondary importance.

LESLIE WHITE

Steward is noted for contributing to a revival of evolutionary theory, and he became the leader of an important movement away from the traditional Boasian views concerning the historical contingency of culture. Leslie White performed a similar role. At a time when evolutionism was rejected by most anthropologists in the United States, and when few were actively engaged in the search for natural laws behind institutions, White proposed an evolutionary and scientific theory of culture. And his approach soon gained considerable ground, especially among some of the then younger members of the discipline. Both Steward and White articulated views which were ready for at least limited acceptance by an important faction of American anthropology.

White was born in Colorado in 1900. He lived in several places as a boy, but attended high school in Zachary, Louisiana.

Not long after his graduation the United States declared war on Germany, and White served in the Navy during World War I. This was an experience which, he comments, "changed my life purpose and outlook profoundly" (quoted in Barnes 1960:xvi), for it turned his interest toward trying to understand why peoples behave the way they do. Upon returning to civilian life in 1919 he entered Louisiana State University to gain a background in the social sciences. After two years at Louisiana State he transferred to Columbia University to study psychology, sociology, and philosophy. In 1924 he received a master's degree from Columbia, writing his thesis in psychology. In addition to his work at Columbia he attended lectures at The New School for Social Research in New York City. In 1924 he went to the University of Chicago to study sociology, but he soon became disenchanted and shifted his focus to anthropology which at that time was taught in the same department. He received his Ph.D. in anthropology from Chicago in 1927.

Between 1927 and 1930 White taught at the University of Buffalo, and in 1930 was selected to replace Julian Steward at the University of Michigan. When he went to Michigan he was the only anthropologist on the staff, but since then he has built the department into one of the most distinguished centers of anthropology in the country (Barnes 1960:xv–xvii). He retired from Michigan in 1970.

At least part of White's influence as an anthropologist must be attributed to his ability as a teacher. His undergraduate classes were traditionally among the largest on the Michigan campus, and they were both lively and controversial. Perhaps much of his appeal is due to his polemic demeanor. He is "unequivocal, and uncompromising, but never arrogantly dogmatic" in his large classes (Barnes 1960:xxi).

White has three principal interests: his researches among the Pueblo Indians, which have resulted in several monographs and an assortment of articles; his evolutionary and cultural theory; and his work on the history of anthropology. Surprisingly, the first two interests have almost no connection with one another. White's Pueblo studies, even the latest (e.g. White 1962), give little evidence of the theoretical side of his thought; they could have been written by any one of a number of Boasians who were dogmatic anti-evolutionists. On the other hand, his theoretical work is broadly comparative and gives scant attention to his own fieldwork. White has written several interpretive studies on the history of anthropology (e.g. White 1963b, 1966), and he has also contributed significantly to the primary literature on the development of the field. For example, he has edited and published the letters from Adolf Bandelier to Lewis H. Morgan (White 1940a), as well as the journals which Morgan wrote during his field expeditions (White 1959b).

White's evolutionary theory began developing shortly after he received his Ph.D., and by 1930, when he started teaching at Michigan, "he had shuffled off his earlier Boasian anti-evolutionary orientation and had espoused the evolutionary approach" (Barnes 1960:xxvi). Barnes cites four primary factors contributing to this conversion. First, when White began teaching he found he could not defend Boasian anti-evolutionism. Second, while at Buffalo he came into contact with a philosopher, Marvin Farber, who was quite interested in evolution. Third, White became involved with the nearby Seneca Indians; this led him to read a classic study of the Iroquois written by Lewis H. Morgan, who at one time was one of the world's leading evolutionists. White was quite impressed with Morgan's work and decided to read more of what he wrote. Fourth, in 1929 White toured Russia and Georgia; in doing so he became acquainted with the writings of Marx and Engels, who had themselves made use of Morgan's evolutionary ideas (Barnes 1960:xxv–xxvi).

In giving an exposition of White's thought it is necessary to distinguish between his two usages of the term "culture." The first meaning refers to the culture of mankind as a whole, the sum total of culture traits the world over. The second refers to specific, delimited aspects of this whole, such as the cultures of the Pueblo Indians or the Shoshoneans. The culture of mankind is "a single fabric"; it constitutes "a self-contained, closed system." In contrast, *a* culture cannot be self-contained, for it is constantly being influenced by the local environment and by the introduction of foreign traits from other societies. Consequently, according to White, it is not always possible to treat *a* culture as a distinct system; nevertheless, he comments, "for certain purposes, and within certain limits, these cultures can be treated as systems" (White 1959a:17–18, 50–52; see also 1945a).

Most of White's theoretical work, and particularly his evolutionary theory, is concerned with the culture of mankind as a whole. In the following, however, I am concerned with his views about the nature of delimited cultural systems; I wish to compare his ideas with those of such anthropologists as Boas, Benedict, and Steward, who never dealt with culture as a world-wide totality.

White's culture concept may be summarized under two main headings, cultural determinism and the utilitarian nature of culture. Before turning to these two aspects of his thought, however, it is necessary to summarize what is perhaps the most prominent part of his work, his evolutionary theory.

CULTURAL EVOLUTION. White's evolutionary theory rests upon the notion that institutions are at bottom utilitarian in nature. Like all animals, man "must come to terms with the external world" (1949b:373). He must secure food, for example, and defend himself against both the elements and his enemies. Subhuman species adapt themselves by the use of their sense organs, muscles, and the like, whereas man has developed culture as an added means of adjustment and control: "The purpose and function of culture are to make life secure and enduring for the human species" (1959a:8).

Not all aspects of culture are equally important in articulating man with the world, however. Culture consists of four distinct sectors or components: the technological, including such features as tools, means of subsistence, and implements of offense and defense; the sociological sector, or the patterns of interpersonal relations; the ideational sector, which encompasses cultural ideas and beliefs; and the attitudinal component, which includes feelings and sentiments (1959a:6–7). Of these, the technological is the most immediately involved in the adaptive process; as a result, it is the most basic, and it determines the rest in at least a general way (1959a:19ff.). For example, a hunting technology will require a form of social organization quite different from that of an agricultural or industrial technology (1959a:20–21). Similarly, "the philosophical component" of culture, as well as the attitudinal, "varies as the technological factor varies" (1959a:23–24).

Although the technological system tends to prevail over the rest of culture in the long run, the other sectors sometimes achieve sufficient momentum of their own to oppose the technological determinants (White 1959a:26–28; see Harding 1960). For example, White regards the modern condition of the world as one in which the social system is holding back changes which are demanded by the technology. "The nineteenth century," he writes, "was one of the expansion and growth of our social system as well as our technology; it was an era of progress." Scientific ideas, including the ideas of the evolutionary anthropologists, were participating in this progressive movement. The colonization of Asia and Africa came to an end, however, and the American frontier disappeared. The social system of Western Europe soon "reached the limits of its capacity for growth." The need now exists for fundamental social change, as evidenced by "unemployment, over-production and glutted markets, relieved only by periodic World Wars." White characterizes the modern condition as "An obsolete social system . . . striving to maintain itself against technological imperatives for change; the old system of capitalism, empire and imperialism" is continuing beyond its natural life. White believes that the Boasian rejection of evolutionary thought arose as part of a reactionary movement linked to the survival of this outmoded social system. Evolutionary theory implies progress and development, whereas anti-evolutionism lends ideological support to the conservative forces of capitalism and imperialism and to the preservation of the status quo in the underdeveloped parts of the world (White 1949a:109–10, 1960b:v–vii).

Although the technological system is the most immediately involved in the adaptive process, the other features of culture are not without value. For example, beliefs and ritual provide man with "a sense of power and of confidence," thereby assisting him in overcoming the suffering, frustrations, fear, and boredom which he is constantly facing (1959a:9). "Philosophy is an instrument devised and used for a purpose. In this respect it is exactly like an axe" (1949a:398). Perhaps the most important functions of the nontechnological components of culture are their contributions toward the effectiveness of the technological system. White remarks that the social system may even be defined "as the way in which a society makes use of its particular technology in the various life-sustaining processes" (1949a:19). The ideational system provides the knowledge necessary for implementing the technological system. Beliefs and sentiments also serve important functions in relation to the social system; for example, they promote social solidarity, a prerequisite to the technological enterprise (1959a:Chapter 10).

Since human beings possess culture, each generation is able to pass its advances on to the next. In addition, cultural improvements spread laterally across the world by means of diffusion, and ultimately the whole of mankind is swept up in the cumulative processes of change (1949b:374). In brief, the culture of man is progressive, "it moves toward greater control over the forces of nature, toward greater security of life for man" (1949a:140). Moreover, this process of evolution is *sui generis:*

Culture has a life of its own, governed by its own principles and its own laws. Flowing down the ages, it embraces the members of each generation at birth and molds them into human beings, equipping them with their beliefs, patterns of behavior, sentiments, and attitudes. Human behavior is but the response of a primate who can symbol to this extrasomatic continuum called culture. Culture is a system that grows by increasing its control over the forces of nature (1949b:379).

Both the measure and source of this growth process is energy. All living organisms are essentially energy-capturing systems; they convert the free energy of the cosmos into forms of energy which sustain their own life processes. For example, by means of photosynthesis plants capture the energy of the sun and employ it in the processes of growth, reproduction, and the maintenance of life (1949a:33–38). Similarly, energy is essential to the functioning of human beings. In brief, all organisms must consume energy in order to live.

The same is true of culture: energy is "the dynamic, living force that animates cultural systems" (1959a:57). All behavior, including cultural behavior, requires effort: "Whether it be chipping an arrow-head, catching a fish, hoeing a hill of beans, avoiding your mother-in-law, . . . or breathing a silent prayer, the event is an expression of energy expended" (1959a:38). Cultural systems do not consume energy for no purpose, however; the energy is used to harness even more of the same, and to put it "to work in the service of man" (1959a:38). For example, the cultural response of drawing a bow consumes a significant number of calories, but presumably the hunter's return is greater than his cost. Religious ritual, although "expensive" in the amount of energy it consumes, promotes a sense of well-being, social solidarity, and the like, which far outweigh the costs.

Cultures differ in the amount of energy they have at their disposal, and cultural advance may be measured as the amount of energy harnessed per capita per year. The simplest societies are those which depend solely on human effort, such as the effort required to draw the hunter's bow. More advanced cultures harness the wind, draft animals, steam, and even the atom (1959a:39ff.). The greater the cultural advance the greater is the material well-being of a people—for, after all, the whole point of cultural evolution is to improve man's adaptation to the world. For example, a people who subsist on domesticated animals enjoys numerous advantages over hunting peoples. Livestock are able to transform the energy of grasses into meat, which is more readily available and more certain than the flesh of wild game. In addition, livestock provide such benefits as milk (1959a:45–47).

White's evolutionary theory had an important influence on American anthropology during and after the 1940s, and it is not difficult to see why. First, according to the Boasian version of culture, institutions were viewed as "purposeless," in that they were thought to be virtually autonomous from the exigencies of life. White decries Boasian anthropology for taking as its mission the demonstration "that there is no rhyme or reason in cultural phenomena" (1949b:368). To White, the diacritical feature of culture is its utility, for both its purpose and function are to promote the welfare of the human animal. Culture is not without meaning or design, after all. Second, the Boasian culture concept denied the scientific status of the discipline, for culture was thought to be infinitely variable and free of necessary or natural laws of development. White chides the Boasians for arguing "that there are no laws of significance in ethnology" (1949b:368). In his view, the utilitarian nature of culture provides the key to history, for culture is progressive in its control over nature. The development of kinship systems, clan organization, philosophical systems, and the like become intelligible when seen in the context of this over-all evolutionary movement (see especially White 1959a). As one critic of White's evolutionism has written, White "has reminded us, as has Julian H. Steward, that as social scientists we cannot immerse ourselves indefinitely in a piecemeal appreciation of the discrete, the exotic, the particular, or the contemporary" (Bock 1952:494).

WHITE'S CULTURAL DETERMINISM. In one sense, at least, White's evolutionary theory imples another part of his scheme, which is his theory of cultural determinism. He conceives evolution as a process which is autonomous with respect to the will or desires of man and which is governed by its own principles. In short, culture is *sui generis*. For example, White remarks that

it is, therefore, culture that determines the behavior of man, not man who controls culture. And culture changes and develops in accordance with laws of its own, not in obedience to man's desire or will. A science of culture would disclose the nature and direction of the culture process, but would not put into man's hands the power to control or direct its course (White 1948c:213).

The germ of this cultural determinism is contained in White's earliest work, and certainly it appears before his conversion to evolutionism. As early as 1925—only a year after receiving his M.A. from Columbia—he was referring to culture as superorganic (1925b:73) and calling for a greater recognition of the role of culture as a determinant of the human personality (1925a). The source of his views about culture and human behavior at this time was probably his contact with such Boasians as Fay-Cooper Cole at Chicago and Alexander Goldenweiser at The New School for Social Research (cf. Barnes 1960:xvi–xvii). However, it is likely that there also were some nonanthropological factors contributing to his early ideas about human behavior. For example, White was strongly influenced by Harry Elmer Barnes, whose approach to history took account "of the great stream of cultural forces upon whose tide civilizations ebb and flow" (White 1925e:645; see also White 1925d and Barnes 1960). Perhaps it is also important that while at The New School White came into contact with the behaviorist psychologist, J. B. Watson. Watson, like White, tended to reject the idea of an independent or autonomous human consciousness.

White's views about cultural determinism are expressed quite forcefully and unequivocally, and yet they have been seriously misunderstood (see especially White 1969). They have also met strong opposition—largely, White feels, because his critics have regarded his views as debasing (1969:xxix). Part of the misunderstanding has arisen from the fact that there are at least two distinct meanings of cultural determinism.

The first meaning refers to the determinism of human behavior. In the extreme or limiting case this usage signifies that the individual's actions are fully a product of cultural conditioning and that he enjoys no individuality whatever. The individual is a "cultural dope." White appears to employ this form of determinism in many places, and a characteristic example is his statement that "it is not human beings who determine their culture by desire and design; it is culture that determines the behavior of peoples" (1963a:115). Nevertheless, White makes it clear that when speaking of the cultural determinism of behavior he is refering to the actions of *peoples* and not individuals. When focusing at the level of society it is possible to disregard individual and noncultural factors; but this is not true when analyzing the actions of a particular person, because the individual's behavior "is a function of his biological make-up as well as of his culture" (1963a:115). White notes that "human behavior is a compound made up of two different elements": culture and biology (1949a:120), or extrasomatic and somatic factors (1959c). To the degree that the individual differs from someone else biologically, he will respond to his cultural stimuli in a somewhat different way (1963a:115). In short, in White's scheme behavior is not wholly determined by cultural conditioning.

White does not view biology and culture as playing equal roles in the make-up of the individual, however; in accordance with the Boasian roots of his thought, he regards culture as the decisive factor in human action. He writes,

Culture exerts a powerful and overriding influence upon the biological organisms of *Homo sapiens,* submerging the neurological, anatomical, sensory, glandular, muscular, etc., differences among them to the point of insignificance (1963a:116).

White does not eliminate biology, but clearly he minimizes it.

Moreover, he denies the existence of a third system which is relatively autonomous from the biological and cultural determinants and which is located in the interstice between the two. In other words, he rejects the idea that man is characterized by a relatively autonomous personality system, consciousness, or will. There is only the organism and culture, with nothing in between. This needs amplification, and I turn first to the issue of the human personality.

Some social scientists have attempted to ascribe the source of human behavior to the organism—William McDougall, for example, wanted to reduce man's behavior to a set of biological instincts. Others, including Freud, regarded the personality as a system which is determined by both inherited and learned elements, welded together to form an organization or pattern which is not wholly reducible to either the properties of the organism or the experiences of the individual. According to this view, the personality is a more or less autonomous system based upon and interposed between two other systems, the organism and culture. Benedict expressed yet another position in her *Patterns of Culture,* for she insisted that it is culture which explains the thoughts and actions of human beings. She did not completely deny that the individual is a distinct entity with the ability to think and reason on his own, or that he has the capacity to react to both cultural and organic stimuli according to his own individuality, but she came close to doing so. To her, the principles behind the individual's behavior are virtually the same as those behind culture.

White comes fairly close to Benedict's position when he stresses the immense importance of culture as a determinant of behavior, but in his theoretical discussions he is careful not to ignore the biological side of man's nature altogether. Like Benedict, however, he does deny the existence of an autonomous personality system. He would not go as far as to argue that the term personality should never be used, or that the study of the individual is an empty undertaking. Rather, he denies that the personality is a *sui generis* system, or a relatively autonomous source of behavior, for he contends that it is resolvable or reducible into two classes of determinants, culture and biology.

An example of White's rejection of the relative autonomy of the personality system is contained in a review of Thompson and Joseph's *The Hopi Way* (White 1945c), in which the authors attempted not to deal with Hopi culture, as White comments, but "with the peoples themselves as human beings and individuals." The study revealed that the Hopi personality adjustment was not altogether satisfactory, as evidenced by a high degree of tension, anxiety, and frustration. White notes that he does "not wish for a second to belittle 'depth psychology' and technical personality analysis." Nevertheless, he feels that there is something that would benefit the people more than psychological studies. He states that the Hopi "live in poverty and chronic hunger and without adequate medical care." If these problems could be alleviated, he writes, "the Hopi personality could take care of itself." Essentially, White is saying that Hopi maladjustments are not to be viewed as features of personality systems at all, but as epiphenomena of the organism. If the organic needs can be satisfied, the personality problems will vanish.

In addition to rejecting the existence of a relatively autonomous personality system, White also discounts the possibility that a more or less independent human consciousness is interposed between the organism and culture. He contends that "mind" is not an entity at all, but that it is the total reactions of the organism to the external world; the mind is simply behavior. White describes searching for the mind as "Philosophic tail chasing, nothing more." Man has a mind only in the sense that oysters, parameciums, radishes, or lichens do—in the sense that he behaves in relation to the external world. In short, White reduces the human consciousness to the level of the biological organism. He acknowledges that he cannot prove "that there is no cosmic entity, mind, which has an existence independent of bodies"; but, he adds, "So far as I know, there is no convincing proof for the non-existence of Santa Claus," either (1949a:51–53; see also 1925c and 1940b).

Similarly, White argues that the individual does not possess a free or independent will. Human behavior is the result "of countless antecedent and concomitant . . . causes"—both cultural and biological. When the causal forces for and against a particular act are equally balanced we refer to the individual's plight as one of indecision, and when one causal force predominates over another we think of him as choosing between alternatives. " 'Free will and choice' is merely the way in which we experience this preponderance of one factor or set of factors over another" (1949a:176). White's rejection of the idea of an independent will is evident in his view that the individual does not have the capacity to alter his culture. White denies that education is an instrument which man can use to improve his society, for any attempt to use education in this way is itself a culturally determined response (1949a:344–47). "The picture of free will and choice is an illusion" (1949a:176).

The second meaning of cultural determinism refers not to

the determinism of behavior, but to that of the cultural system itself. According to this usage of the term, culture is an autonomous or self-determined system. It is governed by its own *sui generis* principles and operates independently of the principles of psychology.

In presenting White's views about the determinism of the cultural system it is necessary to discuss his definition of culture. White contends that there are "three qualitatively different and scientifically significant classes of forms of reality"; these are the physical, biological, and cultural. The latter is an order of reality which came into being with man, for man is peculiar in his ability to use symbols. Culture is defined as those things and events that are dependent on symbols (1949a:15; cf. pp. 22ff. and 1959c:230). "It is the symbol which has transformed man from a mere animal to a human animal" (1949a:35).

The two features of this definition which are important are the concept of the symbol and the term "dependent": a culture trait is anything which would not be perpetuated were it not for symbols. For example, apes frequently invent tools, but they cannot pass on the knowledge and inventions which they have achieved, nor can they retain their insights for long even in their own minds. They lack the symbols necessary for doing so. In contrast, the "tool-experience" of man "is a continuum"; moreover, "it is the symbol, the word-formed idea, that makes this continuity of experience possible" (1949a:47). Man can think and communicate with symbols, and he can thereby preserve his achievements: "and preservation means accumulation and progress" (1949a:39).

A significant aspect of this definition is its inclusiveness, for it embraces phenomena which most other anthropologists would regard as individual, noncultural features. For example, by this definition any concrete and unique action of an individual—including what may appear to be a willful act—is culture, provided that the act requires or entails symbols. An invention or discovery is not the creation of an individual mind; it is a cultural phenomenon, for it is carried out in a medium of cultural beliefs and categories (White 1949a:Chapter 8). White limits the genius' contribution to his native intelligence, which is a matter of biology (e.g., see pp. 294–95), and he regards the invention or discovery itself as an "interactive cultural process" (p. 222). An invention is "a new synthesis of cultural elements" (p. 203), the result of the interaction of culture traits in a particular person's mind; "the individual is merely the neural locus in which the advance occurs" (p. 299). White is emphatic that *"we add nothing to an explanation of this culture process by including man in our calculations"* (p. 210; emphasis in the original). Furthermore, the reason why man cannot willfully alter his institutions is that the motivation which compels him to act and the programs of change which he envisages are actually cultural phenomena. White states that man "is the utensil; the culture supplies the contents" (1963a:158).

White's definition of culture as things and events which are dependent on symbols facilitates his argument that culture is self-determined, for this definition is broad enough to include phenomena which are essential to a cultural analysis but which are normally conceived as individual, noncultural factors. I shall have more to say about White's views concerning the self-determinism of culture in the following section.

White attributes the development of cultural determinism largely to Tylor rather than Boas. White refers to the first chapter of *Primitive Culture,* in which Tylor both defines culture and argues that human thought and behavior are determined by natural laws which leave little if any room for free will. White states that there were others who also contributed to the "culturological point of view"—the view that culture is *sui generis* and the essential determinant of human behavior. Among these contributors were Durkheim, Kroeber, Lowie, Wissler, and Murdock (White 1949a:87–94). In contrast,

White regards Benedict and Boas as representing a trend of thought which he deplores. He writes that "there has been a falling away" or "a definite regression" from the culturological point of view in anthropology; many "have sold their culturological birthright for a mess of psychiatric pottage" (1949a:xix). Boas, like Benedict, was "unable to rise above the level of psychological interpretation and to grasp a culturological point of view" (1949a:95). For example, Boas attempted to explain race prejudice in terms of a tendency of human thought, the tendency to classify people into social categories (White 1947c, 1948b, 1949a:136). Benedict, among others, believed

that man has created culture, that culture is the accumulated product of the creative acts of countless individuals, that the individual is the *fons et origo* of all cultural elements, and, finally, that the culture process is to be explained in terms of the individual (1949a:161).

White's views on these matters are paradoxical, for Boas was far more important than Tylor in developing the idea of the cultural determinism of behavior and the self-determinism of culture. It is necessary to distinguish between two different issues: first, that between determinism and free will, and second, between reductionism and the *sui generis* nature of culture. Tylor was a determinist, and the determinants of human behavior to which he referred were in part the ties of tradition. Another set of determinants even more important in his theory were the laws of the human mind. Tylor's determinism was largely a form of reductionism. It was Boas, not Tylor, who arrived at the position that culture is *sui generis* and has to be understood in terms of its own principles. Moreover, a corollary of Boas' views about culture is that human behavior is largely the product of cultural conditioning. But to Boas this cultural determinism of behavior is not so complete that the individual is totally deprived of an autonomous will. The will might be highly restricted, but it is not absent: for example, Boas held that there is at least a degree of creative imaginativeness behind the development of cultural forms. In brief, White, like Tylor, rejects the idea of free will in favor of determinism; but White's determinism is quite different from Tylor's, and derives instead from the Boasian view of culture as a set of emergent phenomena.

White's misunderstanding of the cultural determinism of Boas' thought is partly explained by the fact that Boas employed the subjective approach; he tended to "reduce" the phenomenal features of culture to subjective thought. These subjective ideas are not "psychological," however; they are cultural and are governed by the same *sui generis* principles as the rest of culture. On the other hand, White locates the governing principles of culture within the technological system. He tends to "reduce" the subjective sphere of culture to the phenomenal sphere.

THE UTILITARIAN NATURE OF CULTURE. To White, culture is a self-determined system, and its guiding principle is that of utility. White's utilitarianism is manifest in his evolutionary theory, according to which the development of culture is conceived as the progressive adaptation of man to the physical world; he writes, "The function and purpose of culture are to make life secure and enduring for the human species" (1959a:8).[11]

White's utilitarianism stands in radical opposition to the ir-

[11] This is not to say that White believes that culture is always perfectly adjusted to best serve man, however, for he notes many occasions in which different sectors of the system acquire a momentum of their own and either resist changes that are needed or develop in ways that are disadvantageous from the perspective of the collective good. An example is his analysis of modern Western society, mentioned earlier, according to which an outmoded social system is preventing changes which are demanded by the technology. Even the cases of dysfunctional institutions that White discusses reveal his utilitarianism, however. On one hand, the concept of dysfunction is defined according to the criterion of utility; an institution is dysfunctional when it goes against the good of the society. On the other, in White's analysis the principle behind the development of dysfunctional institutions is the tendency for each sub-system of culture to attempt to maximize its own advantages and interests even at the expense of the larger whole.

rational culture concept of Benedict, and yet the similarities between their schemes should not be overlooked. First, to Benedict, culture is *sui generis;* it is governed by a more or less pervasive configuration which is virtually autonomous from the natural properties of the human mind. To Benedict, the self-determinism of culture refers to the autonomy of the configuration or ethos, whereas to White it refers to the principle of utility. Second, in Benedict's scheme it is the cultural configuration which supplies the meaning of cultural traits; to White, on the other hand, it is by reference to the function or utility of an institution that it is made intelligible. There is yet a third correspondence between White's and Benedict's schemes: his utilitarianism developed gradually out of an integrational point of view not at all unlike Benedict's. White shifts from a Boasian and integrational form of explanation to a utilitarian form.

Integrationalists like Benedict are functionalists in the sense that they conceive of culture as an integral whole, each trait influencing the rest; culture traits are said to be functionally interdependent. A utilitarian conception of culture posits a further dimension to the interrelatedness of traits. Traits not only condition and delimit one another, but they are also joined together in the pursuit of certain ends. For example, a system of beliefs may be integrated with the economic system in that the beliefs provide a legitimizing rationale for the economic enterprise. According to this form of functionalism a trait is influenced not only by the other traits with which it is combined, but also by the nature of the functions which it performs.

White's work clearly exhibited the integrational form of functionalism during the 1920s and 1930s. In one of his first publications he described a "culture type" as "an organization of culture about a nucleus; the attention is focused upon one, or a few, traits which are then specialized" (1926:546). Behind the "growth and differentiation" of religious systems, for example, we find the same principle operative as in the development of a culture type in general, viz.: the selection of some feature with subsequent elaboration, specialization, and organization of behavior and traits about this nucleus (1926:548).

For example, the Toda religion focuses upon the dairy, Crow religion upon the vision, and Blackfoot religion upon the medicine bundle (1926:548). Compare White's view with Benedict's:

Religion is a spotlight that swings quite indiscriminately, in one region bringing it about that property and all the concepts that center around it are religiously guaranteed, and in another leaving property entirely secular; in one region centering upon weather control, in another upon curing (Benedict 1938:648).

White's ethnography of Acoma, a Pueblo Indian village in New Mexico, gives further evidence of his integrationalism. He speaks of "a very fundamental feature" of the Indian culture, "namely, integration." He describes Acoma culture as "close-knit" and states that it can be envisaged as a unity. He then delineates two cultural emphases or levels in terms of which the social organization may be viewed: "the kinship (and clan) level and the socio-ceremonial level" (1932:140).

Even before 1940, however, White was moving away from the integrational approach toward a functional view more closely akin to Malinowski's and Radcliffe-Brown's. In a paper published in 1939 he attempted to explain different forms of kinship terminology in terms of the relative importance of clans. He seems to imply that the clans become important at a certain stage of evolution because they have utilitarian functions to perform (1939; note his later views in 1959a:122, 149ff.). In 1943 he criticized the mathematical approaches of such sociologists as George A. Lundberg, saying that mathematics can only deal with a limited range of cultural phenomena. He called for a revival of the view of societies as organisms and a concern for the (utilitarian) functions that institutions fulfill.

"In short, we wish to understand the anatomy and physiology, so to speak, of social organisms" (1943b:377).

White's utilitarian functionalism emerges as a healthy bud growing out of his earlier integrationalism. Moreover, he does not distinguish between the two points of view, even though they appear side-by-side in his work during the forties. This suggests that he may have been unaware of the differences between the two as well as the changes taking place in his own thought. For example, in the article in which he criticized the mathematical approach in sociology, he stated that such customs as the dance among the Pueblo Indians and the girls' adolescence rites among the Kwakiutl "cannot be understood without an appreciation of the context in which the ceremony is found." He then quotes from Benedict's *Patterns of Culture:* " 'the significant sociological unit . . . is not the institution, but the cultural configuration' " (White 1943b:376). He is clearly referring to the integrational form of functionalism. However, without suggesting a transition in his argument, he turns to a discussion of the functionalism of Durkheim, Malinowski, and Radcliffe-Brown—in brief, to a discussion of utilitarian functionalism. For example, he quotes the following from Radcliffe-Brown:

Every custom and belief of a primitive society plays some determinate part in the social life of the community, just as every organ of a living body plays some part in the general life of the organism (quoted in White 1943b:377).

White's seeming unawareness of the difference between the two points of view is also evident in a paper published in 1947. He wrote that it was not until the later years of his life that Boas learned that culture was integrated (1947a:184); White suggests that "the influence of the Functionalist schools of Malinowski and Radcliffe-Brown during the late 1920s and early thirties had much to do" with Boas' gradual rejection of the shreds and patches or atomistic view of culture (1947a:185 n.

79; see also 1966:53). White was unaware of the seeds of integrationalism contained in Boas' early work, and he seems to have missed the difference between Boas' version of functional integration on the one hand and Radcliffe-Brown's and Malinowski's on the other.

If it is true that this change was taking place below the level of White's own awareness, then we are led to inquire into the motive or reason for this development in his thought. One factor may have been the very one which White remarked upon in relation to Boas' functionalism: the influence of Malinowski and Radcliffe-Brown. It is possible to suggest yet a deeper reason, however—a reason which explains why such an independent-minded theorist as White would be *predisposed* toward the acceptance of British functionalism. It is important that the emergence of White's utilitarian functionalism is correlated in time with the growth of his evolutionism. He publicly committed himself to evolutionism at least by 1931 (White 1931), but he did not actually begin working out his own evolutionary theory in print until the late thirties (see especially 1939, 1943a, 1943b, 1945a, 1945b, 1947a, 1947b, 1948a, 1949a, 1949b). I suggest that White's utilitarianism arose largely in response to the emergence of his theory of the development of culture. Specifically, White revived the nineteenth-century belief in progress, and this in turn implied that culture is more than an integrated but purposeless body of traits. Human institutions must have some reason for existence, some purpose or utility, if they can be said to show a pattern of advance. White's utilitarianism, and his acceptance of the functionalism of Malinowski and Radcliffe-Brown, may be said to have been stimulated by his contact with the writings of such men as Morgan, Tylor, and Spencer.

Utilitarianism was as fundamental to the nineteenth-century evolutionists' culture concept as it is to White's. For example, Tylor interpreted morality as a means for achieving a higher and better life for man; it serves to promote human happiness by turning the individual away from such vices as alcoholism and laziness. A crucial difference separates the utilitarianism of White and that of his evolutionist predecessors, however. Briefly, White's predecessors assumed that the utility of institutions is to be understood at the level of the individual, whereas to White it is to be viewed at the level of culture.

There were two respects in which Tylor viewed the utility of culture at the level of the individual. First, he thought that the ends which were served by institutions were the ends of individual human beings. For example, morality was supposed to promote the happiness of the members of society, rather than social solidarity. The ends which were served were thought to be "natural" interests and were not implanted in the individual by culture. The motivational features of the personality were not thought to be significantly modified by culture save that man became progressively more discriminating and restrained in pursuing his goals. Second, institutions were thought to have been consciously created by individuals.

Boas' views constituted a rejection of Tylorian utilitarianism in a double sense. First, he rejected Tylor's reductionism. Boas held that the drives or interests which motivate man are implanted in the individual by enculturation and are not natural at all. For example, the Northwest Coast Indian drive for prestige was a cultural response, acquired by learning and autonomous from the natural motivational system of the personality. Second, Boas tacitly denied that culture is to be viewed as a utilitarian system. He did not dispute that culture serves ends of some kind, but these ends are cultural; like the rest of culture they are the result of fortuitous historical processes and vary almost randomly with respect to both the practical interests of individuals and the exigencies of life in general. For example, Boas was explicit that the potlatch served an important interest of Northwest Coast culture, the drive for prestige (e.g.

Boas 1938b:684–85), but the Indian who pursued this interest frequently behaved in ways which went directly counter to both his own practical interests and the collective good.

White accepts Boas' rejection of reductionism and attempts to reestablish the utility of institutions at the level of culture itself. In doing so he locates the purposes behind institutions somewhere other than where Boas found them; he holds that if we are to discover the ends which institutions serve we must look beyond the level of subjective culture—beyond the level of the culturally determined drives, motivations, preferences, or interests of the members of society. Regardless of what a people may think or say about their institutions, the latter have the ultimate purpose of making life "secure, perpetual, and worth-while" (1947a:183) and are to be understood and evaluated by how well they serve these ends. White criticizes the Boasians for thinking

that such things as forms of government, ethical codes, religious beliefs, etc., are to be evaluated, if at all, in terms of the opinions and preferences of tribesmen and citizens (1947a:181).

Who is to judge in scientific matters, the scientist or the folk? People may disagree on the proper way to treat trachoma, but if some are trained physicians while others are preliterate savages, is equal weight to be given to all views? . . . The values of medicines, machines, organizations, philosophies, etc., in the conduct of the life of man as an animal species, are not to be ascertained by appeal to the opinions of laymen or even by taking a poll among experts. They are to be gauged by *objective measurement.* It is curious that Boas . . . should be willing to place the opinions, tastes, and preferences of tribesmen and laymen . . . on the same plane as the investigations and conclusions of the scientific anthropologist (1947a:186; emphasis in the original).

In brief, anthropology is to forsake Boas' subjective point of view, for the *sui generis,* utilitarian principles governing cultural systems are generally beyond the awareness of the people themselves.

White's view that the utility of culture operates independently of human awareness and control is frequently encountered in his work. One case is his account of the manner in which the Australian Kurnai divided their game. The hunter kept the animal's head for his own consumption. However, he gave the ribs of the right side of the animal to his father; the ribs of the left side, as well as the backbone, to his mother; the shoulders to his brothers; the hind legs to his sisters, and so on. White comments that "much of this distribution was done for the sake of promoting social solidarity" (1959a:119–20). Surely the Kurnai themselves were in no position to understand or express the social function of this custom. In another place White explains clan organization in primitive society as a means of achieving social solidarity and cooperation. Moreover, he notes that the solidarity of clans is typically reaffirmed by a variety of ritual and other means:

Clans often employ nonkinship devices to implement their function as integrative mechanisms. Each clan may have certain articles of sacred paraphernalia such as fetishes, altars, or other instruments or utensils. These, together with rituals, establish and reinforce common sentiments among clan members (1959a:157).

Again, the social function of these devices is beyond the conscious awareness of the clan members themselves.

According to White, institutions may also originate without the control or understanding of the members of society. His analysis of the origin of incest rules is illustrative (White 1949a:Chapter 11). He explains incest rules in terms of the need for cooperation, for mutual aid or cooperation offers a number of advantages, including security against enemies and insurance against scarcity. The incest rule forces people to marry outside their immediate group, and it therefore serves to extend kinship ties throughout the locality. White comments that the motivation behind the development of these rules was economic in the broad sense, but that those who originated them were not aware of this motive (1949a:318). Incest and marriage are not to be explained in terms of individuals, but in terms of "the exigencies of a social system that was striving to make full use of its resources for co-operative endeavor" (1949a:320–21). Exogamy and incest rules "were syntheses of culture elements formed within the interactive stream of culture traits" (1949a:329).

There is at least one important reason for the disparity between the cultural beliefs and motivations behind institutions and the true functions which these institutions fulfill: the ends of society often conflict with the ends of individuals, so cultural beliefs and sentiments must be designed to motivate the individual by tricking him and distorting his thinking. White notes that society "must influence or control the behavior of its component members" both "to protect itself from the demands of the individual" and "to serve its own interests." Society is so effective that not only does it enlist people for its own ends, but it leads them to go against their individual interests "even to the point of sacrificing their own lives for others or for the general welfare" (White 1949a:156–57).

A part of the effectiveness of this social mechanism consists in the illusion that surrounds it: the individual is made to feel that it is *he* who is making the decision and taking the proper action, and, moreover, that he is perfectly "free" in making his decisions and in choosing courses of action. . . . His behavior is [really] analogous to a pilotless aircraft controlled by radio. The plane is directed this way and that by impulses external to it (1949a:157; emphasis in the original).

In sum, cultural systems operate according to their own utilitarian principles which are autonomous with respect to the individual.

White's image of man is radically different from that of his predecessors, the nineteenth-century positivists, who viewed the human animal as a rational calculator of advantage. White's view is more like Ruth Benedict's and Franz Boas', both of whom conceived behavior as dominated by traditional patterns which commonly go directly counter to the individual's own interests. According to White's scheme, moreover, the Boasians were in a sense correct in stressing the irrationality of custom, for the Boasians assumed that it was at the level of the individual that the utility of culture should appear if it were to do so at all. To White, the utility of culture operates at a higher level; human behavior *is* sensible, but only in spite of man himself.

If cultural processes are truly autonomous from the human will, and often even from human consciousness, why are institutions not arbitrary? What are the mechanisms which keep them on the track—which bring about a general pattern of progress in history and which insure that cultural systems will "behave in such a manner as to protect and sustain the human organisms within their embrace" (White 1959a:78)?

The mechanism which White refers to again and again is the competitive interaction of culture traits. Culture is

a stream of interacting elements; one trait reacts upon others and is affected by them in return. Some elements become obsolete and are eliminated from the stream; new elements are incorporated into it. New permutations, combinations, and syntheses are continually being formed (1949a:392).

In the interaction of elements in the culture process, those traits less effective in providing adequate adjustment in terms of understanding and control are gradually relinquished and replaced by more effective traits (1949a:356).

For example, the hoe influenced such traits as the sexual division of labor, residence patterns, and food habits. The automobile had a profound impact on American culture. It affected

harness and carriage manufacture, the steel and rubber industries, road building, urban development, road houses and tourist camps, consolidated schools, etc. (1949a:99).

Much of the competitive interaction between elements takes place inside the heads of human beings. For example, the development of mathematics (1949a:Chapter 10) was a conscious process consisting of the interaction and competition of cultural ideas within the nervous systems of men.

White is clear that the individual is irrelevant for an understanding of the process of competitive interaction. He notes that to explain the growth of mathematics "we must rule the individual out completely." Each discovery in mathematics "was something that happened to" the individual and was not something which he himself did (1949a:294). The process of competitive interaction is *sui generis* and cannot be explained by reference to principles which are contained at the level of the individual.

Surely the mechanism of competitive interaction is not adequate for White's theory. Benedict and Boas frequently argued that traits interact with one another and that consequently some are modified and others eliminated from the cultural system. But neither Benedict nor Boas was compelled to say that the more useful cultural forms tend to be the survivors in this process; in their view, the principle of integration is virtually autonomous with respect to the exigencies of life. White's evolutionism and utilitarianism call for an additional principle to explain why the interaction of traits does not result in merely arbitrary changes.

White does provide this additional principle, and in doing so he comes almost to the point of contradicting his cultural determinism. He writes that all forms of life have an urge "to live, to make life secure, more rich, more full, to insure the perpetuation of the species"; because of this urge more effective "means of living and surviving" are seized upon. Man himself has a "biological urge to live, the power to invent and to discover, the ability to select and use the better of two tools or ways of doing something. . . ." Man may not deliberately set out to improve his culture, but once a useful invention or discovery is achieved—even if by chance—it is "seized upon by mankind and employed to make life more secure, comfortable, pleasant, and permanent" (1943a:339–40). In other words, the human brain, a biological organ, has both the capacity and the motivation to select traits which are advantageous. For example, White suggests that "rational and utilitarian considerations"—a desire for more security and abundance of food —played an important part in the domestication of animals (1959a:287–88).

This capacity is a biological constant, and therefore, presumably, it falls outside the purview of the science of culture. Nevertheless, White is clearly bringing the human animal into his analysis of culture, and in a fundamental way. He is explaining cultural phenomena in terms of principles located at the level of the individual.[12]

White's tendency to drop to the level of the individual to explain the nonarbitrariness of culture is especially evident in his treatment of social processes. It has been observed that

when White is dealing with the mechanisms of social class his line of reasoning approaches what is now labeled "game theory" or "decision-making theory." In this context he is less inclined to "disregard the psychological circumstances" (Erasmus 1969:30).

White's analyses of specific social phenomena frequently read as though he sees a conscious or unconscious motivation of individual self-interest behind cultural dynamics. White notes that as wealth increased in society both kinship systems and rules of inheritance were modified, since "Families with greater wealth became increasingly disinclined to share it through inheritance with other family lines of lesser wealth" (1959a:298). Southern whites are opposed to miscegenation because racial intermarriage would "remove the economic and political advantages they now enjoy over Negroes" (1959a:114). Celibacy among the Roman Catholic clergy was probably motivated in part by a desire not to allow the wealth of the church to be

[12] It may also be argued that, although this biological capacity is a constant, the specific instances of selection by men are variable and cannot be excluded from an account of cultural processes. See White 1949a:138–39.

"consumed by wives and children nor dissipated by heirs" (1959a:115–16). The horror of menstrual blood which characterizes many cultures across the world may be nothing more than a "sociological device employed in rivalry between the sexes as social classes to win an advantage for the male sex" (1959a:190). In stratified societies the subordinate class often has a hard life, "and excessive privation and toil, coupled frequently with harsh and brutal treatment, incite them to revolt"; the subordinates are led to reject a system which goes against their fundamental personal interests (1959a:315).

I believe that White would argue that self-interested motivations are culturally determined. For example, he notes that there is no "natural desire" to own property, for there are many societies in which resources are freely available to all members. "Communism has been the dominant note in man's economic life for by far the greater part of human history so far." He continues, "attitudes, sentiments, and behavior toward property are determined by the type of economic system in which one is born" (1949a:126). The expression of self-interest, such as that of the Southern white in relation to the Negro, the Catholic Church in relation to its property, and the subordinate classes of society in relation to their oppressors, are reflexes of economic structures; they are cultural and not individual phenomena.

The difficulty with such an argument is that it represents a shift in the meaning of culture. Self-interest appears too often in White's work and in too many contexts to be a cultural variable like matrilineal descent or Hawaiian kin terms. It does not appear to be acquired by the individual the way ethics and language are. In brief, the self-interested motivations which are evident in White's analyses do not seem to be dependent on symbols; they seem to be natural responses in man which take different forms in different societies because of the different ways in which cultural systems are organized.

In sum, White's utilitarianism is in direct conflict with his cultural determinism.

CONCLUSION

I have suggested that one of Boas' signal achievements was to establish the *sui generis* nature of culture. According to him, traits are constantly being borrowed and modified to fit their new cultural contexts, and they become so thoroughly transformed and widespread that it is impossible to trace them to the original processes of thought upon which they were founded. Culture has to be understood in terms of its own *sui generis* principles—the principles of diffusion and integration; it is these rather than natural processes of thought which make sense out of custom. But the principle of diffusion is quite limited in its capacity to reveal meaning in human affairs. The chief direction which Boasian thought was to take, rather, was that of integration studies.

Much of the accomplishment of Benedict, Kroeber, Steward, and White may be conceived as the elaboration and modification of Boas' principle of integration, and some of the most fundamental differences between these writers are traceable to their divergent views about the nature of this principle.

Benedict's concept of the cultural configuration was an attempt to draw together two elements of Boas' thought: his view that cultures are founded upon emotion, and his idea that they tend to exhibit an internal consistency. To Benedict, it is within the context of the configuration that institutions acquire meaning. Moreover, I have discussed Boas' idea that custom is subject to considerable historical contingency; Benedict's concept of integration continued this point of view. To her, integration is a fortuitous process, in that there is no practical or rational purpose behind the Kwakiutl, Pueblo, or Plains Indian configurations. The integrational pattern of a culture is governed by its own premises which are inherited from the past and which are virtually autonomous from the exigencies of life. The configuration is also virtually autonomous from the natural inclinations of man—or at least so it seems in Benedict's *Patterns of Culture*. Instead of reducing culture to the natural properties or processes of the human mind, she did nearly the reverse by assimilating personality to culture. Particularly in her earlier work, she thought that the individual accepts his traditions almost like a dry blotter, and she all but denied that he has any independence of his own.

Kroeber developed the idea of integration in a somewhat different direction. He distinguished what he called the basic and secondary features of culture: those which are directed toward practical matters such as subsistence and survival on one hand, and those which express playful and creative impulses on the other. He relegated the basic features to a comparatively insignificant place in his scheme and devoted almost all his attention to the less mundane, and more estimable, value culture. The principle which gives coherence to the culture traits of a society is not an emotional theme at all, according to Kroeber, but the playful impulse. The patterns of integration which Boas, Benedict, and others had identified were the result of the fanciful elaboration of an aspect of value culture. One of the distinctive qualities of the secondary features of culture, then, is the attribute of playfulness. For example, in spite of all the horrors of Plains warfare, this complex of traits resembled the excellent basketry of the Pomo Indians and the elaborate systems of kinship, marriage, and descent of the Australian aborigines, in that it was a manifestation of creative and playful urges.

Kroeber's thought resembled Boas' and Benedict's in that he viewed the patterns of value culture as autonomous from the exigencies of life. Plains warfare, Pomo basketry, Australian social organization, and the like, expressed aesthetic and other values, and were not oriented toward such matters as subsistence and survival. Nevertheless, Kroeber did not view secondary culture as totally autonomous: to him, an important motive force behind a stylistic pattern is the natural and playful urge contained within the individual. Kroeber was originally a cultural determinist, but he gradually moved away from that position, possibly because, in his view, the individual has at least some capacity to stand apart from culture and manipulate it in response to his creative urges. It follows that the individual's participation in culture—which at times can be quite demanding—is not motivated by the iron hold of custom to the degree that Boas and Benedict believed, but is prompted in part, at least, by the playful impulse itself.

Steward's scheme may also be conceived as an attempt to develop Boas' principle of integration. Instead of viewing integration in terms of a subjective, emotional theme, however, or in terms of the playful impulse, he drew upon another aspect of Boas' thought: the static conditions of the environment. Steward tried to show that there is an uncompromising framework which circumscribes culture and which significantly reduces the arbitrariness of cultural integration. Furthermore, in his view, institutions acquire meaning when seen within the context of a system of cultural integration which is rooted in environmental factors. In presenting this scheme Steward was led to develop a fundamental revision of the Boasian culture concept. Whereas Boas gave primacy to ideas in his analyses, Steward gave primacy to the phenomenal features of culture and to the environment. He developed the notion that beyond the level of subjective culture is a complex system which contains the key to cultural integration, and that much of this system is even beyond the conscious awareness of the people themselves. Cultural ideas may not be epiphenomena of the ecological system, but these ideas must respond or adjust to the mode of adaptation or the people will not survive; in this sense the subjective features of culture are secondary to the phenomenal features. Moreover, Steward rejected the Boasian view of the "irrationality" of custom in favor of a more practical version. Culture is not virtually autonomous from the hard realities of life, but responds to them in an immediate way. In similar fashion, he tended to see a correspondence between the natural interests and desires of individuals on the one hand and culture on the other. In brief, he tended to de-emphasize the "irrationality" of behavior and to see human actions as more practical than Boas and Benedict thought them to be.

White began his career expressing a view not unlike Benedict's idea of integration at the level of traits. The pressure of his emerging evolutionary theory brought him to make a radical departure, however. His revival of the belief in progress forced him to reject the notion that human institutions are fortuitous or purposeless; they must exhibit some usefulness or value, for otherwise there would be no point to evolution. An examination of White's work reveals a shift from a Boasian and integrational form of analysis, according to which traits are regarded simply as interrelated, to a utilitarian framework, according to which they are thought to be united in the performance of utilitarian functions. Moreover, in White's scheme it is by viewing an institution in terms of its utilitarian aspects that it is made intelligible. This shift in White's thought was accompanied by other changes. Like Steward, he was led to the view that the governing principles behind culture are not located at the level of ideas, and that they are even beyond the awareness of the members of society. The utility of an institution is to be evaluated and understood by standing outside the system and viewing it objectively. Regardless of what a people themselves may think, for example, their technology is the most basic part of their culture. There is another tendency in White's thought which parallels Steward's. White is led away from cultural determinism and toward a more practical image of man, according to which the individual has at least some capacity to shape his culture to his own advantage. If culture is not arbitrary, but is responsive to the exigencies of life, then it is necessary to locate some mechanism by which to explain this responsiveness. White fails to find such a mechanism in culture itself, and tends instead toward the view that it is individual self-interest and the human capacity to choose between alternatives which keeps cultural systems on the track. White does not fully develop this aspect of his thought, however, due to an almost total commitment to the idea that culture is *sui generis*.

--◄ IV ►--

THE TRANSCENDENCE
OF SOCIETY

EMILE DURKHEIM

Boas and Durkheim founded competing schools of thought within the discipline of anthropology, Durkheim's centering mostly in France, Boas' primarily in the United States. One of the contrasts between the leaders of these schools is that Durkheim had a strong philosophical orientation, whereas Boas did not. Durkheim was trained as a philosopher, and even though he engaged in rigorous empirical research of outstanding quality, his work was dominated by an underlying concern with philosophical matters. On the other hand, the central focus of Boas and his students was field research; competence as an ethnographer was valued far more highly than theoretical or philosophical sophistication. Whereas Boas undertook field expeditions periodically throughout his lifetime, Durkheim never engaged in fieldwork, nor did most of his followers. For the most part, the French school relied on the data gathered by others. It seems likely that Boas viewed Durkheim as an armchair speculator, theorizing beyond the limits of scientific respectability, and that Durkheim viewed Boas as a visionless data collector.

The contrast between the learned and profound French philosopher and the hard-headed German-turned-American researcher seems patent. And yet the similarities between their interpretations of behavior are fundamental.

INTRODUCTION

While Boas was developing his criticism of the evolutionary and intellectualist interpretations of institutions, and as a result of his work with actual data, he developed a radically new version of culture. In place of the reductionism of anthropologists like Tylor and Spencer, Boas concluded that culture is *sui generis*. In place of the view that culture is grounded in reason, he substituted the idea that it has an emotional foundation. In place of the idea that culture is a utilitarian construct, fashioned purposefully to serve the interests of men, he tacitly concluded that it is "irrational" in the sense that it varies almost randomly with respect to the interests of the members of society. Finally, Boas rejected the absolutism of Tylor and Spencer in favor of a form of relativity.

Similarly, Durkheim rejected the intellectualist, reductionist, and utilitarian theories of society; he also stressed the emotional basis of culture and behavior, and injected a degree of relativity into the study of human institutions.

When Durkheim began developing his scheme he was decidedly within the positivist camp, for he viewed social phenomena as determined by mechanical, causal forces. However, he gradually moved toward the position that cultural ideas are *sui generis* with respect to their material base or substratum; he increasingly viewed social phenomena as refractory to causal explanation and employed instead an interpretive or subjective approach to his data. Again, this parallels a trend in Boas' work. When Boas began his research in anthropology he believed that cultural phenomena are subject to laws of evolutionary growth, but he soon rejected that view and substituted the idea that cultures vary almost randomly within the limits set by the environment, and that cultural ideas have to be understood in terms of themselves and their history and not in terms of causal laws.

Boas' ideas had considerable influence on the social sciences, for his views about race and culture had fundamental implications for understanding human behavior. But his impact was not fully appreciated during his lifetime, because many of the changes he introduced were so subtle that they escaped recognition. Only recently has the extent of his contributions been clarified by the historical research of George Stocking (1968a). In contrast, Durkheim's role in the development of modern social thought was visible almost from the beginning of his career and is today widely known (e.g., Hughes 1958, Parsons 1937). The reason is probably that his philosophical training prompted him to discuss issues which transcended in scope the limits of sociology and anthropology—the two areas in which he did his empirical research.

Before and during World War I Durkheim was one of the leading intellectuals in his native France. Beginning in 1887 he taught both education and sociology, first at Bordeaux and later at the Sorbonne. Although his pedagogical views left an unmistakable impression on his nation's educational system, it was his sociological work which made him famous. His sociological ideas were widely discussed among French intellectuals, and his arguments with Tarde, in particular, achieved considerable notoriety. Durkheim's eminence was not limited to academic circles, however, for he was very active as a French citizen. He was publicly involved in the defense of Captain Dreyfus; he also lectured on behalf of his troubled country during World War I and served on a variety of committees which were devoted to problems associated with the war (Alpert 1939:60, 72–76).

Durkheim was born in 1858 in the province of Lorraine, in the northeastern part of France. He came from a rabbinical family, and it was planned that he would become a rabbi himself. He decided against the rabbinate while in his youth, however, turning instead to philosophy. In 1879, at the age of twenty-one, he entered the famous Ecole Normale Supérieure. Durkheim did not like the type of education provided by the Ecole Normale, and his performance was remarkably undistinguished. Nevertheless, his experiences there were important in shaping his thoughts, and by the time he graduated he was determined to make sociology his special field of study. Although the idea of a science of society had already been proposed in France—by Comte himself—it was an unpopular subject among French intellectuals, and the discipline of sociology had not yet been established. Durkheim was to be its founder (Alpert 1939:15ff.).

Durkheim enjoyed a notable career as a teacher. After graduating from the Ecole Normale in 1882 he taught philosophy at several lycees near Paris. In 1887 he was appointed to the University of Bordeaux, and fifteen years later, in 1902, he was called to teach at the University of Paris. His courses were quite forceful; they were carefully prepared and masterfully delivered. As a result, Durkheim was regarded as an excellent teacher, and he attracted a circle of outstanding students (Alpert 1939:32ff.).

Durkheim soon became the leader of a gifted group of scholars, including such people as Marcel Mauss, Robert Hertz, Henri Hubert, Célestin Bouglé, Paul Fauconnet, Lucien Lévy-Bruhl, and others (see Bender 1965; Evans-Pritchard 1954, 1960; Levi-Strauss 1945; Peyre 1960:15ff.). The primary organ for the writings of this small but cohesive group was the *Année Sociologique,* a journal which was conceived and instituted by Durkheim and which began publication in 1898. The *Année* was devoted primarily to reviews, for one of its main purposes was to keep social scientists abreast of current ideas and research; but each volume normally included at least one original article, usually by a member of the Durkheim school.

The First World War nearly decimated the *Année* school, for many of the younger members were combatants. Robert Hertz, for example, was killed in battle in 1915 (Evans-Pritchard 1960:10). Durkheim's son, who showed promise of becoming one of his father's brightest followers, died of wounds suffered in the war. The losses were a severe blow to the older Durkheim; his own health was poor, and he succumbed in 1917.

The editorship of the *Année* and the leadership of the school fell to Durkheim's nephew, Marcel Mauss. A more dedicated successor could hardly have been found. His dedication was not enough to sustain the small group, however, because even more misfortune was to come during the Second World War when Paris was occupied by the Germans. To cite one example, Maurice Halbwachs, a Jew, was put to death at Buchenwald during the occupation. Mauss himself was a Jew, and although he survived the Nazi oppression his mind eventually gave way (Evans-Pritchard 1954). Durkheim's influence is still widely felt, but there is no longer a cohesive group of scholars devoted to the methodological and theoretical principles which he laid down.

THE IRREDUCIBILITY
OF SOCIAL PHENOMENA

One of the earliest and most important themes in Durkheim's work was the idea that social phenomena have a distinct nature of their own and cannot be reduced to individual psychology. This theme seems to have animated much of his early work, such as *The Division of Labor in Society* (1893), his Latin thesis on Montesquieu (1892), and his *Rules of Sociological Method* (1895a).

In developing his argument, Durkheim set himself against an assumption which for centuries had dominated much of social thought: this was the idea that society is the product of the human will and that it is no more nor less than what man makes of it. An early discussion of this issue is found in the opening pages of Durkheim's Latin thesis. According to Durkheim, philosophers like Aristotle attempted to arrive at social conclusions through introspection. In order to understand society, they attempted to discover the true nature of the individual. They tried to determine whether man is more profoundly attached to freedom or to security, for example, and then they postulated what type of society should be created to best allow man to fulfill himself. If they concluded that his nature was to desire freedom, a society with minimum restraints was proposed; but if security was taken as the central aim of mankind, then the system of rigorous controls was offered as the ideal.

Durkheim argued that these social thinkers did violence to an important principle of science, which is that it must study things. Science addresses a body of empirical data with the primary purpose of understanding it. The philosophers, however, were offering proposals for the future rather than scientific accounts of actual societies. Their approach was scientific only in relation to the individual, for it was the nature of man that they attempted to understand. The philosophers' discussions about society had closer ties with the arts than with the sciences, for their interest was to create, not to understand, laws, customs, beliefs, and the like.

Durkheim maintained that for a science of society to exist it must study its own subject matter, but also that this subject matter must be resistant or irreducible to the human will. In brief, the social sciences must address a body of data governed by its own principles or causal forces. A central point of his Latin thesis was that one of Montesquieu's main contributions was to treat social phenomena scientifically, for he studied actual societies and he recognized that they have their own nature and causes which are expressions of something other than the human will.

Tylor's cultural theory was a variety of the introspective

approach which Durkheim attacked in his Latin thesis on Montesquieu. To be sure, Tylor attempted to treat cultural phenomena scientifically, for he tried to account for the ethnographic data which had been recorded and seldom attempted to propose the ideal form which society should take. Nevertheless, he tried to explain the ethnographic data as the expression of individual interests and processes of thought. Religion, language, and morals originated and evolved because individuals desired to understand the world, to communicate with one another, and to live wisely and prudently. Rational minds, faced with personal wants, arrived at institutions which served their ends, and the problem was to "re-think" institutions on these grounds in order to understand them.

A large share of Durkheim's attention and criticism was directed against Spencer,[1] but many of the arguments raised apply to Tylor as well. Durkheim opposed Spencer's—and Tylor's—ideas from a number of angles, but essentially his point was that the individual can no more create collective beliefs and practices than he can a live oak tree. Durkheim argued this on two principal grounds. First, he held that the individual simply would not voluntarily rise above a life of animal wants or appetites, and second, that he would not naturally rise above a life of sensations. Durkheim saw a profound gulf between individual and collective life, and he denied that it is possible to explain the superior—collective life—in terms of the inferior.

The first argument, that the individual would never voluntarily rise above a life of animal wants, is perhaps most clearly expressed in *The Division of Labor,* which was largely a polemic against Spencer's analysis of cooperation and social cohesion. Spencer's position was that people gain personal advantages from entering into social relationships, and that conscious reflection therefore provides the explanation for cooperation in

---

[1] Durkheim may be accused of seriously misrepresenting Spencer's theories. I shall not try to correct these errors of interpretation; I simply present Spencer's thought as it was conceived by Durkheim.

society. Any reasonable man would see that it is to his benefit to enter into harmonious relations with others. In the fully developed society, according to Spencer, social order and harmony should come about spontaneously without need for coercion (Durkheim 1893:200–3; Parsons 1937:311ff.).

Durkheim's response was forceful and compelling. He argued that self-interest, unrestrained by an external, moderating influence, does not draw men together; it creates nothing more than transitory bonds between them, and in most cases it pits them against one another. The unleashing of egoism gives rise to the Hobbesian war of all against all rather than to harmony and cooperation. Even the threat of the Hobbesian state of nature would not necessarily lead men to cooperate, for there are advantages to conflict as well as peace (Durkheim 1893:120, 203–4; Parsons 1937:313ff.).

According to Durkheim, cooperation and cohesion in society are brought about because people are controlled by a system of beliefs and sentiments—a collective consciousness—which contains their natural egoism. These beliefs and sentiments regulate and modify, rather than express, the individual's personal interests, and consequently they are a *sui generis* reality.

Parsons suggests that the issue of social cooperation and cohesion (or the problem of order in society) was the central theme in Durkheim's work (e.g., Parsons 1937:307, n. 2, 449). I believe this is too narrow a view, however, for Durkheim's polemic about social order was but one aspect of a much larger anti-reductionist argument. Durkheim was opposed to deriving social phenomena of *any* kind from self-interest or personal expediency; his view of the *sui generis* nature of collective life appears in discussions about ethics, categories of thought, religious beliefs, and the like, as much as it does in his treatment of cooperation and cohesion. In short, Parsons has mistaken one part of Durkheim's general argument about reductionist theories for the motivating force behind his entire system of thought.

The second of Durkheim's arguments against Spencerian reductionism was epistemological, for Durkheim held that an empiricist theory of knowledge could not adequately explain complex systems of thought. According to Spencer and Tylor, social institutions arise out of the individual's interpretations of his own experiences. For example, Tylor's theory of religion postulated that beliefs and rites result from the individual's attempts to interpret such phenomena as dreams, death, and sleep. Tylor even believed that categories of thought arise as a result of the impact of sensations on the human mind. In brief, Tylor, like Spencer and others, tended to equate social institutions with knowledge. To them, cultural phenomena are not merely beliefs and practices passed on by tradition, but are the accumulation of wisdom or practical experience.

Durkheim held that there is an unbridgeable gulf between the level of raw experiences or sensations and that of cultural ideas or collective representations. The real world as it is presented to the senses is in a state of perpetual flux. No two sensations or images are ever exactly alike, and even the same phenomenon is not identical from one instant to the next: if the thing which is observed does not change, the subjective state of the observer does. In contrast to the infinite variability of our sensations, the categories in terms of which we think and arrange our perceptions are stable; they are outside the vicissitudes of our experiences and provide the order and fixity which we perceive in the world (1912:481). Systems of thought or collective representations are *sui generis* and cannot be reduced to psychological processes or individual experiences.

Durkheim's epistemological argument against Spencerian reductionism also appeared in a variety of discussions other than those concerning categories of thought. For example, the argument figured prominently in his criticism of Spencer's utilitarian theory of ethics. Spencer's theory, according to Durkheim, is that moral rules are based upon an objective understanding of what is or is not good for a person. They are like rules of hygiene, in that discoverable consequences result from an infraction: for example, intemperance is harmful to one's health and is proscribed for that reason. According to Spencer, there is no need to punish the child in educating him, since the natural consequences of his actions should be sufficient to teach him right from wrong (Durkheim 1902b:169ff., 1906:44). Durkheim was bound to oppose this theory of ethics because it attempted to derive values from individual calculation and reason. One of his arguments was epistemological. He contended that the interpretation of experience is not as simple as Spencer believed, neither for the child nor for the adult. A child may suffer indigestion from overeating, but how can he determine the cause of his misery? Even an adult has difficulty resolving such a question (1902b:170–73). To Durkheim, moral rules have an altogether different source from experience; they are imposed upon man and do not emanate from within him.

Another illustration of Durkheim's epistemological argument appears in his article on incest, published in the first volume of the *Année*. Durkheim opposed those theories which attempted to explain exogamy and incest rules in terms of the intrinsic consequences of consanguineous marriages, that is, in terms of the debilitating effects which such unions were purported to have. He argued that even if harmful effects were to result from such marriages, it would be extremely difficult for the people to see that it is their matrimonial practices which are at the root of the problem (1898a:64). Durkheim went on to show that incest rules are products of social and not individual processes.

Still a third argument which Durkheim directed against Spencerian reductionism hinged upon the first two. This was his argument concerning the problem of agreement or consensus. Tylor assumed that it is possible to make an objective assessment of the truth or usefulness of an institution, and all people of equal intelligence should therefore agree on the value of a particular belief or practice. For example, sensible, civilized men should agree upon the intrinsic worth of both Victorian morality and an industrial economy based on free enterprise.

Durkheim saw no reason why this should be so. For one thing, he rejected the notion that institutions have a personal utility and therefore that the individual will spontaneously adhere to them. For another, he felt that experience is too equivocal and variable to guide people in selecting their institutions. For example, in arguing against utilitarian ethics, he commented that what is attractive to one person revolts another; life itself is not cherished by all men. Happiness is subjective; it is appreciated differently by each individual (1911a:82; 1911b:63). Even scientific truths are not accepted solely on the basis of objective demonstration, for people will not accept the conclusions of science unless they have an initial faith in the role of the scientist (1912:239). Collective beliefs and practices must be invested with some form of authority or respect in order for men to agree to them, and this authority is *sui generis* in relation to individual reason and calculation.

Each of these three arguments brings Durkheim to the idea that cultural phenomena transcend the individual and are not simply an expression of his nature. Cultural phenomena have a source outside the individual and are imposed upon him. Durkheim was proposing a form of cultural determinism. Man has a dual nature, he asserted, in that part of him is purely individual and natural, whereas the other part is social. The two parts have entirely different natures, and consequently there is tension between them: the social part obliges us to surpass ourselves and to depart from ways of thinking and acting which are natural to us. Durkheim contrasted this dualistic image of man with the monistic view of Spencer and Tylor, who attempted to derive culture from the individual's nature and who therefore saw individual life and social life as a single, continuous fabric (Durkheim 1914).

THE SOCIAL SUBSTRATUM
AND COLLECTIVE LIFE

If social phenomena do not originate in the individual mind, what is their source? If they are not utilitarian in inspiration and form, what is their nature? In short, what scheme did Durkheim propose in place of those he rejected? In presenting his ideas it is convenient to proceed according to a distinction which he emphasized in his own writings, that between the social substratum, or the morphological basis of society, and the collective or social life.

THE NATURE OF SOCIAL PHENOMENA. In one of his most significant papers (1898b), Durkheim draws an analogy between the psychical life of the individual and the collective life of society. The substratum of psychical life is a physiological organ, the brain. Psychical phenomena emanate from the brain and cannot exist without it, but they have properties of their own which are irreducible to the nervous system. Memory, for example, is something more than a neural process; in addition, the individual's ideas react upon one another in terms of their own properties, and these properties are not reducible to the principles of the psychological substratum.

Collective life, which is composed of representations or ideas like the psychical life of the individual, has a material substratum; this is the group, or (more accurately) the collection of concrete individuals who are in association with one another (1898b:24–25). An account of the substratum of a particular society would entail a discussion of the material factors which influence the frequency and quality of association. For example, the account would describe the spatial distribution of the population, water courses and other means of communication, and the physical layout of cities (1900:359–62).

It is by means of the close association or interaction of a

group of people—all of whom sense a common purpose or unity—that collective life emerges. The collective life is a life of religious beliefs, moral rules, categories of thought, values, and the like, which goes beyond anything the individual could create and which forces him to go beyond his own nature. How can a psychical life of such transcendence originate in this way? Durkheim's response was quite sketchy, and it was decidedly unsatisfactory as well, as Gehlke noted over a half century ago (Gehlke 1915:105).

According to Durkheim, when minds come together they react upon one another, and out of this mutual stimulation arises a fundamentally different kind of psychic life. For example, emotional states may be intensified beyond their usual level. A group of men who are affected by the same thing perceive that they have the same response, and this reinforces and intensifies their reactions (1893:99; 1897:125–26). Moreover, if a person recognizes that someone else has an idea similar to his own, this idea acquires a vitality which it did not have originally (1893:99)—just as the most incredible rumor becomes believable once a person finds that others give it credence. Finally, when a group is drawn together for some common purpose, and when its members feel a sense of unity, they set aside their own personal interests in favor of the collective pursuit. In this way they are drawn outside themselves (1899:105). The association of minds is a creative phenomenon, a catalyst, and the psychological phenomena which result are quite different in nature from the psychical life of the isolated individual.

The collective life which emerges consists of ideas or representations; these are in a sense "psychological" phenomena, for they exist exclusively in the mind.[2] But they are very different from the phenomena of individual psychology. Collective representations operate according to their own principles

[2] Even physical actions or overt behavior are "psychological" in the sense that they are the external expression of mental elements.

174

and laws, which will be discussed below. In addition, they surpass the psychic life that the individual is capable of achieving on his own. Durkheim remarks that, although sociology may be referred to as "collective psychology," one should not confuse it with psychology proper, which is the science of strictly individual mentality (1895a:103; 1898b:34, n. 1).

Collective phenomena are essentially traditional or cultural, for they are handed down from one generation to the next and people exhibit a strong attachment to them. For example, although both the social substratum and collective life determine or at least influence behavior, they do so in very different ways. Such morphological facts as river courses or demographic patterns have considerable bearing on a person's way of life, but people do not feel an attachment to them. People do not become morally concerned over the change in a riverbed, for example, although some may suffer personally by its dislocation. It is quite different with respect to collective facts; these constitute a moral rather than a physical milieu surrounding the individual, and people express an intense moral concern about them.

The traditional aspect of the collective life is also illustrated by Durkheim's discussion of the nature of sanctions. The sanctions behind collective life are social and not physical. If a person were to go against a rule of hygiene he would suffer an organic malady; the sanction is a physical and necessary accompaniment of the act. But collective beliefs and practices have a different basis. If a person commits incest or violates a ritual prohibition, the sanctions which come down upon him do not reflect the intrinsic character of the act at all. Rather, the culpable experiences the disapprobation or retaliation of society, a reaction which is brought about consciously by people (1906:42–44).

I have already alluded to the fact that collective life surpasses or transcends the life of the individual, and now I wish to explore in depth how this is so. To recapitulate, according to

Durkheim, social life is transcendent in two ways. Intellectually, it furnishes man with the collective representations which constitute a medium for perception and for the expression of thought, a medium quite different in nature from that of the personal sensations and images which are naturally experienced in the mind. Morally, collective life furnishes man with a set of rules by which to regulate his behavior and to constrain his personal interests.

THE INTELLECTUAL TRANSCENDENCE OF THE COLLECTIVE LIFE. Turning to the intellectual aspect first, the collective representations may be characterized briefly as systems of ideas and belief. According to Durkheim's usage, they always have a referent: they are representations *of* something, such as physical objects or social relations. Moreover, they imply a human consciousness; they imply the existence of sentient minds by which such things as social relations are conceived. Collective representations constitute a conceptual framework or cultural idiom by which the members of the social body represent to themselves both their own society and the objects which affect it (1901:xlix; see Bohannan 1960).

Durkheim's discussion of the collective representations pertaining to blood is illustrative. Durkheim noted that the world over there are taboos surrounding blood, and that it is commonly thought that blood contains potent supernatural powers. He discounted theories which explain these ideas either in terms of a hygienic principle or a natural feeling of repulsion toward blood: in other words, he discounted individualistic interpretations. He suggested that these beliefs and practices should be seen in relation to totemism. The totem is usually some form of plant or animal which is regarded as the sacred ancestor of the clan, and the clan members are thought to be made of the same substance as one another and as their totem. All share the same vital force and are thereby a unity. It is appropriate that this force should be thought to reside in the blood, since the individual dies if a substantial quantity is allowed to spill. By extension, it is logical that blood should be thought to have supernatural power, and that it should be hedged about by taboos.

To understand the representations pertaining to blood, it is not sufficient merely to describe their content—to describe or list the properties which blood is thought to have and the consequences which are supposed to follow if the taboos are violated. Rather, one is to penetrate the beliefs and discover both the meaning which they have in the minds of the human actors and the phenomena to which they refer. What it is that ideas about blood express is the unity of the clan. They are a metaphorical means by which the clan represents its collective unity to itself (1898a:81–89).

To Durkheim, an account of cultural ideas and beliefs that focuses solely on content misses what is most important, which is the meaning of ideas to the members of society. Considering only content is like regarding a scientific theory as a folk tale without reference to the scientist who is trying to come to terms with a body of factual material or to the data that he is confronted with. Such an approach disembodies scientific thought just as it does collective representations.

The existential features which are represented in the mind by collective ideas are not normally represented in an objective way. Rather, they are transfigured or transformed (Durkheim generally used the French verb *transfigurer*), because in the process of representing things to itself society projects both value and meaning onto them. Durkheim's account of the development of the contract is illustrative. Since a contractual relation entails the coming together of several parties to make a willful agreement, the essential element is a declaration of will. Nothing intrinsic in the declaration itself compels the individuals to live up to the terms of the agreement, however, and if the contract is to be binding something has to be added to it. One solution is to endow the declaration with a sacred force, or to transform it from a mere verbal statement into a *sui generis* phenomenon with a power of its own. Once the words leave the lips of the individual they are no longer his. They are uttered in the form of a sacred oath, and failure to meet the terms of the contract amounts to a sacrilege and exposes the defaulter to divine vengeance. Collective thought transfigures the physical act of the contractual agreement by superimposing a sacred quality upon it (1899:184).

In his paper entitled "Value Judgments and Judgments of Reality" (1911a; see also 1912:259ff., 467ff.) Durkheim distinguished between two kinds of concepts. First are those which attempt to represent a phenomenon objectively with the aim of understanding it. An example is scientific thought. Judgments which arise from these representations are judgments of reality, such as the calculation that the volume of a gas varies according to the pressure which is applied to it. Other representations entail judgments of value; these do not present an objective image of reality at all, but transfigure it by the superimposition of values. A flag is a mere piece of cloth, but to the soldier it is worth dying for. A man is a mere system of cells, and yet he is invested with sacred respect. A small piece of paper, a postage stamp, may be worth a fortune, as may a mere stone such as a diamond. The value of a thing does not express its intrinsic worth, as the utilitarians claimed, but is superimposed by collective thought.

It is clear that to Durkheim the vast majority of representations express values and serve to transfigure the world in the mind of the individual. When an individual observes a group of people he does not see human organisms in motion; rather, he sees friends or enemies, people who are aristocratic or common; people who are behaving properly or improperly, who are good or bad. When an individual surveys a landscape he does not merely see land contours, habitations, and vegetation. He sees friendly areas and hostile ones, land both valuable and worthless, beautiful and ugly. In short, "society substitutes for the world revealed to us by our senses a different world that is the projection of the ideals created by society itself" (1911a:95). Or again, social thought "can make us see things in whatever light it pleases; it adds to reality or deducts from it according to the circumstances" (1912:260).

The collective representations transcend the life of sensations in a double sense. On one hand, they superimpose a fixity or stability on the fleeting sensations which we experience; and on the other, they project values onto the things and events around us.

A critical implication of Durkheim's thesis that collective ideas transfigure reality is that the essential features of society cannot be discovered by an examination of the world of real things and events. The reason is that these features are superimposed upon the world of empirical facts by collective thought. In opposition to those like Marx who held that social stratification is grounded in differential access to material power, to Durkheim social hierarchy exists because the collective representations consecrate certain men, groups, or sectors of society with eminence and respect. Similarly, Durkheim opposed the common Victorian view—probably shared by Tylor —that those who are intellectually or physically superior tend to rise to the top of society. To Durkheim, social hierarchy is imposed by thought on the empirical facts and does not emerge from them. Even despotic regimes do not rule through the natural ability of leaders or by virtue of material power, but by the force of the collective beliefs and sentiments. Durkheim suggests that it could not be otherwise, for in the world of objective facts each man is simply a biological organism like the next and no more capable than anyone else of spontaneously inspiring respect or dominating others' behavior (see, among others, 1893:196; 1895a:112, n. 21; 1897:142, n. 25; 1902b:90–91; 1906:58; 1912:243–44). In brief, in the social domain "the idea is the reality" (1912:260). At least in his later writings, Durkheim's was clearly an idealist social theory.

It is possible to suggest the source of this idealism in his mind. Durkheim rejected the utilitarian theory of value, which attempted to explain the value of things in terms of the individual's recognition of their intrinsic nature. For example, according to utilitarian theory, the value of corn is supposed to express its use as food (1911a:82). Such a theory gives individual calculation and reason the authority to distinguish good from bad, worth from worthlessness, beauty from ugliness. This view was intolerable to Durkheim, for he was committed to the proposition that social phenomena are a reality *sui generis* and that they are independent of the human will; the value of a thing has to express something other than its utility in relation to the members of society. Similarly, Durkheim was against interpretations which viewed social phenomena as the reflection of material phenomena. For example, he denied that social stratification reflects differences in the inherent capacities of people or in the distribution of material power. He felt that interpretations such as these assimilate or reduce collective life to its material substratum. Durkheim progressively moved toward the view that social life—collective representations—operates according to its own principles (1912:471–72) and that the social structure is an expression of this *sui generis* system of ideas. Durkheim seems to have been drawn inexorably toward an idealist view of society by the logic of his anti-reductionist thesis.

Durkheim's ideas about the collective representations and the way they transfigure the world appear most clearly in his theory of religion. A theme which runs through this study (1912) was a rejection of all interpretations which attempted to derive religious phenomena from the sensations, or from the reflections of individuals upon their experiences. For example, he rejected Tylor's attempt to derive religious beliefs from the individual's desire to understand such phenomena as dreams and death (1912:66ff.). Durkheim also rejected theories which attempted to derive religion from the awe and admiration which men feel toward the forces of nature (89ff.). To Durkheim, a man is simply a man, even in his dreams, and to postulate a sacred soul within him is to go beyond experience. Similarly, natural forces present themselves to the senses as natural forces and they contain nothing which would suggest the concept of the sacred. In short, both theories attempt to derive from sensations an idea which transcends individual experience. To Durkheim, the transcendent or suprasensational concept of the sacred must have originated in some source other than man's rational faculties (1912:106–7).

Durkheim selected the tribes of Australia for his study. He felt that complex religious systems have a greater development of secondary elements than do the simple religious beliefs. These secondary elements make the more basic and indispensable ones difficult to identify—a point I shall clarify below—and he chose the Australians for his analysis because he believed that they had the most elementary religious system known.

Native Australians are [3] hunting and gathering peoples living in small bands or hordes. Most of the tribes are also organized into clans which cross-cut the hordes and which are therefore dispersed. The clan members, united by strong collective sentiments, regard themselves as kinsmen, and they practice exogamy. They also consider themselves related to the clan totem. This is the pre-eminent symbol or coat-of-arms for the group and it is both sacred and taboo; it cannot be harmed or eaten by any of the members of the clan. Moreover, the clan is the basis of a cosmological system, for everything in the universe is classified according to the clans of the tribe—the kangaroo and the sun are associated with one clan, for example, whereas rain, thunder, and lightning are associated with another (see especially Durkheim 1903). The members of the clan feel a bond with all the phenomena which are associated with it.

[3] I use the ethnographic present, and I do not try to correct the ethnographic errors in Durkheim's account.

The human members of the clan are regarded as sacred, but even more sacrosanct is the totem. The most sacred of all, however, are the churinga. These are pieces of wood or polished stone, sometimes pierced to serve as bull-roarers, and engraved with the design of the clan totem. The churinga are so sacred that among some tribes the uninitiated may not even see them. They are hidden in sacred places where quarrels are forbidden and where women and children may not go. Strictly speaking, it is not the churinga themselves which are sacred, but the images which are incised upon them, the images of the totems. The churinga are actually material symbols of the totem.

The churinga are invested with supernatural power; among other things, they can heal wounds and sickness, make the beard grow, and give men courage and perseverance. This supernatural power is an anonymous and impersonal force, like mana, and Durkheim refers to it as the totemic principle. It is not only the churinga which are invested with this totemic principle, but all things associated with the clan, including the totem, the human clan members, and even the various phenomena which are classified with the clan. The totemic principle is a force which animates all things and beings which are associated with it. It existed prior to the living members of the clan and persists after they have died. This powerful force is the god to which the totemic cult is addressed, so it is the very heart of the Australian religious system.

Durkheim attempted to discover the source of the totemic ideas. Surely they do not reflect the intrinsic nature of the things serving as totems. The lizard, for example, does not have qualities which would arouse religious emotions. In fact, the totem is not even the most sacred thing to the Australians; the most sacrosanct of all is the totem's representation carved on the churinga.

The totem is a symbol of two things. First, it is the visible symbol of a supernatural power, the totemic principle. Second, it is a symbol of the clan, for it is the mark by which the clan distinguishes itself from all others. If the totem symbolizes both the totemic principle, or god, and society, that must mean they are one. The totemic principle is the clan represented and transfigured in the form of a supernatural power (1912:236).

It is clear that society has everything that is necessary to suggest the concept of the divine to people. Like a god, society is superior to men, for it constantly exerts pressure on them and forces them to sacrifice their own personal interests for the collectivity. Moreover, society's demands are not met merely because material coercion is applied, but because of its moral authority: men respect society and follow its dictates without calculation or thought of advantage. The concept of the supernatural and of the sacred is the cultural idiom according to which the members of the clan represent to themselves the power of society over them and the respect which they have for it (1912:236–40).

Why do men represent their society to themselves in such metaphorical or symbolic terms? Why do they not view it realistically? The reason is that social phenomena are too complex to be clearly understood without the aid of a critical and empirical social science. The individual realizes that transcendent influences impinge upon him from the outside; he understands that he experiences a powerful enthusiasm when he participates in collective life and that he is led to transcend his nature as a result. But he does not understand these phenomena clearly enough to represent them to himself in other than distorted images (1912:239–40, 252–53; see also 1899:160–61; 1901:xliv–xlv; 1902b:89, 228–29, 230ff.).

Regardless of the reasons that Durkheim gave to explain the transfiguration brought about by religious representations, this transfiguration was necessary according to the logic of his idealism. To Durkheim, society is not a material phenomenon, for it results from the projection of ideals onto a body of people. In nature, man is no more than a system of cells, a mere organism; he does not have the capacity to stimulate the respect of others. However, the collective beliefs are able to turn him into a sacred being whose opinions are worth hearing, whose feelings are worth respecting, and whose guidance or leadership perhaps is worth accepting. For example, in Australian society the individual is sacralized by being invested with a soul. The soul is the totemic principle incarnate in a clan member (1912:282), and it symbolizes that the individual carries a part of society inside him in the form of beliefs and sentiments (1912:297). The individual is not merely an organism after all, but a sacred being who deserves a share of the respect which we have for society. All things in society are apotheosized in a similar fashion. To Durkheim, it is the religious beliefs which bring society into being, for these beliefs transform a collection of mere physical creatures into a moral and sacred social body.

We now come to a critical point in understanding Durkheim's theory of religion: his theory applies to all societies, even those which may seem to lack religious beliefs altogether, for no society can exist if it is not created by the apotheosis and transfiguration of collective representations. Even in thoroughly secular societies everything that is collective acquires a sacred character. A leader who has the love and admiration of the populace acquires, in their minds, a majesty which makes him appear more a god than a man. He is sacred. Like the churinga, he is also invested with mana-like power; he is thought to have personal ability and dignity which are really a symbolic projection of the power he enjoys in collective thought (1912:243–44). The nation's flag and other social symbols undergo a similar apotheosis. Moreover, everything which stands in opposition to collective life is apotheosized as malevolent or diabolic. There are gods of theft, lust, and death just as there are of virtue (1912:467ff.). Communism is made into Satanism just as capitalism is regarded as the epitome of the good and virtuous. Opponents are transformed into unconscionable rogues just as the actions of friends are thought to express a fundamental integrity.[4]

[4] I do not mean to suggest that Durkheim saw all opinions as irrational or that he denied that one could legitimately and rationally take a stand on social

To Durkheim, religion is not an institution parallel to economics, politics, or kinship. In the anthropological monograph religious facts are not to be treated as a discrete category of cultural data and then sandwiched between chapters on technology and social organization. Religion is the soul of society; it is more fundamental than the other features, and it permeates them all.

THE MORAL TRANSCENDENCE OF THE COLLECTIVE LIFE. Collective life obliges the individual to transcend himself morally by requiring him to limit and constrain his own interests and wants. Moreover, *all* social life requires discipline and sacrifice and therefore requires the individual to rise above his natural self. This is because collective life is altogether different from the life of the individual; if a person is to participate in it at all he must adhere to ideas, beliefs, and ways of acting which are foreign to him.

The discipline and sacrifice required of the individual have a counterpart at the level of society: social constraint. If the individual is to surpass his nature he must receive pressure from outside himself in the form of public opinion and sanctions. Durkheim emphasized repeatedly that constraint is diacritical for distinguishing psychological from social facts, and whenever he referred to a phenomenon as collective he meant that it is also obligatory. He noted that we do not always feel a constraint behind social beliefs and practices, and that we seem sometimes to adhere to them without the need for coercion. But if we try to resist them—if we try to go against social life—we feel how strong the constraint actually is (see especially 1895a:1ff.; 1900:362–70; 1901:liiiff.; 1912:239, n. 6).

If social life is truly foreign to the life of the members of society, and if it must therefore be imposed upon them, why do they not revolt and return to a life more fitting to their nature?

issues. After all, he himself was actively involved in the defense of Dreyfus, and he also worked in the defense of his country during World War I. His point was that even the most defensible ideas and institutions become apotheosized once they become part of collective life.

What makes them willing both to exert social pressure on others and to comply when it is applied to them? The reason is that the collective representations are not simply planted in the mind; they are invested with respect or moral authority, which means that people are passionately committed to them. When the members of society observe a violation of their cherished beliefs they react with moral outrage (e.g., see 1893:85–90). Social life, or culture, is not grounded in man's rational faculties at all, for the individual is governed largely by traditional patterns to which he has a strong emotional commitment. Durkheim's and Boas' ideas were very much alike on this issue.

This similarity between Durkheim and Boas should not be allowed to mask a basic difference, however. Earlier I referred to the contrast which Durkheim drew between his own dualistic image of man and the monistic image presented by Tylor and Spencer. Tylor's and Spencer's view was a form of monism since they saw culture essentially as an expression of individual interests and ideas; social institutions demand little sacrifice on the part of the individual. The dualism of Durkheim's theory implies that social life requires the individual to discipline himself constantly, since collective beliefs and practices are foreign to his natural life of sensations and wants.

Boas' image of man is a form of monism, although radically different from that of either Tylor or Spencer. Implicitly, Boas tended to conceive of man as a formless lump of clay which is almost completely shaped by the impress of culture. Moreover, culture gives the human mind its form almost without resistance. In short, Boas tended to assume that man is almost completely transformed by his cultural milieu, and the mechanism by which this is achieved is habit. Boas' view of man was a form of monism since he all but ignored or denied the natural side of the individual. He placed little emphasis on the idea that culture requires discipline, limitation, sacrifice, abnegation, or constraint—terms which constantly reappear in Durkheim's work. This difference between Boas and Durkheim had major implications for the division between British and American anthropology, as we shall see.

Durkheim did not mean to imply that discipline is without benefits for the individual. A person will not spontaneously choose the limitations demanded by social life, but once he accepts them he is personally better off. Personal wants are infinite, and they result in a craving which is seemingly endless. If he gives complete freedom to his desires, they are a constant source of torment to him. By placing limits on wants, contentment is possible—that is, if the limits are invested with a prestige and authority which makes them legitimate in the person's mind. For example, because of the moral principles regulating conjugal life, the individual's sexual appetites are given limits, and satisfaction is made possible; should this sector of morality break down, passions would be unleashed which would result in considerable personal distress. Periods of rapid economic change unleash men's ambitions and aggravate their frustrations. This is reflected in the rise in suicide rates during periods of economic prosperity (1897:241ff.; 1902b:38–44).

Paradoxically, it is by means of moral discipline that the individual is able to achieve a free and autonomous will. By restraining our interests in deference to the demands of social life we learn to control our passions; instead of being controlled by our natural wants, we subordinate them to the will (1902b:44–46; 1911b:89–90).

THE LAWS AND PRINCIPLES
BEHIND SOCIAL PHENOMENA

Durkheim's theory was extremely complex, and it underwent important changes in the course of his lifetime. In addition, his writings were replete with metaphor and with ambiguities which he never fully resolved. It is no wonder that his interpreters—even the most approving—should disagree among themselves over exactly what he meant.

One of the principal differences of interpretation found among English-speaking anthropologists arises between those who tend to view Durkheim as a positivist and those who regard him as an idealist. According to Radcliffe-Brown's interpretation, Durkheim's was a deterministic social theory in that his analyses focused on the necessary laws which govern the processes of social life. According to Radcliffe-Brown, moreover, Durkheim's theory was a form of utilitarianism in that it explained such institutions as morals and religious beliefs by showing how they fulfill certain requirements of society, and above all how they contribute to social stability and cohesion. On the other hand, Evans-Pritchard contends that Durkheim's theory was not nearly as mechanistic and deterministic as it is often thought. Evans-Pritchard holds that Durkheim was an idealist and voluntarist, in that he viewed society essentially as the objective expression of cultural beliefs and values contained in the minds of its members. By this interpretation, the systems of ideas behind society are a *sui generis* order and cannot be explained by reference to some other order, including the material "needs" or structural requirements of the social body. Therefore, explanation amounts to a kind of subjective interpretation rather than a demonstration of functions or causes (see especially Evans-Pritchard 1960:15–19, 1965a:55; Peristiany 1953:xxviii–xxix).

These differences of opinion provide a springboard for a discussion of Durkheim's views, for each of these interpretations reflects different features of Durkheim's thought and therefore serves to delineate the range of explanations which he actually used and advocated in his work. On one hand, Durkheim employed both causal and functional explanations. These focused explicitly on mechanical factors, since Durkheim excluded the human will or consciousness as a causal force behind social life —in short, he rejected reductionism. By eliminating the human consciousness, his analyses necessarily assumed the objective point of view. On the other hand, Durkheim also presented subjective and interpretive studies, for he attempted to discover the meaning which collective representations have to those who hold them.

CAUSAL ANALYSIS. Durkheim's causal interpretations were presented explicitly in opposition to reductionist theories, including Spencer's, and they should be seen in the context of his attempt to establish the *sui generis* nature of social phenomena. His principal methodological discussion of causal explanations is found in his *Rules of Sociological Method* (1895a: Chapter 5). He began by stating that sociologists (including Spencer) typically thought that to explain a social fact, such as a moral belief, one has to show how it is useful. The assumption was that social phenomena are created willfully in order to serve the ends of the members of society. Durkheim insisted that the question of cause is an entirely separate matter from that of the use to which people willfully and purposefully put their institutions, because willing a social phenomenon is not sufficient to make it appear. People may desire an effective government, but this will not bring it into existence. If it is to be established the people must share a common spirit, and the leaders must be invested with moral authority grounded in tradition (1895a:89–91). Causal analysis amounts to revealing the indispensable and nonvolitional conditions behind a social fact.

The order of phenomena to which we must look to discover causes is the social substratum. Since social life arises out of the act of association it must vary in accordance with the nature of this association. Two variables within the social substratum are particularly important: the size of the society, and the dynamic density or the degree of effective contact between people. The reason these factors are important is that the greater the number of minds which are in contact, and the greater the intensity of their relations, the greater the mutual stimulation between them. The contact must be of a certain nature, however. Relations which are primarily economic or self-interested estrange people from one another and inhibit the mutual stimulation of their minds. If the relations are disinterested, the collective life which develops is rich and vigorous (1895a:112ff.).

The principles of analysis which Durkheim outlined in his *Rules* are exhibited in *The Division of Labor,* which appeared two years earlier. The latter was a causal analysis of the growth of specialization and differentiation, or of the division of labor, in society. A central issue in this work was a rejection of the utilitarian theories (including Spencer's) which explained the growth of differentiation in terms of individual motives, especially in terms of people's desire for the material benefits and human happiness which the division of labor was supposed to offer (1893:233ff.). Durkheim searched instead for a mechanical and nonvolitional cause.

His analysis rested on the distinction he made between primitive societies and civilization. Primitive societies are characterized by a homogeneous system of collective representations: since there is little differentiation within society, the same set of beliefs and sentiments applies to all its members. This homogeneity of collective representations is also the basis of solidarity or cohesion, for each member of society feels a strong attraction to those who share his own sentiments and beliefs. Durkheim refers to this as mechanical solidarity because the thoughts and actions of the "social molecules" (the members of society) are so precisely defined by the collective life that the individual has little autonomy of his own—like the molecules of an inorganic body.

In civilized societies the similarities between people are far less marked. Social and economic roles are highly differentiated, and so are the collective representations. The beliefs and rules which govern people's actions are specialized in accordance with the activities they perform. The solidarity of civilized or organic societies is not based primarily on likeness, but upon differentiation: like the organs of a body, each individual performs a distinctive role and depends on the contributions which others make to the social organism. Organic societies are not totally lacking in common beliefs and sentiments, but those which they do have are considerably more general than those of mechanical societies.

Durkheim tried to explain the development of organic societies in terms of a particular feature of the social substratum, namely, population growth. In the homogeneous, mechanical societies everyone pursues the same ends and has the same needs. Therefore, as the population increases, competition and the struggle to survive become progressively more severe. There are several possible responses to this pressure; one is migration, another is specialization. As people specialize, the points of conflict decrease, because each individual is able to achieve his own ends without keeping others from achieving theirs (pp. 266–68). This morphological cause produces its effect only in societies which already share a common moral life, however. Competition between people who are not connected by moral bonds will only produce further estrangement, so in order for differentiation to develop there must already be a common system of beliefs and sentiments with the power of moderating conflict (pp. 275–82).

There was yet another, subsidiary set of factors which occupied Durkheim in this book; these were the differences between the collective life in primitive and civilized societies. Durkheim held that these differences are due to mechanical causes (1893:302), or to differences in the nature of the social substrata. Briefly, because of the undifferentiated nature of the social substratum of a primitive society, the collective life is both more detailed and more vital, and social constraint is more intense than in a complex society. The individual is more tightly enclosed by tradition. First, the collective life is more detailed or precise in simple societies because all people perform the same activities; even the finest aspects of their behavior become collective and therefore obligatory. On the other hand, the morphological differentiation of complex societies requires a collective life which is abstract enough to be able to transcend the internal diversity. Formalism is more marked in mechanical societies, whereas rational and logical thought is increasingly evident in organic ones; as the collective life becomes increasingly general, the individual mind is given greater latitude to think and reflect independently (pp. 287–91). The reason why Durkheim chose to study the Australians in his *Elementary Forms of the Religious Life* was that he assumed that their societies were the simplest known. He believed that their beliefs and practices were not as highly denatured as the religious systems of complex society, because the aborigines enjoyed less scope for the expression of rational thought. Their religious system more clearly reflected the effects of purely social forces (1912:17–21). The second difference between mechanical and organic societies is that the emotional underpinnings and the authority of tradition are more vigorous among primitive peoples, since the group is so narrowly and rigidly circumscribed. As a result, changes are more difficult and slow in mechanical societies, and the free expression of individual variations is less tolerable (1893:291–97). Third, because of the closeness of group life the social surveillance of behavior is greater in mechanical societies, and hence social pressure is more intense. Consequently, primitive societies are more resistant to change and to individual variation (pp. 297–301; see also pp. 70–110).

Although Durkheim speaks of these factors as the results of mechanical causes, it is clear that it was not their origin that interested him. The causal or necessary basis of these factors means that their effects are discoverable in all societies; the implication is that this framework transcends the vicissitudes of history and reveals the fundamental and objective properties which make up the skeletal structure of the collective life of all peoples. Even though Durkheim turned increasingly to the study of subjective meaning rather than objective cause, he did not forsake this comparative scheme.

An important application of this comparative framework was Durkheim's analysis of what he called the cult of the individual. Among primitives the personality is almost completely absorbed by society, and consequently the human being is given little regard in collective life; his suffering is not a source of pity, and his rights are but little developed. For example, family honor counts more than human life (1899:116), and the individual's rights to property are nonexistent since ownership is collective (1899:159ff.). However, the scope of individual autonomy is far greater in complex society, and the human being begins to acquire a larger share of collective respect and dignity (e.g., see 1899:56). His suffering is increasingly intolerable and his rights are increasingly well developed, which is reflected in the history of law and morals. For example, in complex society the individual has the right to dispose of his possessions at will, since the principle of individual ownership is well developed. In addition, the contractual relationship appears as society becomes complex (e.g., see 1899:171ff.). Morals pertaining to the individual have come to transcend all others, and the individual is now the supreme object of collective sentiments (1899:112). In short, the cult of the individual is not simply an accidental feature of modern Western society. It is causally rooted in the organic structure of the total system and will appear anywhere that social differentiation is advanced.

Although the distinction between mechanical and organic societies is intended for comparative and historical analysis, it also appears implicitly in Durkheim's interpretations of the institutions of single societies. For example, he notes that the punishment of crime is more violent in primitive than in complex societies because of the greater emotional reaction to breaches of custom. In modern Western society punishment is more reflective and thoughtful, and it is therefore better adjusted to the nature of the crime. This does not mean that the nature of punishment is altogether different in complex and simple societies. Even in organic societies punishment is still in part an emotional or passionate reaction to an act which is an outrage to morality (1893:86–89). Punishment may be analyzed along a historical coordinate, revealing a progressive growth of reflection and understanding. But it may also be seen along a synchronic coordinate: both passionate reactions and thoughtful reflection are behind modern practices, and to understand the nature of punishment in organic societies both elements need to be taken into account. The mechanical-organic distinction is a very subtle tool for sociological analysis, for all societies contain elements of both forms of solidarity.

Durkheim wrote as though he were proposing a very rigid or mechanical form of causation, especially in his earlier works, but this was not really the case (see Alpert 1939:85–86). For example, the willful actions of men play a very significant role in producing the division of labor, for it is people who respond in one way or another to the population pressure. But the acts which give rise to specialization in society are only the proximate causes. To understand a historical process such as this, the investigator has to retrace the sequence of factors until he hits bedrock, which is the inflexible set of conditions to which the human wills are responding (1895a:92–93). Moreover, in Durkheim's view, it is possible for the members of society to willfully institute changes, but to do so they have to understand the causal forces behind their social life. Merely desiring an effective government is not enough to bring it into existence; but if people realize that it must be established on a foundation of moral authority, its creation is possible (1895a:90–91).

Durkheim's study of socialism (1895b) clearly reveals the role he assigned to the human agent in causal analysis. During much of European history, according to Durkheim, society and the state were both invested with a religious dignity which dis-

allowed their involvement in profane, economic affairs. Economic pursuits were an individual matter (76–77). Beginning
in the eighteenth century, however, a spate of theories appeared
which argued that economic activities should not be allowed to
remain in the shadows, outside the surveillance and regulation
of society. These socialist doctrines argued that economic functions and the central directive organ of society, the state, should
be wed.

Durkheim suggested that the socialist doctrines arose at this
time in history because of certain objective social conditions
which prevailed then. The economic system was producing
considerable suffering among large sectors of the population,
and the rise of socialist theories represented a moral reaction to
this state of affairs. The impulse which produced these doctrines and which gave them force was

a thirst for a more perfect justice, pity for the misery of the working
classes, a vague sympathy for the travail of contemporary societies,
etc. Socialism . . . is a cry of grief, sometimes of anger, uttered by
men who feel most keenly our collective *malaise* (1895b:41).

The reason for this malaise was that the industrial economy
had emerged as the dominant feature of the social body, but society had failed to bring it under control (pp. 244–45). Consequently, economic life was characterized by deception, strife,
and conflict. According to socialist doctrines, the problem was
that the working classes had become dependent on the "capitalists." The latter, free of social regulation and constraint, had
the power to exploit the workers to their own advantage. To
rectify this situation, according to socialist theories, it was necessary to moderate the power of capital by another force,
namely, the state. The state needed to organize and direct the
economic functions so that the interests of all would be served
equally (pp. 59–61).

In brief, socialist theories were one response to a malady
which had overtaken European societies. It was a reaction on

the part of some people to a set of objective conditions (the conditions of anomie) which were confronting them.

Durkheim agreed with the socialists that the problem was a lack of regulation of economic life, but he felt that their solution would only aggravate matters. They were wrong in thinking that the problems of industrial society could be resolved merely by organizing the economic machine in such a way that it would be controlled by one body of people (the state) rather than by another (the capitalists). The socialists did not see that the regulation and direction that was needed could not be provided by men, but had to consist of a moral power that people would respect. To Durkheim, society should be reorganized into corporations or occupational groups. Each profession or occupation would become an effective social unit with its own affairs. Out of the corporation would emerge a moral life, or a system of ethics, which would govern the behavior of its members and bring an end to the strife and malaise of the times (1895b:245–47; see also 1899 and 1902a).

Although Durkheim brought the human will and consciousness into his analyses, he did not mean to imply that the people's responses are expressions of raw intelligence or native capacity. People's reactions are motivated largely by sentiments which are social in origin. Moreover, the conditions or forces to which the members of society respond are not conceived by them in objective terms. Rather, their understanding is mediated by the collective representations, or by the cultural idiom in terms of which the society represents these phenomena to itself. The human will responds to objective forces, but always through a cultural medium (e.g., see 1899:79–80).

Durkheim's causal approach had important implications for his view of culture. Both Boas and Durkheim severed the connection between personal interests and rational thought on one hand and culture on the other, so culture to them was not anchored in place by the principles of objective truth or usefulness. In Boas' thought, culture was set free and allowed to vary almost randomly, for it was governed almost solely by the *sui generis* and fortuitous historical principles of diffusion and modification; the only objective and necessary restrictions imposed upon cultural variability were the rather broad limitations of the environment.

In a sense, Durkheim's causal scheme is the equivalent of Boas' idea of the limitations imposed by the environment. That is, both Durkheim's causal scheme and Boas' environmental limitations provided them with frameworks by which to tie culture down to the objective world and to define the limits of its variability. Remove these frameworks from each of their theories and culture becomes random.

This parallel between Boas' and Durkheim's thought suggests some essential differences between them, however. First, to Boas, the limitations of the environment are very wide, which means that culture is indeed all but random. To Durkheim, however, such traits as moral rules or religious beliefs are not nearly as fortuitous as Boas believed. They are bound up with the objective conditions of society, and consequently their variation is in part a reflection of variations in the social order. The ideals of individualism which characterize modern civilization, for example, are not products of historical accident at all, but are grounded in certain necessary social conditions of organic societies. Culture seemed random to Boas only because he failed to grasp the causal principles underlying it (e.g., see Durkheim 1906:56–57, 63–65).

A second difference is that Boas and Durkheim thought that culture is attached to entirely different aspects of the objective world. To Boas, the connection—slight though it is—is with the environment, whereas to Durkheim it is with the material form of society. This difference had considerable significance for the future development of anthropology. If a Boasian wanted to avoid subjective analyses like those which Boas and Benedict offered—in other words, if he wanted to move toward a more objective and scientific approach—he would be led immediately to the relationship between culture and the environment. Both the cultural ecology of Steward and the technological determinism of White reflect this option in Boasian thought. On the other hand, if one were a Durkheimian, like Radcliffe-Brown, and wanted to avoid a subjective analysis in favor of a more scientific approach, he would be led to elaborate the notion of social structure. The trend in American anthropology toward ecological, technological, and economic studies, and the trend in Britain toward sociological studies are products of a similar movement, which was to reestablish the positivist approach to human institutions. This movement took different forms in American and British anthropology because of the different versions of culture which became dominant in the two countries.

FUNCTIONAL ANALYSIS. Durkheim also stressed functional explanations in his work, and modern functionalist schools of thought commonly refer to themselves as Durkheim's intellectual heirs. Still, serious reservations have been expressed about the role of functionalism in his theory (see especially Bouglé 1951; Peristiany 1953:xxviii–xxix; Pierce 1960). It is important to know what Durkheim meant by this form of explanation in order to know whether or not, or in what respects, his was a utilitarian version of culture.

Durkheim explicitly excluded all questions of conscious intention from functional explanations, for he felt that the issue of intention is too subjective for scientific treatment. Functional analysis should attempt to discover the objective usefulness or role of a social phenomenon, not the purpose of that social fact as conceived by the members of society (1895a:95).

By function Durkheim meant the contribution which a social fact makes to the needs (*besoins*) of society (1893:49; 1895a:95). Expressed another way, the function of a phenomenon is its role in the establishment of general harmony in society (1895a:97).[5] An illustration is his theory of the function of punishment. According to Durkheim, a crime is an act which offends the moral ideas of society, and punishment is a mechanical and passionate reaction against this offense. It is commonly thought that the function of punishment is to intimidate the criminal and thereby to deter crime, but this is not the case: punishment acts upon the upright and not the culpable, for it serves to reinforce and stimulate the sentiments which are offended by a criminal act. It therefore contributes to the vitality and persistence of social life (1893:108–9).

Another example is Durkheim's analysis of the function of religion. Periodically the Australian clans come together to perform the sacred rites of increase for their totem species. The ritual is paradoxical, however, for it is supposed to ensure the fecundity of the very plants or animals which are taboo to the clan members themselves. The true function of the rite must be something other than that expressed by the people, and it must be hidden from their understanding. When the clan comes together for the ritual, the people experience a strong enthusiasm or effervescence, and they feel themselves transported to another level of reality. Moreover, the collective symbols (including the churinga), to which the social sentiments are attached, occupy a central position in these rites. The display of these symbols excites the sentiments which they express. As a result of the collective ritual, the clan's consciousness of itself and the social sentiments upon which the group is based are reaffirmed. It is this which is the true function of the rite. The Australians' interpretation of the ritual—that it serves to ensure the fertility of the totem species—is simply the metaphorical way in which they represent this function to themselves. It is not the survival of the totem species which is being

---

[5] The English translation of this passage is somewhat inadequate. The original reads: *la part qui lui revient dans l'établissement de cette harmonie générale* (Durkheim 1960:97).

assured, but the survival of the collective life of the clan (1912:240ff.).

A final and somewhat different example of Durkheim's functional analysis is needed in order to show the range of phenomena to which he applied this form of interpretation. Durkheim notes that as society becomes more complex, traditional beliefs and ideas become less constraining; as a result, reflection and free inquiry are given greater scope. This greater intellectual freedom is also necessary, for organic societies are too complex to operate according to blind tradition. The growth of reflective thought therefore has the function of making complex society possible (1895a:96).

It seems inescapable that Durkheim was proposing a functionalist and utilitarian theory, and yet this interpretation seems totally inconsistent with the other features of his thought. A leading theme running throughout his work is that social phenomena cannot be explained in terms of their utility to the members of society. He saw all such explanations as forms of reductionism.

The enigma of his functionalism is even more apparent when his function concept is compared with his theory of social causation. His causal analysis was consistent with his desire to establish the irreducibility of collective life; in proposing his ideas about social causation he was trying to show that collective beliefs and sentiments have a source other than individual interests and reflection. On the other hand, there appears to be nothing in his theory which would lead him toward functionalism and utilitarianism. Not only was utilitarianism inconsistent with his thought, it was uncalled-for.

I believe that Durkheim's functionalism was not an unnecessary and inconsistent appendage tacked onto his theory, however, for I think it performed an important role in his scheme. But before explaining this I must go more deeply into his meaning of function and show that it was not a form of utilitarianism at all.

The function of a social fact, he states, consists in the production of socially useful effects, but he is careful not to imply that this social utility has anything to do with the interests of the members of society (1895a:110). Nor does social utility mean "the greatest possible good for the greatest number of people," for that is still explaining social facts in terms of individuals (1911a:83ff.). By socially useful effects he does not mean what is good for the *members* of society, but whatever makes possible the persistence or existence of the system of collective representations. It is not the physical or material needs of man which functions serve, but the needs of the collective life.

Durkheim differed from other anthropologists, such as Radcliffe-Brown and Leslie White, in refusing to carry the analysis a step farther: he did not go on to assume that the collective life itself serves utilitarian ends. For example, Durkheim argued that religious ritual serves to maintain the collective life of society, but nowhere did he suggest that a vital social life and strong moral cohesion result in economic or political benefits. Nowhere did he try to show that the rituals or beliefs improve the Australians' chances of survival or increase their efficiency in the search for game, or that social solidarity is useful politically.

The value of the collective life to man is apparently "spiritual" in the sense that Durkheim used the term, and not material. Collective life provides man with cultural systems of thought and moral values which allow him to surpass his animal nature. By means of the discipline of collective life the individual is able to surmount the determinism of his organic wants, and by means of cultural ideas he is able to transcend a life of simple and fleeting sensations. To Durkheim, collective life is worthwhile, regardless of the incidental creature comforts it may or may not offer (see Bouglé 1951:xxxix–xli).

Why did Durkheim feel compelled to assert that there are social needs and that social facts serve to satisfy them? Durkheim was determined to show that collective life has its own nature, a nature which is different from the individual's. Having already shown to his satisfaction that it is not possible to explain the *origin* of culture in psychological terms, he tried to do the same with respect to the *operation* of culture. He was proposing the existence of a dimension of social phenomena above the level of human volition and operating according to principles located outside the human mind. This is a dimension, or field of processes and principles, made up of such elements as the functions of punishment and ritual and the role of reflective thought in complex society. This layer of social processes and principles is generally beyond the conscious understanding of the members of society and has to be grasped from the outside: the observer has to assume the objective point of view in order to analyze it. Boas offered no corollary to this level of factors; according to him, it did not exist.

Durkheim's functionalism was not an expression of utilitarianism at all. Instead, it was a manifestation of his relentless drive to avoid reductionism.

SUBJECTIVE ANALYSIS. The third type of explanation which Durkheim used was his subjective form of explanation, or his interpretive analysis of the subjective meaning of behavior and beliefs. I have discussed Durkheim's views about subjective culture or the collective life in a previous section, so the following will be brief.

The reason why Durkheim was led toward the subjective analysis of cultural phenomena is that he viewed collective life as more or less autonomous with respect to its material substratum; it is governed at least in part by its own *sui generis* principles. Causal and functional explanations provide only a partial understanding of social facts, and to complete the analysis collective phenomena have to be viewed in terms of their internal, or subjective, principles.

Two principles in particular are prominent in Durkheim's work. The first may be called the principle of symbolism. I have discussed Durkheim's argument that the collective representations transfigure the world by superimposing meaning and value on it. For example, a flag is simply a piece of cloth, but it is transformed by collective thought into a sacred symbol of society; and a human being is transformed from a system of cells into a moral person deserving respect.

This transfiguration of the empirical world is a product of the collective enthusiasm which is generated in the context of group life. When men come together for collective activities such as rituals, they experience a feeling of effervescence. They also sense that they are dominated by an external force—even in their day-to-day activities they feel a transcendent power impinging upon them. This is actually the collective force of society. The people project these feelings onto the things around them; they attribute value and importance to whatever may seem to be the source of this power. For example, the clan totem is singled out and invested with supernatural properties which are foreign to it. Similarly, a leader, fetish, or even an idea may be apotheosized (see especially 1911a:90ff. and 1912:469–70).

The projection of value and meaning is at bottom a symbolic process, for whatever is apotheosized or transformed by collective thought is a representation of social forces. For example, the supernatural power of the clan totem is a symbolic representation of the collective force behind society, and the totem's sacredness represents the respect which the people feel toward their society. Similarly, the Australian concept of the soul symbolizes that portion of man which is social—it symbolizes the collective beliefs and sentiments which he has acquired in society. To understand a people's beliefs, it is not enough merely to recognize that the world of empirical facts is transfigured by collective thought. One must realize that this transfiguration amounts to the creation of a system of symbols which have society as their referent.[6]

There is, then, a "logic" behind collective representations, and this is the logic of social symbolism. The contrast between Tylor and Durkheim could not be more fundamental, for to Tylor beliefs and practices are to be viewed as rational attempts to achieve specific goals. To Durkheim, collective beliefs are metaphorical representations of collective forces, and if primitive ideas seemed ill-reasoned to Tylor it was because they do not operate according to the principles of rational thought. Even the good sense that Tylor believed was the basis of his own Victorian standards was symbolic. Tylor apotheosized the traditional standards of his society by projecting onto them a reasonableness which did not exist in fact. It was not the power of reason that was behind Victorian institutions, but the moral power of society.

The contrast between Durkheim and Boas was equally marked. From Durkheim's perspective, Boas had a very "flat" view of culture. According to Boas, a culture trait is explained simply by describing its features and then showing how it fits into the larger system of culture traits; there is no need to search for meaning behind it. Custom is habitual and not symbolic. Boas and Durkheim, looking at the same ethnographic datum, saw entirely different things, because they placed the datum in entirely different contexts.

The second principle behind Durkheim's subjective approach may be referred to as his optimism. Some writers, including Marx and, to some extent, Leslie White, interpret beliefs and practices from a cynical perspective, for they see

---

[6] Once the collective ideas are born they acquire an autonomy of their own; they react upon one another and may change their nature altogether. Consequently, their relationship to the group context sometimes becomes tenuous, and may be lost altogether. For example, the idea of force first appeared in human societies as the mana-like totemic principle. This concept was later borrowed by philosophy, and then by science, and in the process it became completely disengaged from its social basis (1912:232–34).

self-interested motivations behind social institutions. For example, in the last chapter I mentioned White's explanation of celibacy among the Roman Catholic clergy. According to White, the celibacy rules were probably motivated in part by a desire to keep the Church's holdings intact and out of the hands of wives, children, and heirs.

Cynical interpretations are completely foreign to Durkheim. In his analyses there is no hint that cultural beliefs may mask selfish interests, or that reputedly disinterested institutions may actually be organized for the pursuit of personal advantage. Self-interest appears in his analyses of social phenomena only when he discusses sectors of society in which the collective life is either undeveloped or has broken down—in short, when he is discussing anomie. An example is his analysis of the malaise of contemporary society, a malaise brought about by an insufficiency of ethics or norms within the economic sphere (1902a).

The reason for his optimism is clear enough. In his theory, collective life is above the life of individual interests; it transcends these interests. To explain beliefs and practices in terms of egoism, and to explain social process in terms of interested manipulations, is to resort to reductionism.

What is the relationship between Durkheim's principles of subjective interpretation and Boas' culture concept? I have said that the field of principles and processes implied by Durkheim's functionalism had no correlate in Boas' thought, but that this was not true of Durkheim's idea of social causation. Durkheim's causal analysis corresponds to Boas' environmental limitations, in that both of these sets of factors are the connecting link between cultural systems and the objective world. Although Boas held that the environmental limitations are quite broad, and that cultures vary almost randomly with respect to the objective world, he did not mean that cultural systems lack governing principles altogether. The principles are *sui generis* and consist of the processes of diffusion and modification. Similarly, when Durkheim held that collective life enjoys a degree of autonomy with respect to the social substratum, he did not mean that it is totally orderless. Collective life is to be viewed in terms of the *sui generis,* subjective principles which I have outlined. These, then, are the analogues of the Boasian principles of diffusion and modification.

It is possible to be even more explicit about this relationship between Boas' and Durkheim's thought, for Boas' principle of modification is actually a subjective principle. Boas' concept of diffusion allowed him to give the historical reason why traits appear in particular cultures, but it could not account for the "shape" that cultures seem to have. Rather, it is the principle of modification which explains the internal character of cultural systems. The principle of modification implies that a subjective theme tends to pervade a culture, and this theme supplies the system with its unity or internal consistency. It is this subjective element which Benedict later called the cultural configuration. To Boas and Benedict, this theme, or "cultural genius," provides the key to subjective understanding, for once it is discovered in a culture the internal coherence of the system becomes apparent. Similarly, the subjective principles in Durkheim's scheme constitute the keys to subjective understanding. In short, Durkheim's principles of subjective analysis and Boas' principle of modification are analogous in a double sense. They are alike in being *sui generis* principles behind culture; and they are also keys to subjective understanding.

Once this relationship between Boas' and Durkheim's schemes is recognized, a similarity between the development of Durkheimian anthropology in England and Boasian anthropology in the United States becomes apparent. Benedict's idea of cultural configurations is a Boasian analogue of the Durkheimian theory of Evans-Pritchard, whom we consider in the next chapter. Benedict and Evans-Pritchard represent a rejection of positivist theory. In place of the objective and causal schemes proposed by Steward, White, and Radcliffe-Brown, among others, they have proposed an interpretive form of cultural analysis. Benedict's cultural configurations represent the logical direction for the subjective approach to take within the Boasian tradition; Evans-Pritchard's scheme represents a similar development within the context of Durkheimian thought. In short, each represents a similar movement in anthropology, and the differences between them follow largely from the different versions of culture which they inherited.

Within Durkheim's own work there was a progressive movement away from positivism and toward the study of ideas, or toward the subjective analysis or interpretation of collective life. In *The Division of Labor* (1893) Durkheim's focus was decidedly upon the causes behind the development of organic society, whereas in his *Elementary Forms* (1912) the emphasis shifted to the subjective interpretation of religious ritual and beliefs. This shift in interest was associated with a significant shift in theory: Durkheim progressively loosened the tie between social morphology and the realm of collective representations. He progressively viewed collective life as autonomous with respect to the material substratum of society (see Benoit-Smullyan 1948: 510ff.). For example, in *The Division of Labor* he held that the rules of conduct regulating the relations between people express the nature of those relations; in other words, the rules are a reflection, at the level of the moral system, of certain features of the social substratum (1893:365–66). By the time he wrote *The Elementary Forms*, however, his position was decidedly nearer idealism. He argued that the moral system transfigures the features of the social substratum and does not simply reflect them, so that society does not even exist outside the realm of collective ideals. The collective life transforms the members of the group—who in fact are physical beings—into moral persons, and it transforms their physical movements into moral relations. Of course, he never completely severed the tie between the social life and the social substratum. In *The Elementary Forms*, for example, it is clear that he thought the religious system of the Australians is consistent with their segmental and mechanical society, and that more complex societies demand different forms of ritual and belief.

This movement in Durkheim's theory—from positivism toward idealism—may be related to his persistent efforts to establish the autonomy of collective life. One of his early arguments for the irreducibility of social life was that it is the product of a distinct set of causes which operate independently of the human will. The collective representations arise from the social substratum and are not willful creations of the individual's mind. However, Durkheim came to feel that an explanation of collective representations solely in terms of the social substratum is itself a form of reductionism (see 1898b), as noted earlier in this chapter. He began to elaborate another argument concerning the irreducibility of collective life, which is that collective representations *transcend* the world of physical facts. They project symbolic meaning and value onto it. Durkheim was led to place increasingly greater emphasis on this second argument, and in doing so to stress the transcendence of the social life in relation to the morphological basis of society.

The increasing autonomy that Durkheim ascribed to the collective life was important in another context as well. The social substratum is not a part of culture; it is not a body of traditional material handed down from one generation to the next. It is the collective life which is the equivalent of culture as that term is used today. In stressing the autonomy of collective life, therefore, Durkheim was emancipating culture and providing for a greater recognition of the role it plays in shaping rather than expressing human experiences.

CONCLUSION: DURKHEIM, BOAS, AND THE MEANING OF HUMAN AFFAIRS

Boas and Durkheim were both participants in the turn-of-the-century revolution in social thought, and consequently their ideas had much in common. First, both developed a form of cultural determinism. They concluded that culture or social life is a vast system of ideas which the individual learns rather than creates, and they thought that the personality is fundamentally transformed by this cultural milieu.

Second, in rejecting the individual as the causal force behind culture, they also rejected the utilitarianism of writers like Tylor and Spencer. To both Boas and Durkheim, culture operates according to its own principles, so to an important degree it is autonomous with respect to the interests of individuals. Culture may provide for the satisfaction of man's needs, but that is not its primary function, the guiding principle behind its development, nor the key to its meaning.

If culture is not grounded in reason and self-interest, what is its basis? Why do people adhere to their customs and institutions if they do not derive benefits from doing so? The third parallel between Boas' and Durkheim's thought is that to both of them culture is grounded in emotion. To Boas, culture traits acquire stronger and stronger emotional associations the more they are repeated, whereas to Durkheim the collective life is invested with moral authority. In either case, the emotional underpinnings of culture are generally powerful enough to overcome any impulse which the individual may have to follow his own inclinations rather than the patterns laid down by society.

Fourth, Boas and Durkheim rejected absolutism and developed a form of cultural relativity. The institutions of civilization are not necessarily more true and useful than those of simple societies because reason and utility are not the mainsprings behind the development of culture. To Boas, each culture is the result of a multitude of fortuitous historical events, and each is therefore qualitatively different from the others. To Durkheim, each society is subject to certain necessary causal factors, including population size and the dynamic density of interpersonal relations; institutions are to be viewed in terms of these forces and not in terms of the absolute standards of truth and usefulness.

Boas and Durkheim were proposing an image of man which was radically different from that of Tylor and Spencer. The human being is not a calculating animal, operating according to more or less enlightened self-interest and governed primarily by his rational faculties. Rather, he is motivated largely by emotional principles which are planted in the mind by culture.

There are also some fundamental differences between Boas' and Durkheim's images of man. Boas proposed a monistic view of the human animal, for he tacitly assumed that the individual is a *tabula rasa* at birth and that his personality is almost completely a product of culture. Once enculturation is complete, the cultural response becomes the natural or automatic form of behavior. In contrast, Durkheim's was a dualistic view of man. To him, social life is superimposed on man's nature and obliges the individual to surpass himself; culture entails discipline and constraint. Mechanisms of social control are an almost incidental aspect of society, in Boas' mind, whereas to Durkheim they are essential; the moral foundations of collective life periodically need to be reaffirmed through religious ritual, for example, and the individual needs to feel the constant pressure of society if he is to surpass his nature.

There is a second difference between the Boasian and Durkheimian images of man. To Boas, behavior is to be seen in terms of simple, learned responses. An individual's attachment to a flag or other social symbol is a pattern of response acquired through habit; it does not differ fundamentally from such patterns as eating with a knife and fork rather than the fingers, or decorating pottery with one design rather than another. To Durkheim, however, behavior is far more complex than Boas recognized. Durkheim agreed that people adhere to custom largely because it is invested with sentiment, but he also saw a second, symbolic dimension behind human behavior. A person's reaction to the desecration of the flag, for example, is more than a customary response. The flag's desecration constitutes an affront to the whole body of sentiments which make up the collective life, and people's reactions to the act surpass what one would expect from a mere breach of custom. It is not only the major social symbols, like flags or clan totems, which can elicit symbolic responses, for symbolic meaning is superimposed upon much of the collective life. For example, according to Durkheim, the breach of a moral norm is not only an offense against moral principles. It represents a symbolic threat to the whole society. A criminal is viewed by society not as a mere rule-breaker, but as a sinister, diabolical person. Moreover, in Durkheim's view, internal divisions of society—such as clans or social classes—exhibit differences in custom, patterns of speech, modes of dress, and the like, and these differences become symbols of the respective segments of the society. Such traits as distinctive pottery designs or lower class speech patterns are symbolic as well as customary patterns.

In arguing that culture is *sui generis* with respect to the natural properties of the human mind, Boas and Durkheim were saying that social phenomena are governed by their own principles; and they implied that it is by reference to these principles that the meaning of human affairs is to be assessed. Moreover, there were several parallels in their thought about the nature of these principles. Both writers began with the notion that there is a set of objective, necessary conditions by which cultural systems are linked to the phenomenal world and which restrict the range of cultural variability. To Boas, these are the limitations imposed by the environment, whereas to Durkheim they are the elements which make up the social substratum. Second, both held that culture cannot be fully explained in terms of these objective factors since cultural systems are partially autonomous with respect to them. Culture is governed by another, strictly *sui generis,* set of principles. To Boas, these are the principles of diffusion and modification, whereas in Durkheim's theory they are the principles employed in subjective analysis.

Durkheim also proposed a third set of factors which was un-

matched by anything in Boas' scheme. This is the field of principles and processes implied by the notion of functionalism. To
Durkheim, it is necessary to postulate this dimension of factors
in order to explain the way in which society works, because
otherwise one is forced to explain the persistence and operation of cultural systems in terms of individual mental processes.
Boas, however, was content to limit himself to these mental
processes. To him, in order to understand a culture as an on-
going or dynamic system it has to be approached subjectively.
There is no need to look beyond the level of subjective culture.
The Kwakiutl potlatch, for example, is adequately explained
solely by reference to the cultural ideas of the people and without reference to the functional significance of money or the
functions which the potlatch performed in relation to the
whole society.

The differences in Boas' and Durkheim's minds about the
objective, necessary conditions which link cultural systems
to the phenomenal world led them to other fundamentally different ideas about the nature and meaning of social institutions.
To Boas, the conditions of the environment are comparatively
broad, and hence they are not very significant for an understanding of cultural systems. To Durkheim, on the other hand,
the social substratum provides the skeletal framework behind
collective life, and this framework is fundamentally different in
complex and simple societies. Any small, compact, and homogeneous society with a high moral or dynamic density exhibits
an elaborate development of formalism, a passionate commitment to even the most detailed aspects of custom, and social
surveillance so intense that deviations of any kind are severely
repressed. In short, it is characterized by a comparatively minor development of individuality. On the other hand, the
conditions are almost the reverse in complex societies. For example, religion in primitive society is less reflective than in
complex society, and it is more closely tied to the social substratum. It was no historical accident that the Australian clans

were characterized by totemism, as Boas would have believed. Moreover, legal systems differ between simple and complex societies. In particular, laws which express the sacredness of the individual are less marked among primitive peoples. It is no accident that human sacrifice passes out of existence with the advent of civilization, or that the punishment of criminals becomes less severe. Nor is it accidental that both the contract and private property develop as complex societies emerge. If Boas missed this necessary framework behind social phenomena it was because he was looking at the data from the wrong angle; he was seeing the wrong sets of features and pursuing the wrong sets of connections. In doing so, moreover, he missed some of the meaning of human affairs, for he failed to recognize that such features as the development of the contract in complex societies are to be seen in the context of the process of social differentiation.

Similarly, Boas and Durkheim conceived the *sui generis* principles behind subjective culture (or behind the collective life) in radically different terms. Boas viewed cultural patterns as learned responses, and he saw no need to penetrate them in order to get at their symbolic meaning. To Boas, it is not the principle of symbolism which makes sense of cultural systems or which constitutes the key to subjective understanding. Rather, it is the principle of modification. When a culture trait is diffused it tends to be modified in order to bring it into conformity with the leading motive or theme of the cultural system. Moreover, Boas would not have agreed with Durkheim's optimism. To Boas, self-interest, competition, and interpersonal conflict can become a basis of institutions just as easily as altruism. Some cultures, such as those of the Pueblo Indians, require an optimistic interpretation; but others, like that of the Kwakiutl, demand a cynical analysis. The principles of cynicism and optimism are culturally variable in the same way as pottery styles.

V

OBJECTIVITY AND SUBJECTIVITY
IN THE STUDY
OF HUMAN SOCIETIES

A. R. RADCLIFFE-BROWN
AND E. E. EVANS-PRITCHARD

Hughes has written that the British played very little role in the turn-of-the-century revolution in social thought (Hughes 1958:12; see also Soffer 1970), for the chief participants were from the Continent. The British reflected but did not actively contribute to the changes which were taking place. Moreover, the way in which the revolution took root in England has not yet received the study it deserves. Whatever the factors may have been which brought British social thought as a whole into conformity with Continental ideas, it is clear that within anthropology the influence of Durkheim was critical.

In this chapter I shall treat two British frameworks for viewing human affairs. The first is that of Radcliffe-Brown, who was strongly influenced by Durkheim early in this century. Radcliffe-Brown was a leading figure in the development of modern structural-functional theory, which has become one of the dominant approaches to society among twentieth-century social scientists. Radcliffe-Brown's theoretical ideas have provided the underpinnings of a large share of the anthropological research which has been conducted since the early 1920s, and his works are also standard reading among sociologists and others beyond the borders of anthropology. The second framework I deal with is that of Evans-Pritchard, who entered the discipline after Radcliffe-Brown's reputation had already been established. Evans-Pritchard was initially trained by Malinowski, but as his ideas matured he became more and more closely aligned with the Durkheim school. Evans-Pritchard's ideas were also strongly influenced by Radcliffe-Brown, but the differences between the two are fundamental. Radcliffe-Brown insisted that society is a natural system and that it is to be studied scientifically, whereas to Evans-Pritchard it is a moral system, and anthropological analysis consists in the subjective interpretation of institutions. Evans-Pritchard enjoys an international reputation both for his African research and for his theoretical views, and within anthropology he is one of the leading opponents both of positivism and of the structural-functional approach to society.

A. R. RADCLIFFE-BROWN

A. R. Radcliffe-Brown[1] was born in England in 1881. In 1901 he entered Trinity College, Cambridge, reading for the Mental and Moral Science examination. He took his degree in 1904, and promptly became the first anthropology student of W. H. R. Rivers at Cambridge. Rivers had recently returned from the Torres Straits Expedition, and he had just changed his emphasis from the study of psychology to anthropology. He was in the process of developing his views about the relationship between kinship and social organization, and his ideas on these matters were to be of fundamental importance in the subsequent growth of Radcliffe-Brown's thought.

[1] The following biographical account was drawn from Eggan and Warner, 1956; Elkin 1956; Fortes 1949, 1956; Stanner 1955.

Radcliffe-Brown undertook two important stretches of fieldwork soon after beginning graduate work in anthropology. From 1906 to 1908 he studied the indigenes of the Andaman Islands in the Bay of Bengal, and from 1910 to 1912 he investigated the Australian aborigines. Between these two periods of research he taught Comparative Sociology and Ethnology at Cambridge and the London School of Economics.

Radcliffe-Brown returned to England after his Australian research, but was back in Australia in 1914. Because of illness he found it necessary to remain there, teaching for a short time at a grammar school in Sydney. From 1916 to 1919, during part of World War I, he served as Director of Education in the kingdom of Tonga in the South Pacific. He again suffered ill health, however, and was forced to resign; he then relocated in South Africa.

In 1920 he returned to university teaching. He occupied chairs at Cape Town, South Africa, from 1920 to 1925; and at Sydney, Australia, from 1925 to 1931. At both institutions he developed anthropological programs from scratch. In 1931 he received an appointment at the University of Chicago, where he had a profound influence. The Department of Anthropology at Chicago is still the center for Radcliffe-Brown's approach in the United States. In 1937 he was selected to occupy the newly created Chair of Social Anthropology at Oxford, which he held until he retired, against his will, in 1946. Radcliffe-Brown was not content to remain idle, however, and from 1947 to 1949 he established a new department at Farouk I University in Alexandria, Egypt; and from 1951 to 1954 he taught at Rhodes University, in Grahamstown, South Africa. He chose to live in South Africa due to a tubercular condition which had bothered him periodically since he was a boy. He returned to England in 1954, and died the next year at the age of seventy-five.

In addition to the principal appointments mentioned above, Radcliffe-Brown served brief periods in Yenching, China (1935–36), and São Paulo, Brazil (1942–44).

Radcliffe-Brown published comparatively little relative to his professional stature. His eminence as an anthropologist was due as much to his teaching as his writing, for he was extremely effective with small groups of graduate students. He had a commanding knowledge of the literature, he was articulate in his dialogue with the students, and he had an unusual capacity to expose what was essential in a complex problem. Moreover, he had an imposing personality, and the image which he projected was that of a man with few intellectual peers. Although he taught very little in England prior to taking the chair at Oxford in 1937, he virtually revolutionized anthropological theory in that country once he became established there. Malinowski was another eminent teacher and had already trained a body of gifted fieldworkers in Britain; in a sense, Radcliffe-Brown reaped Malinowski's harvest.

In spite of his charismatic qualities, Radcliffe-Brown was not universally loved. Stanner has written that "No one . . . responded to him with neutrality or indifference" (1955:117). The same manner that engendered a strong devotion from some alienated others. Benedict, for example, thought he was pompous and hollow. In a letter to Margaret Mead she wrote, "He seemed to me impenetrably wrapped in his own conceit . . ." (Mead 1959:327).

THE DEVELOPMENT OF RADCLIFFE-BROWN'S THOUGHT. Radcliffe-Brown was remarkably innovative. While studying at Cambridge he acquired a decidedly nineteenth-century approach to culture, but largely because of the stimulus from Durkheim he developed an approach which was sufficiently powerful and elegant to catch the attention of social scientists both within and outside of anthropology. His thought, then, was never static, and it is best understood within the context of its growth.

There were at least three distinguishable periods in the development of his ideas: the historical period, his early functional period, and the period of his mature functionalism.

The historical period was brief but important. Beginning with Radcliffe-Brown's initial training at Cambridge, it includes the span of time during which he studied the Andamanese (1906–1908), and it ended upon his discovery of the Durkheimian point of view in 1909–10, just before he undertook field research in Australia (Eggan and Warner 1956:545).

In his historical period Radcliffe-Brown employed what he would later call diachronic explanations. He undertook his research among the Andamanese with an explicit interest in making "a hypothetical reconstruction of the history of the Andamans and of the Negritos in general," and he writes that Appendix A of *The Andaman Islanders* is an example of his earlier historical approach (1933:vii). Moreover, his historical interests verged on evolutionism, even though he was decidedly uncomfortable with evolutionary hypotheses (for example, 1933:468). Not only did he want to show the historical development of Andamanese and Negrito cultures, but he was also tempted to reveal the evolutionary principles behind this development.

A significant feature of his historical approach during this period was an intellectualist framework, rather like Tylor's, by which he analyzed the Andamanese institutions. For example, in his account of the evolution of basketry among the Andaman Islanders he seems to have assumed that basketwork evolved as a result of the progressive, rational, and conscious elaboration of technique (1933:468ff.). His intellectualist approach is even more marked in his 1909 article on Biliku and Tarai, two Andamanese mythical figures. Radcliffe-Brown admitted that his theory was "perhaps somewhat hazardous," and he emphasized that he did "not wish to attribute too much importance to it" (p. 267). Biliku is a sentient, supernatural being which is identified by the Andamanese with the annual monsoons. It is thought that Biliku is angered by the burning or melting of beeswax, among other things, and that it is his anger which brings the yearly storms. Radcliffe-Brown suggests that these beliefs are the result of empirical observations, for the Biliku monsoons occur at approximately the same time as the gathering of honey, for example (267ff.). This explanation is suprisingly close to Tylor's reductionist interpretation of nature myths, according to which beliefs are thought to be rational attempts to explain the natural phenomena which the individual observes around him.

The second period in the development of Radcliffe-Brown's thought, his early functional period, begins with his conversion to the Durkheimian point of view just prior to his Australian fieldwork. An example of this functional period is Radcliffe-Brown's principal monograph, *The Andaman Islanders,* which was completed in 1914 but remained unpublished until 1922 (1933:vii). In introducing the theoretical portion of that book Radcliffe-Brown wrote:

Every custom and belief of a primitive society plays some determinate part in the social life of the community, just as every organ of a living body plays some part in the general life of the organism (p. 229).[2]

The central thrust of his analysis was that certain important sentiments have to be stimulated in people's minds if society is to exist, and his account focused on the role of the Andamanese beliefs and ceremonies in working upon these sentiments.

Most of Radcliffe-Brown's analysis in *The Andaman Islanders* rested upon his concept of social value, by which he meant the effect of a thing on the well-being of society (p. 264). Hunting implements, fire, food, and storms, among other things, have important effects on Andamanese society, and therefore they have social value. According to Radcliffe-Brown, anything of social value is invested with some form of supernatural power:

[2] The assertion that *every* custom and belief performs functions was characteristic of Radcliffe-Brown's earlier work (see 1930, in 1958:40, and 1931, in 1958:72, 78). From 1935 on, however, he avoided this extreme position and argued instead that each custom and belief *may* perform functions and that it is the task of social anthropology to discover them whenever they occur (1935, in 1952:184; 1939.

for example, bows and arrows are supposed to be charged with a mana-like power and to be capable of warding off dangerous spirits (pp. 258–59), and the annual storms are personified as supernatural beings (351ff.). The greater the social value of a thing, the more powerful it is believed to be.

According to Radcliffe-Brown's analysis, the beliefs and rituals which express the social value of phenomena have a double function. On one hand, they serve to impress the importance of a phenomenon on the people's minds (p. 264). The Andamanese man and woman are forced to feel society's concern for storms, hunting technology, and the like. On the other hand, beliefs and rites create what Radcliffe-Brown called a "sentiment of dependence." The individual is made to feel that he depends on society and what it has to offer him, and that he cannot get along without its institutions. For example, the individual depends on the bow and arrow not only for hunting, but also to ward off supernatural dangers. As a result, his adherence to tradition is assured, as is the stability and cohesion of society (pp. 257–58). The beliefs and rites are one means for the creation and maintenance of sentiments which are necessary if society is to persist.

Radcliffe-Brown was converted to functionalism early in his career, and yet the functional approach virtually disappeared from his work from the time he completed the manuscript of *The Andaman Islanders* in 1914 until 1922. It is true that he wrote comparatively little during this period; he published nothing at all during the three years from 1919 to 1921, for example. Nevertheless, his attention seems to have shifted away from his functional theory and toward his ethnographic work on the Australians. Almost all of his published writings between 1910 and 1922 were on the aborigines,[3] and his objectives in these studies were to report his field materials and to untangle the complicated systems of Australian social organiza-

[3] Radcliffe-Brown continued to write on the Australians well after 1922, of course.

tion: he attempted to elucidate the way in which the kin terms, marriage rules, sections, principles of descent, and local groups fit together into a coherent whole (see 1910b, 1912, 1913, 1914a, 1918, 1923, 1927).

In virtually all of his studies of Australian social organization—at least in those which were published prior to 1930—the approach which Radcliffe-Brown used was not at all unlike the Boasian integrational form of analysis. His focus was on the connectedness between the parts of the system, or the way in which they fit together, and not upon their functional role in promoting solidarity and cohesion.

When Radcliffe-Brown returned to the functional analysis of institutions in the early 1920s, his function concept seems to have been far less precise than before. When he wrote *The Andaman Islanders* he described the function of an institution as its contribution to stability and cohesion (1933:234), but during the early 1920s he presented an omnibus definition, placing his emphasis as much on the interrelatedness of institutions as upon their role in promoting an orderly society. For example, in 1922 he defined the function of a custom as

what essential or important relations it has with other institutions, what part it really plays in the economic, moral and religious life of the tribe, and to what important needs of the social organism it is related (1922:40).

A year later he wrote of the functions of institutions as "the place they occupy in the mental, moral and social life" (1923, in 1958:31).

His 1924 article on "The Mother's Brother in South Africa" (reprinted in Radcliffe-Brown 1952) was his first explicit functional analysis since the writing of *The Andaman Islanders*. In this paper he again employed a function concept similar to that which appeared in his book on the Andamanese, for he analyzed a few ritual patterns of behavior in terms of their role in contributing to the stability and cohesion of society. By the late

1920s he seems to have shed his omnibus concept of function altogether.

The third period in the development of Radcliffe-Brown's thought—the period of his mature functionalism—begins in the late 1920s, when he began to focus almost exclusively on the functional analysis of institutions. To him, stability and cohesion should not be taken for granted, for they are contingent or problematic. Radcliffe-Brown noted that societies present the anthropologist with problems parallel to those faced by the physiologist and the electronic physicist. The molecule or atom is composed of constituent units which are repelled and attracted by one another, and the electronic physicist's goal is to discover how these units remain together. Similarly, the persistence of an organism is not automatic, but is to be explained in terms of the functions of such organs as the heart and kidney. The persistence of society, too, is problematic, and the anthropologist must seek the factors which contribute to social stability and cohesion (1937:8off.).

Radcliffe-Brown's work during the period of his mature functionalism was dominated by attempts to ferret out the functions of specific institutions, and some of his analyses have become famous. An example is his analysis of joking and avoidance relationships. The joking relationship is a custom whereby an individual is permitted, and in some cases obligated, to make fun of or tease another, who in turn cannot take offense. It is a relation of "permitted disrespect." The avoidance relationship is the mirror opposite, for it is characterized by extreme respect, often to the point that there is no contact whatever between the individuals involved.

According to Radcliffe-Brown, joking and avoidance relationships occur in a certain type of structural situation; they occur when a social relation is characterized by both attachment and separation, or by social conjunction and disjunction. For example, once a man marries he establishes an important relationship with his wife's kin; his relationship with them is one of conjunction. On the other hand, he is an outsider to them, and consequently the relationship is characterized by disjunction: there is always the possibility of differences of interest between his kin group and theirs, and conflict is a perpetual threat. A relationship of this kind may be stabilized in two ways. One is by institutionalizing the avoidance relationship and requiring the individuals involved to show extreme respect for one another. The other is to establish the joking relationship, whereby hostility is prevented by playful teasing and the obligation not to take offense (1940 and 1949, in 1952:99ff., 105ff.).

Radcliffe-Brown's functionalism implies the existence of a synchronic system of some kind, for it is the persistence of this system which functions serve. In short, Radcliffe-Brown's function concept entails another, namely, social structure. When his thought was first developing he was strongly influenced by Morgan, Rivers, and Durkheim (see Fortes 1969:Part I; and Tax 1960:471–74)—all of whom gave an important place to social structure or social organization. In addition, Radcliffe-Brown showed a decided interest in the structural aspects of society in much of his early work. Nevertheless, the specific nature of this system does not seem to have been clear in his mind until the period of his mature functionalism. In *The Andaman Islanders,* for example, his analysis focused on the functions of specific beliefs and rites in relation to "society"; but he failed to say what he meant by that term, and it appears to have been used with considerable ambiguity.

At least three steps marked the development of Radcliffe-Brown's later views about social structure. First, he conceived this system in increasingly precise terms. In 1914 he referred to social structure as "the way in which the society is divided into social groups of different kinds,—local divisions, phratries, clans, etc." (1914b:622). However, once his ideas matured he was defining it as a network of dyadic, person-to-person relations (e.g., see 1940, in 1952:188ff.). It was now much more specific than simply the organization of society; it was now the social organization viewed explicitly in terms of the system of interpersonal relations.

This conception of social structure seems to have derived from Radcliffe-Brown's studies of the Australians, as Fortes has observed (1969:46). Radcliffe-Brown viewed the Australian kinship system as a network of dyadic relations; he also stressed that their kinship system is coextensive with their social structure:

It is impossible for a man to have any social relations with anyone who is not his relative because there is no standard by which two persons in this position can regulate their conduct towards one another (Radcliffe-Brown 1913:157).

Radcliffe-Brown's analysis of Australian kinship appears to have provided him with the prototype or model for the social structure concept once he began to specify its nature.

A second step in the development of the social structure concept was the formulation of a mode of analysis which has become a hallmark of Radcliffe-Brown's approach. This is the idea that social structures are organized upon a set of internal structural principles. Fortes has drawn the analogy between this approach and that of Mendelian genetics (1969:34ff.). Structural principles are like genetic factors; they are constitutive principles, and by recombining in different ways they result in fundamentally different types of social system.[4]

For example, social relations in primitive societies are frequently ordered and regulated on the basis of kinship, and several principles of descent may be used for this purpose. According to the cognatic principle, ancestry is traced through

---

[4] The terms social structure and social system were not synonymous in Radcliffe-Brown's work. The social system is the broader concept, for it includes both structural and functional aspects (see Fortes 1969:43). The most complete definition of the social system is that it consists of "(a) the social structure, (b) the totality of all social usages, and (c) the special modes of thinking and feeling which we can infer or assume (from behavior and speech) to be related with the social usages and the social relations that make up the structure" (1937:152).

both males and females, and one type of kinship organization which results is that of the bilateral Teutonic sib. The principle of unilineal descent—according to which ancestry is traced either through males or females but not through both—commonly gives rise to a lineage organization. The principle of unilineal descent is often combined with the principle of the unity of the sibling group, according to which siblings are regarded as structurally equivalent in certain contexts. Thus, if I have a kinsman in a lineage other than my own, I may find that I owe his brothers the same obligations as I owe him (Radcliffe-Brown 1950:13ff.).

The structural principles approach was foreshadowed in Radcliffe-Brown's famous paper on "The Mother's Brother in South Africa," published in 1924, but the first fully developed analysis occurs in the 1930–31 monograph entitled "The Social Organization of Australian Tribes." By using his newly conceived approach, Radcliffe-Brown was able to throw considerable light on the internal consistency and interconnectedness of Australian kinship. In Fortes' view, this monograph also firmly established "the modern era in the study of kinship and social organization" (1969:42).

The third step in the development of Radcliffe-Brown's social structure concept involved its separation from the larger concept of culture. Initially, Radcliffe-Brown regarded social organization as but one facet of culture (for example, 1929b: 200). Until the latter half of the 1930s he wrote of social anthropology as the "science of culture" (e.g., 1929, in 1952: 123) and not of social systems at all. However, as his ideas developed he began to emphasize that society is a distinct system and that it is to be set apart from cultural institutions. This tendency reached its climax at the Faculty Seminar which Radcliffe-Brown delivered at the University of Chicago in 1937. In his seminar discussion Radcliffe-Brown initially invoked a taboo on the word culture, for he felt that it had been seriously misused in anthropology. He insisted that culture cannot be understood if disengaged from the structure of society, for it is understandable only "as a characteristic of a social system" (1937:106). What I believe he was trying to establish was that institutions are preeminently utilitarian in nature, in that they serve to ensure the persistence and stability of the social structure. In short, culture is to be understood in terms of its role in relation to the social structure and not in terms of its own, *sui generis* principles.

These three steps in the development of Radcliffe-Brown's idea of social structure provide a brief summary of the essential features of this concept. First, the social structure is a system of dyadic, person-to-person relations. Second, this system of social relations is to be analyzed in terms of the structural principles upon which it is constituted. Third, the institutions of mankind are best understood not in terms of themselves, but in terms of their functional role in relation to the social structure.

The full elaboration of Radcliffe-Brown's concept of social structure took place during the period of his mature functionalism. I suggest that this was no coincidence, and that his views about social structure were contingent on and stimulated by the growth of his functional analysis of institutions. Radcliffe-Brown believed that it is the persistence of the system of social relations which functions serve, and once his interest began to center on functional explanations he was led to focus on the concept of social structure as well.

Radcliffe-Brown's analysis of kinship illustrates how this took place. Almost from the beginning of his career Radcliffe-Brown had been writing that among primitive peoples kinship is an important means for the regulation of interpersonal relations. In 1913 he wrote that kinship among the Kariera of Australia "is not only a system of names or terms of address, but is preeminently a system of reciprocal rights and duties." He continues, "Thus the relationship [or kinship] system regulates the whole social life of the people" (1913:157). The idea that kinship serves to regulate interpersonal relations had also been emphasized by Rivers (for example, see Rivers 1914:12).

Once the problem of the stability and cohesion of society became a central issue in Radcliffe-Brown's mind, however, the idea of the regulation of social relations acquired new importance. The ordering of behavior was now conceived as necessary for the persistence of society: there is little room for conflict when the details of social action are prescribed by custom. The content of kinship relations—the behavior which kinsmen can expect from one another and the rights and duties by which their relations are defined—was no longer a mere ethnographic datum; an account of kinship usages which was at one time purely descriptive was now a functional analysis. In his 1930–31 monograph on the Australians Radcliffe-Brown could analyze the intricacies of kinship with renewed vigor, for he now saw the point to the endless details of the system. Collectively, the complicated rules ensured social stability (e.g., see pp. 431, 443).

Radcliffe-Brown's emphasis on the functional importance of the regulation of social relations reached a climax in his 1935 article on "Patrilineal and Matrilineal Succession" (in Radcliffe-Brown 1952). He wrote,

In any society in which kinship is of fundamental importance in the total social structure . . . it is essential for social stability and continuity that the rights of different individuals over a given individual should be defined in such a way as to avoid as far as possible conflicts of rights (p. 40).

He asserted that the reason for the frequency of patrilineal and matrilineal systems in primitive societies is that these forms of organization allow a very precise definition of rights, and they serve the functional needs of stability and cohesion better than the bilateral forms (p. 46). Radcliffe-Brown developed a penetrating analysis of unilineal kinship and lineage structures, and his motivation was to show the functional advantages of this form of organization.

Radcliffe-Brown's views about functional consistency constitute another example of the way in which his functionalism stimulated his thinking about social structure. According to

Radcliffe-Brown, the various parts of the social system tend to harmonize with one another, since discordances tend to work themselves out over time (e.g., see 1935; and 1935, in 1952:181). For a number of years Radcliffe-Brown had been describing the intricate way in which the parts of the Australian kinship system fit together, but in his 1930–31 monograph this interrelatedness acquired new meaning. Functional consistency was now viewed as necessary if the social system were to persist (see especially 1937:125). The internal concordance which he found was no longer a mere datum to be reported, for an analysis of the way in which the parts of the system fit together was a functional analysis. The integrationalism of Radcliffe-Brown's earlier work was now absorbed by his functionalism.

RADCLIFFE-BROWN AND THE INTERPRETATION OF INSTITUTIONS. Given the key elements of Radcliffe-Brown's thought, we can consider some of their implications for his understanding and interpretation of custom. A useful way to approach this problem is to place his scheme in juxtaposition with those of Durkheim, White, and Boas.

Radcliffe-Brown conceived himself as an intellectual follower of Durkheim, but the theory he developed was in fundamental opposition to Durkheim's scheme. One basic difference between the two is that Radcliffe-Brown tacitly rejected the idealistic view of society. To Durkheim, society cannot be discovered in the phenomenal world, for its essential features are superimposed on the observable facts by collective thought. As early as 1914, however—just two years after the publication of Durkheim's *Elementary Forms of the Religious Life*— Radcliffe-Brown defined social structure in terms of its phenomenal features and explicitly distinguished it from such subjective elements as morals and beliefs (1914b:622). He eventually came to view social structure as a system of actually existing social relations, which is the equivalent, roughly, of Durkheim's social substratum. In short, to Radcliffe-Brown, social structure has an actual, physical existence.

Similarly, little more than a superficial similarity exists between Radcliffe-Brown's and Durkheim's concepts of function. To Durkheim, the function of ritual, punishment, and the like, is to maintain or reinculcate the collective representations, the transcendent or "spiritual" features of society. To Radcliffe-Brown, the function of an institution is its contribution to the persistence of the *phenomenal* features of society; institutions function to promote stability and cohesion within the actually existing system of social relations. Moreover, Durkheim did not assume that the functions of institutions serve man's material well-being. To Radcliffe-Brown, however, institutions promote the common good by ensuring stability and cohesion. Radcliffe-Brown's functionalism had more in common with the work of such writers as Tylor and Spencer, and ultimately Bentham and the Utilitarians, than it had with the theory of Durkheim.

Durkheim originally employed three forms of explanation, causal, functional, and subjective. Radcliffe-Brown placed functional analysis in the center of his scheme, and this form of explanation almost completely usurped the role that Durkheim gave the other two.[5] First, to Durkheim, an institution becomes at least partially intelligible by reference to causal principles: for example, the decreasing severity of criminal punishment in modern times makes sense in view of the changes taking place in the social substrata of organic societies. Durkheim's entire causal framework is virtually neglected in Radcliffe-Brown's

[5] Radcliffe-Brown was probably willing to accept the idea that functional explanations provide only partial understanding, and that there is room for other forms of interpretation. However, his work is marked by a lack of anything other than functional explanations, and it is clear that this was the only kind which was satisfying to him. Radcliffe-Brown may have been willing to accept other forms of interpretation, but in practice he made no room for them.
One could argue that his structural analyses constituted a nonfunctional form of explanation. For example, Radcliffe-Brown was able to offer considerable insight into the nature of kinship systems by ferreting out the structural principles upon which they are based. Nevertheless, these should be viewed as functional studies, for the point of his structural analyses was to show the functional consistency of social systems and the way in which the social relations were defined and regulated by custom. Radcliffe-Brown's social structural approach rested ultimately upon a functional base.

work—he makes almost no mention of the differences between mechanical and organic societies, for example, nor does he attempt to build on the idea of the cult of the individual, which, to Durkheim, is a concomitant of organic societies.

Second, Radcliffe-Brown's functionalism subsumed Durkheim's subjective interpretation. According to Durkheim, collective beliefs and sentiments have an autonomy of their own, and as a result they have to be interpreted in terms of their own internal principles. However, Radcliffe-Brown all but reduced subjective culture to the problem of the maintenance of the social system. He acknowledged that systems of belief and value may have a degree of autonomy and that they may not be wholly explainable in terms of their functional role in the social system (e.g., see 1945, in 1952:177). But in his own work he all but ignored beliefs which are lacking in functional significance, and he provided no framework for their interpretation. The implication is that they are an unimportant and residual category of cultural phenomena. An example of his functional analysis of subjective culture is his discussion of the Australian belief that certain locations contain a supernatural force or power (1937:117ff.); according to this belief, a given rock, water hole, or other physical feature is supposed to contain the life force of such species as the kangaroo. Radcliffe-Brown asserted that he could demonstrate that the whole social structure of the tribe hung on such erroneous beliefs as these. He wrote,

Destroy those beliefs and you destroy the whole structure. The whole system of relationships of the people with one another is maintained and kept going by . . . [these] beliefs and ideas . . . (p. 121).

Subjective culture is not to be interpreted in terms of subjective principles, but in terms of the objective features of society, or in terms of the problem of persistence of the social system (see 1931, in 1958:68).

Radcliffe-Brown's scheme is fundamentally utilitarian, and in this respect his ideas about culture are much closer to White's than to Durkheim's. The similarity between Radcliffe-Brown and White is far from accidental, of course, since White explicitly borrowed from Radcliffe-Brown when he was developing his own utilitarian version of culture.

The differences between Radcliffe-Brown and White should not be ignored, however. Both agree that the meaning of an institution is supplied by discovering the functions it performs, and yet they disagree fundamentally about the framework within which the function concept is to be couched. White views institutions as the means for adapting man to the external world, whereas Radcliffe-Brown focuses on the internal functions of institutions, or their role in adapting man to man in society. Radcliffe-Brown agreed that adaptation has both internal and external aspects (e.g., 1933:ix), but once his ideas matured his interest was directed exclusively toward the issue of internal adaptation.

The difference between the functionalism of Radcliffe-Brown and White is illustrated by their disagreement over the interpretation of incest rules. To White, these regulations serve to promote cooperation in society, which in turn provides for security against enemies and insurance against scarcity during hard times. Radcliffe-Brown explicitly rejected White's interpretation and insisted instead that incest rules serve to promote social integration; they are to be seen in terms of the problem of stability and cohesion and not in terms of the adaptation of a cultural system to its external environment (Radcliffe-Brown 1949a).

There is a sense in which Radcliffe-Brown's utilitarianism is more equivocal than White's. To White, institutions contribute more or less directly to man's security and well-being; for example, incest rules constitute a form of insurance against the threat of enemies and against economic scarcity. To Radcliffe-Brown, however, institutions have an indirect value; the function of an institution is its contribution to order and cohesion, which in turn is supposed to benefit the members of society. Radcliffe-Brown assumed that the material advantages of an orderly and cohesive social system were self-evident, and he never critically examined this assumption. He seems to have been engrossed in the more immediate or empirical question of the actual functions of working institutions.

Associated with the differences between Radcliffe-Brown's and White's forms of functionalism are their fundamental differences over the nature of evolution. To White, evolution amounts to progressive adaptation, and it is measurable in terms of the amount of energy which is placed in man's service. On the other hand, Radcliffe-Brown regarded evolution from the standpoint of social structure, and to him development is to be seen, first, as a process of diversification whereby many different kinds of society originate from a small number of original forms; and, second, as a trend toward increasing social complexity, or toward a progressive extension of the number of people integrated within a system of social relations (e.g., 1930–31:452; 1940, in 1952:203–4; 1949b:322; 1952:7–8; 1958:179). White views evolution in relation to external, and Radcliffe-Brown in relation to internal, adaptation.

An even more illuminating difference between Radcliffe-Brown and White is that of the relationship between evolution and progress. To White, evolution implies the gradual improvement of man's position in relation to the physical world. In view of Radcliffe-Brown's focus on the problem of persistence, however, it is difficult to see how he could have regarded civilized peoples as more highly advanced than the more homogeneous and cohesive societies at the primitive end of the scale. Presumably, the complexity of modern society affords more room for discord and disunity than is found in the simple societies. In short, Radcliffe-Brown's scheme seems to leave little room for the principle of progress. He avoided this dilemma by explicitly eschewing the idea that evolution implies advancement (e.g., 1935, in 1952:183, n. 2; 1940, in 1952:203; 1947:80, 82–83). To him, evolution amounts to the process whereby societies become increasingly diverse and complex, and he left the question of the evaluation of this process to one side.

Some of the most distinctive features of Radcliffe-Brown's interpretation of human affairs emerge when his work is compared with that of Boas. Boas presented a monistic image of man, whereas Radcliffe-Brown inherited the dualism of the Durkheim school, and some of the main differences between the two writers rest upon this foundation.

First, Radcliffe-Brown and Boas arrived at fundamentally different views about the nature of human action. I am not sure that Radcliffe-Brown fully accepted the psychological implications of Durkheim's dualism, the view that the human personality is composed of two parts, the natural and the social, divided by a state of tension. Nevertheless, he clearly accepted another aspect of this framework: the notion that if society is to persist, the individual's behavior must be regulated by a system of obligatory norms, and that the individual cannot be left to himself to select the appropriate response for a given occasion. Radcliffe-Brown emphasized the constraint behind institutions. To Boas, however, custom is simply habitual, automatic behavior. The customary response of an enculturated person is so thoroughly ingrained in him that in a sense it is "natural."

The difference between Boas' and Radcliffe-Brown's interpretations of taboos illustrates their differences on the issue of constraint. Boas viewed taboo as a form of habit, like all other customs; taboos become attached to forms of behavior which are contrary to customary practices. Boas cites American dietary habits as an example. Some animals are regarded as appropriate to eat in the United States, whereas others, such as dogs and horses, are not. The eating of dogs and horses is a violation of a habitual pattern and is therefore regarded with disgust. Similarly, Eskimo life has habituated those people to the eating of seal and caribou meat during different seasons of the year, and they have come to feel that it is inappropriate to eat the flesh of these animals on the same day (Boas 1938c:204ff.). To Boas, a taboo is like an automatic reflex; it is an expression of an internal compulsion.

Radcliffe-Brown's interpretation of taboos emphasized their external constraint. In his 1939 Frazer Lecture he tried to show that taboos are to be explained in terms of their contribution to the maintenance of society; he argued that taboos establish the social value of things and events, and he offered the case of childbirth among the Andaman Islanders as an illustration. The Andamanese man and wife are required to observe a variety of taboos just before and after the birth of a child. The other members of the community are also under certain taboos at this time; in particular, they are not allowed to call the man and woman by name. Radcliffe-Brown writes,

the Andamanese taboos relating to childbirth are the obligatory recognition in a standardized symbolic form of the significance and importance of the event to the parents and to the community at large. They thus serve to fix the social value of occasions of this kind (1939, in 1952:150–51).

A taboo does not express an internal compulsion, and its observance does not rest upon blind adherence to custom, for it is enjoined from without.

Boas would have agreed with Radcliffe-Brown that institutions have the authority of society behind them, for he was explicit that when people observe an infraction of custom they suffer an automatic, negative reaction and are prone to apply sanctions to the wrong-doer. Boas affirmed that customs are characterized by constraint, but he did not evaluate this constraint the way Radcliffe-Brown did. What is theoretically important about customary behavior is the internal, automatic reflex, and external constraint is a subsidiary product, a side effect. To Radcliffe-Brown, however, a stable and cohesive society must be defined and regulated by jural rules and juridical mechanisms.

This difference between Boas and Radcliffe-Brown had considerable importance for the future development of anthropology in Great Britain and the United States. On the whole, British anthropologists have accepted the dualism of Radcliffe-Brown and Durkheim, as well as their emphasis on constraint, whereas American anthropologists have tended to accept Boas' monistic image of man. As a result, British anthropological studies have tended to emphasize the juridical aspects of society, such as the legal and political mechanisms which regulate the social system. I believe that these studies are not received with the same enthusiasm by American anthropologists as they are by the British, for these analyses do not have the theoretical significance from a monistic standpoint that they have from the perspective of dualism. The reverse may also be true, in that the British tend to read American monographs and feel that something is missing. I suspect that when Radcliffe-Brown's followers read Steward's analysis of the Shoshoneans, they see a rather "flat" account of custom, an account which lacks emphasis on the very juridical features which constitute key elements in the system.

A second important difference between Radcliffe-Brown's and Boas' interpretations of human affairs is that they had basically different views concerning functionalism. Boas' image of man must have made him quite skeptical of the idea that there is a problem of persistence at all. To Boas, stability and cohesion are not problematic, for adherence to custom is automatic. It is no more likely for the system of social relations to collapse than it is for Americans suddenly to discard their knives and forks and to begin eating with their fingers. Social behavior is the only form of conduct that enculturated people know, and the only way they know how to live is in society. To Boas, functional analysis cannot be the basic form of explanation in anthropology, because the problem of persistence is not the fundamental and ubiquitous issue that Radcliffe-Brown thought it was.

From Boas' perspective, institutions may indeed perform functions of the type which Radcliffe-Brown focused upon; but if so, it is sheer chance, a lucky coincidence. The function which an institution performs is an incidental matter and not the key to its interpretation.

The importance of the difference between Boas and Radcliffe-Brown on the issue of functionalism becomes clearer when it is realized that they both held that cultural systems are *governed* by the respective principles which they singled out. At least implicitly, they held that the principles which they located have the capacity to influence both the course of cultural development and the nature of a given custom or institution. To Boas, once a new trait, such as a myth, is acquired through diffusion, its form is at least partially determined by the subjective premises behind the cultural system. For example, the myths of the Kwakiutl Indians tended to reflect the Northwest Coast emphasis on social competition (e.g., see Boas 1933, in 1940:448). On the other hand, to Radcliffe-Brown, it is the principle of function which guides institutions. He noted that cultural elements are frequently diffused from one society to another, and that they are then "worked over and modified in the process of fitting them into the existing cultural system" (1931, in 1958:73); but all changes in culture, including the modifications which take place subsequent to diffusion, "are not properly comprehensible until we know the functions of those institutions" (1931, in 1958:77). In *The Andaman Islanders* Radcliffe-Brown distinguished between major and minor motives in myth (pp. 339ff.). Minor themes are those which vary between the different groups of Andamanese peoples, whereas the major ones are those which are consistent or stable from one group to another. The reason for the stability of certain themes is that they perform important functions and are thus fixed in place. The minor myths perform less crucial functions, and as a result they are comparatively free to vary. It follows that when a new trait is modified after being introduced into an existing cultural system, what it has to be adjusted to is the more essential or basic institutions, those with important functions to perform.

Radcliffe-Brown's notion that the principle of function is a governing factor behind institutions is expressed even more clearly in his view that "the *raison d'etre* of an institution or custom is to be found in its social function" (1950:62). In 1939 he wrote,

My own view is that the negative and positive rites of savages *exist and persist* because they are part of the mechanism by which an orderly society maintains itself in existence, serving as they do to establish certain fundamental social values (in 1952:152; emphasis mine).

Elsewhere he asserted that unilineal forms of succession occurred in the great majority of primitive societies; he remarked that the reason for this frequency, and the "sociological 'cause' or 'origin' " of unilineal succession, was the functional value of unilineality. In particular, unilineal succession allows a precise definition of rights and duties and it thereby serves to avoid unresolvable conflicts in society (1935, in 1952:46). The "cause" of the high incidence of matrilineal and patrilineal forms of society is to be sought in the functional advantages which these modes of descent have to offer.

Radcliffe-Brown's thesis that the principle of function is the governing factor behind institutions implies that cultural systems are not subject to the vicissitudes of history to the degree that Boas believed. In Radcliffe-Brown's scheme, the necessary, objective conditions which constitute the sociological "cause" of custom and which anchor institutions in place are the "needs" for stability and cohesion. To Boas, on the other hand, the only objective, necessary, and present conditions to which the *sui generis* cultural system has to yield are the rather broad limitations of the environment; the emphasis on social stability and cohesion in society is a cultural variable, like pottery designs or kinship terms. Some peoples, like the Kwakiutl, tolerate a considerable degree of conflict, whereas others, including the Pueblo Indians, do not.

Radcliffe-Brown's and Boas' disagreement over whether or not anthropology is a science is to be seen in the context of their disagreement over the issue of historical contingency. To Boas, each culture is the product of a unique history, and it is futile to search for general laws behind culture. To Radcliffe-Brown, on the other hand, the problem of persistence is both fundamental and ubiquitous. It is not important that societies have different histories, for institutions are to be interpreted by reference to the exigencies of the present and not the vicissitudes of the past. The problem of persistence provides a set of fixed points for a comparative analysis of institutions and the establishment of cross-cultural regularities or laws.[6]

According to Radcliffe-Brown, the central goal of social anthropology is to compare societies in order to discover both the features which are common to all social systems and those which characterize societies of a particular type (1937:71ff.). For example, Radcliffe-Brown suggested that it is a natural law that all societies have a system of morals (1937:72). The existence of morals is not a cultural variable, but is necessary if society is to persist. A law of narrower applicability is that, in societies characterized by a hunting and gathering economy, the animals and plants which occupy an important place in the subsistence system become objects of ritual attitude, and the social value of these species is thereby established (1929, in 1952:117ff.). The recurrence of totemism, joking and avoidance relationships, taboos, ritual attitudes, morality, and the like, in societies which are highly remote from one another,

[6] There were other bases as well for the disagreement between Radcliffe-Brown and Boas over whether or not anthropology can be a science. For example, whereas Radcliffe-Brown analyzed custom by means of objective categories which apply cross-culturally, Boas attempted to view cultural systems in terms of the categories of the people he studied, and consequently he was confronted with data of bewildering diversity. Radcliffe-Brown's framework led him to see uniformities behind the variability of custom, whereas Boas' did not.

merely demonstrates that the forms of functional adaptation are finite.

Even though all societies have to come to terms with the problem of persistence, there is no logical reason why Radcliffe-Brown had to assume that different peoples will adapt in similar ways. It would have been legitimate for him to accept the Boasian notion that each culture is unique and to assert that each people achieves a unique mode of accommodation.

What was it that led him to the idea that there are cross-cultural regularities and that society is based upon natural laws? From the beginning of his career—even before the full development of his theory—Radcliffe-Brown wanted to view anthropology as a science and to discover natural laws behind human institutions (e.g., see 1910a; and 1931, in 1958:86). Moreover, since the 1860s, at least, it had been almost a truism in British anthropology that cultural forms recur with an almost monotonous regularity across the world. Tylor, for example, accepted the existence of cross-cultural similarities as a self-evident truth (e.g., see Tylor 1871, I:1, 6). Radcliffe-Brown's view that anthropology is a natural science and that societies are natural systems was logically unnecessary in the context of his theory; rather, these ideas are to be traced to the general intellectual milieu in which his thought took shape.

E. E. EVANS-PRITCHARD

Evans-Pritchard was born in 1902 in the town of Crowborough, in Sussex, England. He attended one of England's old and eminent public schools, Winchester College, after which he enrolled at Exeter College, Oxford. Upon receiving his M.A. from Oxford in 1924 he went to the University of London, where he and Raymond Firth became Bronislaw Malinowski's first two students in anthropology.

Evans-Pritchard conducted a number of field expeditions between 1926 and the outbreak of World War II. These took

him to much of Central, East, and North Africa, although he is
best known for his work among two peoples in particular, both
in the Sudan. The first were the Azande (singular, Zande),
whom he visited during three different field trips between
1926 and 1930. He spent a total of twenty months among the
Azande, and the material collected during the first of his expeditions constituted the basis of his Ph.D. thesis at London. The
second people were the Nuer, whom Evans-Pritchard visited on
four occasions between 1930 and 1936. His total residence with
them was about a year. His work among the Azande was not
marked by great difficulty, and he found the people themselves
generally hospitable and friendly. By contrast, the Nuer were
hostile and irritatingly uncommunicative, at least in the early
stages of his research. The physical discomforts of fieldwork in
Nuerland were extremely trying as well, and Evans-Pritchard
had to contend with severe bouts of illness while there.

In the early 1930s Evans-Pritchard was appointed to a teaching position at the Egyptian University in Cairo. This enabled
him to become intimately acquainted with that part of Africa,
for much of his leisure time was spent studying the desert. He
next served briefly as a Leverhulme Research Fellow, and then
received an appointment at Oxford as a Research Lecturer. He
held the Oxford post throughout the last half of the 1930s.

In 1940 Evans-Pritchard left teaching and research in order
to enter active military service. He served for a period with the
Sudan Defense Force, and in 1942 became the Political Officer
of the British Military Administration of Cyrenaica in North
Africa. Evans-Pritchard served in Cyrenaica for over two years,
spending most of his time among the more nomadic Bedouin
groups. Later he was to publish an important historical account of the Cyrenaicans (1949).

Upon returning from military life in 1945 Evans-Pritchard
was appointed Reader in Social Anthropology at Cambridge.
The following year he was elected to succeed Radcliffe-Brown

in the Chair of Social Anthropology at Oxford, a position which he held until his retirement in 1970.

Evans-Pritchard's thought has undergone marked changes during his lifetime. His early work was influenced by the functionalism of his teacher, Malinowski (e.g., see Evans-Pritchard 1929a). He also made frequent reference to Radcliffe-Brown (e.g., see 1928, in 1965b:188–89; 1929, in 1965b:94; 1929b; 1931c), whose influence was both patent and decisive by 1933 (see 1932–33:97ff.). During the mid-1930s, however, his thought began to take a significant turn, which is most clearly exemplified by his *Witchcraft, Oracles and Magic among the Azande,* published in 1937. Essentially, the shift was from a positivistic and functional interpretation of institutions toward an idealistic one. According to Evans-Pritchard, society is a moral and not a natural system, and anthropology is not a science but one of the humanities. Today Evans-Pritchard explicitly identifies himself with the Durkheim school—"though with serious reservations" (1960:24)—and it is clearly the idealistic elements of Durkheimian theory, and not the positivism, which attracts him.

These changes did not come about all at once, and possibly the various strands of the development did not knit together until the 1940s. Moreover, this drift remained implicit at first, and most of Evans-Pritchard's colleagues, including Radcliffe-Brown, apparently were not fully aware that it was taking place. Evans-Pritchard did not publicly express his disagreement with the positivistic view of society, which had dominated social anthropology for so many years, until he delivered his Marett Lecture in 1950 (1950, in 1964:139ff.)—four years after succeeding Radcliffe-Brown at Oxford. However, he did offer a few guarded hints somewhat earlier (1946:412, 413; 1948:9).

At the time of this writing it has been over twenty years since Evans-Pritchard first spelled out his departure from Rad-

cliffe-Brown's framework, and yet his position is still not altogether clear. He has sketched his ideas in bold outline but remains silent on many of the crucial aspects of his theory—
apparently in part because of a predilection for empirical research over philosophical and theoretical matters. In 1952
Raymond Firth expressed the following view about Evans-
Pritchard's position: "My own general impression, as an analogy, is that of an underexposed photographic plate—strong
contrast, with brilliant passages in the high lights but lack of
detail in the shadows" (Firth 1952:37). The same analogy could
be drawn today. Consequently, it is difficult to summarize
Evans-Pritchard's ideas and to compare them with others'.

In presenting Evans-Pritchard's scheme I shall begin by discussing one of the most prominent and basic developments in
his work: his restoring the integrity of subjective culture. I
shall then discuss the broader theoretical context within which
this development is to be seen.

THE INTEGRITY OF SUBJECTIVE CULTURE. Closely associated
with Evans-Pritchard's ideas about subjective culture are his
rather strong feelings about free will. In Evans-Pritchard's view,
Radcliffe-Brown reduces man to an automaton by attempting
to explain human actions, ideas, and beliefs in terms of necessary sociological laws (Evans-Pritchard 1950, in 1964:154).
Evans-Pritchard writes that, to Radcliffe-Brown, "societies are
natural systems in which all the parts are interdependent, each
serving in a complex of necessary relations to maintain the
whole" (p. 145). This, he feels, is a scientifically sterile and
pernicious form of positivistic determinism. I am not sure how
Evans-Pritchard acquired his commitment to the principle of
free will, but his strong Catholic convictions must have played
a part. His religious beliefs require that he view the individual as a morally free agent, for if the individual is not responsible for his actions Christianity is nonsense. Evans-Pritchard

writes, "sociological determinism and the teachings of Jesus are irreconcilable" (1959, in 1964:170).

Evans-Pritchard's personal religious convictions are important as background, perhaps, but his sociological or theoretical views stand or fall independently of them. What is significant is that, associated with his views about the freedom of the human will, he is introducing into social anthropology the German idealist distinction between the cultural and natural sciences. This distinction rests upon the premise that ideas and human actions do not operate according to the laws of nature, and the cultural sciences are therefore fundamentally different from the natural sciences. These notions were taken up by the Italian historian and philosopher Benedetto Croce, and spread into English historical thought largely through Croce's follower, R. G. Collingwood, who, like Evans-Pritchard, was an eminent Oxonian. In certain respects Evans-Pritchard's position seems quite close to Collingwood's, and the similarity has been remarked upon by such writers as Firth and Fortes (Firth 1952:37; Fortes 1953:33).

According to Collingwood, nature can be understood only as a phenomenon, that is, from the outside, whereas the events of history may be apprehended from the inside as well. He writes, "the events of history are never mere phenomena, never mere spectacles for contemplation, but things which the historian looks, not at, but through, to discern the thought within them." Moreover, it is the main task of the historian to discern the thought which is within or behind the actions of human beings (1970:213–14). Collingwood gives the example of an historian of Rome who is trying to understand an edict of the Theodosian Code. In order to understand this edict the historian must envisage the situation the emperor was trying to deal with, and he must envisage it as the emperor himself envisaged it. The historian must see the alternatives which were open and the reasons for making one decision rather than another.

243

In other words, "he must go through the process which the emperor went through in deciding upon this particular course" (p. 283). For the historian, explanation amounts to reenacting the past in his own mind (pp. 282ff.).

This version of historical explanation follows from Collingwood's view of the nature of historical events. The things that history investigates, he wrote, are *"res gestae:* actions of human beings that have been done in the past" (1970:9), and human beings are "free to order their activities in accordance with the demands of reason," at least to some extent (Dray 1964:10). To Collingwood, history is an expression of thought or mind (Walsh 1967a:49). Actions or historical events are not predictable or understandable because they are necessitated by natural laws, but because the thoughts and considerations of the historical agent conform to the principles of reason. The events of history are rationally, not naturally, necessitated (Dray 1958:209).

Collingwood wrote about the events of history and not about culture or society, and consequently there are difficulties in applying his ideas to anthropology. Nevertheless, it is clear that, in his view, Radcliffe-Brown approached society as a phenomenon. To Radcliffe-Brown, the structure of society has an existence which is as concrete and real as the structure of a sea shell.[7] Moreover, subjective culture is explained by showing its functional contributions to the persistence of the social structure, and these functions are apparent only when one stands outside the society and views it as a phenomenon: it is necessary to enter into the inside of the system only to explain it in terms of the outside. In addition, to Radcliffe-Brown, institutions are rooted in certain structural exigencies and are naturally and not rationally necessitated.

By implication, at least, Radcliffe-Brown's theory denies the integrity of subjective culture. If cultural beliefs persist it is

---

[7] See Radcliffe-Brown's letter to Lévi-Strauss in Tax, ed., 1953:109.

because they have functions to perform and not because they are compelling in themselves. The believability of subjective culture entered into his scheme negatively—if people cannot be made to believe in and adhere to their subjective culture, then the stability and cohesion of society is in jeopardy.

It is precisely this integrity which Evans-Pritchard has restored, and by doing so he developed a form of explanation quite at variance with Radcliffe-Brown's. Evans-Pritchard regards subjective culture as having an internal coherence and validity which makes it compelling to the members of society; exotic beliefs and values can therefore be explained by making them intelligible to the nonbeliever.[8] Explanation need not end at this point, but at least it must begin here.

Evans-Pritchard implies that all social institutions are to be viewed from the inside, for it seems that, to him, the phenomenal features of culture and society are manifestations of subjective factors. People do things willfully—at least within limits —and are not automatons whose thoughts and actions are governed by the laws regulating some larger social system. Evans-Pritchard implies that the working or operation of social institutions is to be understood largely by grasping the goals, aspirations, ideas, values, and decisions of the individual members of society, just as historical explanation, to Collingwood, amounts to a reenactment of the past in the historian's mind. Collingwood writes that there is no need to search for laws or causes behind history, for

an historical fact once genuinely ascertained, grasped by the historian's re-enactment of the agent's thought in his own mind, is already explained. For the historian there is no difference between discovering what happened and discovering why it happened (1970:176–77).

I believe that Evans-Pritchard is making a similar point when he asserts that social anthropology "interprets rather than ex-

---

[8] Pocock aptly describes this development in Evans-Pritchard's thought as a "shift from function to meaning" (Pocock 1961:72ff.).

plains" (e.g., 1950, in 1964:152; 1951a:62). Evans-Pritchard has all but turned Radcliffe-Brown on his head—or, perhaps, he has turned society inside-out.

These features of Evans-Pritchard's thought first clearly appeared in his book on Zande witchcraft (1937). This book was the culmination of a series of articles which he wrote on the Azande, the first of which was published in 1928 (1928, 1929a, 1929c, 1931a, 1931b, 1932–33, 1934b, 1935). By following these studies it is possible to get an intimate look at the growth of his ideas.

All of Evans-Pritchard's witchcraft studies which were published prior to 1934 exhibit a decidedly functionalist orientation, and this was clearly a result of the influence of Malinowski (Evans-Pritchard 1929a:621) and Radcliffe-Brown (Evans-Pritchard 1932–33:97). For instance, Evans-Pritchard argued that the Zande beliefs function to promote confidence and assurance in people's minds. According to the Azande, witches are men and women who have inherited a certain substance inside their bodies and who therefore have the power to bring misfortune to others, and whenever a man is beset by troubles he immediately thinks of witchcraft. He may then set out to discover the identity of the witch by means of oracles or witchdoctors and to ask him to withdraw his malign powers. Evans-Pritchard asserts that these beliefs enable a man to feel that his misfortunes are not due to "ignorance, incompetence, or bad luck," but that they are due to people whom he can identify and then influence (1932–33:98–99). In another context Evans-Pritchard writes that these beliefs "have a common function in stretching out man's capabilities rather further than they actually reach. They lengthen his arm, so to speak . . ." (1929c:188). Evans-Pritchard also held that witchcraft beliefs serve to uphold the moral standards which are necessary for the persistence of Zande society. A witch is not an evil person merely because he has inherited the powers of witchcraft, for his possession of the witchcraft substance is beyond his control. He was born with it. He is blameworthy only if he uses his power against people. When a person suffering from misfortune seeks to discover the witch who is causing him harm, he only places before his oracle the names of those who bear him malice. The one to be accused, therefore, is the neighbor or acquaintance with whom the individual has bad feelings. Consequently, the Zande man or woman who exhibits antisocial behavior—who often quarrels and is difficult to get along with —receives social opprobrium and humiliation (1929c:210ff.).

A theme which runs through all these studies of witchcraft, and which seems to have occupied an increasingly important position in Evans-Pritchard's mind, is how the Azande could adhere to such patently absurd ideas and practices. He asks whether the Azande can "really believe in all this hocus-pocus" concerning witchdoctors (1932–33:320). In reference to the belief in witches themselves he writes:

how is it that men can so firmly believe in something which seems to us so remote from reality as to appear almost pathological? Through what mental processes does such a fiction arise, and how is it maintained in culture in spite of the enormous waste which it appears to engender? (1929c:198).

Evans-Pritchard accounts for this in part by reference to function: the functional value of the institution provides at least a partial explanation for both its existence and its retention (see 1929c:198ff.). Like Radcliffe-Brown (and Malinowski), he regarded the utilitarian value of a trait as a measure of its viability.

Even in his earliest writings Evans-Pritchard was not satisfied with this functional explanation by itself, however; he attempted to show that the beliefs, absurd though they seemed to the outsider, were logically coherent and intellectually defensible given the point of view of the believer himself. For example, he tried to show that empirical contradictions of the beliefs could be explained away by the people. Contradictory verdicts of the oracles were resolved by invoking the idea that the oracles could lose their potency, by asserting that certain taboos were not adhered to when the oracles were consulted, or by reference to the work of hostile witches. Not only were the beliefs maintained because of the functions they performed, but also because they were perfectly credible. They provided an intellectually satisfying and reasonable idiom of thought.

In 1934 Evans-Pritchard delivered a paper in London on witchcraft, published the next year in *Africa* (1935), which seems to represent a shift in his thinking about Zande beliefs. He placed less emphasis than before on functionalism, and relatively more on understanding Zande beliefs as a system of ideas. Moreover, between 1933 and 1936 Evans-Pritchard published a series of articles on Frazer, Tylor, Levy-Bruhl, and Pareto (1933, 1934a, 1936) in an attempt to delineate these writers' theories concerning the nature of primitive thought (see 1937:5, n. 1). These articles suggest a growing concern for understanding belief systems from the inside, rather than in terms of such outside factors as the functions they perform. This development in Evans-Pritchard's thought reached its culmination in his book on Zande witchcraft (1937).

This book was written specifically with Levy-Bruhl in mind (Evans-Pritchard 1970). According to Levy-Bruhl, primitive peoples view the world in terms of mystical influences and give little scope to natural causation. He also held that primitives are comparatively uncritical in their thinking, having little tendency to reflect upon the empirical validity of their ideas. Evans-Pritchard thought that Levy-Bruhl presented a distorted image of primitive beliefs (see 1934a), and in his book on the Azande he attempted to correct Levy-Bruhl's mistakes.

Evans-Pritchard argued that savage systems of thought are not as thoroughly dominated by mystical elements as Levy-Bruhl believed. Evans-Pritchard described what he called the dual causality in Zande beliefs, by which he meant that Zande thought incorporated both mystical and natural causation. He cites the case in which a group of people were sitting beneath a granary which, unknown to them, had been weakened by termites. The granary collapsed, causing injury, and witchcraft was blamed (1937:69ff.). The Azande were aware that the natural cause of the granary's collapse was the action of termites, but to the people this merely explained how, and not why, the structure fell. Why was it *this* granary which happened to collapse, and why did it do so precisely when these persons were beneath it?

Evans-Pritchard also rejected Levy-Bruhl's view that primitives were uncritical in their thought, for he held that the Azande are quite skeptical within the limits of their beliefs. They are critical of the actions of their oracles, and carefully check or test them to make sure they are working properly (pp. 329ff.). They are critical of their witchdoctors, and are aware that there is a good deal of fakery in their performances (pp. 183ff.). But the existence of chicanery among some practitioners does not lead the Azande to assume that all are quacks; indeed, their traditions suggest that at least some witchdoctors are highly successful in their professional roles (pp. 194ff.).

In presenting the Zande witchcraft beliefs Evans-Pritchard shows that they constitute a logically tight and circular system, for each part is dependent upon and supports the others:

Witchcraft, oracles, and magic form an intellectually coherent system. Each explains and proves the others. Death is proof of witchcraft. It is avenged by magic. The achievement of vengeance-magic is proved by the poison oracle. The accuracy of the poison oracle is determined by the king's oracle, which is above suspicion (1937:475).

Moreover, these beliefs are impervious to contradictions from empirical evidence. I noted above how the contradictory oracular verdicts are explained away. Evans-Pritchard remarks that the blindness of the Azande to the inefficacy of their oracles is not due to stupidity, but rather "they reason excellently in the idiom of their beliefs, but they cannot reason outside, or against, their beliefs because they have no other idiom in which to express their thoughts" (1937:338).

Like his 1934 paper on witchcraft, this book shows little evidence of the functionalism which was so important in his earlier studies. To be sure, he specifically avoided theoretical issues in this work (1937:5); nevertheless, the weight of his argument was upon the intellectual force of the beliefs. In short, the system of ideas—and the actions associated with these ideas, including the accusation of witches, the consulting of oracles, and the like—are explainable by seeing them from the inside rather than by viewing the larger social system from the outside.[9]

It should now be clear what I mean when I assert that Evans-Pritchard has restored the integrity of subjective culture and has elaborated a form of explanation quite different from that which Radcliffe-Brown employed. I do not want to overlabor this point, but neither do I wish to give the impression that Evans-Pritchard is solely concerned with the logical coherence of beliefs and that he feels that all subjective analyses must follow the pattern of his book on Zande witchcraft. Evans-Pritchard actually investigates systems of thought in a number of ways, as illustrated by the analysis contained in his *Nuer Religion* (1956).

A substantial portion of this book is concerned not with beliefs specifically, but with a few Nuer conceptions or representations. Evans-Pritchard attempts to convey the meaning of a few key terms or categories of thought, and particularly the concept of Spirit, or *kwoth*. *Kwoth* is conceived by the Nuer as having an intangible quality, like air, and as being ubiquitous. Everything in nature, culture, and society—and everything

[9] It is impossible in a few pages to convey the power of Evans-Pritchard's analysis. In over 500 pages of text, crammed with data, virtually every facet of Zande witchcraft beliefs is examined; both the coherence of the system and its capacity to resolve empirical contradictions are exhaustively considered. For a philosopher's comments on Evans-Pritchard's analysis, see Polanyi 1958:286ff.

having to do with man—is the way it is because *kwoth* made or willed it that way. For example, Spirit gives and sustains life; he also brings death, largely by means of natural circumstances such as lightning (see 1956:Chapter 1). Although there is a single idea of Spirit, this idea has a variety of manifestations. There are the spirits of the air, *colwic* spirits, totems, and the like, all of which may be conceived as "refractions of God in relation to particular activities, events, persons, and groups" (p. 107).

Evans-Pritchard is explicit that these religious ideas are *sui generis* (pp. viii, 92, 121–22); he implies that "the essential nature" of Nuer religion cannot be understood by reference to the functions the system performs in relation to the larger society (p. 122). Indeed, the relationship between Nuer social structure and Nuer religion—such as the association of certain totems with lineages and clans—is fortuitous. Evans-Pritchard writes that the Nuer "had first the conception of Spirit and it was a quite fortuitous event which . . . brought about a religious connection" between the social groups and totems (pp. 92–93). An understanding of the essence of Nuer religion is not acquired by means of a functional analysis, but by discovering the meaning of the religious conceptions themselves.

In another work Evans-Pritchard speaks disparagingly of writers like Radcliffe-Brown and Durkheim who regarded religion as an illusion and whose theories attempted to account for this illusion. Writers such as these were nonbelievers, and therefore they needed to explain "how everywhere and at all times men have been stupid enough to believe" in souls, spirits, and gods. By contrast, Evans-Pritchard proposes that the believer need not regard religious conceptions as illusions and therefore does not feel compelled to explain them away by psychological or sociological theories. The believer accepts them for what they are and then simply attempts to understand them (1965a:121). What is important about this argument is that it assumes that religious ideas have a validity and integrity which are to be respected. Understanding, by itself, is a legitimate form of explanation.

Nuer Religion is also a study of symbolism, and a prime example is Evans-Pritchard's discussion of sacrifice. In order to understand the nature of this rite it is first necessary to understand the meaning of cattle in Nuer thought as well as the relationship between the men and their herds, since, ideally, the sacrificial victim is an ox.

Nuer have more than a utilitarian interest in cattle, for there is a symbolic identification between men and their livestock. For example, when a boy is initiated he is given an ox by his father as a sign of manhood (pp. 250ff.), and the animal becomes closely associated with the youth. Among other things, the boy acquires the ox's name, or a derivative, for his own. The relationship between oxen and men is manifest at a more general level as well (pp. 254ff.), for all the cattle which belong to the members of a single clan are thought of as a common herd. The clan, and each of its component lineages, is identified with its livestock. Indeed, the splitting of a clan is represented in Nuer tradition as a cleavage in the herd (pp. 258ff.).

There are several forms of sacrifice in Nuer religion, and Evans-Pritchard focuses on the piacular form, which he regards as the most important for an understanding of the people's beliefs. The piacular sacrifices are made either to prevent danger or misfortune or to bring an end to some misfortune which has already fallen, such as a plague or serious illness (p. 198). The Nuer believe that misfortunes are due to God who brings suffering to those who sin. Incest, for example, may result in death within a few days if the persons involved are closely related. The piacular sacrifice is a means for propitiating God or expiating sin.

At the heart of this rite is the idea that the oxen are symbolically substituted for men, and the consecration of the victim, whereby ashes are rubbed on the animal's back, has precisely this meaning. Moreover, ideally, cattle should only be killed for sacrifice, and never solely for food; in Nuer thought they are specifically allotted a sacrificial role in life. The symbolic equivalence of men and cattle can now be properly understood, for it is in the context of sacrifice that the identification takes its most crucial form (pp. 269–71).

Evans-Pritchard is explicit that the rite cannot be interpreted as the giving of an animal to God, for Spirit gains nothing from the slaughter. *Kwoth* has no use for the flesh of oxen. Besides, the cattle are his to take whenever he pleases. The sacrifice, rather, is a gift of oneself to God. The individual gives his life to expiate for sin: he does so symbolically by offering that with which he is identified. The Nuer say that whatever is evil—the sin which is being expiated—is placed on the cow's back, or is transferred to the victim, and flows away with its blood into the earth. It is the ox, not man, who gives its life for man's transgressions (pp. 276ff.).

According to Evans-Pritchard, an understanding of an institution from the inside must take account of such symbolic factors as these. He is critical of writers like Levy-Bruhl and Tylor who, he feels, never fully understood this. Evans-Pritchard speaks of "an imaginative level of thought where the mind moves in figures, symbols, metaphors, analogies, and many an elaboration of poetic fancy and language" (p. 142). Speaking of the Nuer in general, he notes that in their poetry and singing they show a facility for playing on words and images, and that it is the same with respect to their cattle- and dance-names. He writes, "Lacking plastic and visual arts, the imagination of this sensitive people finds its sole expression in ideas, images, and words" (pp. 142–43).

STRUCTURE, FUNCTION, AND ANTHROPOLOGICAL EXPLANATION. Some of the key differences between Radcliffe-Brown's and Evans-Pritchard's points of view can be traced to the latter's attempt to restore the integrity of subjective culture. One of the most fundamental differences separating these two writers is that, at least by implication, Evans-Pritchard has redefined or reformulated the function concept.

Evans-Pritchard is clearly a functionalist, as he himself testifies (1951a:58). A striking example of his functionalism is his analysis of exogamy in Nuer society. The Nuer live in small hamlets, which in turn are organized territorially into political units of greater and greater inclusiveness. This political structure is closely tied to the lineage system. In particular, the lineages and clans provide the conceptual framework upon which the political system is built; it provides the idiom for expressing and directing political relations. Each political unit is referred to by the name of a specific lineage and is identified with that lineage in people's minds. Moreover, the lineages articulate with one another according to the principle of patrilineal descent, and patrilineality also provides the framework for organizing the political units of Nuer society. However, not everyone living in a political group is a member of the lineage with which that group is identified, for movement between territorial divisions is not at all uncommon. Although the political and lineage systems are closely associated, the membership of the two is hardly identical.

Exogamy serves several functions in relation to the political system. For one, by requiring that people marry outside their body of kin it binds together the members of a local group into a complex network of kinship relations. In addition, it results in the extension of kinship relations even beyond the limits of the local community, since the kinship ties within the group eventually become so extensive that spouses must be sought from outside. Exogamy therefore functions both to weld together the members of a local group and to bridge the gaps between political entities (1940:225–28; 1951b:46–48).

This analysis bears a strong resemblance to Radcliffe-Brown's functionalism, but the similarity is misleading.

Evans-Pritchard has not changed the concept of function itself, perhaps, but the larger conceptual context surrounding it has been fundamentally modified.

The obvious departure which Evans-Pritchard takes is that he rejects the idea that the functions of an institution help guide its development and shape its form, for he is opposed to "functional determinism" (1950, in 1964:146). The theoretical consequences of this are far-reaching. Radcliffe-Brown's function concept may be analyzed into at least two discrete factors. First, the function of an institution entails a relationship between that institution and other parts of the social system; a functional relation in this sense simply means that two parts of a system are interdependent. For example, Radcliffe-Brown postulates a functional relation between ancestor worship and lineage organization. Second, these functional relations in turn relate to an ulterior end, for they contribute either positively or negatively to the stability and cohesion of society. Not only is the problem of persistence universal to all societies, it is also the principle by which institutions are rooted in the conditions of the present and which limits their variability. To Radcliffe-Brown, the ulterior end which institutions serve occupies a superordinate position in relation to the simple interdependencies between the parts of the social system. The first aspect of his function concept is to be seen in reference to, and as a manifestation of, the second.

Evans-Pritchard hardly denies that there are functional relations between the elements of the social system or that these interdependencies may be critical for an understanding of that system. He accepts the first aspect of Radcliffe-Brown's function concept. But he must reject the second, for if this ulterior end were indeed the governing principle behind institutions it would reduce man to an automaton; it would mean that his behavior is an expression of the properties or "needs" of some entity other than himself, of which he is not fully aware. It would seem, then, that the logic of Evans-Pritchard's thought must lead him to reject Radcliffe-Brown's conception of the problem of the persistence of society.

An example will illustrate the importance of this point. Evans-Pritchard holds that the legal machinery which is brought into operation in cases of witchcraft in Zande society is "one of the main supports of royal authority." This is because the final verdict in a case is that of the king's oracle, beyond which no appeal is possible (1951a:101–2; see also 1937:288–93; 1963, in 1965a:118). Presumably, the authority of the king would be seriously threatened if the system of oracles were discredited. By knowing this we achieve insight into the total system, for we begin to see what would happen to one part of the system (the kingship) if we changed another part (the system of oracles). However, Evans-Pritchard regards this simply as an instance of a functional interdependence between the elements of a system. To Radcliffe-Brown, of course, it is something more, for in his scheme an interdependence of this kind is oriented toward the ulterior goal of social stability and cohesion.

In short, Evans-Pritchard appears to be rejecting the entire framework within which Radcliffe-Brown's function concept is couched.

In rejecting the idea that institutions are largely oriented toward and governed by the ulterior end which Radcliffe-Brown stressed, Evans-Pritchard virtually divests his scheme of utilitarianism. Institutions such as the Nuer rules of exogamy may have socially useful effects, of course, and anthropological analysis should reveal them, but the utility of an institution is not its primary feature nor the key to its understanding. Moreover, because he has tacitly rid himself of utilitarianism, his function concept has more in common with Boasian integrationalism than it has with any part of Radcliffe-Brown's thought. To Evans-Pritchard, the function of an institution is one type of relationship between the parts of a system and is therefore simply one link in a pattern of integration. I shall return to this point below.

The difference between Evans-Pritchard's and Radcliffe-Brown's functionalism has important implications for their views about the role of history in anthropological studies. When Evans-Pritchard first publicly expressed his difference with Radcliffe-Brown's and others' views about the methods and goals of anthropology, he did so by raising the issue of history, because, he remarks, this difference "is perhaps at its sharpest when the relations between anthropology and history are being discussed" (1950, in 1964:139).[10]

To Radcliffe-Brown it was not necessary for the anthropologist to work out the history of the people he was studying. In his view, it is to the present constitution of the social structure that we must look in order to understand an institution's features, for that institution's nature and form are an expression of on-going structural exigencies. Evans-Pritchard is reluctant to accept Radcliffe-Brown's causal and utilitarian framework. To him, institutions are not rooted primarily in the functional exigencies of the present, and there is room for a good deal more contingency in history, and in social institutions, than Radcliffe-Brown recognized. The antecedent forms of an institution must be taken into account for a full explanation.

Evans-Pritchard is opposed to Radcliffe-Brown's functionalism since it entails an objective and causal framework for which his own voluntaristic and subjective view of human action have little countenance. He is led to modify Radcliffe-Brown's social structure concept for much the same reason: to Evans-Pritchard, society is to be apprehended subjectively, in terms of the categories and values of the culture.

Does this mean that Evans-Pritchard is committed to a form of idealism, according to which society exists solely in the mind? Surely it does not, and I believe that Collingwood again

---

[10] Some tend to minimize the importance of the issues which Evans-Pritchard raises with respect to history (for example, Forde 1950, Fortes 1955:21, Lewis 1968, Schapera 1962). M. G. Smith feels that the issues raised are important, but that Evans-Pritchard has failed to resolve them in his own scheme (Smith 1962). Bidney (1953:Chapter 9) presents one of the most sympathetic discussions of Evans-Pritchard's position.

offers a clue to Evans-Pritchard's views. According to Collingwood, the historian is not concerned with either the inside or the outside of events exclusively. He is concerned not solely with the thought behind Caesar's crossing the Rubicon, but also with the physical event itself. The historian is concerned with "the unity of the outside and inside of an event," although of course the outside is to be understood by penetrating the inside (1970:213). Similarly, to Evans-Pritchard, society has an objective, phenomenal aspect (see Schneider 1965:26, 79, n. 2); but if the system is to be adequately understood it must be apprehended from within.

For example, Evans-Pritchard represents the Nuer political segments as actual, concrete groups with corporate actions or functions. Nevertheless, in his view, the political structure is made intelligible largely by elucidating a few key terms or concepts, such as that of *cieng*. Roughly, this word means "home," but it is a highly relative term. Depending on the context, it can refer to one's homestead, hamlet, village, tribal section, tribe, or even to all of Nuerland (1940:136). Nuer society is highly segmented, for it is composed of political units of varying span; moreover, there is an important element of relativity with regard to these units, for a given political group takes objective form only when it stands in opposition to another of similar span: the emergence of political groups *as* groups is relative to definite political contexts, notably the feuds. This segmentation and relativity of Nuer political organization is reflected in, and made intelligible by, the term *cieng*.

As early as 1934 Evans-Pritchard remarked that he and others had originally misunderstood both the political organization and the system of marriage and descent among the Nuer because of a misinterpretation of this term. Although *cieng* refers to a territorial or political entity within which one lives, it had been confused with the lineage or clan into which one was born. The problem was not a failure to observe the phenomenal social relations carefully enough, but was due to an "incorrect translation of the Nuer word" (1934, in 1933–35:4ff.).

The importance of the study of concepts for an understanding of society is heightened by the fact that, to Evans-Pritchard, values are embodied in words (1940:94, 114, 135), and values define the political and social structure. The Nuer political system is the organization of the people into territorial entities, but a given political unit is not a mere expression of the physical distribution of the members of society—although, to be sure, the facts of demography and ecology affect the political order. Superimposed on the facts of distribution are a set of values which define and differentiate the various units of the political system (see especially 1940:108–10). Evans-Pritchard writes,

The nature of the country determines the distribution of villages and, therefore, the distance between them, but values limit and define the distribution in structural terms and give a different set of distances (1940:110).

In sum, Evans-Pritchard attempts to view political and social structure from the inside, and he does so through the analysis of linguistic categories as well as the values which they embody. Pocock describes Evans-Pritchard's approach in *The Nuer* as one which

works through the relativities of Nuer language so that what is meaningful and therefore systematic to the Neur becomes meaningful and systematic for the observer (Pocock 1961:74).

He continues,

Since Malinowski, social anthropologists had laid great stress upon the importance of learning the language of the people studied. Now the social aspect of language became a clue to a new kind of analysis (1961:75).

At this point I need to return to a question to which I have already alluded: *why* must we view society from the inside? Are there compelling reasons for doing so, or is Evans-Pritchard's subjective analysis simply a useful but optional methodological principle? Clearly, in Evans-Pritchard's scheme it is a necessary

principle if for no other reason than that his voluntarism requires him to view human behavior in terms of the ideas,
thoughts, and aspirations of the individual. Evans-Pritchard
might argue that there is another reason as well. If we do not
view the system from within we will not see its sensibleness,
and consequently we will be tempted to impose false explanations and meaning upon the data. In other words, by failing to
view the system in terms of the categories and values of the
people being studied, we will want to create social or psychological theories in an attempt to make sense out of institutions
which have been made to appear senseless. Evans-Pritchard nowhere raises this argument as a *general* criticism of Radcliffe-
Brown and his followers, but it does appear in his discussions
of functionalist theories of religion; I have mentioned Evans-
Pritchard's view that, since religion is an illusion to the nonbeliever, the free-thinking anthropologist must fashion theories
which allow him to make ritual and belief intelligible without
focusing on the point of view of the people themselves. This argument may be extended to apply to Radcliffe-Brown's analysis
of joking relations, avoidance relations, taboos, and the like—
the reason why these customs invite functionalist explanations
is that they have not been thoroughly understood from the inside. Perhaps it is in this context that we are to understand
Evans-Pritchard's comment that the "constructions" of functionalist anthropology are "posited dialectically and imposed
on the facts" (1950, in 1964:146).

Besides inverting the relationship between the subjective
and phenomenal features of the system, Evans-Pritchard has
modified the social structure concept in yet another respect: by
implication, at least, he has removed much of the theoretical
weight which social structure had to bear in Radcliffe-Brown's
scheme. To Radcliffe-Brown, social structure constitutes the
necessary frame of reference for anthropological analysis. The
governing principle behind institutions is their functional role
in relation to the social structure, and consequently to explain

an institution it has to be seen in the context of the organization of society. This is not to say that social structure is the exclusive framework: Fortes remarks that Radcliffe-Brown's theoretical approach "requires us . . . to accept the inevitability of a plurality of frames of reference for the study of society" (1955:26; see pp. 26–29). However, in Radcliffe-Brown's view, these other frames of reference were to explain the residuum left over after the structural and functional analysis was complete; for example, Fortes states that "It is only *after* we have made the sort of analysis of ritual customs" that Radcliffe-Brown calls for "that the way is opened for the psychological study of a ritual system" (1955:29; emphasis in the original).

I have said that Evans-Pritchard rejects the idea that institutions are governed by the ulterior end which Radcliffe-Brown's theory focused upon. If the guiding principle behind institutions is not their functional role in the maintenance of the social structure, then it follows that social structure ceases to constitute the necessary frame of reference for anthropological analysis. The theoretical importance of social structure is reduced in direct proportion to the changes brought about in the function concept.

Why, then, does Evans-Pritchard continue to produce and advocate social structural studies? He contends that analyses which take culture rather than social structure as their frame of reference inevitably become bogged down by the "heavy load of cultural reality" which they must carry (1951a:40), whereas the social structure framework allows us to achieve far higher levels of abstraction. The structural approach provides greater understanding of institutional systems because it enables us to see them as abstract wholes (see for example 1951a:16–20, 40, 95–96, 104). This point will become clearer after I have discussed the relational analysis which he advocates.

Evans-Pritchard's structural and functional studies clearly place him within the orbit of the Radcliffe-Brown school, and if he had never drawn attention to the differences separating him from Radcliffe-Brown it is likely that few would have been fully aware of them. Nevertheless, these differences are fundamental. Among other things, Evans-Pritchard rejects Radcliffe-Brown's utilitarianism, including the idea that institutions are governed and anchored in place by structural exigencies. Does this mean that institutions are not grounded in objective conditions of any kind and that they are free to vary almost randomly within the broad limitations of the environment, as Benedict believed? And if institutions are not random, what is it that limits their variability, according to Evans-Pritchard?

The answer to these questions, I believe, is provided by Evans-Pritchard's insistence upon the principle of free will. Evans-Pritchard gives far greater scope to human intelligence and conscious thought than Benedict did, and consequently he rejects her view that culture is attached to the real world by the slenderest of threads. According to Benedict, institutions are virtually unhampered by reason and are governed instead by the *sui generis* cultural configuration. To Evans-Pritchard, however, man is at bottom a sensible creature; his behavior is predictable and intelligible because of this reasonableness, which is also reflected in his social institutions. The Zande witchcraft beliefs are not a set of fantastic delusions, but they are grounded in, and limited by, intellectual processes: they are not free to change in directions which run counter to reason. The Zande beliefs are entirely worthy of a sensible-minded people and are to be understood by seeing the sense which is behind them. Economic factors are not a domain of culture which may be emphasized in one way or another, or all but ignored, according to the seemingly capricious demands of culture, as Benedict suggested; the economic life of the Nuer, for example, fits the requirements of their ecology in a way which allows us to see the people as anything but tradition-bound (1940:Chapter II; see also 1937–38).

The reasonableness of man is also reflected in social structure. As I have noted, Nuer lineages perform important func-

tions in relation to the political organization, for they constitute the conceptual framework on which the political system is
built. The association of the lineage system with the political
organization is manifest by the fact that the lines of cleavage
and levels of segmentation within the one correspond with
those of the other. However, some lineages have no tribal associations at all, for they are not identified with any political segment in Nuer society. These lineages typically have fewer
branches and less depth of segmentation than the others—it is
as if they were imperfect specimens. Evans-Pritchard attributes
this characteristic to their lack of political functions. In short,
the political significance of lineages—the political functions
they perform—affects the form which they assume (1940:
240–48; 1950:360–61).

Is this evidence that in Evans-Pritchard's view the principle
of utility plays a guiding role behind institutions, after all? I
think not. I think that the key to understanding this analysis is
contained at the end of his 1950 Marett Lecture. He argued
against the positivistic approach which was inherited from the
Enlightenment and which conceives society as a natural system
subject to natural laws; he identified himself with an older tradition of thought which views societies

as systems only because social life must have a pattern of some kind,
inasmuch as man, being a reasonable creature, has to live in a
world in which his relations with those around him are ordered and
intelligible (1950, in 1964:154).

It would seem that it is man's intellect, and not the ulterior
end that Radcliffe-Brown emphasized, which has the capacity
of shaping institutions; it is the intellect which removes the
randomness from social structure.

However, it should not be thought that Evans-Pritchard is
reviving the intellectualistic theories of writers like Tylor. One
critical difference between Tylor and Evans-Pritchard—among
others—is that Tylor had not truly discovered culture. To

Tylor, the exotic customs which seemed absurd from the Victorian point of view were simply based upon faulty logic. Differences between societies could be resolved into quantitative differences in the people's power of reasoning. To Evans-Pritchard, however, there are cultural or qualitative differences between the categories, values, and beliefs of different societies. These differences, or cultural points of view, are idioms in terms of which people think and interpret the world, and they must be understood before the reasonableness of man and his institutions is to be appreciated. Evans-Pritchard's analysis of Zande witchcraft beliefs is an excellent example.

To Evans-Pritchard, the conscious, rational mind of man is to be taken into account in the analysis of institutions; but the mind does not create institutions out of nothing, for it works with the cultural materials at hand.

If I were to end my discussion of Evans-Pritchard at this point I would leave the reader with a serious misunderstanding of his ideas; for ease of presentation I have tended to imply that to him an account of the point of view of the actor, or of the actor's conception of his society and its institutions, constitutes the goal of anthropological research. This is hardly the case, for he believes that an understanding of an institution from the inside is only the beginning of the anthropologist's task.

The forms of explanation which Evans-Pritchard advocates should be seen in the context of his radical opposition to positivism. He protests against the view that anthropological explanation amounts to subsuming facts under universal and empirical laws, and that the anthropologist is to deduce necessary relations between facts. He asserts that, so far, "nothing even remotely resembling" natural laws has been adduced in the social sciences; the generalizations which have been developed are "so vague and general" that they are "of little use," and tend to be "mere tautologies and platitudes on the level of common sense" (1951a:57). Like Kroeber, he proposes a form of explanation which is commonly used by historians who try to achieve understanding, either of a succession of events or of the events of a particular period, by integrative rather than analytical techniques. It is usual for them to organize their accounts around major themes or general historical movements, and to make specific events intelligible by tracing their relations with other elements and hence by placing them in their historical contexts (see Walsh 1967:59–63). Similarly, Evans-Pritchard attempts to view society as an intelligible whole in which each element falls into its natural place (see 1950, in 1964:148–51).

According to Evans-Pritchard, there are three phases to the work of the social anthropologist, and these differ according to the levels of abstraction which they achieve (see especially 1950, in 1964:148–51; 1951a:61–62). The first is that of description and consists of translating from one culture into another. The anthropologist lives among a people "as intimately as he can, and he learns to speak their language, to think in their concepts and to feel in their values" (1950, in 1964:148). Then he attempts to make their culture meaningful in terms of the categories and values of his own. In short, he attempts to interpret their culture from the inside.

The second phase of the anthropologist's task entails the structural or relational method—and it is to this level that Evans-Pritchard directs most of his own research. In this phase the anthropologist attempts "to discover the structural order of the society, the patterns which, once established, enable him to see it as a whole, as a set of interrelated abstractions." The structural account makes the society "not only culturally intelligible," that is, intelligible from the point of view of the actor, but "sociologically intelligible" as well, intelligible from a perspective which the members of that society do not share (1950, in 1964:148).

Evans-Pritchard's account of Zande witchcraft beliefs illustrates his relational approach. This study was not simply an attempt to translate a system of Zande ideas into the categories of our own culture, nor was it an attempt to go deeper into the mind or thoughts of a typical individual. Rather, the account was a composite or synthesis made from many people's statements and many different observations. The cultural ideas and actions which were brought together in this way form a complex system "which makes sense only when thay are seen as interdependent parts of a whole." For example, the belief in oracles is intelligible only when viewed in relation to the belief in the power of witches. The system "has a logical structure," and this appears as a result of investigation but is not obvious to the people themselves (1951a:99). In other words, the account moves in a different plane from that in which the individual operates in his day-by-day affairs. Furthermore, these beliefs have relations with other facets of the culture and society, including the social structure, and by tracing these relations we are able to achieve an even fuller understanding.

Evans-Pritchard's *The Nuer* provides another illustration of his structural approach. The political system is described in terms of such abstract concepts as tribe, segmentation, and the like, and it is then related to such other features—also represented in general terms—as the ecology, lineage system, and feud. Evans-Pritchard writes, "what the method amounts to is to make some part of the social life intelligible by showing how it is related with other parts. This can only be done by making abstractions and interrelating them logically" (1951a:104). Pocock, referring to Evans-Pritchard's relational method, writes that "one can begin to speak of the structural analysis of social life as opposed to the functional analysis of social structures" (1961:73).

By moving to this more abstract level Evans-Pritchard does not mean to discount the importance of the individual within the system. Rather, the purpose of his method is to achieve greater understanding by enabling us to see the system as a whole. It provides the perspective of a road map, for it presents a highly simplified, birds-eye view and enables us to apprehend relations and implications which are not apparent to the person "on the ground."

Historically, Evans-Pritchard's relational approach can be traced to the influence of Malinowski and Radcliffe-Brown, both of whom insisted that culture (or society) is a system. However, his approach also bears a strong resemblance to Boasian integrationalism.[11] Evans-Pritchard is opposed to the view that institutions are naturally necessitated, or that "in the given circumstances no part of social life can be other than what it is" (1950, in 1964:146). He is against the view that an institution is governed by its contribution, or relation, to the ulterior end which Radcliffe-Brown singled out. Rather, the elements of the system are conditioned by one another, and the structural approach consists in tracing the relations between them. Social and cultural systems are integrated, and this is largely because man is a "reasonable creature" and "has to live in a world in which his relations with those around him are ordered and intelligible" (1950, in 1964:154).

Associated with Evans-Pritchard's relational method are his views concerning the relativity of explanation. The causality of Radcliffe-Brown's scheme seems to have led him to emphasize the objectivity of anthropological analysis. Radcliffe-Brown seems to have conceived the anthropologist as a scientific "discoverer" who faithfully observes and reports what is intrinsically important; the study of a single society by two independent observers should lead to similar results. Evans-Pritchard's image of the anthropologist more closely resembles that of an artist, for to him the investigator attempts to convey the meaning of social facts, or to present them in such a way as to make them intelligible (see 1951a:123). The anthropologist contrib-

---

[11] Evans-Pritchard's relational approach also has ties with Durkheimian thought. Evans-Pritchard notes that Durkheim did not focus primarily on causal explanation, but that more commonly he tried to view cultural systems of idea and value as intelligible wholes (1960:15–18; see also 1953a:214, and 1954).

utes something of himself to the study, and in particular he selects and organizes his material according to subjective criteria. For example, in making abstractions he must pare away detail in order to throw into relief those features of the system which are significant in the context of the investigation. Although the anthropologist is more like an artist than a scientist, this does not release him from the scientist's obligation of remaining faithful to the data: Evans-Pritchard's account of Nuer social structure may exhibit an important degree of creativity, but his book was not a creative production in the same way as a novel.

In the third phase of anthropological research the investigator undertakes comparisons in order to determine the "essential features" of structural forms as well as "the reasons for their variations" (1950, in 1964:149). For example, Evans-Pritchard suggests that future fieldworkers may wish to apply the conclusions of his study of Zande witchcraft to other societies in an attempt to determine which of these conclusions are generally valid and which apply only to Zande society. He writes, "If a sufficient number of studies of that topic are made we end up with certain general conclusions about it, though I do not claim for them the status of universal laws" (1963, in 1965b:31). An example of his own use of the comparative method is his study of Zande sacrifice, in which he discusses the theories of Robertson Smith, Tylor, Spencer, and others, in order to see what light his material sheds on their schemes (1956:Chapter II). He feels that comparative studies are necessary, for without them "we have just a long succession of descriptive field monographs which in the absence of theory bear little relation to each other" (1967:177).

Although he calls for comparative studies, he does not conceive them the same way Radcliffe-Brown did (see especially 1960:12ff.; 1963, in 1965b:13ff.), and the reason seems to be his rejection of positivism. Radcliffe-Brown analyzed social systems by relating their component features to the exigencies of the social structure. For example, he explained the joking relationship in terms of the need to stabilize an inherently brittle social tie. He next viewed the isolated trait within the comparative dimension, since functionally similar institutions (or parts of institutions) are expressions of the same necessary principles. Given Radcliffe-Brown's framework, a feature such as a joking relationship could be viewed just as meaningfully within this comparative dimension as it could within the social context from which it was extracted.

According to Evans-Prtichard, institutions are not based upon functional exigencies, cross-cultural or otherwise, and both history and society are characterized by more contingency than Radcliffe-Brown allowed for. An explanation of the elements of social life is not achieved by Radcliffe-Brown's analytical method, but only by viewing these elements within the contexts in which they occur in society. Consequently, Evans-Pritchard is opposed to the wide-ranging comparative analyses attempted by Radcliffe-Brown and others, largely because these studies necessarily wrench the data from the contexts in which they belong. He calls instead for what he terms intensive comparative studies, which are conducted on a limited scale and in which the comparison involves societies that are basically quite similar. Studies such as these, he writes, "would seem to offer the best opportunity for detailed and controlled comparative treatment" (1963, in 1965b:27). Moreover, he is apparently looking for "narrow range low level conclusions" and not the broad generalizations attempted by writers like Radcliffe-Brown (1967: 179). What seems to be in the back of his mind is to retain as much of the social context as possible without giving up the comparative method altogether.

A question which is difficult to avoid concerns the nature of the general conclusions which comparative research is to develop. If history and society are subject to a good deal of contingency, and if institutions are not analyzable into universal or recurrent functional exigencies like those which Radcliffe-Brown envisaged, what is the basis for assuming that general

conclusions will ever emerge? What is the cross-cultural principle which brings about similarities of the kind which Evans-
Pritchard seeks? Perhaps it is that man is a conscious and rational agent and that different people respond to similar
situations in like manner. However, it seems that this would be
an uncongenial position to someone who, like Evans-Pritchard,
has stressed the rich diversity of cultural worldviews and hence
the variability of human responses.

CONCLUSION

Perhaps one of the most important differences between Radcliffe-Brown and Evans-Pritchard is that they located the meaningfulness of institutions at different levels. To Evans-Pritchard, institutions make sense when viewed subjectively. Radcliffe-Brown would not have denied that this is true, but
he would have disagreed about its theoretical significance. The
essence of anthropological explanation, to Radcliffe-Brown, is
to reveal the functions of the various parts of the social system;
the credibility or reasonableness of subjective culture was of
secondary importance to him.

To Evans-Pritchard, the anthropologist begins his study by
understanding institutions at the level of the individual in society; he then moves to a more general plane by employing the
relational framework which allows him to view the system as a
whole. In place of Radcliffe-Brown's analytical and scientific
method, Evans-Pritchard employs an integrative approach—
whereby each part of the system is made intelligible by relating
it to the other parts. Not only is this consistent with his idealism, it is also compatible with his Boasian-like view of the interrelatedness of the parts of the social system.

Like Radcliffe-Brown, Evans-Pritchard uses the concept of
social structure and function in his work, but he modifies them
fundamentally. The function of an institution is not its contribution to an ulterior end, but is simply one kind of relation

which that institution has with other parts of the system. The function concept loses much of the significance it had in Radcliffe-Brown's scheme, and the same is true of the social structure concept. Social structure is no longer the necessary framework for analysis, since the problem of the persistence of society is not the explanatory principle behind institutions. The social structural approach is employed simply because it is a useful way to organize and view one's data.

There are also differences between Evans-Pritchard's and Radcliffe-Brown's images of man, or at least between their views about the role of man in society. Perhaps Radcliffe-Brown did not conceive man as an automaton, as Evans-Pritchard believes. Perhaps Radcliffe-Brown's theory, although focusing upon the highly standardized aspects of the social system, left considerable room for the free play of individuality (see Fortes 1955:23ff.). Nevertheless, it was unimportant to his theory whether or not the human being is a conscious and rational agent, whereas Evans-Pritchard seems to place human consciousness and intelligence in the center of his scheme and to build around them. To Evans-Pritchard, man plays a role in the operation of the social system which Radcliffe-Brown either denied or ignored.

In sum, Evans-Pritchard believes that Radcliffe-Brown's framework leads us to miss the sense or meaning of human affairs; Radcliffe-Brown imposed on the data characteristics which were not there, and then he paid little attention to what was essential. To Evans-Pritchard, institutions express human ideas and values, not utilitarian principles; they are made intelligible by discovering the thought which is within them, not by locating the functions they perform.

VI

CULTURE AND MAN'S
INBORN CHARACTER

BRONISLAW MALINOWSKI

Radcliffe-Brown's and Malinowski's theories grew out of the same intellectual milieu. They were of the same generation— not only in age (they were born three years apart), but also in terms of the period in which they entered the discipline. Radcliffe-Brown undertook graduate studies in anthropology at Cambridge in 1904, and Malinowski's formal training began in 1910 at the London School of Economics. Moreover, at that time only a handful in England were seriously engaged in anthropological research, and most of them were located within a comparatively short distance of one another, at London, Cambridge, and Oxford. Anyone trained in British anthropology during that period was subjected to the same intellectual stimuli and was influenced by the same group of scholars, including A. C. Haddon, W. H. R. Rivers, and C. G. Seligman, among others.

Another parallel between Malinowski and Radcliffe-Brown is that both expressed considerable esteem for Durkheim early in their careers. Radcliffe-Brown's almost total conversion to Durkheimian theory took place in about 1909–10. Malinowski never fully committed himself to the French school, but by the time he published his first book, *The Family Among the Australian Aborigines* (1913), his debt to Durkheim was both patent and explicit (see especially 1913:192 n., 300–1). In the same year Malinowski published a review of Durkheim's *Elementary Forms of the Religious Life,* and, although it was not altogether favorable, he referred to the author as "one of the acutest and most brilliant living sociologists" (1913, in 1962:288).

Radcliffe-Brown's enthusiasm for the French school never slackened, whereas Durkheim's influence on Malinowski was only temporary. In the *Argonauts of the Western Pacific,* published in 1922, Malinowski hardly mentions Durkheim. Even his earliest works show little *fundamental* influence of the French sociologist. Malinowski's theory instead elaborates certain ideas about human behavior and culture which pervaded British anthropology during the first few decades of this century. Even at the beginning of his career in anthropology the gulf separating his thought from Durkheim's was considerable, and in developing his scheme he eventually arrived at an image of man, culture, and society which is radically non-Durkheimian and markedly different from anything considered so far.

INTRODUCTION

Bronislaw Malinowski was born in Cracow, Poland, in 1884. His parents were of the landed gentry and nobility, and he himself inherited the title of Count (although he declined to use it). His father was a professor, and the young Bronislaw decided that he, too, would pursue an academic career. He studied mathematics and physical sciences at the University of Cracow, receiving the Ph.D. *summa cum laude* in 1908. Ill health prevented him from engaging in research after he completed his degree, but while recuperating he read Frazer's *The*

Golden Bough. He writes, "no sooner had I begun to read this great work, than I became immersed in it and enslaved by it" (1926, in 1948:94). He then decided to devote himself to the science of anthropology. He went first to the University of Leipzig to work under Karl Bücher and Wilhelm Wundt, but in 1910 he decided to move to England where anthropology was much better established. He studied at the London School of Economics under C. G. Seligman and E. Westermarck, among others, and conducted library research on the Australian aborigines.

In 1913 he became a lecturer at the London School of Economics, and in the following year left for the Pacific with the Robert Mond expedition. He did not return to Europe until after the war, in 1920. Because he was an Austrian subject, he was technically an enemy alien when the conflict broke out; but throughout World War I he was allowed to pursue his research and to remain in Australia during the intervals between expeditions, and as a result he was able to complete the most detailed study ever made of an exotic society. He first spent about six months studying the inhabitants of Mailu, a small island located off the southeast coast of New Guinea. He then shifted his research to the Trobriand Islands, located about 100 miles northeast of New Guinea. He spent approximately twenty-six months with the Trobrianders, and in doing so he set a new precedent for field research:

he actually pitched his tent in the middle of the village, learned the language in its colloquial form, and observed directly at first hand just how his Trobriand neighbors behaved throughout the 24 hours of an ordinary working day. No European had ever done this before and the kind of ethnography that resulted was completely new (Leach, in Malinowski 1935, I:ix).

Because of Malinowski's skill and industriousness as a field anthropologist and his productivity as a writer, the Trobrianders are among the most fully reported of all primitive peoples.

Upon returning to England in 1920 Malinowski again took a

position at the London School of Economics, and in 1927 he was appointed to the newly created chair of anthropology. He continued at this position until 1938, making London his home. He also traveled widely on the Continent and in the United States, both touring and lecturing; and once he flew across Africa visiting his students who were in the field. Moreover, he "hurried each vacation [from London] to the more congenial atmosphere of the Tyrol," where he maintained a villa (Richards 1943:1).

In 1938 Malinowski decided to spend his sabbatical leave in the United States. He taught briefly at Yale, and he engaged in research among Indians in Arizona and Oaxaca, Mexico. He was about to return to London in 1939 when war broke out once more, and friends advised him that it would be safer to remain in this country. He accepted an appointment at Yale, where he died in 1942.

Soon after returning to London after the First World War Malinowski became a towering figure in British anthropology, and virtually everyone who was trained in that country during the 1920s and 1930s came under his influence. He was a demanding but enthusiastic teacher; he viewed himself "as the leader of a revolutionary movement in anthropology; and such was his magnetism, his wit and his virtuosity that he made us, his pupils, fall in eagerly with that view" (Fortes, in Firth, ed., 1960:157). He could also be intolerant of criticism, insensitive to another's feelings, and prejudiced. He made enemies as well as followers.

Relations between Malinowski and Radcliffe-Brown were strained. This was possibly due in part to a personality clash, for they were both strong-willed. It was also due in part to their rivalry within the field, as well as to their fundamental theoretical disagreements. Radcliffe-Brown was in England comparatively little from the time he entered anthropology until the time he assumed the chair at Oxford in 1937, but his influence was keenly felt nevertheless. During the 1940s it became clear that in theoretical matters it was his viewpoint which would prevail in British anthropology (Richards, in Firth, ed., 1960:26–30; Gluckman 1963:244–52).[1]

The problem of the nature of man was a residual issue in Radcliffe-Brown's scheme. In his view, the social system is based upon its own distinctive principles and can be understood without reference to the nature of the individual members of society. Almost the exact opposite is true of the work of Malinowski, who wrote, "The most important thing for the student, in my opinion, is never to forget the living, palpitating flesh and blood organism of man which remains somewhere at the heart of every institution" (1934:xxxi).

Malinowski had an abiding interest in what he sometimes referred to as the "psychological principles" behind social institutions, or the factors which drive or move the human actor in society. The branch of anthropological thought with which he is identified—and which he helped pioneer—was the functional approach, and the type of functionalism he espoused rested on the premise that social institutions ultimately serve the interests or needs of the individual members of society and that they must be seen from that perspective. Malinowski brought the individual into his analysis in a way which was totally illegitimate to Radcliffe-Brown (e.g., see Radcliffe-Brown 1946); moreover, because he drew social institutions and the individual into such a close relationship in his scheme, the image of man contained in his work cannot be ignored if his thought is to be properly understood.

MALINOWSKI'S IMAGE OF MAN

Malinowski's image of man has several ingredients; one of the most dominant is what Durkheim would have referred to as a monistic conception of human nature.

[1] For accounts of Malinowski's life and work, see especially Association of Polish University Professors, 1943; Firth 1942; Firth, ed., 1960; Gluckman

MONISM AND BEHAVIOR. It will be helpful to review some points already made concerning the distinction between monistic and dualistic views of behavior. Tylor and Spencer were monists, for they conceived culture as a human creation; to them, culture is derived from, expresses, and is consistent with man's nature. In response, Durkheim contended that the human being is largely (though not entirely) formed by the collective milieu and that the collective representations which the individual acquires in society constrain him to transcend himself. There is a fundamental cleavage between the natural and social aspects of the personality; man has a dual nature. Boas and Benedict exceeded Durkheim's views by tacitly assuming that the individual is so thoroughly transformed by culture that there is virtually nothing of the natural self remaining in the normal, enculturated individual. They introduced a new form of monism, although it had more in common with the Durkheimian view of the transcendence of the collective life than with the reductionism of Tylor and Spencer.

Malinowski's monistic view of behavior resembled Tylorian reductionism more than Boasian determinism. In Malinowski's view, culture is consistent with man's nature for the most part —neither is there a breach between the two, as Durkheim contended, nor is man's natural self virtually obliterated, as Boas and Benedict implied. Sometimes Malinowski even tried to explain the origin of institutions by reference to man's inborn character. Nevertheless, he did not do so consistently, and from the early 1920s, at least, he shunned searching for the origins of institutions in preference for an analysis of the way they work. There was one principle that he was consistent about, however, and this may be regarded as the most critical feature of his monism: regardless how an institution may have come about, once in existence it serves as a vehicle for the expression of

1963:207–52; Jarvie 1967; Kluckhohn 1943; Leach 1958, 1966; Murdock 1943; Powell 1960; Richards 1943; Uberoi 1962. See also the references cited in Firth, ed., 1960:271–72.

man's nature. The motivation behind the individual's participation in a cultural system consists largely in ambition, self-interest, and the like. Culture is not imposed on the individual, nor must his personality be fundamentally modified if he is to accept the privations which it entails.

Malinowski's emphasis on inborn tendencies is consonant with the personality theories which helped shape his thought. He was influenced by a wide variety of psychological schools during his lifetime: for example, he was attracted to Wundt very early in his career, and to behaviorism many years later. But the most fundamental and subtle influence of all seems to have come from Alexander F. Shand, a British psychologist whose ideas enjoyed wide favor during the first few decades of this century. Both Westermarck and William McDougall, among others, borrowed from his scheme. Shand's theory of sentiments first appeared in 1896, and his *Foundations of Character* was published in 1914. Malinowski was apparently acquainted with Shand's work while in the Trobriands (1967:264 [for clarification see *ibid.*, p. xxi]), and Shand's influence on Malinowski was apparently at its peak during the mid- to late-1920s (e.g., see 1927b:18, 155–57, 207–9). Raymond Firth, who became Malinowski's student at London in 1924, writes that "At the time I first knew Malinowski, Shand's *Foundations of Character* . . . was one of his household books" (in Firth, ed., 1960:7).

Shand and Malinowski had very similar conceptions of human motivation. According to Shand, instincts or innate dispositions are among the mainsprings of human behavior. Shand refers to the instinctive systems of fear, for example, and the various tendencies which make up the parental instinct. Whether or not Malinowski was influenced by this aspect of Shand's thought is difficult to say, but clearly he did accept it.[2]

---

[2] Malinowski also employed Shand's idea that the human "character" or personality is composed of many impulses and emotions which are organized into sentiments. According to Malinowski, this organization is fostered by culture,

Malinowski frequently referred to the work of William McDougall (e.g., 1927b:155), whose ideas about the instinctive basis of human behavior are even better known than Shand's. In 1921 Malinowski wrote a favorable review of McDougall's *The Group Mind,* and he refers to McDougall as "a pioneer in the domain of instinct and emotion and their influence on custom and belief" (1921b:109).

Malinowski was also attracted briefly to Freudian thought, which, like the theories of Shand and McDougall, places a heavy emphasis on inborn qualities. Seligman introduced Freudian theory to Malinowski while he was in the field, and Malinowski published several articles which dealt with his Trobriand data from a psychoanalytical point of view (Malinowski 1924b, 1925b; see also 1923, in 1962:114–16).[3]

Malinowski's image of man emerges quite clearly in his *Argonauts of the Western Pacific,* and by concentrating on this book it will be possible to place his monistic view of behavior within the context of the development of his thought and to set the stage for a more detailed analysis of his views.

The *Argonauts* was written shortly after Malinowski returned to England from his field expeditions in the Pacific, and it was published in 1922. It is primarily an account of the kula ring, an elaborate system of trading linking the peoples of eastern New Guinea and the neighboring archipelagoes. The principal items of exchange are ceremonial objects—necklaces and arm bands—which are highly prized but which have no utilitarian value, and which are passed between regular trade partners during more or less elaborate and extensive kula expeditions. Malinowski devoted the largest portion of his book to the Trobrianders' role in the kula system.

---

which directs and stimulates the natural tendencies and channels them in the appropriate directions (1927b:207). An example is the couvade, which is supposed to organize the father's sentiments toward his offspring.

[3] These articles were slightly revised to form Parts I and II of *Sex and Repression* (1927b), but by the time he wrote the last portion of this book he fully dissociated himself from psychoanalysis (1927b:6–7).

The focus of this work was cultural and not psychological, and yet Malinowski tried persistently to get beneath the surface of custom (beneath "the definite, crystallized legal frame" [1922b:19–20]) in order to discover the motives and feelings which governed the people in their everyday lives. As Frazer wrote in the Preface, Malinowski "sees man, so to say, in the round and not in the flat" (1922b:ix).

This interest in motives appears quite early in Malinowski's work and seems to have been a stimulus behind much of his field research. In November, 1917, while stopping briefly on the small island of Samarai (off the eastern tip of New Guinea), he wrote the following in his diary: "What is the deepest essence of my investigations? To discover what are his [the native's] main passions, the motives for his conduct, his aims. . . . His essential, deepest way of thinking" (1967:119).

One of the principal goals of the *Argonauts* was to revise the ideas then current in the literature about the economic motivations of savages. The common view depicted the primitive as guided primarily "by the desire to satisfy his wants" (p. 62), but more generally as "lazy, individualistic and selfish" (p. 175). It was assumed that the savage would expend only the minimum effort necessary in order to satisfy his immediate wants (pp. 6off.), and that he loathed sharing anything he had troubled to acquire (pp. 96ff.). He was supposed to want "nothing but to satisfy his simplest needs and [to do] it according to the economic principle of least effort" (p. 516).

Malinowski argued that Trobriand economics do not operate according to strict utilitarian principles: the Trobriander does not rationally calculate his material interests or set out to satisfy them in the most economical way, for he adheres to traditional usages and customary procedures. He does not produce just enough food to eat, but grossly overproduces and exhibits the results of his labor in lavish displays. Funerals entail ostentatious food exhibitions, for example, and the wealthy Trobrianders display their yams throughout the year in comparatively elaborate storehouses. The quantity of food contained in these bins is a matter of considerable pride, and the best or most impressive tubers are placed to the outside where they can be appreciated (pp. 166–73). About three quarters of a man's yam crop is given away, partly to his chief and partly to kinsmen (p. 61). He gives most of what he grows to the household of his married sister, with whom he has little direct contact due to a stringent brother-sister avoidance relationship. The Trobriander also expends considerable effort solely to make his gardens attractive: he does more than is necessary in clearing them of debris, and he divides each plot into small squares measuring only a few yards in length and width, even though this is completely unnecessary on practical grounds (pp. 58–59).

In the Trobriand Islands, at least, the people are not governed primarily by unfettered self-interest and petty selfishness; rather, "the real force which binds all the people and ties them down in their tasks is obedience to custom, to tradition" (p. 158). In a resume of lectures Malinowski gave at the London School of Economics in 1920, he wrote that in the Trobriands "we find a state of affairs where production, exchange and consumption are socially organized and regulated by custom, and where a special system of traditional economic values governs their activities and spurs them on to efforts" (1921a:15).

Malinowski's argument concerning economic incentives grows in significance when seen in the context of the development of his own thought. He may have been debating not only against what others had to say about the savage, but against himself, or against the views which he had held before his field work. In one of his earliest publications, written during the period in which he was studying anthropology at London prior to his first field expedition, Malinowski noted that savages are not capable of the forethought, self-restraint, and effort required by civilized economic life. The savage's "attitude at work approaches much more nearly our attitude at play or sport"

(1912:104). Civilized forms of labor "are normally repugnant to his nature" (p. 105). In a book review written at about the same time, he commented that "the savage's mode of working is pre-eminently irregular, unsystematic and desultory" (1914a).

It was apparently as a result of his field experiences that Malinowski changed his mind. In the monograph which he wrote after his first field expedition (to the island of Mailu) he notes that the people there are quite capable of hard labor, and that some of them "actually like work" (1915:629–31). His field work also persuaded him "of the complete futility of the theories which attribute to the savage a different type of mind and different logical faculties" (1916, in 1948:273, n. 75). Malinowski may have found the subjects of his researches irritating and offensive at times, as passages in his diary suggest (e.g. 1967:272–73), but clearly he acquired a respect for their capabilities which he did not have earlier.

The development of Malinowski's ideas about the processes of thought and motivations of savage peoples raises tantalizing questions concerning his role in the development of twentieth-century views about race and human behavior, for upon returning to London after his field work he exhibited a much keener appreciation for the role of culture as a factor in both thought and action. Another set of questions is even more critical for the present discussion, however: if Malinowski established the idea that the savage is governed not primarily by pure self-interest and native intelligence, but by custom, what is the grounding of this custom? What are the bases for the savage's adherence to traditional usages? Malinowski's monistic view of behavior is clearly revealed by the way in which he approached this issue.

Statements can be gleaned from Malinowski's writings which appear to offer totally contradictory views about the grounding of custom. On one hand, he frequently seems to suggest that people acquire respect or esteem for their traditions by learning. Although this idea appears in the *Argonauts,* it is even more explicit in other works which appeared at about the same time. For example, in a book review published two years after the *Argonauts,* Malinowski wrote of "a number of traditional motives" which have "been inculcated" in men (1924a:81). Elsewhere he wrote that "the automatic, self-acting moral rule is of the greatest importance for forming the very foundations of primitive organization and culture," and he makes it clear that these moral rules are taught (1925, in 1948:67). In still another place he wrote of certain ideals being "impressed upon the mind," and of the "moulding and gradual inculcation of ideals" (1927b:203).

On the other hand, it is clear that Malinowski placed most of his emphasis upon another principle, which is that custom is not rooted in a process of learning at all but is grounded in innate or natural tendencies of the human mind. It is in this sense that his is a monistic interpretation of behavior. The following are a few examples drawn from the *Argonauts:* Malinowski speaks of a "natural acquisitive tendency" in man (1922b:96), a "love of accumulation for its own sake" (p. 173), a "deep desire to possess" (p. 510), a "love of give and take for its own sake" (p. 173), and a "fundamental human impulse to display, to share, to bestow" (p. 175). According to Malinowski, inborn tendencies or impulses such as these are at the basis of a good deal of cultural behavior, including the kula exchange. The Trobriander is driven to engage and compete in this system of ceremonial trading not primarily because of the inculcation of cultural values, but because of such inborn tendencies as these. Similarly, the overproduction and accumulation of yams among the Trobrianders, and the generous gifts of agricultural goods to kinsmen, are motivated largely by the same impulses.

Perhaps the best illustration of Malinowski's propensity for viewing behavior in terms of inborn tendencies is his analysis of the father-son relationship, which appeared in the *Argonauts* and was elaborated upon in other publications (e.g., 1922b:

179–80, 1926c:100–11, 1927b:183–90, 1929:94–103). According to Malinowski, a father has a natural fondness or affection for his child, and this is illustrated with particular poignancy among the Trobriand Islanders because of their matriliny. Descent, authority, and inheritance follow the maternal line in the Trobriand Islands, and consequently a child's maternal uncle is particularly important to him. It is the maternal uncle, not the father, who wields authority over the child, and it is the maternal uncle from whom the young man will inherit. In the idiom of Trobriand culture, the father is a "stranger" to his children, since the child's most important kinship ties are on his mother's side. The child's father has sororal nephews of his own who are not only under his authority but who will inherit his wealth when he dies. Malinowski emphasized that the Trobriand father not uncommonly tries to circumvent the institutionalized rules of inheritance by offering gifts to his children prior to his death. In short, the father's natural attachment to his own children is expressed by a desire to benefit them instead of his sister's sons and daughters.

A discussion of the *Argonauts* cannot be complete without mentioning what to Malinowski was one of the most important motivating forces in Trobriand society: ambition and the desire for social renown. This discussion must be deferred until later in the chapter, however, for reasons which will become apparent.

KINSHIP AND THE MONISTIC VIEW OF BEHAVIOR. Malinowski's analysis of the father-son relationship in the Trobriands played a comparatively incidental role in the over-all scheme of the *Argonauts,* but it appears prominently in his general theory of kinship. I shall now consider this theory in detail, for it is a telling illustration of his views about the grounding of culture.

The key element of Malinowski's theory of kinship is the family, which he described as early as 1914 as the elemental building stone of society (1914b:1080).[4] Among all mammals, he notes, the helplessness of the infant and the burden of motherhood make the continuing care of an adult male necessary. In nonhuman species the relationship is established by instincts. But "instincts alone never determine human behaviour" (1927b:189), for the instincts of man are quite plastic. This plasticity permits a greater variety of responses to the same set of situations and thereby facilitates more adequate forms of adaptation. Man's instinctive patterns of response have been replaced largely by culture, although the innate tendencies have by no means disappeared. Malinowski does not express himself in these terms, but he implies that instinct provides the motivation, whereas culture provides the form which the response takes (see 1927b:161–238). For example, Malinowski notes that natural endowment does not provide man with concrete forms of behavior by which to express the natural concern and affection which he feels toward his child, and instead it is culture which does so. The couvade, for example, "provides the necessary stimulus and expression for paternal tendencies" (p. 189). The rites and taboos which make up the couvade focus the father's attention on the child and stimulate his interest in it, but "once forced into this position, the male responds invariably with strong interests and positive feelings for the offspring" (p. 187).

Malinowski offers a similar analysis of the mother-child relationship. Among all mammals "there exists a passionate instinctive interest of the mother in the child," although in the case of

---

[4] Due to the influence of Westermarck, Malinowski stressed the importance of the family from the very beginning of his work in anthropology: "The subject of kinship, and above all the fact that it invariably originates in the family, was the starting point of my anthropological work" (1930, in 1962:153, n. 5). His first book was *The Family Among the Australian Aborigines*, published in 1913, an important attack on the view that the original domestic organization of mankind was based on the principle of group marriage (Fortes, in Firth, ed., 1960:158). Malinowski's book presented convincing evidence that the domestic group among the Australians—who were regarded as one of the simplest peoples known—was the nuclear or biological family, composed of mother, father, and offspring.

human beings this interest is not left solely to the instincts. Rather, "society hastens to step in and add its at first feeble decree to the powerful force of nature." The pregnant woman must keep certain taboos and observances, for example, and she may perform rites which are intended to promote the welfare of the unborn infant. Among the Trobrianders an elaborate ceremony is performed at a woman's first pregnancy, and following birth the mother and child are secluded together for about a month (1927b:29–33, 184–85). Culture focuses and stimulates the natural motivations and provides the form for their expression, but this does not deny that the mother's commitment to her role is based ultimately upon a natural disposition.

Of particular importance for the kinship system are the child's emotional reactions toward the mother and father. The child's bonds with the mother are very strong and are firmly rooted in biology (e.g., Malinowski 1927b:29). Malinowski writes, "the child responds with an exclusive personal attachment to the mother, and the mutual bond remains one of the strongest sentiments in any human society" (1930, in 1962:46). Throughout life the son or daughter regards the mother with an attitude of tenderness and affection.

The child's sentiments toward the father are somewhat more complicated, although still rooted in natural tendencies. In our society, and in those which are based on the principle of patriliny, the father's position vis-a-vis his children includes two aspects. The first, that of protector, derives from natural paternal affection: the father's attachment to his children impels him to look after them. This aspect of the father-child relationship is characterized by tenderness and warmth. The second is that of authority, for if the family is to adequately fulfill its educational function there is need for authority and discipline within the household. The father must be "the lawgiver within the family" (1927b:224; see pp. 191–93). The combination of these two aspects in the father means that he must be both "tender friend and rigid guardian of law" (p. 231), which results in the phenomenon which Freud identified but misunderstood: the Oedipus complex. The child displays ambivalence toward his father, but this is not due to a sexual desire for the mother and a deep-seated jealousy over the father's access to her, as Freud contended. It expresses the child's natural reaction toward someone who combines the roles of protector and lawgiver.

In matrilineal societies the roles of protector and lawgiver are divided (see 1927b:22–39, 45–51, 71–77, 218–33), for in these societies it is the maternal uncle who is in a position of authority over the child. In the Trobriands, the child learns at an early age that he belongs to his mother's kin group, upon which his station in life depends, and that he must display respect and obedience toward his principal within that group, the maternal uncle. He also learns that his father is someone with whom he can share a warm and intimate relationship:

To the father, therefore, the children look only for loving care and tender companionship. Their mother's brother represents the principle of discipline, authority, and executive power within the family (1927b:24).

The sentiments which develop toward the father in patrilineal societies, and toward the father and maternal uncle in matrilineal societies, are natural responses: for example, the impulse to clash with and to rival the lawgiver is natural and is not taught or imposed by culture.

Both the patterns of behavior and the sentiments upon which the kinship system is based are extensions of these inborn tendencies which are rooted in family ties. The family is the mainspring and source of the bonds linking kinsmen. As the child passes beyond infancy he comes into contact with members of other households. Among the most important of these people, according to Malinowski, is the mother's sister, who often assists the mother and sometimes replaces her in case of illness or death. The child experiences an intimacy with his mother's sister like that which he has with his mother, and as a result the maternal aunt becomes the focus of sentiments in the child's mind which are similar (but not identical) to those which attach to the mother. In many societies the mother and mother's sister are referred to by the same kin term, so the mother-child relationship is extended to the mother's sister at the linguistic and conceptual level as well as that of sentiments.

Other extensions of the bonds of kinship take place. The father's brother may become a substitute father, and in patrilineal societies his sister may become a substitute mother (1929, in 1962:141–48). According to Malinowski, "Kinship invariably begins in the family" (1929, in 1962:145): "The household is thus the workshop where kinship ties are forged, and the constitution of the individual family supplies the pattern upon which they are built" (1929, in 1962–141).

The sentiments and motivations behind the bonds of kinship are largely inborn tendencies. If the individual is conscientious in discharging his kinship obligations—such as extending economic assistance in time of need, providing political support in time of conflict, or simply offering the normal, day-to-day courtesies which are expected between kinsmen—it is not solely because of an acquired commitment to a set of cultural ideas and patterns of action.

Isolated hints in Malinowski's work suggest that his analysis of family and kinship had applications beyond the limits of the kinship system. Even in his earliest publications he indicated that he felt the household played a critical role in society, but as his theory of kinship developed this idea began to acquire more definite shape. Malinowski eventually arrived at the view that the family is not only the basis of kinship sentiments, but that it is also the source of interpersonal relations of all kinds, at least in primitive societies:

[The social anthropologist] must establish the final triumph of parenthood as the only stable force working right throughout life, as the pattern of most relations, as the foundation on which even the religious cults and dogmatic conceptions of a community are based (1930, in 1962:70).

In primitive societies the individual does build up all his social ties upon the pattern of his relation to father and mother, to brother and sister. . . . Thus the endurance of family ties beyond maturity is the pattern of all social organization, and the condition of co-operation in all economic, religious, and magical matters. . . . [S]ocial bonds . . . must have been derived from the development of the only relationship which man has taken over from his animal ancestors: the relationship between husband and wife, between parents and children, between brothers and sisters, in short the relationship of the undivided family (1927b:194; see also 1929, in 1962:146; 1930, in 1962:158).

Malinowski goes on to assert that the social bonds which develop in society are not wholly innate and that in this respect culture "steps beyond instinctive endowment" (1927b:194–95). Nevertheless, it is clear that in his view these bonds are not without an important innate aspect, for they are extensions of natural, inborn sentiments into new and diverse contexts.

The difference between Malinowski's and Radcliffe-Brown's approaches to kinship is revealing. Radcliffe-Brown held that the kinship system cannot be explained by reference to how people naturally *feel* toward one another, for kinship usages are imposed from without: they are defined and regulated by jural rules which are maintained by a system of effective sanctions. The whole system of usages reflects, not personal feelings, but the structural exigencies of society. Kinship is to be seen in relation to structural alignments and cleavages, political relations, and the like, and not in terms of the inborn characteristics of the personality system.

INTERESTS AND THE MONISTIC VIEW OF BEHAVIOR. Malinowski's foregoing views on natural tendencies or motivations have led to a dead-end in anthropology: his theory of kinship was virtually stillborn, for example, in contrast to Radcliffe-Brown's, which has given rise to a vigorous program of research. On the other hand, some natural dispositions which appear in Malinowski's work—and which we have yet to consider—are far from outmoded, and may even be gaining in acceptance.

Malinowski did not explicitly distinguish between these two classes of motivation, and yet they are substantially different from one another. The first—those which I have considered above—are of the nature of predispositions, for they constitute inclinations to behave in a certain way in a given context. The second are a form of interests, for they consist in a desire to further one's own advantages. A principal difference between the two is that the interests evoke a comparatively cynical view of human behavior, whereas the predispositions do not. For example, the mother's affection for her offspring—a predisposition— is a relatively straightforward impulse and gives rise to little calculation or scheming. The same is true of the relationship between father and child (except that in favoring his child the father sometimes infringes on others' rights). Even the clash between child and lawgiver is presented by Malinowski with little emphasis on the cunning or guile in which the child may feel moved to indulge. On the other hand, an interest consists of a desire to profit oneself even at the expense of others. Whenever Malinowski touched upon this class of motivations he tended to represent the individual as a self-interested calculator of advantage, rationally manipulating the objects of gratification and weighing the alternatives open to him.

These two types of motivation—predispositions and interests—entail fundamentally different conceptions of the relationship between the individual and culture. The idea of predispositions implies that institutions manifest or express the individual's nature, in the way that the institutionalized role of the father manifests the man's natural inclinations toward his offspring. On the other hand, the idea of interests implies a utilitarian relationship between individual and culture: the individual finds the institution useful to him, and that is why he accepts or adheres to it.

Furthermore, the interests are more prone than the predispositions to engender competition between the members of society, for a person's interests lead him to seek "scarce goods" which are desired by others as well. When Malinowski referred to the interests, then, he stressed that contention, rivalry, and controversy are characteristic of the social system.

There are two contexts in particular in which interests appear in Malinowski's work. The first is in his discussions of ambition and social honor, and the second is in his analyses of law and reciprocity.

A theme which runs throughout the *Argonauts* is that the Trobrianders are characterized by a strong desire for renown and social esteem, and that this desire is the principal motivation behind Trobriand economics and the kula system. Malinowski reports that the overproduction of garden crops in the Trobriands is due primarily to a concern for social distinction; a successful harvest brings "much praise and renown" to the gardener, and a lavish display of yams brings prestige to its owner (pp. 60–62, 166–73). Similarly, the kula trade objects are not valued on purely utilitarian grounds, Malinowski remarks, but largely for the renown they bring (pp. 88–91, 94–95); he writes that it is "through being the means of arousing envy and conferring social distinction and renown, that these objects attain their high value" (p. 511). To the Trobrianders, "to possess is to be great" (p. 97). The act of giving is also motivated largely by a desire for esteem, for generosity brings renown (p. 97, 174–75). One of the main bases of the chief's position in Trobriand society is his wealth, most of which he does not consume but which he redistributes to his people (pp. 64–65).

Prestige and renown are "scarce goods," for an individual's social position will suffer relative to the success of another.

Hence, in addition to representing the Trobrianders as having a strong interest in social honor, Malinowski regarded them as relatively competitive in their interpersonal relations. Speaking of the participants in the kula, Malinowski writes:

It is obvious that, however much a man may want to give a good equivalent for the object received [in the kula exchange], he may not be able to do so. And then, as there is always a keen competition to be the most generous giver, a man who has received less than he gave will not keep the grievance to himself, but will brag about his own generosity and compare it to his partner's meanness; the other resents it, and the quarrel is ready to break out (1922b:97–98).

There are suggestions that Malinowski thought the desire to gain prestige and to avoid humiliation constituted an important motivation behind the adherence to custom of all kinds, including sexual mores. In a discussion about the Trobrianders' views concerning sexual aberrations Malinowski writes,

To ask a man seriously whether he had indulged in such practices would deeply wound his vanity and self-regard, as well as shock his natural inclination. Vanity would be especially wounded, by the implication that he must be unable to procure the full natural enjoyment of his impulse if he has to resort to such substitutes. The Trobriander's contempt for any perversion is similar to his contempt for the man . . . who suffers hunger because there is nothinng in his yamhouse (1929:469–70).

The second important context in which Malinowski's cynical view of human behavior appears is in his discussions of law and reciprocity.[5] Malinowski strongly opposed those who contended that savages "automatically" accept the rules and laws of their society; he rejected the

[5] Malinowski's analysis of the basis of law was initiated when he was invited to present a paper before the Royal Institution of Great Britain in 1925 (Malinowski 1925a). He later published several other essays on the topic, the most important of which are his *Crime and Custom in Savage Society* (1926c) and his introduction to Hogbin's *Law and Order in Polynesia* (Malinowski 1934). See also 1925c, 1926a, 1936, and 1942.

assumption that in primitive societies the individual is completely dominated by the group—the horde, the clan or the tribe—that he obeys the commands of his community, its traditions, its public opinion, its decrees, with a slavish, fascinated, passive obedience (1926c:3–4).

Malinowski attributed this assumption to Durkheim,[6] among others. I have indicated that in Durkheim's scheme the ultimate grounding of law consists in the disinterested and passionate commitment which people have to the moral life of their society. To Malinowski, however, primitive custom and law are grounded in reciprocity, based upon self-interest:

In the Trobriands I had found that people keep to what custom— or, more correctly, law—bids them to do because they know that not far ahead there looms the occasion when in the name of the same law they will be entitled to demand the counter-service (1934:xli).

The individual feels compelled to accept the legal maxims of his society and the legitimate claims of others for if he does not he will have to suffer sooner or later:

The serial balancing of services, the reciprocal interlocking of claims, which makes up the personal bond of husband and wife, of chief and subject, of economic partners, supplies the real compulsion for their respective contributions to the joint work or enterprise (1934:xxxv).

Malinowski offers the institution of chieftainship as an illustration of his ideas about law and reciprocity (1934:xxxviii–xxxix). He notes that it might appear to the unsympathetic observer that primitive societies are dominated by despotic rulers. He himself was impressed at first by the enormous tribute which the Trobriand chief received, by his prerog-

---

[6] Malinowski seriously distorted Durkheim's views about the way in which primitive people are dominated by custom. This is not to say that there was no substance to the differences which Malinowski saw between his own ideas and those of Durkheim, however.

atives, and by the conspicuous patterns of deference which the people owed him. The authority of the chiefs is so exaggerated that the British colonial administrators once felt that the power of the local officeholders should be reduced for the good of the people. However, after Malinowski had begun to understand Trobriand culture it became clear to him that the chief's prerogatives are not as one-sided as they seemed. In particular, the chief is not free to consume his tribute as he pleases, for much of his wealth must be redistributed on ceremonial occasions, and most of the rest is used to finance tribal undertakings. The chief's prerogatives are balanced by a set of duties, and the common man in Trobriand society, no less than the chief, derives advantages fron the system. Without the institution of chieftainship, Malinowski writes, the commoners in Trobriand society "would be deprived of most of the things which make life worth living for them."

Malinowski also cites the family to illustrate the basis of law (1934:liii–lv). As I have indicated, Malinowski believed that the bonds which link the family members are manifestations of natural sentiments of kinship; in addition, he held that the household is bound together by an interlocking system of reciprocities. For example, the parents sacrifice heavily for their children; and yet, Malinowski writes,

I am confident that wherever there are any data on this subject in literature it can be shown that parents are repaid by their children for the early cares by what might be termed various forms of old age insurance in filial duties (p. liii).

Children may also assume domestic and economic duties early in life. The marriage relationship itself entails "a constant flow of services, claims, gifts" between the kinsmen of the husband and wife.

In brief, people derive advantages from entering into social relations, and to a large extent this is why they adhere to the rules and legal principles which define these relations:

The man who would persistently disobey the rulings of law in his economic dealings would soon find himself outside the social and economic order—and he is perfectly well aware of it (1926c:41).

In Durkheim's theory the breach of custom or law in primitive society is an offense against moral sentiments and results in a strong and disinterested reaction against the culpable. However, if legal principles are held in place by the interests of the individual members of society, then an offense which harms no one will go unpunished. That Malinowski's thought was leading him in this direction is manifest by a case which he described. A young Trobriander was having sexual relations with one of his maternal relatives and was therefore violating one of the most basic moral principles of his society, the principle of clan exogamy. Although this affair was common knowledge in the community, and although it was disapproved of, nothing was done to prevent it. However, the girl had previously had a lover whom she was now ignoring, and he felt injured. He threatened to use black magic against his rival, but since this had no effect he accused and insulted the young man in public. The case took a dramatic turn at this point, for the breach of exogamy was now forced into the open where it could not be discreetly ignored, and the culpable was dishonored. The young man who was disgraced had no alternative but to commit suicide. Even as serious a crime as a breach of exogamy, then, does not result in punishment unless someone—"an interested party"—is injured by the act and is motivated to blow the whistle on the wrongdoer. In Malinowski's view, sanctions hardly work in the disinterested manner envisaged by Durkheim (1926c:77–80).

THE RELATIONSHIP BETWEEN ACQUIRED AND INBORN MOTIVATIONS. Earlier it was suggested that Malinowski employed two very different principles with regard to the grounding of custom. He held that culture is rooted in a process of learning on one hand, and in natural predispositions and interests on the other. It is necessary to show the relationship between these two seemingly contradictory principles.

Malinowski was explicit about the way he conceived this relationship. He writes that the Trobriander has "the greatest respect for his tribal custom and tradition as such," and that "the rules of his tribe . . . are regarded by him with reverence and felt to be obligatory." The Trobriander exhibits a disinterested, moral respect for his cultural norms. Nevertheless, Malinowski continues, "the force of custom, . . . if it stood alone, would not be enough to counteract the temptations of appetite or lust or the dictates of self-interest." The force of tradition alone is adequate to enforce manners and other customary usages, but it is effective only when it is not in conflict with the more basic, natural dispositions—that is, "where there is no need to encroach on self-interest, inertia or to prod into unpleasant action or thwart innate propensities." In brief, the principle of learning is of comparatively little theoretical importance in explaining the grounding of culture, for in important matters it is the natural response which prevails (1925c:234, 1926c:64–65; see also 1926a:14; 1926c:51–54; and 1927b: 174, 188). Malinowski writes,

direct knowledge of native life reveals the underlying strata of human conduct, moulded, it is true, by the rigid surface of custom, but still more deeply influenced by the smouldering fires of human nature (1929:505–6).

These views were not incidental to Malinowski's work; they are evident in an argument which he frequently raised, the argument that a large discrepancy usually exists between the ideals which people express and the actualities of their behavior, or between theory and practice (see Fortes, in Firth, ed., 1960:159–61). He writes that the most surprising upshot of his fieldwork was "the gradual perception of an undercurrent of desire and inclination running counter to the trend of conven-

tion, law and morals" (1927b:96). A principal concern of his
Sexual Life of Savages was

not only to state the norm [of Trobriand behavior], but to indicate
the exceptions, to trace what might be called the amplitude of de-
viation, the margin within which people usually try, and sometimes
succeed, in circumventing the strict rule (1929:281; see also pp.
294–95, 385–86, 505–14, 522, 538).

Malinowski notes that the Trobriander is exactly like a civilized business man, for whenever he "can evade his obligations
without the loss of prestige, or without the prospective loss of
gain, he does so" (1926c:30).

It might appear that Malinowski's views about the discrepancy between theory and practice contradict his monistic conception of behavior. In emphasizing this discrepancy is Malinowski not contrasting inculcated moral standards with
self-interest and personal dispositions? Is it not true that this
distinction between theory and practice rests upon the dualistic
assumption that conformity is motivated by a fundamentally
different set of factors from those which prompt deviance and
the evasion of custom?

However sensible this interpretation may be to someone
schooled in the Durkheimian tradition, I do not believe it is a
faithful rendering of Malinowski's thought. To Malinowski,
cultural ideals are grounded primarily in natural motivations.
People fulfill their legal obligations, adhere to kinship usages
and sexual standards, and overwork themselves in the economic
system because of personal inclinations, ambition, and self-interest; they do not do so primarily because of an inculcated,
disinterested, moral respect for the principles of their society.
In brief, conformity is a product of inborn predispositions and
interests—and entails calculation and the weighing of
alternatives—in the same way as deviance. The discrepancy between theory and practice in human behavior need not imply a
dualistic image of man at all.

EMOTION AND THE DYNAMIC NATURE OF BEHAVIOR. This discussion of Malinowski's monistic view of behavior suggests an important similarity between his ideas about human action and those of Spencer and Tylor, for all three conceived the individual as motivated primarily by natural interests and inclinations. The similarity is no accident, for historically this conception of behavior has been a basic principle of many British social, political, and economic thinkers, among whom Locke and Bentham are prominent.

Nevertheless, there is a fundamental difference between Malinowski on one hand and Tylor and Spencer on the other, a difference which reflects the fact that Malinowski's ideas belong to the twentieth and not the nineteenth century. Tylor and Spencer placed their emphasis on the intellect, the *means* by which the individual achieves his interests, and not on the interests or ends themselves. They derived social order and cohesion, cultural institutions, and human behavior from man's rational faculties and allowed the problem of man's motivations and emotions to remain a virtually unexplored, residual issue. In Malinowski's work, however, these emotional and motivational factors moved to the foreground, and he conceived man as governed primarily by emotional tendencies or forces and not by reason; moreover, he tended to regard reason as subordinate to, and the instrument of, the passions. To Malinowski, man is essentially an emotional and not a rational creature.

Malinowski's emphasis upon emotions is quite apparent in the *Argonauts*. He notes that when a group of men undertakes a kula expedition they are apprehensive about visiting their trade partners—who are members of an alien society—even though invited and expected by their hosts. Malinowski asks rhetorically why they should experience these fears, and he answers that the question assumes "a logical way of reasoning" whereas "custom is not logical." He writes,

the emotional attitude of man has a greater sway over custom than has reason. The main attitude of a native to other, alien groups is that of hostility and mistrust. The fact that to a native every stranger is an enemy, is an ethnographic feature reported from all parts of the world (1922b:345).

This conception of the role of emotion behind human behavior was shared by others who influenced Malinowski. In Shand's work the main forces behind the human character are emotional tendencies which influence perception, thought, and will. Shand notes that "every strong sentiment has a tendency to develop a strong will in its support" (1914:65), and he offers the following as a fundamental law of the human character: "All intellectual and voluntary processes are elicited by the system of some impulse, emotion, or sentiment, and are subordinated to its end" (1914:67).

Malinowski's view of the role of emotions and of their control over the intellect is particularly evident in his discussion of the belief in an afterlife. Like all men, the primitive has an intense fear of death—perhaps due to "some deep-seated instincts common to man and animals"—and the belief in a life after death provides comfort in the face of this terrifying emptiness. The belief is valuable as well, for it enables the individual to overcome his debilitating fears. A theory of immortality is not "a primitive philosophic doctrine" or an expression of rational thought; rather, "the substance of which the spirits are made is the full-blooded passion and desire for life." The senses seem to contradict these beliefs by testifying to "the gruesome decomposition of the corpse, the visible disappearance of the personality," but "religion steps in" and overrides the sensual experiences. The same beliefs which Tylor explained by means of intellectual processes are accounted for in terms of "the deepest emotional fact of human nature, the desire for life" (1925, in 1948:50–51).

Malinowski's analysis of magic is another illustration of the importance he ascribed to emotion in human behavior and culture. The Trobrianders believe that magic is an indispensable accompaniment of many of their activities; for example, they hold that their gardens will not grow unless the proper rites have been performed. Nevertheless, horticultural success is not attributed solely to magic, for the people know that if a crop is not adequately weeded and fenced, among other things, it will suffer. No one is foolish enough to rely on magic alone. What, then, is the context in which the individual resorts to ritual? In spite of the considerable technical knowledge which the Trobrianders have acquired, certain natural factors (such as weather and soil fertility) are beyond their control or understanding. The same plot of ground will produce substantially different yields from one year to the next according to variations in rainfall, temperature, and sunshine, and adjacent plots will differ consistently in productivity. It is these unpredictable aspects— "the unaccountable and adverse influences, as well as the great unearned increment of fortunate coincidence" (1925, in 1948:29)—to which magic applies.

Malinowski cites fishing among the Trobriand Islanders to illustrate his thesis. Fishing within the enclosed lagoon is easy, reliable, and safe, whereas fishing on the open sea is both dangerous and unpredictable. When the individual fishes on the lagoon he relies solely on his technical knowledge and skill, for he employs no magic whatever, but an extensive body of magical belief and technique is associated with the perils and vagaries of open-sea fishing (pp. 28–32).

Malinowski is emphatic that magic does not arise from some "abstract conception of universal power," such as the notion of mana. It is not a product of purely intellectual processes (p. 78). Rather, magic arises when there is a gap in man's knowledge—when the hunter fails to locate game, or when the sailor finds himself drifting in windless weather. The individual feels forsaken and baffled, but "his desire grips him only more strongly; his anxiety, his fears and hopes, induce a tension in his organism which drives him to some sort of activity" (p. 79). He reproduces the action which is suggested by his desire: for example, the man who is thwarted in love imagines that he addresses his loved one and that she accepts him. The tension is then partially relieved. Magic is an institutionalized manifestation of this spontaneous emotional response in man.

One reason why the individual continues to believe in magic even though it has no effect at all on crops, weather, and the like, is because the ritual relieves the person's anxieties and fears and he therefore *feels* that the performance has been efficacious. His thinking and perception are somewhat perverted by the emotional forces within him (pp. 79–84).

According to Malinowski, magic and primitive science are distinguished by the fact that magic is founded on emotion, whereas science is based on intellectual processes. Magic is associated with situations which provoke anxiety, while science occurs in the context of the predictable and commonplace. Unless Malinowski's discussion is read with care, it appears that he implies that the savage is quite rational and unemotional within the sphere of life in which he employs science. For example, Malinowski argued that the Trobrianders are intelligent and clear-headed in their grasp of the technical aspects of gardening, fishing, and canoe-building, and that the knowledge they have acquired is based upon empirical inquiry and logical inference. Their accomplishments are not distorted or perverted by a mystical and emotional mode of thought. He also notes that the Trobrianders make a distinction between magical causes and influences on one hand and natural ones on the other, and that they do not confound the two. Furthermore, according to Malinowski, every primitive society has its equivalent of the European naturalist, the man who engages in careful, empirical observations for their own sake and who then relates his conclusions to the other knowledge which he has acquired (1925, in 1948:35; see also pp. 25–36, 85–87).

A closer reading of Malinowski's analysis reveals that, in his view, primitive science is not emotion-free and disinterested after all. Although primitive knowledge may indeed be rational, on the whole this rationality is not a product of disinterested observation and speculation; rather, the rudimentary science of savages is motivated by deep-seated desires. Malinowski compares magic with science, in that each "always has a definite aim intimately associated with human instincts, needs, and pursuits" (p. 86). He notes that

science, even as represented by the primitive knowledge of savage man, is based on the normal universal experience of everyday life, *experience won in man's struggle with nature* for his subsistence and safety, founded on observation, fixed by reason (p. 87; emphasis added).

In short, the intellectual operations upon which primitive knowledge is built are manifestations of people's predispositions and interests; the intellect is wed to, and serves, the emotions and appetites.

This interpretation of Malinowski's analysis of primitive science is confirmed by his comments about totemism (1925, in 1948:44–47). Malinowski asks why certain species of plants and animals are selected as totems in primitive societies, and the explanation he offers is that, for the primitive, "the world is an indiscriminate background against which there stand out the useful, primarily the edible, species of animals or plants" (p. 44). The savage has a selective interest in natural phenomena; every species of animal which a people hunts, for example, "forms a nucleus round which all the interests, the impulses, the emotions of a tribe crystallize" (p. 45; see also 1927b:20, 1923:329–31).

The emotional background of human behavior is a distinctive attribute of Malinowski's monistic view of behavior, setting it apart from Tylor's and Spencer's. It is also a definitive aspect of his image of man in general, for to Malinowski a critical principle to grasp in understanding the actions of people is that the mainsprings of behavior are enshrouded in emotion and that the latter tends to dominate all thought and action.

Another definitive aspect which needs comment is his dynamic view of human behavior. Boas tended to conceive man as passive, whereas Malinowski viewed him as active. To Boas, human behavior is dominated by habitual or customary responses to which emotional associations became attached; the principal ends which the individual seeks are learned or traditional, and the individual is thus conceived as the agent of culture. For example, to Boas, there is no point or purpose to a taboo—it offers no advantages and serves no personal ends; it is "passively accepted," to use Malinowski's expression. Moreover, a custom is adequately described once its form is reported: there is no need to delve into the personal goals or intentions of individuals in order to discover its nature.

Malinowski held that, above all, man is goal-oriented. The Boasian tendency to focus on the form of cultural ideas and behavior, and to allow the individual's personal ends to recede into the background, must have seemed to him to miss what is essential for understanding. Boas' approach may be likened to a description of automobile driving which simply lists habitual responses—such as the unconscious habit of depressing the clutch pedal before shifting gears. What would stand out in a description written by Malinowski would be that the driver is effectively controlling a complex machine on one hand and intentionally driving himself somewhere on the other.

The dynamic view of behavior is particularly evident in Malinowski's analysis of myth. Malinowski opposed both theoretical and descriptive accounts of myth which remove the tale from its living context. He cited Boas' *Tsimshian Mythology* as an example of a study "in which the texts are given as if from the beginning they had led a flat existence on paper" (1928, in 1962:290), and he rejected theories like Tylor's which attempted to explain myth as the expression of a contemplative, thoughtful frame of mind, or "as a primitive armchair intellectual operation." These approaches tear the mythological narratives "out of their life context" and view them as what "they look like on paper" and not in terms of "what they do in life (1926, in 1948:110–11). According to Malinowski, the savage "is above all, actively engaged in a number of practical pursuits, and has to struggle with various difficulties; all his interests are tuned up to this general pragmatic outlook" (1926, in 1948:98). Myths must be viewed from this perspective, for they "are told with a purpose, and they are deeply rooted in the savage's interest and his social organization and culture" (1928, in 1962:290). Malinowski invites the reader "to step outside the closed study of the theorist into the open air of the anthropological field" and see the way in which myths function in real life (1926, in 1948:98–100).

For example, the Trobrianders have an elaborate system of beliefs concerning death, the afterlife, sickness, and health (see 1926, in 1948:126–38). Malinowski insists that each of these myths is "very far removed from a mere intellectual explanation," for they express man's reaction "toward disease and death" (p. 132). Malinowski remarks that the Trobrianders often felt sorrow and even dread at the prospect of dying, and that they would like to have had the end postponed if possible. He notes that they "would clutch at the hope given to them by their beliefs. They would screen, with the vivid texture of their myths, stories, and beliefs about the spirit world, the vast emotional void gaping beyond them" (p. 138). The tales themselves mean nothing when transcribed as "just so" stories for it is when they are seen in relation to the fears and motivations of real people that their significance appears. When the Trobriander tells the myth of the afterlife he is not passively responding to habit, but actively striving for solace.

Malinowski's analysis of meaning (1923; 1935, II) also reveals his dynamic view of behavior. He holds that language is not simply a "mirror of reflected thought" (1923:312); it is not to be viewed in relation to the purely ideational or reflective side of human behavior. Rather, it is an instrument or tool which people use in concrete situations, and it is shaped by the uses to which it is put (1935, II:52). Malinowski writes that language is "embedded" in a "course of activity" (1923:311), and it is "against the background of human activities and as a mode of human behavior in practical matters" that it is to be understood (p. 312). Speech is "meaningless" outside "the context of the activity in which it is enveloped" (1935, II:8).

Malinowski illustrates this principle with the example of "free aimless social intercourse," such as when a group of people sits idly around the village fire. The literal meaning of the words which are used in this social context is of little importance: Malinowski mentions such phrases as "How do you do," "Ah, here you are," and "Nice day to-day." The purpose of these expressions is not to convey abstract thoughts, but to surmount "the strange and unpleasant tension" which arises when people face one another in silence (1923:313–16).

The vocabulary of a language does not reflect principles of abstract logic or the accidents of history, but rather the interests and activities of enterprising people. For example, in the Trobriands, the types of distinctions which are made between categories of crops correspond to the requirements for the organization of activities. A gap in linguistic terminology—a nonexistent word in a language—reflects the fact that the concept is never used in practical affairs. In short, "gaps in abstract concepts," "gluts in concrete words," and "other vagaries in terminology" are not "an insoluble puzzle, for . . . native terminology is determined by the needs and interests of everyday life" (1935, II:66–67). Even the structure of language reflects the purposiveness of human behavior. Malinowski asserts that the "Peculiarities, exceptions, and refractory insubordination to rule" so often manifest in the study of grammatical systems is "the reflection of the makeshift, unsystematic, practical outlook imposed by man's struggle for existence in the widest sense of this word." Moreover, the "fundamental outlines of grammar" reflect the fact that language is an instrument which people use in their everyday lives (1923:328).

Malinowski's analysis of language was of considerable significance for British social anthropology. By viewing speech in terms of people's goals Malinowski successfully connected language with the practical affairs of society. The linguistic dimension was to him not merely an aspect of culture to be reported in the literature, but an essential guide to the understanding of the activities and concerns of people, and therefore their institutions. For example, the ethnographer may achieve important insight into the structure of a primitive society by discovering the meaning of certain key terms, such as those used in reference to clans or local groups. Evans-Pritchard's use of linguistic categories in his analysis of Nuer society is illustrative. American anthropologists may be less prone than the British to assimilate the linguistic dimension into their studies of society. If so, it may be because the Boasian approach to linguistics was more formal and less dynamic than Malinowski's and did not direct the anthropologist's attention toward seeing the interrelatedness of language and practical social affairs (see Bohannan 1956).

Malinowski's dynamic view of human behavior is apparent in many other aspects of his work, such as his theory of magic. The primitive magician is actively oriented in a direction laid down by internal compulsions, and his behavior is not a mere reflection of custom. The same idea is behind Malinowski's discussion of the Trobriand economic system, a primary motivation of which is ambition. Even the adherence to law, in Malinowski's view, is due to the active pursuit of one's interests.

CONCLUSION. It is possible now to pull together the main threads of my discussion of Malinowski's image of man and to suggest some of its implications for other aspects of his thought.

Malinowski's image of man was monistic in the sense that he held that behavior is a manifestation or expression of natural inclinations and interests: to him there is no true cleavage between culture and man's nature. Sometimes he implied that the origin of specific institutions is to be explained in terms of certain tendencies of the personality. An illustration is his theory of magic, according to which the source of both rite and spell is the general tendency for anxiety to be expressed in overt action. What is crucial is not Malinowski's more or less implicit theories of origin, however, but his view that the primary *motivation* behind behavior consists in natural predispositions and interests. For example, Malinowski never attempted to speculate about the origins of the patterns of exchange in the Trobriands, or about the inborn trait or complex of traits which brought about these patterns. Nevertheless, in his view, people are motivated to participate in the system largely by ambition. Regardless of how the system originated, its persistence or grounding is explained in monistic terms.

The distinctiveness of Malinowksi's monistic view of behavior is highlighted by comparing his and Boas' ideas about what is required to understand human activities. In Boas' view, it is culture which makes behavior intelligible. An individual behaves in a particular way because he has acquired the patterns of response which characterize his society, so if we are to grasp what he is doing we are to inquire into the customs of his people. To Malinowski, on the other hand, when we become acquainted with custom we have still not achieved full understanding; we cannot say that we see the point to an individual's behavior until we go *behind* culture and discover the natural predispositions and interests which it expresses. In order to grasp what a Trobriander is doing when we see him carrying the most select portion of his crop to someone else's yamhouse it is necessary to realize that he is activated by ambition. If we are to fully comprehend what he is doing when he adheres to kinship usages, law, and sexual mores, or when he practices magic or expresses a belief in the afterlife, we are to inquire into his fundamental, precultural inclinations.

According to Boas, human motivations are acquired through enculturation, and an investigation of the mainsprings of human behavior is therefore an investigation into cultural patterns. To Malinowski, the investigation of human motivations reveals man's animal nature—it exposes his natural, inborn predispositions and interests. This is not to say that man does not undergo a process of enculturation, or that he does not acquire both a reverence for tradition and a feeling that it should be followed for its own sake. However, if tradition conflicts with inborn tendencies, there is no question which will give way.

It follows that Boas and Malinowski had different views about the universal nature of man. To Boas, each culture has a distinct history and is therefore unique. If man is basically a product of culture, each society will exhibit a different type of personality. To Malinowski, however, all men are basically alike; when we inquire into the inner dynamics which motivate the Trobriand horticulturalist or magician we discover the same factors which move the American businessman or university student. The fundamental contrasts in personality which the Boasians thought they had discovered—such as the differences between the moderate, unassuming Zunis and the individualistic Plains Indians—are differences of style and not substance. The Plains Indian who achieves social honor by means of his skills in the arts of war, and who indulges in exotic self-torture to achieve visions, supernatural power, and temporal renown, is not fundamentally different from the Zuni elder who avoids dissension and ostentatious exhibitionism. The Zuni is equally motivated by ambitious desires, but if he were to behave like a Plains warrior he would soon be ostracized; consequently, he operates according to the mode which prevails in his own society.

Malinowski did not imply that culture has no significant influence on the individual, however. Whereas to Boas and Benedict the total personality is transformed by culture, Malinowski's monism implies that only one portion is substantially changed: namely, the intellectual features, the motivational structure remaining unmodified for the most part. All people have the same desire for renown, but each culture has different rules concerning the manner in which it is to be achieved. The individual must learn the rules appropriate to his own society and he must train himself in the proper modes of behavior if he is to compete effectively. Similarly, all people have a deep-seated fear of death, but each society provides a different set of beliefs by which to account for human mortality and to assuage these fears. The successful Zuni cannot become a successful Plains Indian overnight, but the problems he would encounter in making the transition would not be as difficult as the Boasians might have thought. Indeed, the *type* of problems which the Pueblo Indian should experience in moving to another culture would be different from those which Boas and Benedict anticipated. A successful transfer to another way of life requires retraining and not a fundamental restructuring of the personality system.

A problem central to Durkheim's work is that of conformity: why do people adhere to the standards of their society? One critical context in which this issue emerges is in his discussion of social order, and it was his view that if the individual is allowed to govern his behavior primarily by his own interests and desires society would be impossible. Unfettered self-interest must give rise to the war of all against all. The basis of order and social solidarity is that people acquire an emotional commitment to the collective life of their society, and this commitment is powerful enough to compel the individual to rise above his animal nature. This set of ideas has become important in modern sociology and social anthropology, due especially to the influence of Talcott Parsons (see Parsons 1937).

To Malinowski, asking why the individual conforms or adheres to the norms, laws, and beliefs of his society is like asking why a hungry man eats. The Trobriand economic system—with all the privations and hard work which it entails—satisfies a man of ambition in the same way that food satisfies a man with an empty stomach.

Moreover, in Malinowksi's view, the Durkheimian ideas

about conformity will lead us to completely misunderstand what we observe in society. The commitment which people express—the ideal which they are quick to relate to the anthropologist—is a facade which disguises their true motives and feelings. If the observer does not look into the way people use the system for their own ends and the way in which they evade the rules when it is to their advantage to do so, he will mistake form for substance. For example, Malinowski was strongly opposed to the Durkheimian notions of solidarity and cohesion (e.g., 1926b:132). When ideas such as moral cohesion and collective consciousness are investigated closely their emptiness becomes manifest, and what emerges instead is "personal resentment, thwarted ambition, jealousy, economic grievance, and so on" (1934:xxv). In another context Malinowski writes,

the hasty field-worker, who relies completely upon the question and answer method, obtains at best that lifeless body of laws, regulations, morals, and conventionalities which *ought* to be obeyed, but in reality are often only evaded. For in actual life rules are never entirely conformed to, and it remains, as the most difficult but indispensable part of the ethnographer's work, to ascertain the extent and mechanism of the deviations (1929:509; emphasis in the original).

In Malinowski's view, sociological analyses like those of Durkheim and Radcliffe-Brown presented the shape of social life but missed its true meaning.

The problem of social constraint was a residual issue to Boas and Benedict—to them the enculturated person is so thoroughly modified by culture that it is his nature to conform to the cultural ideal. In the view of Durkheim and Radcliffe-Brown, however, social ideals are constantly at odds with the refractory interests of the individual, and the ideals therefore need the buttressing of social sanctions. Malinowski is led to underline the importance of constraint, like Durkheim and Radcliffe-Brown, for in his view culture leads the individual to limit his wants and to participate in activities which he would avoid if possible. For example, Malinowski dwelt on the fact that the Trobriander is required to produce much more food than he needs, and he was clear that the rules and laws of Trobriand society require the individual to forego or limit the satisfaction of some of his most basic and immediate wants. Nevertheless, Malinowski's version of constraint is quite different from Durkheim's and Radcliffe-Brown's. To Malinowski, what moves the individual to curb his impulses and to go beyond his immediate interests is the realistic appreciation of what is necessary to achieve his own ends. The Trobriander may desire to keep his harvest for his own use, or even to cut down on production, but to do so would bring on humiliation and loss of prestige. He may also want to default in his obligations toward kinsmen, friends, and chiefs, but to do so would result in a prohibitive net "cost." Culture exhibits constraint, but it is not the constraint of a moral authority "imposed" from the outside in the Durkheimian sense.

The issue of constraint carries this discussion beyond the level of the individual to that of the larger social system. To Radcliffe-Brown, it is by reference to this larger whole that jural norms and legal mechanisms are to be understood: the principles which govern law and social constraint in general are the needs for stability and cohesion in society, or the structural exigencies of the social system. For example, a jural norm which is pivotal in maintaining the relations between important segments of society is to be understood by reference to its structural role in the total system, and any account which views that norm solely in relation to the level of the individual is fundamentally incomplete. Radcliffe-Brown did not deny that certain features could be explained by reference to the individual, of course, for he would have agreed that in all societies individuals attempt to circumvent the rules and to manipulate them for their own ends. However, in his view, these factors are merely imperfections in the system and are therefore residual—unless the society is approaching collapse. No social system works perfectly, just as no machine is free of friction. Moreover, just as friction does not run the machine, the manipulating, self-interested actor is not the key to the way in which the social system works.

To Malinowski, it is at the level of the individual that the system makes sense. It is the actor's subterfuges, evasions, as well as his self-interested conformity, which constitute governing principles behind law, custom, and the social system as a whole. The legal norms which define the relations between chief and commoner in the Trobriands, for example, are grounded in the interests and predispositions of living human beings and do not reflect the structural exigencies of the larger whole. The commoner accepts his burdensome role in relation to the chief largely because of the advantages he receives, and the chief stands by his obligations for the same reason.

Malinowski's tendency to focus on the level of the individual rather than that of society would have had major implications for his concept of social structure if he had pursued this issue. In Radcliffe-Brown's scheme the structure of society is defined and regulated by jural rules; the stability or equilibrium which exists is therefore contingent primarily on the juridical system, together with the aid of such institutions as religion. Ultimately, the grounding of all these factors is the people's acquired, emotional commitment to the moral values of their society. Malinowski tended to view human behavior in terms of individual incentives, not social morals. The implication is that social equilibrium consists in a delicate balancing of actual and potential interests, advantages, and opportunities. Each individual is engaged in pursuing his interests, and the structural relations which result are a type of stalemate. The commoner in Trobriand society would like to press himself forward and assume the prerogatives and fame of a wealthy chief, but he does not have the resources to do so. On the other hand, the system offers him sufficient advantages and potential opportunities that it pays him to accept his position, at least for the moment. The Trobriand chief would like to improve his position also, but like everyone else he is caught in a web of duties and obligations which he cannot avoid if he is to maintain the benefits he already enjoys. Malinowski's focus on the individual was leading him to the view that social equilibrium or stability is the outcome of competitive self-interest, not jural rules or disinterested morality.

Malinowski's tendency to direct his attention to the level of the individual may have left its mark on the work of his student, Evans-Pritchard. Evans-Pritchard turned away from Malinowski's framework early in his career, for he came under the influence of the social structural approaches of Robertson Smith, Durkheim, and Radcliffe-Brown, as well as the theories of Levy-Bruhl and others. The relations between Evans-Pritchard and his former teacher eventually grew cold (Evans-Pritchard 1953b: 18). Nevertheless, traces of Malinowski's influence may be evident in Evans-Pritchard's scheme. We do not know the source of Evans-Pritchard's commitment to the principle of free will, or its concomitant, the rejection of "sociological determinism"; perhaps these ideas derive in part from his religious beliefs, according to which the individual is morally responsible for his actions. But certainly Evans-Pritchard's ideas parallel Malinowski's view that the actor is the dynamic ingredient in the social system and not a slavish follower of custom. Similarly, Evans-Pritchard's rejection of the idea that social structure is to be seen in terms of the objective categories of the scientist, who analyzes the system from the outside, reflects Malinowski's focus on the level of the individual in society. According to Evans-Pritchard, society is to be viewed from the perspective of the person who lives within it, or in terms of his systems of belief and categories of thought.

A critical difference between Malinowski and Evans-Pritchard is that the latter does not present a cynical image of social institutions and human behavior. Evans-Pritchard's position seems to be nearer Durkheim's optimism, according to which the ultimate basis of law and custom is not the self-interested calculations of the members of society, but the disinterested moral commitment which is instilled in their minds.

MALINOWSKI'S FUNCTIONALISM

Malinowski's image of man was far from an incidental aspect of his thought; not only does it appear at least implicitly in all his descriptive and theoretical studies, but it seems to have been a relatively stable element to which the other facets of his thinking had to adjust. Nevertheless, his approach to human behavior would hardly be exhausted by giving an account of his image of man, for something crucial would be left out. This is his culture concept.

Malinowski's theory of culture is above all a functional theory: he is commonly regarded as one of the founders of functionalism in anthropology and the social sciences, and his functionalism was a leading aspect of his approach to human behavior. His notion of culture may therefore be described by giving an account of his functionalism.

There is a problem in approaching his idea of culture from this perspective, however: the term "functionalism" has many different meanings in his work. In the following pages three of the primary ones have been singled out, and an attempt is made to show the different patterns of explanation or interpretation which each entails.

The types of functionalism which are differentiated below were not explicitly distinguished by Malinowski himself. They were tightly interwoven in his work, and even when they appeared separately Malinowski was able to jump from one to another without being consciously aware that he was shifting perspective. The term "functionalism" remained imprecise enough to cover a number of forms of interpretation which actually had little in common. It might even be said that it was the elasticity of the term which made it possible for his cultural framework to cohere. He was able to ignore the discontinuities and incompatibilities between the modes of interpretation which he employed because, somehow, the label of "functionalism" could be stretched to fit them all.

INTEGRATIONALISM. The first form of functionalism may be designated as Malinowksi's integrational approach; I use this term to stress its similarity to the integrationalism of the Boasians. Function in this sense denotes a relationship or interdependence between the parts of a larger whole, in that if one of the elements is changed or removed the others will be affected. It follows that if a trait is to be understood, it must be seen in its cultural context. As I use the terms here, integrationalism and utilitarianism are mutually exclusive; the latter implies that the relations between the parts of the whole have beneficial results, whereas integrationalism does not. Integrationalism simply entails the notion that the elements of culture are interrelated, whereas utilitarianism adds the idea of an ulterior end behind this interconnectedness.

Malinowski's integrationalism is a guiding theme in all his descriptive studies. As early as 1913, in his monograph on the Australian family, he stated that "the essential features" of the family "depend upon the general structure of a given society and upon the conditions of life therein" (1913:6). In the same book he wrote:

It is undoubtedly one of the most valuable discoveries arrived at by modern sociological science that each institution varies in accordance with the social environment in which it is found (p. 168).

Integrationalism is even more important in his writings on the Trobrianders, for it is the basis of the organization of each of his descriptive works. He labeled the method which he employed in his ethnographic publications "organic presentation" (1932:xxviii). For example, what stands out about his article on "Baloma" (1916, in 1948) is that the beliefs he describes are presented as a coherent whole. In his *Argonauts* the kula sys-

tem is the central theme, but it is presented by tracing its interconnections with other aspects of Trobriand culture, such as
gardening, magic, canoe building, and chiefship. In *The Sexual Life of Savages* (1929) his focus was upon sexual behavior
in Trobriand society, but his account carried him into discussions about divorce, marriage, chiefship, matriliny, love magic,
and a variety of other topics; the cohesiveness of the book derives from the fact that all these elements are interrelated. The
central theme of *Coral Gardens and Their Magic* (1935, I) is
land tenure, but this really is a point of departure for wide-
ranging discussions about gardening, magic, and kinship,
among other things.

Closely associated with Malinowski's integrationalism and
his method of "organic presentation" was the distinctive field
technique which he developed. This method was of inestima-
ble importance both in the training of students and in the development of the high standards of field research which has
characterized the work of British anthropologists. The approach which he fostered was that of organizing the field data
into synoptic charts (see 1922b:13–15; 1935, I:339, 436–43).
This allowed the researcher to view a fact not as an isolated
phenomenon—as a mere "curio," as Malinowski would say—
but as an aspect of a larger whole, for the synoptic chart served
to emphasize the interconnections between elements. The technique is applied at all levels of analysis, from simple ritual
practices to entire cultures. One value of the method is that it
brings gaps in the data to the attention of the field investigator.
For example, in collecting information on gardening practices
the anthropologist may inadvertently overlook the rules regulating an individual's rights to land, or possibly the belief or
"charter" by which the person's rights are legitimized. If the
material is organized and summarized in the form of synoptic
tables, lacunae such as these are immediately apparent (see
Richards, in Firth, ed., 1960:24–26).

Concerning the actual sources of Malinowski's integrationalism, two factors may be mentioned. First, the idea that culture is an integral whole was apparently "in the air" during the early part of this century. Malinowski refers to W.H.R. Rivers of Cambridge as one who both employed and emphasized this principle in his own work (Malinowski 1913:6, 1922a:218). Second, Malinowski's field work may have been a contributing factor, as he himself suggests (1931:655–56). He engaged in the most intensive field work which had been conducted until that time, and it may have been inevitable that he would recognize the importance of the context within which each trait is found.

Regardless of how his integrationalism originated, it is clear that one of the reasons it became important in his writing is that it performed several crucial functions. For one thing, it was a useful literary device in that it enabled him to present coherent monographs rather than disjointed cultural inventories. More important here, however, is that his integrationalism enabled him to make sense of native practices which otherwise seemed absurd or even immoral. He could show that it is not possible to dismiss polygamy as a disgusting savage custom, for among the Trobrianders, at least, the practice is a basis of the political order. In a paper published in 1922 Malinowski presented a stinging criticism of missionaries and colonial administrators who had done injustices to native peoples by misunderstanding them. A sample sentence reads: "Yet the ignorant and pedantic morality-monger, whether clerical or official, cannot help scenting some sexual mischief, wherever he finds amusement and pleasure" (1922a:210). Near the end of the article Malinowski remarks: "A belief, which appears crude and senseless in isolation, a practice which seems queer and 'immoral,' becomes often clear and even clean if understood as part of a system of thought and practice" (p. 218). In brief, the integrational method enabled Malinowski to make exotic beliefs and practices intelligible. I suggest that this served to give the method vitality in his work and to convince him of its importance:

For we are now more and more interested in the connections between the component parts of an institution, in the relations of institution to institution and of aspect to aspect. We are interested,
that is, rather in meaning and function than in form and detail
(1932:xxix).

Anyone who reads Malinowski's accounts of the Trobrianders will be convinced that the cultural context does indeed
provide a form of understanding. And yet it is difficult to say
in what sense it does so, for Malinowski employs the method in
so many ways that it seems to defy all attempts at systematization. For example, in some cases the context he emphasizes is
that of the subjective ideas behind an act or belief, in others it
is the complex of practical pursuits of which the act or belief is
a part, and in still others Malinowski merely cites customs
which exhibit a pattern similar to that which he wishes to elucidate. During the 1930s he developed the concept of institution, which is discussed below, and this may be viewed as an attempt to specify or refine his integrationalism. However, he
never applied this concept to his own data in a rigorous fashion. Furthermore, the diacritical aspect of the institution is its
utilitarian and not its integrational features, and its development therefore represents an elaboration of something other
than his integrationalism, as I use that term.

The inchoate and undeveloped nature of Malinowski's integrationalism presents a striking contrast with the scheme of
Ruth Benedict. In her view it is the configuration which makes
a culture trait intelligible. For example, warfare among the
Plains Indians makes sense when seen in the context of the
Dionysian tendency of those peoples. Evans-Pritchard, whose
structural approach itself is a form of integrationalism, characterizes Malinowski's method as no more than "a literary device
for integrating his observations for descriptive purposes." According to Evans-Pritchard, Malinowski "never showed himself
capable of using it with any clarity when dealing with the abstractions of general theory" (1951a:54).

Perhaps one reason why Malinowski's integrationalism remained unelaborated is that it did not fit with his monistic image of man, according to which the principal context within which to view custom is that of the interests and predispositions of the individual. An implication of his monistic conception of behavior is that the cultural context is of secondary importance for understanding. The integrational approach is more consistent with the cultural determinism of Ruth Benedict, according to whom a given custom is to be seen in terms of other customs: either in terms of cultural history or in terms of the synchronic, cultural context in which it is found.

Another factor which may have deflected Malinowski's thought away from the integrational approach was his dynamic view of human behavior. Boas' passive image of man is consistent with an integrational analysis which focuses upon pattern and form in culture. On the other hand, Malinowski's thought calls for a mode of analysis which regards culture as an instrumental apparatus which *does* something (see 1936, in 1962:329–30). His ideas about behavior require that culture be viewed as a working system of some kind. Malinowski frequently described his functionalism as a "dynamic study" which attempts to determine "how ideas, customs, and institutions actually work in tribal life" (1931:655–56).

THE MONISTIC FORM OF UTILITARIANISM. When Malinowski began to elaborate his functionalism his thought moved in the direction of utilitarianism rather than integrationalism. His earliest writings were dominated by the integrational form of interpretation, although utilitarianism did appear in a few early articles (see especially 1912). It was not until 1925, when his "Magic, Science, and Religion" appeared (reprinted in Malinowski 1948), that the utilitarian pattern of explanation became a dominant theme. Once the shift occurred, however, his new theoretical focus was quickly elaborated in such works as "Myth in Primitive Psychology" (1926, in 1948) and Part IV of *Sex and Repression* (1927b). There are other suggestions that the mid-1920s was a period of fundamental change in Malinowski's thought. Herskovits first met him in 1924, and "was impressed with the vividness of Malinowski's interest in what was being done by American anthropologists, and his awareness of how their concepts and methods fitted in with his own point of view." However, when the two spoke again in 1926 in New York City, Herskovits "was bewildered" by "the abrupt change in [Malinowski's] attitude." Malinowski's hostility toward historical studies had begun to appear, as had his strong preference for the synchronic, functional analysis of culture (Herskovits 1965:410–11). It may be that the change in attitude which Herskovits notes was associated with a controversy between Malinowski and the British diffusionists, G. Elliot-Smith and W. J. Perry (Malinowski 1927a). The argument revolved around the issue of the functional vs. historical approaches to culture, and it may have sharpened Malinowski's utilitarian ideas.

Malinowski's utilitarianism was predominantly monistic, in that he conceived culture as an instrument serving man's biological and psychological needs: the end served by functions is individual imperatives, and not social stability and cohesion as Radcliffe-Brown held. The monistic and utilitarian form of Malinowski's functionalism is consistent with his monistic image of man, according to which the context for viewing custom is the system of motives and desires of the individual human being. It is also consistent with his dynamic view of behavior, for customs are viewed both in terms of how they work and as instrumentalities which people use.

Like integrationalism, the utilitarian approach offered manifold possibilities for understanding. Malinowski's analysis of magic is illustrative. Malinowski was able to show that magical practices are neither unintelligible nor silly, for they perform a critical function. They help the individual cope with his fears and uncertainties. Similarly, Malinowski could see the significance or meaning behind beliefs in the afterlife; these, too, assist the individual in overcoming debilitating anxieties.

I suggested that Radcliffe-Brown's functionalism revolutionized his view of the Australian kinship system. It occurred to him that the endless rules which governed the system were not pointless cultural miscellany, for they functioned to regulate the relationships between people and thereby to maintain a stable system of interaction. Once this insight came to him he could return to his analysis of the particulars of Australian social organization with renewed vigor. Similarly, I think that Malinowski's utilitarianism was motivated and given vitality by its capacity to make sense of what may have seemed to others pointless custom. In an article written in opposition to the work of Elliot-Smith and Perry, Malinowski insisted that culture "is not a heap of trinkets which can be peddled about across oceans and round continents." Rather, it "is constantly at work," for it is "there for the satisfaction of elementary human needs" (1927a:36). The implication is that the diffusionists' scheme reduced culture to a lifeless, pointless mass of traits, the result of fortuitous historical principles. Elliot-Smith and Perry attempt to "explain away" culture "as a mere result of 'diffusion' " (p. 42) instead of trying to understand it. Malinowski wrote that anthropology as a whole "has for the most part tried to evade the live issues and the problems of life: it has tried to shelter behind the Chinese Wall of mere antiquarian curiosity." He argued that there is a tendency within all the humanities "to play about with dead remains instead of grappling with actualities" (p. 26).

Malinowski's analysis of magic and of the belief in an afterlife are possibly the best concrete examples of his monistic and utilitarian form of functionalism. However, at a more abstract level, he developed a general scheme within which his particular analyses of magic, religion, myth, and the like, were to fit. The central element of this general framework was his notion of institution.

Malinowski described the institution as the concrete isolate of cultural analysis: all cultures are composed of institutions and are best described by giving an account of those institutions (1944a:49). A total culture may be conceived either as a single institution, or as a "related system of institutions" (1944b:253). Furthermore, each aspect of culture is to be defined or understood "by placing it within . . . its institutional setting" (1944a:54). The institution, then, constitutes the framework behind the organization of culture and a scheme for anthropological research. "[I]nstitutional analysis is not only possible but indispensable" (p. 54), and in the best work done by historians, economists, political scientists, and others, the institutional approach has always been used, at least implicitly (p. 49).

Malinowski defines the institution as "an organized system of purposeful activities" (1944a:52). The following are examples of institutions: a tribe or nation; a clan which is not a mere category of people but which has a body of common affairs; a household; a group which is engaged in magical or religious rites; a university; a firm or business.

Each institution has six aspects: first, the charter, which is a set of values, myths, or beliefs which legitimize the activity; second, the personnel, the people who engage in the pursuit; third, the norms which the group follows; fourth, the material apparatus which is employed; fifth, the activities themselves; and sixth, the function of the institution. Malinowski presented these aspects in diagrammatic form, and one of the distinctive characteristics of the chart he provides is that the whole is directed toward the institution's function (p. 53):

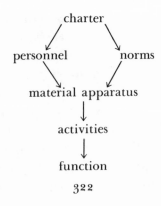

Malinowski contended that there is an immediate and fundamental relationship between the functions of an institution and the biological needs and drives of human beings. He lists seven "basic needs" (metabolism, reproduction, bodily comforts, safety, movement, growth, and health; 1944a:91–95). The individual satisfies these by cultural and not natural means. For example, people eat food which has been prepared by the use of cultural utensils and techniques, and they do so in the context of a social group, normally the household. The food is also produced and distributed by means of traditionally established forms of organization. A consideration of the hunger drive (a metabolic need) therefore leads directly to the institutions which function in relation to eating. The reverse is also true: the analysis of any institution leads eventually to the biological needs which it serves. This is not to say that there is a point-by-point correspondence between institutions and needs, however, for the same need may be served by several institutions, and an institution will normally serve a wide variety of needs simultaneously. The family alone functions in relation to the need for food, shelter, and sex, among other things.

Not all needs are purely biological; culture is a complex apparatus, and if it is to operate effectively certain conditions must be met. There are "derived needs" in addition to the biological imperatives. For example, there must be a system for the training of children in the traditional practices and techniques of society; some form of economic and political organization is also needed, as is a system of social control (1944a:120–31). Furthermore, each culture has integrative needs, and these are met in part by religious beliefs and practices and by systems of knowledge, among other things. An institution may function in relation to these derived needs in addition to the more basic biological imperatives.

According to Malinowski, the institutional framework provides the basis for cross-cultural comparisons. All cultural systems must satisfy the same needs, and consequently different societies have analogous institutions. People like Benedict are wrong when they assert that each culture tends to emphasize one potential human characteristic, such as megalomania or individualism, and that it may do so to the exclusion of all other human responses. Cultures do not specialize in this way, for each serves the entire range or spectrum of human needs. Malinowski writes that some institutions "seem very strange at first sight," but they "are essentially cognate" to other, less exotic forms. By recognizing the analogous nature of institutions we are able to understand them (pp. 40–41).

The utilitarianism of Malinowski's scheme is patent. He writes that culture "is a system of objects, activities, and attitudes in which every part exists as a means to an end." It "is essentially an instrumental apparatus by which man is put in a position to better cope with the concrete specific problems that face him in his environment in the course of the satisfaction of his needs" (1944a:150).

Malinowski's attempt to bring the institution into direct relationship with biological needs may be one of the most unfortunate aspects of his work, for he was able to do no more with this scheme than offer such platitudes as the notion that the family functions to promote the health and security of the child. It was an embarrassing failure, and yet it has become one of the well-known features of his thought. It may have attracted attention away from some of the more enduring ideas which his writing contains.

Radcliffe-Brown and Malinowski both developed utilitarian versions of culture, but their thoughts were moving in radically different directions. One held that the function of any part of the social system was to be seen in relation to the *sui generis* social structure, and the other argued that if you pursue the functions of an institution far enough you will ultimately be led to the individual. This contrast may be expressed by saying that Radcliffe-Brown employed a dualistic form of utilitarianism, whereas Malinowski's was monistic in form. This cannot be dismissed as a mere difference in emphasis or theoretical interest, for it entails fundamentally different views about the nature of culture, society, and the individual.

To Radcliffe-Brown, social institutions are attached to the real world primarily by means of their role in relation to the objective and natural exigencies of the social structure. For example, to him the principle which explains the prevalence of unilineal descent among primitive peoples is the effectiveness of this form of organization in the ordering of society. Unilineality does not vary in random fashion precisely because of its structural value.

Malinowski tended to stress yet another principle, for he implied that custom is fixed in place by means of the natural motivations of human beings. An illustration is his theory of magic, according to which the magical rite receives its orientation from the emotional response which it taps (see 1925, in 1948:71–72, 79–82). On one hand, the form which the rite assumes is associated with the psychological factor behind it: a magical rite which expresses a man's anxieties over his crops will exhibit different features from that which expresses his concern over sexual success, for example. On the other hand, psychological conditions determine where magic will occur within the cultural system. In the Trobriands, a rich body of magical beliefs is associated with the dangers and uncertainties of deep-sea fishing, but none at all exists in connection with the fishing activities in the sheltered lagoon.

Radcliffe-Brown all but rejected Malinowski's theory of magic (Radcliffe-Brown 1939, in 1952:148ff.). He argued that the point of such practices as magical rites and taboos is to emphasize things and events which are important to society as a whole, and he illustrated his thesis by reference to the Andamanese taboos which must be observed by an expectant mother and her husband. The function of these taboos is to stress the social importance of birth; the custom reflects a structural exigency, the need to incorporate new members into society. Radcliffe-Brown contended that such rituals as these can hardly offer the individual reassurance, for they evoke chimerical fears: the Andamanese father expects that sickness will follow if he breaks the food taboos, for example. Furthermore, the rite does not emanate from within the individual, for it is imposed on him from without; it is obligatory, and the father is expected to show concern for the birth of his child even if he is completely indifferent. Although Radcliffe-Brown does not make this point, it is clear that, according to his analysis, rituals do not occur in random fashion in society, for they attach to matters of structural importance. It is because they serve the structural exigencies of society that they do not vary randomly.

George Homans suggests that Radcliffe-Brown's and Malinowski's interpretations are complementary rather than incompatible, for the two theories are merely directed toward different levels of analysis. A rite may be obligatory and contribute to social solidarity and cohesion and also promote confidence and relieve anxieties in the individual. The father in Andamanese society may be obligated to observe his food taboos and still gain a measure of reassurance from them, for example. Homans concludes his discussion by commenting that the disagreement between Radcliffe-Brown and Malinowski represents a common phenomenon in science,

two distinguished persons talking past one another rather than trying to find a common ground for discussion, presenting their theories as alternatives when in fact they are complements (Homans 1941:172).

Homans' attempt to reconcile Radcliffe-Brown and Malinowski is seductive, but the problem is not as simple as he makes it appear. The two theories of ritual are compatible only if we ignore the theoretical and conceptual contexts within which each occurs. For example, Radcliffe-Brown might accept the idea that there are occasions when rites alleviate anxieties, but he could not accept the Malinowskian thesis that it is this which gives the rite its vitality and which anchors it in place. Nor could Malinowski accept Radcliffe-Brown's views about the nature of constraint and the grounding of custom. To Malinowski, the Andamanese taboo may be obligatory, but it would be naive to think that the rule is anything more than an empty formula unless the rite taps a natural response of some kind. People are quite adept at evading what is obligatory in society if prompted to do so by interests or inclinations. Homans' attempt to show the complementarity of the two theories of ritual can be successful only by modifying Radcliffe-Brown's and Malinowski's general views about society, culture, and the individual.

The fundamental contrast between Radcliffe-Brown's and Malinowski's functionalism is brought into focus when it is recognized that the historical roots of their ideas were quite different. There was one thing they did have in common: utilitarian assumptions have been deeply embedded in British social thought for many years, and the schemes of both Radcliffe-Brown and Malinowski are manifestations of this historical current. When Radcliffe-Brown aligned himself with Durkheimian theory he emphasized the principles derived from his own intellectual tradition. His dualistic form of functionalism was the result: the dualism reflects Durkheim, the utilitarianism reflects his British heritage. However, Malinowski's attraction to Durkheim was fairly brief and inconsequential, and his monistic form of utilitarianism derives instead from certain trends which were occurring in psychological theory during the early part of this century in Britain. It reflects the views of such writers as McDougall, Westermarck, Rivers, Marett, and Shand.

The latter was particularly influential in the development of Malinowski's thought. It was pointed out above that, to both Shand and Malinowski, the mainsprings of human behavior are innate. What is more, these innate behavior patterns or motivations were conceived as adaptive, for they were thought to serve the interests of the organism or species. This utilitarian aspect of Shand's theory is particularly evident in the emphasis he placed on the role of instincts in human behavior. The instinct concept is at bottom a utilitarian idea, for what is significant about the instinctive response is that it is "directed to the end of self-preservation or to the preservation of the race" (Shand 1914:183).

When Malinowski wrote the concluding portions of his *Sex and Repression* (1927b) he repeatedly referred both to Shand and to the innate bases of behavior. Like Shand, he assumed that instincts are adaptive in nature. For example, he noted that among many species of animal the male and female set up relatively permanent relationships, resembling marriage, and that this benefits the mother, the offspring, and the species as a whole. Malinowski wrote,

In the higher animals marriage is necessary because the longer the pregnancy, the more helpless the pregnant female and the new-born infant and the more necessary it is for them to have the protection of the male (p. 180).

The behavior of animals is determined by these instinctive patterns, according to Malinowski, whereas human behavior is somewhat more complex. Man's actions, though motivated largely by inborn tendencies, adhere to the forms laid down by culture. Nevertheless, culture and instinct are analogous: culture "duplicates the instinctive drive" (p. 185):

But as the family passes under the control of cultural elements, the instincts which have exclusively regulated it among pre-human apes become transformed into something which did not exist before man: I mean the cultural bonds of social organization (p. 171).

Culture and instinct are thus two different means for achieving the same ends:

The preservation of species through selective mating, conjugal exclusiveness, and parental care is the main aim of human institutions as well as of animal instinctive arrangements (p. 196).

In sum, Shand tended to interpret the innate psychological response in terms of its practical value in relation to the individual and species; Malinowski took a broader view by drawing custom into the same framework.

Edmund Leach has tried to place Malinowski's functionalism in a broader intellectual context by relating it to the Pragmatism of William James. Leach argues that Pragmatism was enjoying its "maximum vogue" in England precisely when Malinowski went to London to study anthropology, and that this was one of the principal influences behind his work (Leach, in Firth, ed., 1960:121). In support of his argument Leach refers to an incisive discussion of James's work written by W. B. Gallie (Gallie 1952:21–31). According to Gallie, when James developed his Pragmatic philosophy he elaborated two important psychological principles. The first is "that the sole function of thought is to satisfy certain needs of the organism, and that truth consists in such thinking as satisfies these interests." The second is the idea that when these interests "are faced with issues which cannot be settled on strictly intellectual grounds, . . . other factors, deriving from the 'passional and volitional' side of our nature, should be allowed to determine our opinions" (Gallie 1952:25). The similarity between James and Malinowski is clear: man's thoughts and actions are a reflection of biological needs and emotional impulses; moreover, the validity of ideas and actions need not be judged solely on rational and empirical grounds, for they may also be evaluated according to their practical usefulness in relation to these biological and psychological factors. Magic may have no value in promoting the growth of crops, but its pragmatic value with respect to the emotional nature of the gardener may be considerable.

THE DUALISTIC FORM OF UTILITARIANISM. I have now described two fundamentally different forms of functionalism which appear in Malinowski's work: his integrational approach and his monistic utilitarianism. There is yet a third; this is utilitarian like the last, but it is also dualistic and hence not at all unlike the approach employed by Radcliffe-Brown. Function in this sense refers to the contribution which any aspect of culture makes to the persistence or integrity of the larger cultural system.

An example of Malinowski's dualistic and utilitarian functionalism is his analysis of myth; he notes that myth functions "to strengthen tradition and endow it with a greater value and prestige by tracing it back to a higher, better, more supernatural reality of initial events" (1926, in 1948:146). Myth serves as a charter which establishes, affirms, and legitimizes patterns of social organization and custom in general.

Malinowski illustrates this theory by citing the Trobriand myths of origin (1926, in 1948:111–26). According to Trobriand belief, the people originally lived beneath the surface of the earth, having emerged only a few generations ago. The holes through which they came can be identified—they are marked by grottoes, heaps of stone, springs, and the like—and are regarded with respect.

One of these holes, Obukula, is especially important, for it is associated with the myth by which the comparative rank of the Trobriand clans was established. There are four clans in Trobriand society, and the totemic representatives of each emerged from Obukula. These totems included the iguana, dog, pig, and crocodile. The dog represented the Lukuba clan which enjoyed the highest rank of all prior to the time of emergence, and the pig was totem of the Malasi clan which has held the highest rank since that time. The critical feature of this myth is that after the dog arose from the hole he saw a piece of fruit growing on the *noku* plant, and he ate it. He was severely reproached for this by the pig, for the fruit of the *noku* is taboo to people of high rank. The pig accused the dog of eating dirt and declared that he would be low-bred from then on, whereas he, the pig, would be chief. Since that time the members of one particular lineage of the Malasi clan—the clan represented by the pig—have been the chiefs of Trobriand society. According to Malinowski, this myth is not a mere story, for it serves to establish and affirm the comparative rank of the Malasi and Lukuba: the incident "settles once for all the relation between the two rival clans" (1926, in 1948:113).

The origin myth also performs important functions in relation to land tenure and village organization. The Trobrianders' forebears emerged from the ground at many different locations, and once they were on the surface of the earth they founded villages near the holes from which they arose and claimed the surrounding territory for their own use. Community membership and the ownership of property were thereby established; if a man can trace descent to the original founding ancestors of a village, he has the right to settle there and to acquire a parcel of land for himself and his family. Malinowski contends that the myth

conveys, expresses, and strengthens the fundamental fact of the local unity and of the kinship unity of the group of people descendent from a common ancestress. . . . [The myth] contains the legal charter of the community (p. 116).

A number of other examples of Malinowski's dualistic form of utilitarianism could be cited, including his theory of religion. He held that religion focuses upon the important features of culture, and that, by means of its public pomp and ceremony, it sacralizes, reinforces, and maintains customary practices and beliefs (1925, in 1948:54–69).

Malinowski's use of the dualistic function concept raises serious difficulties for his scheme. It has been suggested that his monistic form of utilitarianism coheres with his monistic image of man: a useful trait, such as a magical rite, taps an emotional response in the individual, and this response supplies the motivation which maintains the custom. People are not likely to ignore even the most onerous magical practices because the ceremony is rooted in their emotional make-up. However, Malinowski's dualistic form of utilitarianism fails to supply a connection between function and motivation. According to the dualistic mode of interpretation, a custom serves the ends of the larger society and not the interests of the individual; but if this is so, why do the people not evade or ignore the practice?

The difficulties of Malinowski's dualistic form of utilitarianism are illustrated by his theory that myth serves as a charter for social affairs. This theory assumes that the myth is accepted by the individual in a disinterested way. Malinowski writes that the myth is both "venerable and sacred" (1926, in 1948:107). It overcomes the selfishness of individuals, who embrace the belief even though it is not in their interest to do so. Malinowski reports that when a Trobriand community was driven from its land by hostile neighbors, "their territory always remained intact for them; and they were always . . . allowed to return to the original site, rebuild their village, and cultivate their gardens once more" (p. 116). He implies that this was due largely to the effectiveness of myth. Malinowski also writes that in the event of a quarrel over land, "the testimony of myth would be referred to" (p. 113). Moreover, he notes that "myth functions especially where there is a sociological strain"—such as where there are differences in power and rank, or where there are restrictions on the use of land (p. 126).

This analysis comes very close to the view which Malinowski attacked with so much vigor: the view that the savage is a "model of the law-abiding citizen," willingly submitting to the demands of custom (1926c:9). It fails to explain how myth can function effectively when its precepts are contrary to the natural inclinations of the individuals in society.

Malinowski's theory of myth as charter is decidedly dualistic, and yet a monistic sub-theme is occasionally hinted at. He sometimes implies that these myths may be used interestedly by individuals to assert their claims in opposition to rivals. For example, Malinowski wrote that the Trobriand myth which established the relative rank of clans is actively used

in discussion and squabbles in reference to the relative superiority of the various clans, and in the discussions about the various food taboos which frequently raise fine questions of casuistry (1926, in 1948:113).

When myth is employed in this way it does not support tradition, but validates the claims of the teller. According to this interpretation, the principle which gives the myth vitality and which provides its motivation is the self-interest of the individual.

If Malinowski had consciously developed this theory he would have arrived at a fully cynical view of beliefs, and in this respect he would have stood in direct opposition to writers like Durkheim, Evans-Pritchard, and Radcliffe-Brown. Malinowski apparently did not recognize the possibilities of the cynical interpretation of tales, however, although others have done so. According to Leach, for example, the contradictory versions of myth "are more significant than the uniformities." Among the Kachins of Burma, whom he studied, story-telling always has a purpose, for "it serves to validate the status of the individual who tells the story." However, when one person validates his claim by invoking a myth, someone else is likely to dispute him: "if the status of one individual is validated, that almost always means that the status of someone else is denigrated." Consequently, each tale occurs "in several versions, each tending to uphold the claims of a different vested interest" (1954:265–66). Leach writes that myth "is a language of argument, not a chorus of harmony" (p. 278).

CONCLUSION

A theme which runs through all of Malinowski's work and which binds it into an integral whole is his thesis that both culture and human behavior are dynamic. A typical illustration of this dynamism appears in a discussion of the Trobriand emergence myth; Malinowski writes that the myth "is not an idle fairy-tale. It is a live force, active, effective, co-ordinating human work, integrating human grouping, and conferring very definite economic benefits on people" (1935, I:350). Culture and the individual are always in motion, never stationary. The individual is activated by strong desires to satisfy his needs, to advance himself in society, and to achieve other personal goals. Culture not only conforms to these inborn motivations, it serves them. To Malinowski, culture hardly needs to be imposed on the individual, for it is a complex instrumental apparatus which the individual uses in his everyday affairs.

The coherence of Malinowski's scheme is more fragile than he supposed, however, for his thought was actually moving in several different directions at once. On the whole, he tended to have a monistic image of man; he regarded the mainsprings of human behavior as natural, innate drives and inclinations. These drives and inclinations are the basis of the grounding of culture, in that they provide the compulsion behind the individual's conformity to traditional patterns. However, two distinguishable kinds of inborn motivations appear in Malinowski's analyses of action. The first are interests and are illustrated by the desire for social honor and prestige. The interests entail a cynical view of behavior, for they imply that the individual derives benefits from the adherence to custom and that his conformity is the product of a more or less conscious process of calculation. The second are predispositions, which entail the idea that culture is an expression of man's nature. An example is the bond between father and son; this relationship is based upon the natural affection which they feel toward one another. Whenever Malinowski assigns a prominent role to the predispositions in his work, conformity is not conceived as a product of calculation at all.

The coherence of Malinowski's scheme is even less secure at

the level of the cultural system itself. His functionalism rested on the idea that culture is a dynamic, integral whole: each part has a role to play in the working system, and each is to be seen in terms of its contribution. A closer look at his scheme reveals that his idea of the wholeness of culture is made up of several different features, however. The first is his integrationalism, which simply entails the notion that the parts of the culture system are interrelated. The second is his dualistic form of utilitarianism, according to which each aspect of culture is conceived as contributing to an ulterior end; this end is the persistence and integrity of the larger whole. Third is his monistic form of utilitarianism, according to which the end which institutions serve is the needs and interests of human beings. The first element of Malinowski's holism is in disagreement with his image of man, and the second receives even less support from the rest of his theory. Only the third is fully compatible with the other parts of Malinowski's scheme; it constitutes the chief feature of his functional approach to culture.

VII

CONCLUSION

The writers considered in this book employed a wide variety of explanatory principles in their work—cultural evolution, cultural ecology, functionalism, and configurationalism, to name a few. Nevertheless, their schemes are alike in at least one respect. Behind all the diversity, each of their theories explains human affairs in the sense that it makes them intelligible. Each theorist seeks by his or her theory to reveal the point or significance of behavior and social institutions, or to make sense of beliefs and practices which at first seem alien and opaque. In short, each thinker assumes that he has located the principle of meaning (see Chapter 1).

This interpretive or meaningful form of explanation is distinguishable from scientific explanation, according to which the thing that is explained is subsumed under a general covering law. A characteristic of scientific explanation is that it allows predictions, since it attempts to supply the causal factors behind a phenomenon so that when the appropriate conditions exist the phenomenon can be expected. By contrast, meaningful explanation attempts to make a phenomenon intelligible, and the issue of prediction does not arise. For example, if I observe a person in a foreign society engaging in activities that make no sense to me, I do not necessarily search for the causal conditions which necessitate his actions and which allow me to predict when they will occur again. I simply try to discover what he is doing. Suppose the person I am observing is performing an esoteric rite over what appears to be a small bundle of leaves. At first his behavior is opaque to me, and I ask someone to explain his actions. I might be told that he is performing magic over some of the remains of last year's crop and that the performance is intended to insure the abundance of his next crop. I later learn that this rite is part of a complex system of magical beliefs and practices. I have now achieved a degree of understanding. Scientific explanations answer "why" questions—why an event occurs, for example, or why a phenomenon behaves in a certain way. Meaningful interpretations answer "what" questions, such as "What is this person doing?"

To supply a meaningful explanation of a phenomenon is to see it in context. A magical rite may seem puzzling when seen in isolation, but it becomes intelligible when viewed in relation to a system of beliefs and cultural pursuits. A social usage which at first seems absurd makes sense when viewed as part of a larger system of social relations.

A principal goal of this book is to show that the culture concept and image of man that an anthropologist employs guide him in the meaning which he sees in his data. His ideas about culture and man lead him to portray human affairs in a certain light by viewing them in relation to one context rather than another.

Tylor's views about human affairs reflect the British tradition of utilitarian thought. According to Tylor, the feature which stands out about human institutions is that they express the goals and interests of the members of society. For example, language is essentially a tool which people use in communicating with one another, and it is to be understood in that context. Linguistic systems are purposefully designed to serve, and are more or less adequate for, the needs of human discourse. Similarly, morals are a means for promoting human happiness, and, if not adhered to, the individual will suffer. Victorian sexual standards express an intelligent desire to improve man's condition. Religion and myth are to be seen in the same light. The belief in souls and gods originated in man's desire to understand such phenomena as dreams, death, and sleep, and nature myths arose as a result of the savage's need to account for the natural phenomena around him. In short, cultural phenomena are oriented toward certain ends; remove the ends and the institutions appear meaningless.

The meaning of culture is not fully revealed by reference to the ends served, however, for institutions also express rational, intellectual processes: language, moral principles, religion, and myth all represent more or less rational, more or less intelligent attempts to come to terms with certain issues which people have faced through the ages. The meaningfulness of beliefs and practices, then, is discoverable by grasping both the intellectual processes of thought by which they developed and the human ends toward which they are oriented.

Tylor's interpretation of behavior rests upon the assumption that, by and large, human action is rational. The less gifted individuals and societies are encumbered by ignorance and error, and by a disinclination or inability to think through the problems before them. Nevertheless, even their simple-mindedness is a form of rationality, a low-grade form. If behavior is to be made intelligible, it is to be seen in terms of intellectual principles of thought and interpreted according to a single scale of reason. The ne'er-do-well, the drunkard, or the irascible is not someone who is suffering from emotional problems or rebelling against society; he is simply a person who has not sense enough to understand where his actions are leading him. Those who are industrious, upright, and thrifty, and who display a tempered compassion toward the less fortunate, exhibit the wisdom that civilization has to offer.

One of the most distinctive features of Tylor's scheme is that it minimizes the significance of culture as a determinant of human behavior. To Tylor, it is native intelligence and not the

inculcation of values which guides the civilized, Victorian Englishman. It is an intellectual deficiency and not an emotional
attachment to custom which makes the savages behave as they
do.

On the other hand, Boas elevated culture to the position of
the primary determinant of man's behavior. To Boas, the actions of human beings are not interpretable according to the
principle of reason, but by reference to social tradition. An individual's actions are to be understood by inquiring into the
customs of his society.

For the most part, the reasoning which an individual offers
in order to justify his actions and institutions is nothing more
than a form of rationalization. For example, the Oxonian is deceiving himself when he asserts that his dialect is a more effective instrument of communication than that of a coal miner. A
key factor behind the rationalization of custom—and a critical
principle to recognize in attempting to understand human
behavior—is that man is an emotional and not a rational creature. Tylor's preferences for the languages, arts, and refine-
ments of modern Europe, and for the standards of thrift, industriousness, and self-discipline of his society, were not based
upon rational considerations at all, but upon an emotional attachment to custom. Tylor's vision was perverted and deceived
by the sentiment within him. The anthropologist must penetrate beyond the level of intellectual reflection to that of habit
and emotional associations—or to the level of subjective
culture—in order to throw light upon the individual's behavior.

If behavior is made intelligible by reference to culture, how
are social institutions themselves to be understood? In Tylor's
scheme, institutions are fixed in place by their effectiveness in
resolving the problems which men face. For example, the persistence of Victorian standards of morality is explained by the
fact that these standards are useful in promoting human happiness. Boas' cultural determinism severed the tie between cus-

tom on the one hand and individual reason and human ends on the other. Culture is *sui generis* in relation to man's nature; it is irrational, for it is free to vary almost randomly with respect to rational thought and natural human goals, and this irrationality is an important principle to grasp in assessing the meaning of human affairs. The Kwakiutl potlatch, the religious wars in European history, and even the voting patterns of modern Western democracy illustrate the irrationality of tradition.

Institutions are not entirely unintelligible, however, according to Boas. In order to understand them they must be analyzed according to their own *sui generis* principles. The first of these is diffusion. A specific trait, such as a form of basketry or a type of myth, acquires at least a degree of meaning when it is conceived as a local variety of a more generalized culture element that has been diffused throughout a region. However, the depth of meaning which is afforded by diffusion studies is quite limited. In addition, distributional analyses tend to lead to the view that a culture is utterly meaningless, that it is a pointless jumble of elements, the result of countless historical accidents.

The second and more important principle for the understanding of culture is that of modification, according to which a newly diffused trait is altered to fit the context in which it has become established. A custom makes sense once it is recognized how it fits or articulates with the other elements with which it is associated. For example, among the Kwakiutl Indians, legends are owned and jealously guarded by kin groups. This custom may appear meaningless when viewed in isolation, but it is intelligible when seen in relation to the social competitiveness of these people. The exclusive ownership of legends reflects the Kwakiutl emphasis on prestige and rivalry. Similarly, the zeal of the Kwakiutl chief in destroying and giving away his property at the potlatch acquires significance in relation to the larger cultural context. The principle of modification, or integration, offers almost unlimited possibilities for the interpretation of custom and behavior, and it constituted one of the primary lines of development open to Boasian anthropology.

There is a third principle behind culture in Boas' scheme: the limitations of the environment. To Boas, the limits imposed by the environment are quite broad, and this aspect of his scheme was therefore comparatively unimportant for the interpretation of culture and human behavior.

Like Boas, Benedict attempted to explain culture in terms of its internal principles and not by reference to such external factors as human goals, the conditions of the environment, or the exigencies of life. The explanatory principle which became paramount in her work was the cultural configuration, a concept which she developed by elaborating two key features of Boas' thought: his view that human behavior is fundamentally emotional, and his idea that the elements of culture are progressively modified to fit the context in which they occur. Benedict's configurational approach consists in an integrational analysis according to which emotional consistency is the principle behind the unity of the cultural whole.

The configuration constitutes the key to the meaning of both custom and behavior. The frenzied and masochistic vision quest, and the aggressive patterns of warfare of the Plains Indians, may appear to be foolish, even grotesque, institutions; the people themselves may seem senseless and cruel when engaging in them. However, these patterns are perfectly intelligible when seen in relation to the cultural configuration, which emphasizes individual achievement and renown. Both war exploits and the attainment of visions are means for acquiring personal glory, and they are perfectly consistent with the emotional bent of Plains culture. Tylor made custom and behavior appear nonsensical when he used rational principles of thought as the guide for understanding human affairs, for the meaning of man's actions is impenetrable from that point of view.

It was largely a desire to discover the meaning in culture and behavior which motivated Benedict to develop her theory of cultural configurations, for she was not content with mere descriptions of opaque customary practices. Moreover, it was no accident that the approach she selected was an integrational approach, for within Boas' scheme it was the principle of modification or integration which provided the greatest opportunities for seeing meaning in human affairs.

Kroeber explicitly noted the close similarity between Benedict's ideas and his own (1935:555–58), and yet their views were far from identical. Kroeber divided most of culture into two categories, the basic and secondary features. The former are directed toward the practical matters of life; they are to be understood in relation to the problems of subsistence and survival. For example, the dominant type of subsistence pattern in aboriginal California focused on the gathering and preparation of acorns; this pattern acquires meaning when it is viewed as a mode of adjustment to the exigencies of life in that region. On the other hand, value culture is an expression of creative impulses, and its distinctive attribute is the quality of playfulness. It is important to recognize this quality in interpreting or assessing the meaning of an institution. For example, much of the social organization of a primitive society does not manifest practical considerations at all, but the desire for playful innovation and elaboration; this is true of the system of clans among the Zuni, and the systems of kinship, marriage and descent among the Australian aborigines. Kroeber made sense of social organization, ceremonial life, and much of the rest of culture by viewing them as one would an elaborate game.

Kroeber placed a definite value on the secondary features of culture, and this had further implications for the meaning which he saw in human affairs. Value culture, to him, is not merely frivolous or light-hearted play, for it represents human achievement. The complicated social organization of the Australian aborigines represents the flowering of human creativity in the same way as Renaissance art or modern philosophy.

Steward focused on what Kroeber referred to as the basic features of culture. Moreover, Steward developed his scheme partly in response to a view which was common among Boasians during the first few decades of this century: the view that the traditions of a society are a pointless accumulation of traits fortuitously assembled by diffusion. Like Benedict and Kroeber, Steward conceived culture as a more or less coherent and meaningful whole. However, he also believed that anthropology should attempt to become a science, and he wanted to avoid developing a subjective approach to human affairs. Consequently, he focused upon phenomenal and not subjective factors in his interpretation of institutions: he turned to the unbending limitations of the environment in order to make custom intelligible.

Steward distinguished between the culture core—those elements of culture which are closely related to subsistence and economic activities—and the secondary features. The secondary features, which include myth, pottery designs, ritual practices, and the like, are not directly tied to ecological factors and are governed primarily by such fortuitous historical principles as diffusion. Steward tacitly regarded the secondary features as meaningless: they simply exist, and little more can be said about them.

On the other hand, the culture core is made intelligible by viewing it in relation to the natural environment. The family level of organization of the Shoeshone Indians is related to such ecological factors as the limited and uncertain food supply, which makes it impossible to have a sedentary way of life or for more than a few people to live in close proximity. Shoshone family organization becomes intelligible when viewed in the context of ecological factors. Similarly, Steward's framework gives meaning to Shoshone property rights: the principle of "first come, first served" is ideally suited to a society characterized by a high degree of physical mobility.

To Steward, the environmental limitations are not nearly as indeterminate and unimportant as Boas believed, for culture is closely tied to the features of the natural world. Culture is practical, not irrational; it is responsive to the exigencies of life, and this is an important principle to grasp in assessing the meaning of human affairs. In order to discover the relations between culture and the environment, however, it is necessary to step outside the sphere of subjective culture and to analyze the system objectively. What is critical for an understanding of Shoshone property rights and family organization is not the subjective patterns which Boas, Benedict, and Kroeber focused upon, but the causal, ecological factors which provide the context for these traits. The subjective approach concentrates on the trivial or contingent, and not on the fundamental, features of culture.

In developing his ecological approach Steward was on the verge of revising the Boasian view of human behavior. To Steward, culture is more practical and less irrational than Boas believed, and behavior is less dominated by irrational tradition. Compared to Boas, Steward implicitly gave greater scope to the dictates of reason and personal interests. To Steward, then, the meaning of behavior cannot be understood solely in relation to custom; individual interests and creative thought need to be given an emphasis which they did not receive in Boas' work.

White's earliest writings exhibit an integrational approach which reflects his Boasian roots. However, his thought gradually moved toward an altogether different mode of interpretation, for he eventually arrived at a fully utilitarian view of culture. This shift was probably due to the development of his evolutionary theory. By 1930 White was convinced that the history of culture is characterized by progress, which in turn calls for the view that institutions serve man's general welfare: it was difficult for him to evaluate a custom as better or more advanced than another unless he could assert that it was a benefit to society. The form which White's utilitarianism took reflected the functionalism of such writers as Durkheim, Malinowski, and Radcliffe-Brown, but the stimulus was provided by the logic of his own thought.

Within the utilitarian framework, the significance or meaning of custom is not established simply by tracing the relations between traits and showing how they fit together. The relations between the elements of the system are thought to serve an ulterior end, and it is by reference to this end that intelligibility is achieved. For example, a religious ritual is only partially explained by showing its connections with economic and political factors, for it is necessary to go a step farther and show how the interrelatedness of the system is beneficial. The religious system may provide a rationale and sanction for economic activities, and it may contribute to political cohesion; and in doing so it promotes the physical security of the people and the effective utilization of their technological system.

From the perspective of White's utilitarianism, culture is conceived as having a shape or structure which Boas tacitly rejected. Within White's framework it is the function of customs which is given prominence, and all institutions are viewed by him in relation to their functional contributions to the effectiveness of the technology. The technological system is therefore foundational: sentiments, beliefs, social organization, and the like all support and promote its operation. Boas implicitly denied the existence of the utilitarian dimension behind cultural integration, and in doing so he tacitly denied that the technological system is necessarily the basis of the total culture. He saw only the particular relations between the elements of the system and not the general structure which appears when the data are seen from White's utilitarian point of view.

According to White's frame of reference, the utility of institutions is discoverable at the objective and not the subjective level, for the value of cultural practices is beyond both the awareness and the control of the members of society. Moreover, the ends of society are often in conflict with those of the individual, and his conformity must be achieved by instilling cultural beliefs and values in him. In a sense, then, White agrees with the Boasian view that individual behavior is dominated by custom and that it is irrational. It is only at the level of the total system that the value and meaning of man's actions become apparent.

Whereas the central concept of Boasian anthropology was the notion of culture, in Durkheimian thought it was the collective life, the system of collective representations. There are substantial differences between the Boasian culture concept and the collective representations of Durkheim's theory, and yet they are alike in that each constitutes a framework for the interpretation of man's thoughts and actions. Each may be seen as an expository notion for assessing the meaning of human affairs.

Within Durkheim's scheme there are three ways to interpret behavior. First, according to his causal framework, the collective life varies in relation to the social substratum, which is the system of physical relations linking the members of society. Societies which are small and whose members engage in intense social relations are characterized by a high degree of formalism and social surveillance, and the people exhibit a strong emotional commitment to their traditional patterns—in short, individualism is given little scope. Complex societies consist of large numbers of people who do not engage in intense social relations, and the individual enjoys considerable latitude and freedom. The collective representations—or culture—are to be seen in the context of this causal framework. For example, in simple societies the individual is submerged within his social milieu: he is accorded less respect or dignity than the social segment of which he is a member, and it is even required that he give his life, if necessary, for the honor of the group. In complex societies the individual is relatively autonomous; increasingly he becomes an object of concern, and more and more his suffering becomes a matter of social importance. For example, the pain inflicted on criminals is becoming less in modern societies. The meaning of such collective or cultural phenomena as patterns of punishment and feelings of family honor is to be assessed by reference to this causal scheme. If Boas thought that culture varies almost randomly within the rather broad limits set by the environment, he was mistaken; he failed to view custom and behavior in terms of the appropriate causal framework, and as a result he failed to unlock some of the meaning contained in the data.

The second principle for the interpretation of human affairs is that of function, by which Durkheim meant the role which an institution plays in maintaining or perpetuating the collective life. The full significance of a religious ritual, for example, cannot be appreciated unless viewed in relation to the social function it performs. Durkheim's functionalism is not adequately described as a form of utilitarianism, however. To him, the collective life enables man to surpass the determinism of his animal nature and to transcend the life of simple, fleeting sensations, and it therefore enables him to lead a higher "spiritual" existence; but the collective representations, or culture, do not necessarily adapt man to the natural world or contribute to his physical well-being. The function of an institution is its service in relation to man's "spiritual," not his material, life.

Durkheim's causal and functional analyses do not exhaust the meaning of social phenomena, for the collective life is partially autonomous from its material base and it must be interpreted according to its own internal, subjective principles. Durkheim's subjective interpretation was both an optimistic and a symbolic mode of analysis. Neither collective activity nor an individual's behavior can be understood primarily in terms of habit and emotion, as Boas believed, for there is another dimension altogether which must be grasped: this is the dimension of social symbolism. The reverence which people feel toward their clan totem is not a simple manifestation of habit; the totem is invested with supernatural power and elicits feelings of awe in people's minds because it is a representation of the social milieu to which they are passionately attached. Tylor's feelings about the dialect and morals of his social class were more than simple, customary responses. These patterns of speech and moral principles were symbols of Tylor's social milieu, and when he praised their virtues he was engaging in symbolic behavior. The customs of a people, and the actions of an individual, cannot be fully understood until this symbolic dimension has been penetrated and interpreted.

Although Radcliffe-Brown thought of himself as a follower of Durkheim, a gulf separates the views of the two writers. Three forms of interpretation are contained within Durkheim's scheme, and Radcliffe-Brown focused on one of them, the function concept. He then reinterpreted this concept along utilitarian lines and made it the central feature of his own approach. To Radcliffe-Brown, all societies are faced with problems—the threat of internal disruption, disorder, and disintegration. The function of a custom is the role it plays in minimizing these problems, or in contributing to the stability and cohesion of society and therefore to the welfare of its members.

To Radcliffe-Brown, then, the principal way in which the meaning of human activities is revealed is by the use of the functional method, or by discovering the role which the institution plays in maintaining the social structure. If an anthropologist should come upon a joking relationship in a foreign society, the custom may appear to him as a peculiar but insignificant trait, a mere oddity. However, the practice acquires substance when viewed in the context of the functional needs of the social system. The custom serves to minimize the danger of an open breach in the social fabric; and it occurs at precisely that point where conflict is liable to occur but is important to avoid. Similarly, unilineal descent systems acquire significance when it is realized that they are a particularly effective means for avoiding ambiguity in social relations. A system of unilineal descent allows the rights and duties of the members of society to be defined with precision, and it therefore minimizes the possibility of internal conflict.

There is a secondary key to understanding in Radcliffe-Brown's scheme. This is the social structure concept itself, for a particular feature of the social system acquires significance when seen in relation to the larger social organization. For example, it is possible to achieve a greater understanding of the family structure of a given society by discovering how it fits with the clan system; an understanding of the clan system itself is increased when it is viewed in relation to the political organization. The social structural form of interpretation is not entirely separate from the functional mode of analysis, however; behind the purely structural explanation is the assumption that it is functionally advantageous for the parts of the system to fit together into an ordered whole. The greater the consistency between the aspects of society, the less the opportunity for conflict to arise or for social disintegration to occur. In the final analysis, a social structural explanation is equally, but implicitly, a functional interpretation.

According to Radcliffe-Brown, institutions make sense in terms of the objective exigencies of the social system and not by reference to the thoughts and sentiments of the members of society, for the people need not be aware of the functions their institutions serve nor of the exigencies which have to be met. In a sense, even subjective culture is to be seen objectively, for it must be analyzed in terms of its functional contributions to the total system and not by reference to its credibility or cogency. Beliefs may indeed make sense by themselves and without reference to the functions they perform; but that is beside the point. What is crucial is the contribution they make to the persistence and maintenance of society.

According to Evans-Pritchard, however, it is by reference to subjective culture that understanding is achieved. Man is a free agent, and he is morally responsible for his actions. His behavior and institutions are not governed by the functional needs of the social system, as Radcliffe-Brown maintained. Rather, human activities are to be understood in terms of the beliefs, values, and sentiments of the individual: institutions make sense when viewed from the inside. For example, Zande witchcraft beliefs are internally coherent and logically tight; they are *believable* to the Azande, and it is not necessary to resort to a functional analysis to discover their meaning. Magical rites, the consulting of oracles, witchcraft accusations, and the like, can be made intelligible by grasping the ideas and sentiments which are behind them. Similarly, the ritual of sacrifice among the Nuer becomes quite intelligible by examining the cultural ideas and values it expresses. Even the physical organization of society is to be seen from the inside, or according to the cultural categories and values of the people. Nuer social structure is elucidated through the analysis of certain key terms, such as *cieng,* and by learning the values which define the lineages and local groups. In Evans-Pritchard's view, Radcliffe-Brown's functional analysis superimposes an illegitimate meaning or significance on the facts, for it views institutions in terms of a nonexistent ulterior end.

Evans-Pritchard was a student of Malinowski, and there are some distinct similarities between their ideas. Both built their theories on the premise that the individual must occupy a central position in anthropological thought, and in doing so they rejected the view that a person is not his own master. When they assert the autonomy of the individual, however, Malinowski and Evans-Pritchard are actually moving in very different directions, and they attack fundamentally different types of "determinism." It even appears that they regard one another's theories as prime examples of what they are against. Malinowski tended toward a cynical view of behavior, according to which the individual is conceived as using and manipulating culture for his own ends. Human action is not adequately described as a reflection of cultural values and beliefs. Malinowski was particularly virulent in his attacks against Durkheim, who, he felt, reduced man to a slavish follower of custom. I suspect that Malinowski would have included Evans-Pritchard in his list of those who committed the errors of cultural determinism, for Evans-Pritchard presents an optimistic view of behavior. The individual is conceived as exhibiting a disinterested commitment to his cultural values. Moreover, to Evans-Pritchard, man is not governed by the principles of biology, culture, or society. Evans-Pritchard directs his own attacks primarily against the sociologism of Radcliffe-Brown, but he includes Malinowski's cultural theory as an example of functional determinism.

To Malinowski, understanding at the level of individual behavior is achieved by penetrating to the level of interests and predispositions. It is necessary to see behind custom and to discover the natural motivations which are the mainsprings of human action. For example, to understand the activities of the Trobriand gardener, it is necessary to grasp the ambitiousness and the desires for advantage which motivate him. To understand the behavior of the primitive magician it is necessary to recognize the emotional needs which compel him to act.

Malinowski employed still another set of principles in his interpretation of the cultural system itself. The first is integrationalism, an approach which is not very different from that used by the Boasians. An understanding of the chiefship in the Trobriands is achieved when it is seen in relation to village organization, economic activities, the kula exchange, and the like. Second, Malinowski offered a dualistic form of utilitarianism, according to which meaning is revealed by discovering the way in which an aspect of custom, such as a myth, contributes to the persistence of the total cultural system. The third and most important mode of interpretation of culture is Malinowski's monistic form of utilitarianism, according to which meaning is discovered by locating the functions which a trait serves in relation to the emotional and biological needs of man. For example, magic is made intelligible when it is recognized that its performance relieves the anxieties of the human actor, and that in doing so it enables him to better cope with the problems he faces.

All the anthropological approaches considered here supply the meaning of human affairs, even though the writers themselves did not always intend to do so and were unaware that they had. For example, Tylor's attention was directed toward his evolutionary approach, and he devoted the majority of his work to demonstrating progressive sequences of development in the cultural record—in short, he focused primarily on how and why institutions evolved. He virtually ignored the utilitarian and intellectualist assumptions by which he interpreted human thought and action. White focuses his attention on evolution, and Steward on ecology. Both seem to have missed the distinctive kinds of meaning which their ideas project onto custom and behavior.

Even though the interpretation of meaning may not be the conscious goal of a writer's work, it may still occupy a central place in his approach. For example, White would argue that cultural evolution is one of the leading aspects of his scheme. Nevertheless, what is most important may not be his evolutionary theory at all, but the utilitarian interpretation of institutions. If his evolutionary theory were eliminated altogether, his utilitarianism would remain an important influence within the field, and most of his interpretations of specific institutions, such as the analyses which are contained in *The Evolution of Culture* (1959a), would be virtually unaffected.

In the introductory chapter I raised the possibility that two anthropologists looking at the same datum need not "see" the same thing, for the different frames of reference which they use in viewing human behavior may lead them to interpret it in very dissimilar ways. What occupies the foreground in one scheme fades into the background in another.

There are some who would argue that the observer's point of

view is so fundamental in structuring his perception and understanding that the "facts" can never be fully distinguished from "theory." Empirical data must be viewed from a perspective of some kind, and in that sense they do not have an existence independent of the observer. If this line of reasoning is followed to its logical conclusions, it is difficult to avoid the view that the observer's scheme can never be tested scientifically: the data are *part* of his perspective and cannot be used to verify or discredit it. On the other hand, some would argue that the distinction between "fact" and "theory" is clear enough that scientific discriminations are indeed possible.

I do not wish to enter into this argument here, but simply to assert that an anthropologist's frame of reference *does* tend to shape his view of the data, and that this often occurs without his realizing it. The explanation of human affairs is not an entirely objective procedure.

For example, to Malinowski, man is goal-oriented, and an adequate account of custom must include an elucidation of the ends which the individual is seeking when he participates in cultural activities. To understand gardening in the Trobriands, for example, it is not enough merely to describe the customary patterns of thought and behavior which have been handed down from generation to generation. The account must move to the level of individual goals and reveal the dispositions and interests—such as the desire for social esteem—which motivate the actor in his role. On the other hand, Boas' frame of reference throws a very different set of factors into relief. In his view, behavior follows the grooves carved by habit, and a custom is adequately accounted for by describing its form. Gardening practices are manifestations of traditional patterns, not self-interest. Boas did not automatically exclude individual ends from his analysis, but in the context of his scheme personal goals always remained in the shadows. Even if they were observed and noted by the anthropologist, they were ascribed comparatively little significance.

Boas' and Malinowski's disagreement over the interpretation of myth also illustrates that the understanding of human affairs is not an entirely objective procedure. When Boas wrote his monographs on the tales of the Northwest Coast tribes, he conceived himself as a scrupulous recorder of facts, presenting the data as accurately and fully as possible. He explicitly avoided all preconceptions derived from his own background. To Malinowski, however, the myths of the Northwest Coast are presented in disembodied form in Boas' books, for, among other things, the motivations behind the tales are completely ignored. Boas' presentation was not a faithful rendering of the data after all, but manifested his own more or less implicit views about culture and behavior. Since custom is a type of habit, according to Boas, an account which concentrates on the form of the response and which ignores the Malinowskian interests and predispositions is fully complete.

In sum, two anthropologists, observing the same person at the same time, may not agree what that individual is doing. To Boas, the Trobriand Islander who assiduously accumulates and redistributes his yams is manifesting the traditional patterns of his society, whereas in Malinowski's view he is pursuing his own self-interest. To Tylor, the civilized European who expresses distaste for the standards of etiquette or the patterns of speech of the uneducated classes is behaving sensibly and rationally; to Boas, he is manifesting the habitual and emotional preferences he has learned; to Durkheim, he is expressing an attachment to his social milieu through the symbols which set it apart from the other segments of society.

A chief goal of this book has been to focus on a particular way in which anthropologists disagree over what they see in their data. The emphasis here has been on differences in the interpretation of meaning.

The issue of meaning has exerted an influence on and given direction to some important theoretical developments in the field. It is perhaps a truism that an approach is compelling in

354

proportion to its explanatory power; the capacity of a theory to supply satisfactory explanations is a measure both of its influence within the discipline and of the conviction of its supporters. Since the interpretation of meaning is one form of explanation, it follows that an approach will enjoy a degree of support and influence as a result of its capacity to supply the sense of behavior.[1] The growth of Benedict's ideas is illustrative. Initially, she employed a general integrational approach to culture, but she was not fully satisfied with the results. She was drawn toward a more comprehensive framework in her desire to explain why cultures exhibit their distinctive forms of organization, and she eventually arrived at the idea of the cultural configuration. Her configuration concept had the capacity of showing the sense of a wide variety of customs—from Plains warfare and Pueblo divorce patterns to Dobuan gardening practices. Her configurationalism has been severely criticized for its lack of rigor, and she must have been aware of its problems; nevertheless, something convinced her that the scheme had value in spite of its defects. The persuasion may have come from its ability to supply the meaning of custom and behavior.

Even if the expressed goal of an anthropologist is to trace causal sequences, locate evolutionary or social laws, and the like—in short, even if his expressed goal is to provide answers to the question "why" and not "what"—the pursuit of meaning may still be a critical stimulus behind both the work of that individual and the development of his thought. Radcliffe-Brown's work is illustrative. One reason why Radcliffe-Brown embraced Durkheimian theory may have been that the function concept proved to be highly successful in showing that Andamanese religion is not a pointless assemblage of rites and beliefs. Radcliffe-Brown probably would have argued that his

---

[1] Other forms of explanation, including the scientific, may also offer compelling accounts of the anthropologist's data and acquire an enthusiastic following as a result. In excluding these other forms of explanations from the present discussion I do not mean to deny their importance.

convictions about functionalism arose from the scientific demonstration of its validity, but few today are convinced of the rigor of his analyses. His certainty of the value of the approach must have come from elsewhere, at least in part, and possibly the source was the sense which his utilitarianism made of custom. After Radcliffe-Brown completed his work on the Andamanese, he proceeded to apply this method to an increasingly wider range of phenomena, such as joking and avoidance relationships, taboos, and ancestor worship; in each case he could show the meaning of the customs he focused upon.

Steward's theory is also suggestive. Clifford Geertz has criticized Steward for committing the fallacy of assuming what it was he was trying to prove, namely, that "the adaptive realities a given sociocultural system faces" are more important in influencing cultural development "than various other realities with which it is also faced" (Geertz 1963:11). According to Geertz, Steward merely asserted and did not demonstrate that social change is traceable to cultural ecological factors. Steward's ideas about the role of ecology in culture history exhibited "a mere prejudice" (Geertz 1963:11) and did not reflect actual research.

If Geertz' criticism is valid, what was so compelling about Steward's scheme, both to Steward himself and to the large number of anthropologists he influenced? In part, at least, it may have been that his framework enables the investigator to see meaning in human affairs. Steward could not only point to the Shoshone and assert that they failed to develop beyond the family level of organization because of ecological factors; in addition, he could show that the family organization of these people made sense in the context of Shoshone life. The issue of why they had failed to develop beyond the family level is a historical problem, and Steward had very little historical data in support of his analysis. On the other hand, the interpretation of meaning is a wholly synchronic matter and needs no historical evidence at all.

Divisions within the field may also be interpreted as differences of opinion over the meaning of behavior. For example, when Boas initially expressed his disagreement with the nineteenth-century evolutionists, he framed his argument primarily in terms of methodology. He urged abandonment of wide-ranging comparative studies in favor of detailed historical research. He held that if evolutionary patterns are to appear, they will do so as a result of the historical understanding of specific regions. Boas' students joined the dialogue in the first and second decades of this century, when the argument had begun to revolve around the issue of diffusion vs. evolution. The Boasians argued that the historical record does not reveal evolutionary stages and that the evolutionary approach is therefore invalid. In its place they proposed diffusionism, which is both a method and a view of history.

The issues involved were far more fundamental than appeared on the surface, however. By the early part of this century Boas had developed the view that behavior reflects custom far more than reason, and that the human animal is comparatively emotional and unreflective in his thoughts and actions. He also developed an irrational version of culture, according to which custom reflects fortuitous historical processes and is relatively autonomous from the exigencies of life. In short, the issue of diffusionism vs. evolutionism was only the tip of the iceberg, for what was also involved was a rejection of the Tylorian views concerning the rationality of human behavior and the utilitarianism of institutions. What was taking place was a fundamental revolution in ideas about the *meaning* of behavior.

The principle of meaning has implications for the future of anthropology as well as its past, for the goal of research may be profitably conceived as the attempt to locate an adequate framework for interpreting human affairs. This view provides an alternative to the positivistic conception of what the field should achieve.

A powerful current running through the discipline has been a desire to go beyond the level of description and arrive at general statements about human behavior. Unlike the historian, for whom the goal of research is typically a deeper and more detailed understanding of specific events, the anthropologist is commonly dissatisfied if his findings do not have broad significance. In seeking generalizations, anthropologists have usually taken the sciences as their model and have attempted to arrive at causal, natural laws behind human behavior. According to this positivistic viewpoint, explanation consists in bringing what is to be explained under a general covering law.

The contrast between the historian and the anthropologist is suggestive, for although the former may feel little need to search for general laws, he certainly employs generalizations in his work. If nothing else, he operates according to a more or less implicit image of man which he assumes has a degree of generality. In giving an account of political events, for example, he may need to judge whether an utterance expresses genuine convictions or if it is a subterfuge masking ulterior motives, and his image of man will guide his interpretation.

In seeking general principles behind human behavior the anthropologist need not take as his goal the search for natural laws, for the framework by which the meaning of man's actions is assessed is another form of generalization that merits attention. The investigator may attempt to work out or establish an adequate framework of this kind. In short, not only has the issue of meaning actually been an important force behind the development of anthropological thought, it also offers rich possibilities as the focus of research.

REFERENCES

ABERLE, DAVID F.
1960   "The Influence of Linguistics on Early Culture and Personal-
        ity Theory." In Gertrude E. Dole and Robert L. Carneiro,
        eds., *Essays in the Science of Culture in Honor of Leslie A.
        White* (N. Y., Crowell), pp. 1–29.

ALPERT, HARRY
1939   *Emile Durkheim and His Sociology.* N. Y., Columbia Univer-
        sity Press.

ASSOCIATION OF POLISH UNIVERSITY PROFESSORS
AND LECTURERS IN GREAT BRITAIN
1943   *Professor Bronislaw Malinowski.* London, Oxford University
        Press.

BARNES, HARRY ELMER
1960   "Foreword" to Gertrude E. Dole and Robert L. Carneiro, eds.,
        Essays in the Science of Culture in Honor of Leslie A. White
        (N. Y., Crowell), pp. xi–xlvi.

BARNOUW, VICTOR
1949   "Ruth Benedict: Apollonian and Dionysian." *University of To-
        ronto Quarterly,* 3:241–53.

BARTH, FREDRIK
1959a   "Segmentary Opposition and the Theory of Games: A Study of
        Pathan Organization," *Journal of the Royal Anthropological
        Institute,* 89:5–21.
1959b   *Political Leadership among Swat Pathans.* London, Athlone
        Press.

BEALS, RALPH
1968   "Kroeber, Alfred L." *International Encyclopedia of the Social
        Sciences.* N. Y., Macmillan.

BENDER, DONALD
1965   "The Development of French Sociology," *Journal of the His-
        tory of the Behavioral Sciences,* 1:139–51.

References

BENEDICT, RUTH

1923   "The Concept of the Guardian Spirit in North America." *Memoirs of the American Anthropological Association*, No. 29.

1928   "Psychological Types in the Cultures of the Southwest." Reprinted in Mead 1959:248–61.

1929   "The Science of Custom." Reprinted in V. F. Calverton, ed., *The Making of Man*. N. Y., The Modern Library (1931).

1931   "Tales of the Cochiti Indians." *Bureau of American Ethnology*, Bulletin 98.

1932   "Configurations of Culture in North America," *American Anthropologist*, 34:1–27.

1934   *Patterns of Culture*. Boston and N. Y., Houghton Mifflin.

1935   "Zuni Mythology." 2 vols. *Columbia University Contributions to Anthropology*, No. 21.

1936   "Marital Property Rights in Bilateral Society," *American Anthropologist*, 38:368–73.

1938   "Religion." In Franz Boas, ed., *General Anthropology* (N. Y., D. C. Heath & Co.), pp. 627–65.

1939a   "A Reply to Dr. Aginsky," *Character and Personality*, 7:344–5.

1939b   "Sex in Primitive Society," *American Journal of Orthopsychiatry*, 9:570–73.

1942   "Anthropology and Cultural Change," *American Scholar*, 11:243–48.

1943a   "Franz Boas as Ethnologist." In "Franz Boas: 1858–1942," *Memoirs of the American Anthropological Association*, No. 61.

1943b   Thai Culture and Behavior, An Unpublished War-Time Study Dated September, 1943. Data Paper No. 4, Southeast Asia Program, Dept. of Far Eastern Studies, Cornell University, Ithaca. February, 1952.

1946   *The Chrysanthemum and the Sword*. Boston, Houghton Mifflin.

1948   "Child Rearing in Certain European Countries." Reprinted in Mead 1959:449–58.

1956   "The Growth of Culture." (Edited by Margaret Mead, written in 1948). In *Man, Culture, and Society*, Harry L. Shapiro, ed. N. Y., Oxford University Press.

BENNETT, JOHN W.

1946   "The Interpretation of Pueblo Culture: A Question of Values," *Southwestern Journal of Anthropology*, 2:361–74.

BENOIT-SMULLYAN, EMILE

1948   "The Sociologism of Emile Durkheim and His School." In Harry Elmer Barnes, ed., *An Introduction to the History of Sociology* (Chicago, University of Chicago Press), pp. 499–537.

References

BIDNEY, DAVID

1953   *Theoretical Anthropology.* N. Y., Columbia University Press.

BOAS, FRANZ

1889   "On Alternating Sounds," *American Anthropologist,* 2:47–53.

1894   "Human Faculty as Determined by Race," *Proceedings of the American Association for the Advancement of Science,* 43:301–27.

1897   "Northern Elements in the Mythology of the Navaho," *American Anthropologist,* 10:371–76.

1898a   "Introduction," *Publications of the Jesup North Pacific Expedition,* 1:3–11.

1898b   "Facial Paintings of the Indians of Northern British Columbia," *Publications of the Jesup North Pacific Expedition,* 1:13–24.

1901a   "The Eskimo of Baffin Land and Hudson Bay," *Bulletin of the American Museum of Natural History,* Vol. 15, Part I.

1901b   "The Mind of Primitive Man," *Journal of American Folk-Lore,* 14:1–11.

1904   "The History of Anthropology," *Science,* n.s., 20:513–24.

1908   *Anthropology* (A Lecture Delivered at Columbia University in the Series on Science, Philosophy and Art, December 18, 1907). N. Y., Columbia University Press.

1909   "The Kwakiutl of Vancouver Island." *Publications of the Jesup North Pacific Expedition,* Vol. 5, Part 2, pp. 301–522.

1910   "Psychological Problems in Anthropology." *American Journal of Psychology,* 21:371–84.

1911   *The Mind of Primitive Man.* N. Y., Macmillan.

1927   *Primitive Art.* Cambridge, Harvard University Press.

1932   *Anthropology and Modern Life.* Revised edition. N. Y., W. W. Norton & Co. (1962).

1935   "Kwakiutl Culture as Reflected in Mythology," *Memoirs of the American Folk-Lore Society,* Vol. 28.

1938a   "An Anthropologist's Credo," *Nation,* 147:201–4.

1938b   "Methods of Research," in Boas *et al., General Anthropology.* N. Y., D. C. Heath.

1938c   *The Mind of Primitive Man.* Revised edition. N. Y., Free Press (1965).

1940   *Race, Language and Culture.* N. Y., Macmillan.

BOCK, KENNETH E.

1952   "Evolution and Historical Process," *American Anthropologist,* 54:486–96.

BOHANNAN, PAUL

1956   "On the Use of Native Language Categories in Ethnology," *American Anthropologist,* 58:557.

References

1960 "Conscience Collective and Culture." In Kurt H. Wolff, ed., *Essays on Sociology and Philosophy*. N. Y., Harper and Row (1964).

BOUGLÉ, CÉLESTIN

1951 "Preface to the Original Edition." In Emile Durkheim, *Sociology and Philosophy* (translated by D. F. Pocock). Glencoe, Ill., Free Press (1953), pp. xxxv–xli.

BRINTON, CRANE

1963 *The Shaping of Modern Thought*. Englewood Cliffs, N. J., Prentice-Hall.

BURROW, J. W.

1966 *Evolution and Society, A Study in Victorian Social Theory*. Cambridge, Cambridge University Press.

CODERE, HELEN

1966 "Introduction," to Franz Boas, *Kwakiutl Ethnography*. Chicago, University of Chicago Press.

COLLINGWOOD, R. G.

1970 *The Idea of History*. London, Oxford University Press.

DALTON, GEORGE

1965 "Primitive Money," *American Anthropologist*, 67:44–65.

DRAY, WILLIAM H.

1958 "Historical Understanding as Re-thinking." *University of Toronto Quarterly*, 27:200–15.

1959 " 'Explaining What' in History." In Patrick Gardiner, ed., *Theories of History*. N. Y., Free Press, pp. 403–8.

1964 *Philosophy of History*. Englewood Cliffs, N. J., Prentice-Hall.

DRIVER, HAROLD E.

1962 "The Contribution of A. L. Kroeber to Culture Area Theory and Practice." *Indiana University Publications in Anthropology and Linguistics,* 18. Baltimore, Md., Waverly Press.

DRUCKER, PHILIP, AND ROBERT F. HEIZER

1967 *To Make My Name Good*. Berkeley and Los Angeles, University of California Press.

DURKHEIM, EMILE

1892 *Montesquieu and Rousseau: Forerunners of Sociology*. Translated by Ralph Manheim. Ann Arbor, University of Michigan Press (1960).

1893 *The Division of Labor in Society*. Translated by George Simpson. Glencoe, Free Press (1960).

1895a *The Rules of Sociological Method*. Translated by Sarah A. Solovay and John H. Mueller. Glencoe, Free Press (1958).

362

References

1895b   *Socialism.* Translated by Charlotte Sattler, edited by Alvin W. Gouldner. N. Y., Collier Books (1962). (Originally presented as lectures in 1895–96; first published in French in 1928).

1897   *Suicide: A Study in Sociology.* Translated by John A. Spaulding and George Simpson. Glencoe, Free Press (1963).

1898a   *Incest: The Nature and Origin of the Taboo.* Translated by Edward Sagarin. N. Y., Lyle Stuart, Inc. (1963).

1898b   "Individual and Collective Representations." In *Sociology and Philosophy,* translated by D. F. Pocock. Glencoe, Free Press (1953).

1899   *Professional Ethics and Civic Morals.* Translated by Cornelia Brookfield. Glencoe, Free Press (1958).

1900   "Sociology and Its Scientific Field." Translated by Kurt H. Wolff. In Kurt H. Wolff, ed., *Essays on Sociology and Philosophy.* N. Y., Harper and Row (1964).

1901   "Author's Preface to the Second Edition." In Durkheim 1895a:xli–lviii.

1902a   "Preface to the Second Edition." In Durkheim 1893:1–31.

1902b   *Moral Education.* Translated by Everett K. Wilson and Herman Schnurer, edited by Everett K. Wilson. Glencoe, Free Press. (Originally presented as lectures in 1902–3; first published in French in 1925.)

1903   *Primitive Classification* (with Marcel Mauss). Translated and edited by Rodney Needham. Chicago, University of Chicago Press (1963).

1906   "The Determination of Moral Facts." In *Sociology and Philosophy,* translated by D. F. Pocock. Glencoe, Free Press (1953).

1911a   "Value Judgments and Judgments of Reality." In *Sociology and Philosophy,* translated by D. F. Pocock. Glencoe, Free Press (1953).

1911b   "Education: Its Nature and Its Role." In *Education and Sociology,* translated by Sherwood D. Fox. N. Y., Free Press (1968).

1912   *The Elementary Forms of the Religious Life.* Translated by Joseph Ward Swain. N. Y., Free Press (1965).

1914   "The Dualism of Human Nature and Its Social Conditions." Translated by Charles Blend. In Kurt H. Wolff, ed., *Essays on Sociology and Philosophy.* N. Y., Harper and Row (1964).

1960   *Les Règles de la Méthode Sociologique.* 14th edition. Paris, Presses Universitaires de France.

EGGAN, FRED, AND W. LLOYD WARNER

1956   "Alfred Reginald Radcliffe-Brown, 1881–1955," *American Anthropologist,* 58:544–47.

ELKIN, A. P.

1956   "A. R. Radcliffe-Brown, 1880–1955," *Oceania,* 26:239–51.

References

ERASMUS, CHARLES J.

1961   *Man Takes Control.* N. Y., Bobbs-Merrill.

1969   "Explanation and Reconstruction in Cultural Evolution," *Sociologus,* 19:20–38.

EVANS-PRITCHARD, E. E.

1928   "Oracle Magic of the Azande," *Sudan Notes and Records,* 11:1–53.

1929a   "The Morphology and Function of Magic." *American Anthropologist,* 31:619–41.

1929b   "The Study of Kinship in Primitive Societies," *Man,* 29:190–91 (148).

1929c   "Witchcraft *(Mangu)* Among the Azande," *Sudan Notes and Records,* 12:163–249.

1931a   "Sorcery and Native Opinion," *Africa,* 4:22–55.

1931b   "Mani, a Zande Secret Society," *Sudan Notes and Records,* 14:105–48.

1931c   "An Alternative Term for Brideprice," *Man,* 31:36–39 (42).

1932–33   "The Zande Corporation of Witchdoctors," *Journal of the Royal Anthropological Institute,* 62:291–336; 63:63–100.

1933   "The Intellectualist (English) Interpretation of Magic," *Bulletin of the Faculty of Arts* (Egyptian University, Cairo), 1:282–311.

1933–35   "The Nuer: Tribe and Clan," *Sudan Notes and Records,* 16:1–53; 17:1–57; 18:37–87.

1934a   "Levy-Bruhl's Theory of Primitive Mentality," *Bulletin of the Faculty of Arts* (Egyptian University, Cairo), 2:1–27.

1934b   "Zande Therapeutics." In Evans-Pritchard, *et al.,* eds., *Essays Presented to C. G. Seligman* (London, Kegan Paul), pp. 49–61.

1935   "Witchcraft," *Africa,* 8:417–22.

1936   "Science and Sentiment: An Exposition and Criticism of the Writings of Pareto," *Bulletin of the Faculty of Arts* (Egyptian University, Cairo), 3:163–92.

1937   *Witchcraft, Oracles and Magic Among the Azande.* Oxford, Clarendon Press.

1937–38   "Economic Life of the Nuer." *Sudan Notes and Records,* 20:209–45; 21:31–77.

1940   *The Nuer: A Description of the Modes of Livelihood and Political Institutions of a Nilotic People.* Oxford, Clarendon Press.

1946   "Social Anthropology," *Blackfriars,* 27:409–14.

1948   *Social Anthropology: An Inaugural Lecture Delivered before the University of Oxford on 4 February 1948.* Oxford, Clarendon Press.

1949   *The Sanusi of Cyrenaica.* Oxford, Clarendon Press.

References

1950   "Kinship and the Local Community Among the Nuer." In A. R. Radcliffe-Brown and D. Forde, eds., *African Systems of Kinship and Marriage* (London, Oxford University Press), pp. 360–91.

1951a   *Social Anthropology.* Glencoe, Free Press.

1951b   *Kinship and Marriage Among the Nuer.* Oxford, Clarendon Press.

1953a   "Religion in Primitive Society," *Blackfriars*, 34:211–18.

1953b   "Anthropology at Oxford." *Proceedings of the Five-hundredth Meeting of the Oxford University Anthropological Society, Held on February 25, 1953.* London, Oxford University Press.

1954   "Introduction." In Marcell Mauss, *The Gift.* Glencoe, Free Press.

1956   *Nuer Religion.* Oxford, Clarendon Press.

1960   "Introduction." In Robert Hertz, *Death and the Right Hand.* Glencoe, Free Press.

1964   *Social Anthropology and Other Essays.* Glencoe, Free Press.

1965a   *Theories of Primitive Religion.* Oxford, Clarendon Press.

1965b   *The Position of Women in Primitive Societies and Other Essays in Social Anthropology.* Glencoe, Free Press.

1967   "Social Anthropology and the Universities in Great Britain," *Universities Quarterly*, 21:167–81.

1970   "Bergson and Witchcraft," *Man*, 5:131.

FIRTH, RAYMOND

1942   "Prof. B. Malinowski." *Nature*, 149:661–62.

1952   Review of *Social Anthropology*, by E. E. Evans-Pritchard, *Man*, 52:37–39 (53).

1960   *Man and Culture: An Evaluation of the Work of Bronislaw Malinowski* (editor). London, Routledge and Kegan Paul.

FORDE, DARYLL

1950   "Anthropology, Science and History," *Man*, 50:155–56 (254).

FORTES, MEYER

1949   "Preface." *Social Structure: Studies Presented to A. R. Radcliffe-Brown*, Meyer Fortes, ed. N. Y., Russell and Russell (1963).

1953   *Social Anthropology at Cambridge since 1900, An Inaugural Lecture.* Cambridge, Cambridge University Press.

1955   "Radcliffe-Brown's Contribution to the Study of Social Organization," *British Journal of Sociology*, 6:16–30.

1956   "Alfred Reginald Radcliffe-Brown, F.B.A., 1881–1955: A Memoir," *Man*, 56:149–53.

1969   *Kinship and the Social Order.* Chicago, Aldine Publishing Company.

References

FRAKE, CHARLES O.

1962 "Cultural Ecology and Ethnology," *American Anthropologist*, 64:53–59.

FREIRE-MARRECO, BARBARA W.

1907 "A Bibliography of Edward Burnett Tylor." In *Anthropological Essays Presented to Edward Burnett Tylor*. Oxford, Clarendon Press.

GALLIE, W. B.

1952 *Pierce and Pragmatism*. Harmondsworth, Middlesex, Pelican Books.

GEERTZ, CLIFFORD

1963 *Agricultural Involution: The Process of Ecological Change*. Berkeley and Los Angeles, University of California Press.

GEHLKE, CHARLES ELMER

1915 *Emile Durkheim's Contributions to Sociological Theory*. N. Y., Columbia University Press.

GLUCKMAN, MAX

1956 *Custom and Conflict in Africa*. N. Y., Barnes and Noble (1967).

1963 *Order and Rebellion in Tribal Africa*. N. Y., Free Press.

GOLDSCHMIDT, WALTER, ED.

1959 "The Anthropology of Franz Boas." *Memoirs of the American Anthropological Association*, No. 89.

GOODENOUGH, WARD H.

1964 "Introduction." In Ward Goodenough, ed., *Explorations in Cultural Anthropology*. N. Y., McGraw-Hill.

HARDING, THOMAS G.

1960 "Adaptation and Stability." In Marshall D. Sahlins and Elman R. Service, eds., *Evolution and Culture*. Ann Arbor, University of Michigan Press.

HARRIS, MARVIN

1968 *The Rise of Anthropological Theory*. N. Y., Thomas Y. Crowell.

HERSKOVITS, MELVILLE J.

1965 "A Genealogy of Ethnological Theory." In Melford E. Spiro, ed., *Context and Meaning in Cultural Anthropology* (N. Y., Free Press), pp. 403–15.

HOMANS, GEORGE C.

1941 "Anxiety and Ritual: The Theories of Malinowski and Radcliffe-Brown," *American Anthropologist*, 43:164–72.

References

HUGHES, H. STUART

1958 *Consciousness and Society: The Reorientation of Social Thought, 1890–1930.* N. Y., Vintage Books.

HYMES, DELL H.

1961 "Alfred Louis Kroeber," *Language*, 37:1–28.

JARVIE, I. C.

1967 *The Revolution in Anthropology.* London, Routledge and Kegan Paul.

KARDINER, ABRAM, AND EDWARD PREBLE

1963 *They Studied Man.* N. Y., New American Library (Mentor Books).

KLUCKHOHN, CLYDE

1943 "Bronislaw Malinowski 1884–1942," *Journal of American Folk-Lore*, 56:208–19.

———, AND OLAF PRUFER

1959 "Influences During the Formative Years." In Walter Goldschmidt, ed., "The Anthropology of Franz Boas." *Memoirs of the American Anthropological Association*, No. 89, pp. 4–28.

KROEBER, ALFRED L.

1917 "Zuni Kin and Clan." *Anthropological Papers of the American Museum of Natural History*, Vol. 18, Part 2, pp. 39–204.

1919 "On the Principle of Order in Civilization as Exemplified by Changes of Fashion." *American Anthropologist*, 21:235–63.

1925 "Handbook of the Indians of California." *Bureau of American Ethnology*, Bulletin 78.

1935 "History and Science in Anthropology," *American Anthropologist*, 37:539–69.

1939 *Cultural and Natural Areas of Native North America.* Berkeley, University of California Press.

1940 "Three Centuries of Women's Dress Fashions; a Quantitative Analysis" (with Jane Richardson), *Anthropological Records*, vol. 5, no. 2, pp. i–iv, 111–153.

1944 *Configurations of Culture Growth.* Berkeley and Los Angeles, University of California Press.

1948 *Anthropology.* Revised edition. N. Y., Harcourt, Brace.

1952 *The Nature of Culture.* Chicago, University of Chicago Press.

1957 *Style and Civilizations.* Ithaca, Cornell University Press.

1962 "A Roster of Civilizations and Culture." *Viking Fund Publications in Anthropology*, 33.

1963 *An Anthropologist Looks at History* (edited by Theodora Kroeber). Berkeley and Los Angeles, University of California Press.

References

————, ET AL.

1943   "Franz Boas: 1858–1942." *Memoirs of the American Anthropological Association*, No. 61.

KROEBER, THEODORA

1970   *Alfred Kroeber: A Personal Configuration.* Berkeley, Los Angeles, and London, University of California Press.

KUHN, THOMAS S.

1962   *The Structure of Scientific Revolutions.* Chicago, University of Chicago Press.

LEACH, EDMUND

1954   *Political Systems of Highland Burma.* Cambridge, Harvard University Press.

1958   "Concerning Trobriand Clans and the Kinship Category *Tabu.*" In Jack Goody, ed., "The Developmental Cycle in Domestic Groups." *Cambridge Papers in Social Anthropology,* 1, pp. 120–45.

1966   "On the 'Founding Fathers'," *Current Anthropology,* 7:560–76.

LESSER, ALEXANDER

1968   "Franz Boas." *International Encyclopedia of the Social Sciences.* N. Y., Macmillan.

LÉVI-STRAUSS, CLAUDE

1945   "French Sociology." In Georges Gurvitch and Wilbert E. Moore, eds., *Twentieth Century Sociology.* N. Y., Philosophical Library.

LEWIS, I. M.

1968   "Introduction." In I. M. Lewis, ed., *History and Social Anthropology.* N. Y., Tavistock Publications.

LOWIE, ROBERT H.

1936   *Essays in Honor of Alfred Louis Kroeber* (editor). Berkeley, University of California Press.

1937   *The History of Ethnological Theory.* N. Y., Holt, Rinehart and Winston.

MALINOWSKI, BRONISLAW

1912   "The Economic Aspect of Intichiuma Ceremonies." In *Festskrift tillagnad Edvard Westermarck,* Helsingfors.

1913   *The Family among the Australian Aborigines.* N. Y., Schocken Books (1963).

1914a   Review of *Rest Days,* by Hutton Webster, *Man,* 14:46 (26).

1914b   "Sociologie der Familie," *Die Geisteswissenschaften,* 32:883–86, 33:911–14, 1080–82.

1915   "The Natives of Mailu: Preliminary Results of the Robert

References

Mond Research Work in British New Guinea," *Transactions of the Royal Society of South Australia,* 39:493–706.

1921a   "Primitive Economics of the Trobiand Islanders," *Economic Journal,* 31:1–16.

1921b   Review of *The Group Mind,* by William McDougall, *Man,* 21:106–9 (61).

1922a   "Ethnology and the Study of Society." *Economica,* London School of Economics, 2:208–19.

1922b   *Argonauts of the Western Pacific.* N. Y., E. P. Dutton & Company (1961).

1923   "The Problem of Meaning in Primitive Languages." In *The Meaning of Meaning,* by C. K. Ogden and I. A. Richards. London, Kegan, Paul, Trench, Trubner & Company.

1924a   "Instinct and Culture in Human and Animal Societies," *Nature,* 114:79–82.

1924b   "Psychoanalysis and Anthropology," *Psyche,* 4:293–332.

1925a   "The Forces of Law and Order in a Primitive Community," *Proceedings of the Royal Institution of Great Britain,* 24:529–47.

1925b   "Complex and Myth in Mother-Right," *Psyche,* 5:194–216.

1925c   Review of *Primitive Law,* by E. Sidney Hartland, *Nature,* 116:230–35.

1926a   "Primitive Law and Order," *Nature,* Vol. 117, Supplement, pp. 9–16.

1926b   "Anthropology." *Encyclopaedia Britannica,* 13th Edition, Vol. 1, pp. 131–40.

1926c   *Crime and Custom in Savage Society.* Patterson, N. J., Littlefield, Adams & Company (1959).

1927a   "The Life of Culture." In *Culture: the Diffusion Controversy,* by G. Elliot-Smith and others (N. Y., W. W. Norton & Company), pp. 26–46.

1927b   *Sex and Repression in Savage Society.* N. Y., Meridian Books (1959).

1929   *The Sexual Life of Savages in Northwestern Melanesia.* London, George Routledge and Sons.

1931   "The Anthropology of Africa," *Nature,* 127:655–57.

1932   "Introduction," to *The Sorcerers of Dobu,* by Reo Fortune. N. Y., E. P. Dutton & Company (1963).

1934   "Introduction," to *Law and Order in Polynesia,* by H. Ian Hogbin. N. Y., Harcourt Brace & Company.

1935   *Coral Gardens and Their Magic.* 2 vols. Bloomington, Indiana University Press (1965).

1936   "Primitive Law," *Man,* 36:55–56 (74).

1942   "A New Instrument for the Interpretation of Law—Especially Primitive," *Yale Law Journal,* 51:1237–54.

References

1944a   *A Scientific Theory of Culture and Other Essays.* N. Y., Galaxy Books (1960).

1944b   *Freedom and Civilization.* Bloomington, Indiana University Press (1960).

1948   *Magic, Science and Religion and Other Essays.* Garden City, N. Y., Anchor Books.

1962   *Sex, Culture, and Myth.* N. Y., Harcourt, Brace & World.

1967   *A Diary in the Strict Sense of the Term.* N. Y., Harcourt, Brace & World.

MARETT, ROBERT R.

1936   *Tylor.* N. Y., J. Wiley & Sons.

MEAD, MARGARET

1942   "Anthropological Data on the Problem of Instinct," *Psychosomatic Medicine,* 4:396–97.

1959   *An Anthropologist at Work: Writings of Ruth Benedict.* Boston, Houghton Mifflin Co.

MOORE, OMAR KHAYYAM

1957   "Divination—A New Perspective," *American Anthropologist,* 59:69–74.

MURDOCK, GEORGE P.

1943   "Bronislaw Malinowski." *American Anthropologist,* 45:441–51.

NISBET, ROBERT A.

1965   *Emile Durkheim.* Englewood Cliffs, N. J., Prentice-Hall.

PARSONS, TALCOTT

1937   *The Structure of Social Action.* Glencoe, Free Press.

PERISTIANY, J. G.

1953   "Introduction." In Emile Durkheim, *Sociology and Philosophy,* translated by D. F. Pocock (Glencoe, Free Press), pp. vii–xxxii.

PEYRE, HENRI

1960   "Durkheim: The Man, His Time, and His Intellectual Background." In Kurt H. Wolff, ed., *Essays on Sociology and Philosophy.* N. Y., Harper and Row (1964).

PIERCE, ALBERT

1960   "Durkheim and Functionalism." In Kurt H. Wolff, ed., *Essays on Sociology and Philosophy.* N. Y., Harper and Row (1964).

POCOCK, DAVID F.

1961   *Social Anthropology.* N. Y., Sheed and Ward.

POLANYI, MICHAEL

1958   *Personal Knowledge: Towards a Post-Critical Philosophy.* Chicago, University of Chicago Press.

References

POWELL, H. A.

1960   "Competitive Leadership in Trobriand Political Organization," *Journal of the Royal Anthropological Institute,* 90:118–45.

RADCLIFFE-BROWN, A. R.

1910a   "Puluga: A Reply to Father Schmidt," *Man,* 10:33–37 (17).

1910b   "Marriage and Descent in North Australia," *Man,* 10:55–59 (32).

1912   "Marriage and Descent in North and Central Australia," *Man,* 12:123–24 (64).

1913   "Three Tribes of Western Australia," *Journal of the Royal Anthropological Institute,* 43:143–94.

1914a   "The Relationship System of the Dieri Tribe," *Man,* 14:53–56 (33).

1914b   "The Definition of Totemism," *Anthropos,* 9:622–30.

1918   "Notes on the Social Organization of Australian Tribes. Part I," *Journal of the Royal Anthropological Institute,* 48:222–53.

1922   "Some Problems of Bantu Sociology," *Bantu Studies,* 1:38–46.

1923   "Notes on the Social Organization of Australian Tribes. Part II," *Journal of the Royal Anthropological Institute,* 53:424–47.

1927   "The Regulation of Marriage in Ambryn," *Journal of the Royal Anthropological Institute,* 57:343–48.

1929a   "Bride Price, Earnest or Indemnity," *Man,* 29:131–32 (96).

1929b   "Bilateral Descent," *Man,* 29:199–200 (157).

1930–31   "The Social Organization of Australian Tribes," *Oceania,* 1:34–63, 206–46, 322–41, 426–56.

1933   *The Andaman Islanders.* N. Y., Free Press (1967).

1935   "Kinship Terminologies in California," *American Anthropologist,* 37:530–35.

1937   *A Natural Science of Society.* Glencoe, Free Press (1957).

1946   "A Note on Functional Anthropology," *Man,* 46:38–41 (30).

1947   "Evolution, Social or Cultural?" *American Anthropologist,* 49:78–83.

1949a   "White's View of a Science of Culture," *American Anthropologist,* 51:503–12.

1949b   "Functionalism: A Protest," *American Anthropologist,* 51:320–23.

1950   "Introduction." *African Systems of Kinship and Marriage,* Radcliffe-Brown and Daryll Forde, eds. London, Oxford University Press.

1952   *Structure and Function in Primitive Society.* Glencoe, Free Press.

1958   *Method in Social Anthropology.* Chicago, University of Chicago Press.

RAY, VERNE F.

1956   "Rejoinder," *American Anthropologist,* 58:164–70.

References

RICHARDS, AUDREY

1943   "Bronislaw Kaspar Malinowski," *Man*, 43:1–4 (1).

RIVERS, W. H. R.

1914   *Kinship and Social Organization*. London, Constable & Co.

ROWE, JOHN H.

1962   "Alfred Louis Kroeber, 1876–1960," *American Antiquity*, 27:395–415.

SCHAPERA, I.

1962   "Should Anthropologists Be Historians?" *Journal of the Royal Anthropological Institute*, 92:143–56.

SCHNEIDER, DAVID M.

1965   "Some Muddles in the Models: Or, How the System Really Works." In Michael Banton, ed., *The Relevance of Models for Social Anthropology* (N. Y., Tavistock Publications), pp. 25–85.

SHAND, ALEXANDER F.

1896   "Character and the Emotions," *Mind*, 5:203–26.

1914   *The Foundations of Character*. London, MacMillan & Co.

SHIMKIN, DEMITRI B.

1964   "Julian H. Steward: A Contributor to Fact and Theory in Cultural Anthropology." In Robert A. Manners, ed., *Essays in Honor of Julian H. Steward*. Chicago, Aldine Publishing Co.

SMITH, M. G.

1962   "History and Social Anthropology," *Journal of the Royal Anthropological Institute*, 92:73–85.

SOFFER, REBA N.

1970   "The Revolution in English Social Thought, 1880–1914," *American Historical Review*, 75:1938–64.

SPIER, LESLIE

1931   "Historical Interrelation of Culture Traits: Franz Boas' Study of Tsimshian Mythology." In Stuart Rice, ed., *Methods in Social Science*. Chicago, University of Chicago Press.

STANNER, W. E. H.

1955   "A. R. Radcliffe-Brown." *The Kroeber Anthropological Society Papers*, No. 13, pp. 116–25.

STEWARD, JULIAN H.

1936a   "The Economic and Social Basis of Primitive Bands." In *Essays on Anthropology in Honor of Alfred Louis Kroeber*, Robert H. Lowie, ed. (Berkeley, University of California Press), pp. 311–50.

1936b   "Shoshoni Polyandry," *American Anthropologist*, 38:561–64.

References

1937 "Ecological Aspects of Southwestern Society," *Anthropos*, 32:87–104.

1938 "Basin-Plateau Aboriginal Sociopolitical Groups." *Bureau of American Ethnology*, Bulletin 120.

1939 "Changes in Shoshonean Indian Culture," *The Scientific Monthly*, 49:524–37.

1940 "Native Cultures of the Intermontane (Great Basin) Area." In "Essays in Historical Anthropology of North America" (Published in Honor of John R. Swanton). *Smithsonian Miscellaneous Collections*, 100:445–502.

1941 "Determinism in Primitive Society?" *The Scientific Monthly*, 53:491–501.

1950 "Area Research: Theory and Practice." *Social Science Research Council Bulletin*, 63.

1955 *Theory of Culture Change: The Methodology of Multilinear Evolution*. Urbana, University of Illinois Press.

1956a *The People of Puerto Rico* (with Robert A. Manners, Eric R. Wolf, Elena Padilla, Sidney W. Mintz, and R. L. Scheele). Urbana, University of Illinois Press.

1956b "Cultural Evolution," *Scientific American*, 194:69–80.

1959 *Native Peoples of South America* (with Louis Faron). N. Y., McGraw-Hill.

1960 "Evolutionary Principles and Social Types." In Sol Tax, ed., *Evolution After Darwin*, Vol. II (Chicago, University of Chicago Press), pp. 169–86.

1961 "Alfred Louis Kroeber 1876–1960," *American Anthropologist*, 63:1038–60.

1965 "Some Problems Raised by Roger C. Owen's 'The Patrilineal Band'," *American Anthropologist*, 67:732–34.

1967 *Contemporary Change in Traditional Societies* (editor). 3 volumes. Urbana, University of Illinois Press.

1973 *Alfred Louis Kroeber*. N. Y., Columbia University Press.

STOCKING, GEORGE C., JR.

1968a *Race, Culture, and Evolution: Essays in the History of Anthropology*. N. Y., Free Press.

1968b "Edward Burnett Tylor." *International Encyclopedia of the Social Sciences*. N. Y., Macmillan.

SUTTLES, WAYNE

1960 "Affinal Ties, Subsistence and Prestige among the Coast Salish," *American Anthropologist*, 62:296–305.

TAX, SOL

1953 *An Appraisal of Anthropology Today* (editor). Chicago, University of Chicago Press.

References

1960 "From Lafitau to Radcliffe-Brown: A Short History of the Study of Social Organization." In Fred Eggan, ed., *Social Anthropology of North American Tribes*. Chicago, University of Chicago Press.

TYLOR, EDWARD B.

1861 *Anahuac: Or Mexico and the Mexicans, Ancient and Modern.* London, Longman, Green, Longman, and Roberts.

1866 "The Religion of Savages," *Fortnightly Review*, 6:71–86.

1867 "On Traces of the Early Mental Condition of Man," *Proceedings of the Royal Institution*, 5:83–93.

1871 *Primitive Culture.* 2 volumes. N. Y., Harper Torchbooks (1958).

1873 "Primitive Society," *Contemporary Review*, 21:701–18, 22:53–72.

1878 *Researches into the Early History of Mankind and the Development of Civilization.* 3d ed., revised. London, John Murray.

1881 *Anthropology: An Introduction to the Study of Man.* N. Y., D. Appleton & Co. (1898).

UBEROI, J. P. SINGH

1962 *Politics of the Kula Ring.* Manchester, Manchester University Press.

VAN KAAM, ADRIAN

1969 *Existential Foundations of Psychology.* Garden City, N. Y., Image Books.

VAYDA, ANDREW P., AND ROY A. RAPPAPORT

1968 "Ecology: Cultural and Non-Cultural." In James A. Clifton, ed., *Introduction to Cultural Anthropology*. Boston, Houghton Mifflin Co.

WALSH, W. H.

1967a *Philosophy of History: An Introduction.* N. Y., Harper Torchbooks.

1967b "Colligatory Concepts in History." In W. H. Burston and D. Thompson, eds., *Studies in the Nature and Teaching of History* (London, Routledge and Kegan Paul), pp. 65–84.

WHITE, LESLIE A.

1925a "Personality and Culture," *The Open Court*, 39:145–49.

1925b "The Concept 'Social': A Critical Note," *Social Forces*, 4:72–74.

1925c "Knowledge Interpreted as Language Behavior," *The Open Court*, 39:396–404.

1925d Review of Harry Elmer Barnes, *The New History and the Social Studies*, *Social Forces*, 4:432–34.

1925e Review of Harry Elmer Barnes, ed., *The History and Prospects of the Social Sciences*, *Social Forces*, 4:643–46.

References

1926   "An Anthropological Approach to the Emotional Factors in Religion," *Journal of Philosophy*, 23:546–54.

1931   Review of Bernhard J. Stern, *Lewis Henry Morgan, Social Evolutionist*, *American Journal of Sociology*, 37:483.

1932   "The Acoma Indians," *Bureau of American Ethnology, 47th Annual Report*, pp. 17–192.

1939   "A Problem in Kinship Terminology," *American Anthropologist*, 41:566–73.

1940a   *Pioneers in American Anthropology, The Bandelier-Morgan Letters 1873–1883*. 2 volumes. Albuquerque, University of New Mexico Press.

1940b   "Mind Is Minding—But or Still?" *The Scientific Monthly*, 50:365–66.

1943a   "Energy and the Evolution of Culture," *American Anthropologist*, 45:335–56.

1943b   "Sociology, Physics, and Mathematics," *American Sociological Review*, 8:373–79.

1945a   "Diffusion vs. Evolution: An Anti-Evolutionist Fallacy," *American Anthropologist*, 47:339–56.

1945b   "History, Evolutionism and Functionalism: Three Types of Interpretation of Culture." *Southwestern Journal of Anthropology*, 1:221–48.

1945c   Review of Laura Thompson and Alice Joseph, *The Hopi Way*, *The Scientific Monthly*, 60:473–74.

1947a   "Evolutionary Stages, Progress, and the Evaluation of Cultures," *Southwestern Journal of Anthropology*, 3:165–92.

1947b   "Evolutionism in Cultural Anthropology: A Rejoinder," *American Anthropologist*, 49:400–13.

1947c   Review of Franz Boas, *Race and Democratic Society*, *American Journal of Sociology*, 52:371–73.

1948a   "The Definition and Prohibition of Incest," *American Anthropologist*, 50:416–35.

1948b   Reply to Bernhard J. Stern, *American Journal of Sociology*, 53:497–98.

1948c   Review of Grahame Clark, *From Savagery to Civilization*, and V. Gordon Childe, *History, Antiquity*, 22:217–18.

1949a   *The Science of Culture: A Study of Man and Civilization*. N. Y., Grove Press.

1949b   "Ethnological Theory." In *Philosophy for the Future: The Quest of Modern Materialism*, R. W. Sellars, V. J. McGill, and M. Farber, eds. (N. Y., Macmillan), pp. 357–84.

1959a   *The Evolution of Culture: The Development of Civilization to the Fall of Rome*. N. Y., McGraw-Hill.

1959b   *Lewis Henry Morgan. The Indian Journals*. Ann Arbor, University of Michigan Press.

References

1959c "The Concept of Culture," *American Anthropologist*, 61:227–51.

1960a "Introduction," to E. B. Tylor, *Anthropology*. Abridged edition. Ann Arbor, University of Michigan Press.

1960b "Foreword," to Marshall D. Sahlins and Elman R. Service, eds., *Evolution and Culture*. Ann Arbor, University of Michigan Press.

1962 "The Pueblo of Sia, New Mexico," *Bureau of American Ethnology*, Bulletin 184.

1963a "Individuality and Individualism: A Cultural Interpretation," *Texas Quarterly*, 6:111–27.

1963b "The Ethnography and Ethnology of Franz Boas," *Bulletin of the Texas Memorial Museum* (University of Texas), 6.

1966 "The Social Organization of Ethnological Theory." *Rice University Studies*, Vol. 52. no. 4, Houston, Texas.

1969 "Preface to the Second Edition." *The Science of Culture*. Revised edition. N. Y., Farrar, Straus and Giroux.

INDEX

Index

Index

Pragmatism, and Malinowski, 329
Predispositions, defined, 290-91
Problem of order, 169, 309
Problem of persistence, 222, 230, 235, 238, 239, 255-56, 271
Progress, 13-37 *passim*, 40, 134, 135-36, 148, 160, 232-33, 344
Psychic unity of mankind, 31-32
Psychology, 49, 139, 174-75, 215, 261
Pueblo Indians, 80-86 *passim*, 90-91, 129-30, 146, 147, 157, 213, 238, 355
Puerto Rico, 114, 120, 122
Punishment, *see* Sanctions, social

Race, 31-32, 49
Rationalizations, *see* Secondary interpretations of custom
Reality culture, 94, 95-100, 107-8, 112, 117, 158, 342
    defined, 95-96, 342
Reason: and nineteenth-century positivism, 38-39; and the turn-of-the-century revolution in social thought, 6, 39-40, 298
    Benedict and, 84, 89, 262
    Boas and, 51, 53-57, 72, 84, 163, 339, 357
    Durkheim and, 204
    Evans-Pritchard and, 262-64, 267
    Malinowski and, 298, 301-2
    Steward and, 344
    Tylor and, 18-37 *passim*, 50, 55, 71, 84, 298, 338
Reciprocity, 292-95
Reductionism: defined, 18; of intellectualism, 19; *see also* Culture, autonomy of
    Boas and, 143-44, 149-50, 163
    Durkheim and, 163, 166-172 *passim*, 180, 188, 200, 202, 205, 208
    Tylor and, 18-24, 37, 143, 149, 163, 219
    White and, 150
Relational method, 265-68, 270
Relativity, 16, 26, 39, 163, 209, 267
Religion: *see also* Animism
    Durkheim and, 180-85, 192, 199-200, 201, 203-4, 251
    Evans-Pritchard and, 242-43, 251-52, 260
    Malinowski on, 331
    Radcliffe-Brown on, 319-20, 325-27, 355

Revolution in social thought, turn of the century, 13, 37-40, 42, 53, 208, 214, 282, 298
Rhodes University, 216
Rivers, W. H. R., 215, 223, 226, 317, 327
Robertson Smith, William, 313
Royal Ethnographic Museum (Berlin), 41, 45

Sacred, 178, 181-84, 203, 213
Sanctions, social, 175, 188, 193-94, 199
Sauer, Carl, 113
Science, Malinowski's theory of, 301-2
Scientific explanation: contrasted with meaningful interpretation, 9-10, 336-37, 355; *see also* Historical explanation; Positivism
    Boas and, 43
    Kroeber and, 94-95, 112
    Radcliffe-Brown and, 215, 238-39, 267, 270
    Steward and, 10, 112-13, 343
    Tylor and, 20-21, 24
    White and, 135-36
Secondary features of culture, *see* Value culture
Secondary interpretations of custom, Boas on, 55-56, 57, 69-70
Self-interest, 8
    Durkheim on, 169, 190, 205
    Malinowski on, 290-95, 306, 309-14, 333, 334, 353, 354
Seligman, C. G., 274, 279
Sentiment of dependence, 220
Shand, Alexander, 278-79, 299, 327-29
Shoshone Indians, 9, 10, 115-19 *passim*, 124, 235, 344, 356
Smith, M. G., 257
Smithsonian Institution, Institute of Social Anthropology, 113
Social facts, 185
Socialism, 194-96
Social life, *see* Collective life
Social order, *see* Problem of order
Social structure:
    Evans-Pritchard and, 257-61, 262-63, 270-71
    Kroeber on, 96, 97, 109
    Malinowski and, 312-13
    Radcliffe-Brown and, 84-86, 223-28, 244, 260, 312, 324, 349
Social substratum: and causal analysis,

Index

theories of man & culture

ELVIN HATCH

This unusual and ambitious book will be welcomed by readers everywhere who wish to understand exactly what anthropology is and what anthropologists do. It summarizes, compares and contrasts the ideas of ten prominent anthropologists. One of these, Edward B. Tylor, is representative of the kind of thinking which predominated among English-speaking anthropologists during the late nineteenth century, when the science was formulated; but a distinctly twentieth-century view of humanity is embodied in the works of the other nine: Franz Boas, Ruth Benedict, A. L. Kroeber, Julian Steward, Leslie White, Emile Durkheim, A. R. Radcliffe-Brown, E. E. Evans-Pritchard, and Bronislaw Malinowski. Dr. Hatch has selected these figures because their works are important in themselves, their names are familiar even beyond anthropology, and their influence has been decisive and lasting. Each of the ten, in the author's view, offers a fundamentally different interpretation of human behavior. Were they observing the same person at the same time, none would fully agree on what that person was doing. Dr. Hatch's goal, in summarizing their works and views, is to reveal the